DATE DUE

PRINTED IN U.S.A.

CRITICAL INSIGHTS

Nature and the Environment

CRITICAL INSIGHTS

Nature and the Environment

Editor
Scott Slovic
University of Idaho

SALEM PRESS
A Division of EBSCO Publishing
Ipswich, Massachusetts

Library of Congress Cataloging-in-Publication Data
Nature and the environment / editor, Scott Slovic.
    p. cm. -- (Critical insights)
  Includes bibliographical references and index.
  ISBN 978-1-4298-3738-5 (hardcover) -- ISBN 978-1-4298-3786-6 (ebook) 1.
American literature--History and criticism. 2. Environmentalism in literature. 3.
Ecology in literature. 4. Nature in literature. 5. Environmental protection in lit-
erature. 6. Environmental literature--History and criticism. I. Slovic, Scott,
1960-
  PS169.E25N38 2912
  810.9'36--dc23

                              2012019662

Contents_____

Critical Contexts

Critical Readings

Resources

About This Volume

Scott Slovic

When the editors at EBSCO contacted me about compiling this book, I was in Taipei, Taiwan, having just participated in the Fifth International Conference on Ecological Discourse at Tamkang University, where the focus was on Asian environmental literature and environmental issues. I had spent several days listening to colleagues talk about writers from mainland China, India, Japan, Korea, and Taiwan, confirming my sense that important environmental literature exists throughout the world and that ecocritical scholars have plenty of work to do beyond North America and Western Europe. We considered the possibility of including in this book some chapters devoted to writers from countries other than England and the United States, but in the end we decided to focus on authors, texts, and literary traditions most likely to be represented in literature curricula at the high school and introductory college levels in the United States. This explains the fairly canonical scope of the topics represented here. But I would venture that there is something subversive, even radical, in the very application of ecocritical approaches to writers at the core of the American and British literary canons, such as Wordsworth, Whitman, and Hemingway. With more space, we could have included chapters on green approaches to Shakespeare, Faulkner, and Morrison, among others, and on luminaries in the field of environmental literature, such as Rick Bass, Annie Dillard, and Barry Lopez.

Some readers might find the title of this volume, *Critical Insights: Nature and the Environment*, a bit perplexing. Isn't it redundant to say "nature *and* the environment"? I felt this way initially, but it has occurred to me that using both of these terms makes sense in order to expand the scope of the book to include authors whose work came before we began routinely using such words as "environment" and "environmental issues" in the latter half of the twentieth century. Also, some of the authors featured here, even modern writers, really have focused their work on natural phenomena and processes ("nature") rather than on the human relationship with the surrounding world ("the environment"), or sometimes they explore nature as a discrete, nonhuman entity, and at other times they contemplate human beings in the context of the environment around them. Philosophers and ecocritics such as Kate Soper, Leo Marx, and many others have written at length about the various definitions of nature and the environment. For the purposes of the present book, however, using both terms in the title facilitates the inclusion of an exciting range of authors and literary texts.

As I mentioned above, the seventeen chapters included in this volume are intended to cover rather familiar authors, texts, and literary traditions. We hope teachers and students will be able to use these essays as a way of quickly getting up to speed in the field of ecocriticism. Perhaps individual students who happen to have a special concern for or fascination with the environment will be able to adopt ecocritical approaches in some of their essays for high school or college classes. Perhaps teachers will be inspired to include units on environmental literary traditions, or to take an environmental approach to writers or texts they've normally presented in classes without explicitly environmental perspectives. The field of ecocriticism is not new at all, as I've tried to explain in my introduction, called "On Nature and the Environment." Scholars have been exploring environmental aspects of literature for many decades, even during the nineteenth century, but the field really began to surge with the new environmental consciousness following the first Earth Day in 1970, attracting many new scholars in the 1980s and finally developing its self-consciousness as a critical movement in the 1990s with the founding of the Association for the Study of Literature and Environment (ASLE) in 1992.

This particular book is designed specifically to help students who are just beginning to study literature in a serious way and who may never have heard of ecocriticism before. The first four chapters are examples of special kinds of critical articles. Richard J. Schneider, one of the leading experts on the major American writer Henry David Thoreau, has prepared a "critical reception" study that shows how various literary critics and writers have responded to Thoreau's mid-nineteenth-century writings in the subsequent century and a half, focusing especially on the impact of Thoreau's work on later environmental thought and expression. Prominent British ecocritic Terry Gifford wrote the book on the pastoral tradition in European and American literature—I mean, he literally wrote the book *Pastoral* (1999), which helped to clarify the ongoing importance of pastoral forms of thought even as we enter the twenty-first century. His contribution to this collection exemplifies the critical practice known as comparison and contrast, and he specifically explores the subtle overlaps and distinctions between pastoral, antipastoral, and postpastoral literary traditions. If Professor Gifford wrote the book on pastoral literature, Priscilla Solis Ybarra can be said to have written the book on Mexican American environmental literature; her article for this book demonstrates how a scholar can apply a specific critical lens (like feminism, Marxism, or ecocriticism) to literary texts that could also easily be read in different ways. She has chosen to show how ecocriticism can illuminate two modern classics of Chicano fiction, Tomás Rivera's *. . . And the Earth Did Not Devour Him* (1973) and Rudolfo Anaya's *Bless Me, Ultima* (1972), emphasizing agricultural themes in these novels and also the ethnobiological tradition of herbal medicine (*curanderismo*) in Anaya's book. The fourth article in the book, David Landis Barnhill's introduction to the major contemporary environmental writers Gary Snyder and Peter Matthiessen (both winners of the Pulitzer Prize and other lofty awards in the United States), demonstrates how a literary critic might apply a specific cultural or historical context to the reading of certain texts. In this case, Professor Barnhill, who was trained in both literary scholarship and religious studies, shows how the Buddhist philosophical and spiritual tradition from East Asia permeates the environmental writing of these two important American writers.

After these first four chapters, I have organized the book in a loosely chronological fashion, keeping in mind when the featured authors lived and when they published their major work. Ashton Nichols, an expert on English and American romantic literature, has provided a thorough introduction to William Wordsworth's extraordinarily influential environmental ideas in both lyric (short) and epic (long) poems published in the late eighteenth century and the first half of the nineteenth century in England, highlighting the fact that Wordsworth's special sensitivity to the impact of nature on the human mind would provide a foundation for later environmental consciousness. M. Jimmie Killingsworth, who, yes, wrote the book on Walt Whitman as an ecological poet, argues that this giant figure in nineteenth-century American letters was "*the* ecological poet," showing in particular how Whitman's fascination with the physical connection between the human body and nonhuman nature anticipated the twenty-first-century development of "material ecocriticism."

Jack London's *The Call of the Wild* was first published in 1903; the story of a dog stolen in California and brought to work in the rugged Yukon Territory is interwoven with evolutionary theory, biological determinism, radical socialism, and transcendentalist philosophy. Tina Gianquitto, who provided the notes and introduction for a new edition of London's novel (2003), has explored these themes in the work, with a particular emphasis on the paradoxical patterns of evolutionary progress and devolutionary primitivism embodied in the canine protagonist Buck. A similar tension between *progress* and *conservation* emerges in Cather scholar Matthias Schubnell's analysis of the early-twentieth-century novels *O Pioneers!* (1913) and *A Lost Lady* (1923)—except that these works focus less on the evolutionary trajectory of individual characters than on human behavior toward the land. Two of the major paradigms in ecocriticism are *animality* (what does it mean to be human, how do our bodies intersect with the physical environment, what is our relationship with other species, etc.) and *place* (the physical, psychological, and philosophical implications of location; human impacts upon landscape; how particular authors/artists grant agency to the land and represent it as something more than background "setting" for human action; etc.). These important foci are highlighted in the studies of Jack London and Willa Cather in this book.

Another significant emphasis in ecocritical readings of literature is the tracing of observations and concepts as they make their way from natural science into literary form. Robert Bernard Hass, who has written at length (yes, *the* book) on Robert Frost's familiarity with science and the influence of science upon his poetry, not only points out the scientific elements in several of Frost's well-known poems but shows how the author subtly reveals a special philosophy of nature through the literary expression of science.

The science of evolutionary biology is central to the next two articles in the book: Bert Bender's reading of Ernest Hemingway's *The Old Man and the Sea* (1952), among other works, and Brian Railsback's treatment of several major works by John Steinbeck. Prominent ecocritic Glen A. Love wrote in 2010 that one of the most important theories available to ecocritics is Charles Darwin's theory of evolution—several of the articles in this book apply Darwinian theory, and other evolutionary perspectives, to major works of literature. Professor Bender has written perhaps the central work of "evolutionary literary criticism," *The Descent of Love: Darwin and the Theory of Sexual Selection in American Fiction, 1871–1926* (1996), and Professor Railsback has coedited an entire encyclopedia of material about Steinbeck. (I think I should stop saying that so-and-so wrote the book or the major article about this or that author, as I selected all of the contributors for this volume because they are prominent experts on these writers, texts, and literary themes.)

As David J. Rothman (president of the Robinson Jeffers Association from 2009 to 2011) explains in his chapter, the poet Jeffers was deeply influenced by natural science. One of the most prominent modernist poets in the United States during the middle decades of the twentieth century, Jeffers had worked in the field of comparative literature and studied not only half a dozen ancient and modern languages but also medicine, forestry, and a smattering of astrophysics. So fascinated was Jeffers with the preeminent importance of the "world out there" that he developed an entire philosophy of *inhumanism* to explain the relative unimportance of human affairs (including the two world wars that he lived through). Following Professor Rothman's explanation of Jeffers's eloquent inhumanism, we have David Copland Morris's analysis of how the tonal and philosophical dimensions of Edward Abbey's famous *Desert Solitaire: A Season in the Wilderness* (1968) intersect inextricably. Abbey was also an inhumanist, a believer in the ultimate importance of nature rather than the trivial, ephemeral concerns of human beings, but that didn't stop Abbey from enjoying the beauty of the world, the pleasure of human company, and the dance of language and ideas, nor did it stop him from arguing fiercely against civilization's destructive treatment of rivers and wild country. Many of the essays in this book focus on the representation of nature or the theme of environmental protection in literature without always offering explicit stylistic analysis of the texts in question. Professor Morris's study of style and tone in a book that some consider the cornerstone of recent American environmental literature is an excellent model of both stylistic and thematic discussion.

It is difficult to mention Edward Abbey without referring in the next breath to his contemporary, the Kentucky farmer, poet, essayist, and novelist Wendell Berry. Wes Berry, who also comes from Kentucky but is not related to the author (despite sharing his family name), routinely teaches Wendell Berry's works to university students in Kentucky, telling them to pay attention to the writer's ideas if they want to protect the places and communities of their home state. The strong pedagogical motif in ecocritical research (Berry mentions his students in the article included here) is another routine aspect of the field. If some readers encounter the works of authors like Robinson Jeffers and Edward Abbey and assume that inhumanist skepticism toward human culture is the predominant feature of environmental literature, they should, as Wes Berry suggests, turn to such novels as *The Memory of Old Jack* (1974) and observe how the author articulates through story a philosophy of family, community, and place. Humanism and environmentalism co-exist absolutely in Wendell Berry's life and work. The same could be said of the Native American poet, essayist, and novelist Linda Hogan, whose work is explained in Barbara J. Cook's chapter, in which the critic highlights the ecofeminist facets of Hogan's thinking and the author's great interest in animals. As I mentioned above, place and animality are two of the key paradigms in ecocritical research, along with science and pedagogy. Another major facet of ecocriticism is the study of how literature and other artistic media express social critique and seek to motivate readers to become engaged citizens, even activists. If Wendell Berry's writing tends to provoke readers to think seriously about place and community, Linda Hogan's work does much the same in the context of human relationships with other species, from horses to panthers to whales. Priscilla Leder's chapter on bestselling novelist and essayist Barbara Kingsolver's *Prodigal Summer* (2001) further highlights the inextricability of human experience from the complex layers of the nonhuman ecosystem. Like that of Berry and Hogan, Kingsolver's work frequently has an activist dimension; environmental consciousness, acquired through the careful reading of eloquent literature, is not a neutral condition of intellectual cultivation but a moral imperative. If we know that all is not right in the human relationship with nature, we are compelled to do something about this knowledge *with* this knowledge.

Doing something other than simply reading, thinking, talking, and writing is precisely the emphasis in the Integrated Outdoor Program at South Eugene High School in Eugene, Oregon, an innovative example of how literature and outdoor activity can be thoughtfully brought together in an educational context. Jeff Hess's article about the IOP brings home several essential aspects of ecocriticism: a focus on teaching; an acknowledgment of both canonical works of environmental literature (Abbey's *Desert Solitaire* is the centerpiece of the class's reading list) and avant-garde texts (or less well known texts); a guiding principle of linking textuality and engagement with the physical world;

and an interweaving of story and analysis—as shown in other chapters as well, such as Terry Gifford's and Wes Berry's.

Looking over the essays here, I think to myself, "There could be more gender balance in the contributors and featured authors, more multicultural representation, more of an international dimension. More experimental theory and analytical approaches—ecopoetics, feminist environmentalism, critical animal studies, green postcolonial theory, ecocosmopolitanism, new approaches to bioregional theory, and on and on." I do think, however, that these articles by leading scholars (the book is a Who's Who of specialists on the particular authors, texts, and themes) will provide an accessible and authoritative foundation for students and teachers who may want to know something about the Anglo-American traditions of ecocriticism and environmental literature. This book represents the tip of the iceberg of world ecocriticism and environmental expression. Please start here and then expand your horizons!

On Nature and the Environment_____

Scott Slovic

Try to imagine a society, or even an individual human being, that does not require some form of interaction with the natural world in order to exist. At the moment, I'm reading Sharman Apt Russell's *Hunger: An Unnatural History* (2005), and she speaks in her opening chapter about certain individuals—eccentrics, desperately overweight individuals, and even "hunger artists" who perform by abstaining from food—who have avoided *eating* for extraordinary periods of time. An American magician, for instance, had himself suspended in a six foot by six foot by three foot box near the Tower Bridge in London, England, for forty-four days without food in 2003. But did this "entertainer," David Blaine, go without water? Without air? And what about the 465-pound Scottish man, known to the public simply as "A. B.," who fasted for thirteen months in the mid-1960s in order to lose 276 pounds? Even during this long period of hunger, Mr. A. B. relied upon the planet, upon nature, for his very survival. All human beings throughout history have relied upon their relationship with nature in order to exist.

The problem, some might say, is that many cultures have either come to take nature for granted or have, as the ecological literary critic (ecocritic) Simon Estok has recently written, developed an adversarial attitude toward nature, believing that human success and comfort require us to dominate and exploit nature rather than live in a kind of symbiotic, or cooperative, relationship with the nonhuman world. Estok refers to this antagonism toward nature as *ecophobia* and argues that it is an essential condition of many contemporary societies—a condition that we may need to overcome if humans are to continue living on this planet well into the future.

What I've begun to describe above is a kind of paradox, a strange and ironic situation by which we know that we all need nature but for some peculiar reason like to think of ourselves as being free from the encumbrances of physical needs. We like to imagine that we are clever enough to overcome the physical realities of our planet: living in cool, comfortable dwellings even in hot regions of the world; eating any foods we desire no matter the time of year or what's "in season;" jetting vast distances in a single day; consuming all other species for food or other purposes, even animals that are much larger and stronger than we are, and even animals that are, like chimpanzees, our close genetic relatives. I'd guess that all of us, in some way or another, fit the patterns I've just described. I know I do, even though I'm a so-called environmentalist. Some scholars, in this age of the Internet, have gone so far as to argue that physical place is no longer meaningful, that we truly inhabit *cyberspace* rather than the world of nature; and yet we eat, drink, and breathe. We require physical space for our bodies. Many would claim that we are not spiritually satisfied unless we can feel the breeze brush across our skin, hear birds chittering in the yard or near the city streets we walk along on the way to school or work. To counter Simon Estok's notion of ecophobia, we have what biologist Edward O. Wilson has described as *biophilia*, an intrinsic love of living things; some might expand upon this and suggest that there is, in human beings, an essential love of the world that motivates many of our behaviors, even perhaps our wish to continue living and to produce students and biological offspring who might similarly love and celebrate the Earth.

The point of showing that these biophilic and ecophobic impulses compete with each other in the human mind is to suggest that our relationship with the natural world is complicated, and often contradictory. In reality, this is not simply a twenty-first-century first-world urban situation, a result of industrialization and the skeptical reasoning of the postmodern age. From the very beginning of our existence as a species, human beings have pondered our relationship with other beings in pragmatic, aesthetic, and philosophical ways. How can we grow certain plants in order to eat them, or hunt animals that are larger and swifter than ourselves? What kind of pigment might be used to depict deer or ox-like animals on the walls of caves in the Pyrenees mountains of southern Europe? What is the difference between domestic animals that live among humans and wild animals that exist, with a different degree of agency, apart from our own kind?

A few months ago, while giving a series of lectures in Toulouse, France, I visited a place called Grotte de Niaux, where people imprinted colorful images of antelope-like animals on cave walls half a mile underground some fourteen thousand years ago; other nearby caves, such as the famous ones in Lascaux, are thought to be thousands of years older. A few days after visiting Niaux, I went to Seattle, Washington, to talk with photographer and digital artist Chris Jordan, who uses cutting-edge computer software to manipulate thousands of images of SUV logos, cell phones, and plastic bags in order to create works of art, such as those in his 2009 book *Running the Numbers: An American Self-Portrait*. These images aim to spur citizens in one of the world's most intensely consumerist societies to wake up to the implications of our vast exploitation of planetary resources and the pollution that is resulting from our discarded consumer goods; Jordan refers to the process of his work as "the trans-scalar imaginary." Although I've mentioned a few examples of visual art to represent the "environmental art" that has existed from the most ancient human cultures to the present, the same fascination with and confusion about the human relationship with nature has inspired songs, stories, and reports about nature and our relationship with the world beyond ourselves in all human cultures across the planet. In the modern academic context, we tend to speak about poetry, fiction, nonfiction, and drama to describe major types of literature, but in some ways we're really talking about the same categories of communication—song, story, and informative report—that humans have always relied upon to convey meaningful, delightful, and useful ideas to each other.

What I've tried to describe above is the need for environmental art—which includes not only literature and visual art, but music, theater, film/TV, and other forms of human expression—to help us understand our complicated and sometimes paradoxical relationship with the natural world. How is this connected to ecocriticism? If environmental art is a mode of human communication that explores and describes human relationships to nature in beautiful or aestheticized ways, then ecocriticism is the mode of scholarship that seeks to explain or contextualize this art. In other words, a poem about seasonal processes, such as Robert Frost's "Spring Pools," would be an example of environmental literature; the 2006 article by Glenn Adelson and John Elder titled "Ecosystems of Meaning in Robert Frost's 'Spring Pools'" (and discussed by Robert Barnard Hass in his article on Frost in this book) is a work of ecocriticism. The articles in this book, although some of them include storytelling and are rather elegantly, even poetically, crafted, are works of ecocritical scholarship. They study a wide range of authors and literary texts but only a fraction of the works that ecocriticism could potentially examine—I will explain this in a moment.

First, though, let me discuss some of the varieties of ecocritical scholarship. The term *ecocriticism* was first used in the title of a 1978 article by William Rueckert, "Literature and Ecology: An Experiment in Ecocriticism." This article floated the term out to the scholarly community, but few people picked up on the word until years later. Scholars had actually been studying natural themes and environmental issues in literature for many years prior to Rueckert's use of the word. David Mazel, for instance, published a collection of protoecocritical writings called *A Century of Early Ecocriticism* in 2001, identifying many works written between 1864 and 1964 that provide a foundation for contemporary ecocritical work. Although Rueckert may have been the first scholar to use the term *ecocriticism*, it wasn't until the 1990s that critics rescued the word from obscurity and began to apply it to the field of environmentally focused literary scholarship that was rapidly developing at that time. One of the well-known definitions that emerged in the 1990s was Cheryll Glotfelty's statement in the introduction to *The Ecocriticism Reader* in 1996: She wrote that ecocriticism is "the study of the relationship between literature and the physical world" (xviii). Responding to the previous tendency of literary scholars to focus their work on the artistic design of literary works and the *human* contexts of such texts (gender, psychology, social class, ethnicity, and so forth), Glotfelty and the writers whose articles she and Harold Fromm collected in *The Ecocriticism Reader* recognized that it's important to think about the even larger "environmental context" of literature and other forms of human expression. After all, as David Mazel playfully and profoundly remarks at the beginning of his book *American Literary Environmentalism* (2000), ecocritics simply study literature "as if the earth mattered" (1)—and since the earth does matter to all of us (including everyone doing literary criticism), perhaps all of us should try to keep the earth in mind when we think about literature.

Perhaps the central debate in ecocriticism today has to do with the merits of narrowing the scope of the field (i.e., pinning down an identifiable methodology, a body of acceptable texts to study, or a political ideology that would fit within the boundaries of the field and thus help to define the enterprise) or maintaining the broad and somewhat baggy definition that has so far defined who ecocritics are and what they do. When British scholar Peter Barry included ecocriticism as the topic of the final chapter in the 2002 edition of his popular book *Beginning Theory*, he articulated several specific tactics that he associated with the environmental approach to literary studies, such as rereading canonical literary works "from an ecocentric perspective," applying "ecocentric concepts" such as "growth and energy, balance and imbalance" to a variety of conditions and phenomena, placing "special emphasis [on] writers who foreground nature," appreciating "factual" or even scientific writing that has often been neglected by literary critics, and pushing aside certain critical theories that highlight the social and/or linguistic construction of reality (264). But after outlining certain approaches that seem to be displaying a limited array of practices, Barry concludes his introduction to the field by quoting my own comment that ecocriticism, as the poet Walt Whitman once said of himself, is large and "contain[s] multitudes" (269).

This, in fact, is what ecocritic Lawrence Buell is getting at when he states, in *The Future of Environmental Criticism* (2005), "The environmental turn in literary studies is best understood . . . less as a monolith than as a concourse of discrepant practices" (11). Buell suggests that ecocriticism could better be described as a group of scholars who are looking or moving in the same general direction, although they are practicing their scholarship in a variety of ways. This "concourse" (think of an airport terminal as an area through which passengers and workers are moving in recognizable directions, although individuals may be weaving this way and that) may suggest a general interest in environmental matters, although the particular concerns of readers and critics may differ.

In recent years, some ecocritics, such as Camilo Gomides at the University of Puerto Rico and Simon Estok (mentioned above) from Sungkyunkwan University in South Korea, have argued that we need a narrower, more precise methodology for the field. Gomides put a "new definition of ecocriticism to the test" in a 2006 article, writing, "Ecocriticism: The field of enquiry that analyzes and promotes works of art which raise moral questions about human interactions with nature, while also motivating audiences to live within a limit that will be binding over generations" (16). This is an elegant and fascinating definition, admirable in various ways, not the least of which is the possibility that art and scholarship might work together to guide audiences to more careful ways of living on the Earth. When I read this definition I find myself thinking of Native American author Joseph Bruchac's lovely essay "The Circle Is the Way to See" (1993), in which he tells the story of Gluskabe, the trickster figure in northeastern North American indigenous traditions, who in one instance captured all the animals in the forest in his "game bag," leaving nothing for future hunts and therefore threatening his people with starvation. After telling the traditional story, Bruchac unpacks the implications of the story for late-twentieth-century readers, applying the moral aspect of Gluskabe's unthinking exploitation of nature to our own contemporary habits. In a way, Bruchac's interpretation of this particular story is the perfect demonstration of what Gomides is calling for.

Along similar lines, Estok, in the same 2009 article I mentioned at the beginning of this introduction, states:

> The strategic openness that characterizes early ecocriticism has become to a certain degree ambivalent, garnering success for ecocriticism in its bid to gain footing and credibility in academia, but also resulting in some uncertainty about what ecocriticism does or seeks to do, some sense that "we'll work it all out as we go along," to borrow a phrase from Dr. Sarvis in Edward Abbey's *The Monkey Wrench Gang*. The Edge seems to have become blunted. (10)

Estok uses this concern as the foundation for his argument for a new term, *ecophobia*, which he believes might lend focus and purpose to future ecocritical efforts. Ecocritics, he implies, should become "ecophobia hunters," identifying and condemning ecophobic tendencies (nature fearing/hating/destroying) wherever they exist in modern society. I've been reading cultural critic Curtis White lately—see his 2007 essay "The Ecology of Work," for instance, in which he says that our lives in countries like the United States are entirely controlled by corporations and the capitalist system, and that there is no way capitalism can ever "become green," because "the imperatives of environmentalism are not part of its way of reasoning." In other words, in many societies today ecophobia is rampant, and since our modern way of life originated centuries ago, at least dating back to the beginning of the industrial revolution, we can probably keep ourselves busy identifying ecophobic attitudes toward nature in various artistic representations of nature from the past two or three centuries.

But other ecocritics, while recognizing the power of ecophobia as an idea and a source of environmental damage, would continue to argue for a more ecumenical or broad-minded view of ecocriticism. I belong to this latter group. For one, I have found over the years that scholars, like artists, do not like to be herded together. We don't follow directions especially well, being of independent personalities and imaginative tendencies of mind. Take a look at the contributions to this book, for example; the seventeen contributors in the pages that follow have each followed rather different approaches to their topics, texts, and writers. It would not have worked well, I can tell you, if I had prescribed a specific way of reading and writing to each of these critics—you'd probably be holding a very thin book in your hands right now!

Even more importantly, though, in my frequent travels around the world to interact with ecocritics and environmental artists from various cultures, I have noted striking differences in terminology and aesthetic and political priorities. Let me sketch out briefly what I mean by this. In Australia, a country that has produced some of the world's leading ecocritics, there are dramatic geographical extremes, ranging from fiercely dry deserts to lush tropical forest, from alpine heights to a vast seacoast. Ecocritics in that part of the world are naturally prone to what I would call "geographical determinism," a way of understanding literature and experience that foregrounds the effects of place on language and state of mind. Perhaps the most explicit statement of this view is Mark Tredinnick's 2005 book *The Land's Wild Music: Encounters with Barry Lopez, Peter Matthiessen, Terry Tempest Williams, and James Galvin*, in which he argues that these American writers derive their very literary styles from their home territories (in the compendious doctoral dissertation that preceded the book, Tredinnick included Australian writers in his discussion). Tasmanian scholar Peter Hay, the author of *Main Currents in Western Environmental Thought* (2002), has made comparable claims about his native island and about island cultures more generally. Meanwhile, Roslynn D. Haynes makes powerful claims for the influence of heat and aridity on artistic expression in Australia's "red centre" in her study *Seeking the Centre: The Australian Desert in Literature, Art and Film* (1998). These are just a few examples from Down Under.

In the People's Republic of China, where the field of ecocriticism is currently booming (of course, out of 1.4 billion people you'd expect there to be hundreds of literary scholars taking environmental approaches to their work!), there are some uniquely Chinese angles. For instance, in his 2006 book *The Space for Ecocriticism* (published in Chinese), Lu Shuyuan has an entire chapter analyzing the "semantic field" of the Chinese character that means "wind"—a particularly rich and multilayered concept in Chinese geomancy (known as "feng shui"). There are diverse approaches throughout Chinese ecocriticism, but another conspicuously local one is the tendency of eco-aestheticians such as Zeng Fanren and Cheng Xiangzhan to discern some of the core precepts of classical Chinese philosophy in literature and art—precepts that include the Song Dynasty (969–1279 CE) phrase *"tien ren he yi"* ("the harmonious oneness of the universe and man") or fourth-century BCE thinker Chuang-zi's *"ziran da mei"* ("nature is the most beautiful")—and to use the elegant expression of such ideas to sway the juggernaut of contemporary Chinese consumer society toward a new path.

In India, on the other hand, ecocritic Nirmal Selvamony leads a group of scholars who are intent on applying *tinai* (the body of traditional Tamil ecological thought from the southeastern region of the subcontinent) to the study of literary works. In South Africa, Dan Wylie has tried to imagine how "Bushman" views of nature might help to shape a locally appropriate southern African insight into texts and place. French scholar Bertrand Westphal developed the idea of *la géocritique* as a way of applying theoretical concepts like Deleuze's *transgressivity* and Derrida's *referentiality* to spatial experience, while across the border in Germany, Hubert Zapf leads a research group at the University of Augsburg dedicated to understanding *Kulturökologie*, a quasi-Hegelian mode of analysis that finds ecological tensions in literary works. The list goes on and on, from Turkey to Argentina, Finland to Japan. The difficulty—no, the diplomatic and practical impossibility—of squeezing so many different perspectives into a narrow mode of ecocriticism explains why I strenuously support a more pluralistic view of the field.

One of the strongest tendencies in contemporary ecocriticism is the application of environmental perspectives to local literatures around the world, or the comparison of literary works across languages and cultures. Patrick D. Murphy recognized the importance of this approach in 2000, when he wrote the following in his book *Farther Afield in the Study of Nature-Oriented Literature*:

If ecocriticism has been hindered by too narrow an attention to nonfiction prose and the fiction of nonfictionality, it has also been limited by a focus on American and British literatures. In order to widen the understanding of readers and critics, it is necessary to reconsider the privileging of certain genres and also the privileging of certain national literatures and certain ethnicities within those national literatures. Such reconsideration will enable a greater inclusiveness of literatures from around the world within the conception of nature-oriented literature. It will also enable critics and readers such as myself, who focus primarily on American literature, to place that literature in an internationally relative and comparative framework. I see such reconsideration as one of the ways by which we can refine our awareness and expand the field of ecocriticism. (58)

Indeed, leading international ecocritics, such as Ken-ichi Noda and Katsunori Yamazato in Japan and Won-Chung Kim and Doo-ho Shin in South Korea, were trained as specialists in American literature, but in recent years they have begun to write articles about environmental aspects of Japanese and Korean literature or have performed comparative studies of such authors as Miyazawa Kenji and Gary Snyder. I have found myself drifting increasingly toward comparative ecocritical studies, although I also was a specialist in American literature as an undergraduate and graduate student. I have described some of my courses in comparative ecocriticism in the essay "Teaching United States Environmental Literature in a World Comparatist Context."

In fact, when I began contemplating the authors and literary works that should be highlighted in this book, I was in the midst of preparing a seminar for graduate students on the topic of comparative ecocriticism and international environmental literature, and it was a struggle for me to narrow the focus here to North American (and a few English) writers. In recent courses, I have included such authors and texts as Bashō's *The Narrow Road to the Deep North* (1966, translated by Nobuyuki Yuasa), Gao Xingjian's *Soul Mountain* (2000, translated by Mabel Lee), Marjorie Agosín's *Of Earth and Sea: A Chilean Memoir* (2008), and Homero Aridjis's *Eyes to See Otherwise/Ojos de otro mirar: Selected Poems* (1998, edited by Betty Ferber and George McWhirter). Each of these authors—and many others from East Asia and Latin America, Africa, and South Asia—would merit inclusion in a volume such as this one and in a high school or university course on environmental literature. In my recent course, because I had just attended a conference on Scandinavian environmental studies at the Swedish Embassy in Washington, DC, I decided to use such works as Peter Hoeg's *The Woman and the Ape* (1997, translated by Barbara Haveland) and Kerstin Ekman's *Blackwater* (1997, translated by Joan Tate), along with a diverse assortment including Alejo Carpentier's *The Lost Steps* (2001, translated by Harriet de Onís), J. M. G. Le Clézio's *The Prospector* (1993, translated by Carol Marks) and *The Round and Other Cold Hard Facts* (2002, translated by C. Dickson), Zakes Mda's *The Whale Caller* (2006), Witi Ihimaera's *The Whale Rider* (1987), Orhan Pamuk's *Istanbul: Memories and the City* (2004, translated by Maureen Freely), and Tim Winton's *Dirt Music* (2003) and *Breath* (2008), among others. (For many more examples of global environmental literature, see the "Booklist of International Environmental Literature" published in *World Literature Today* in January 2009.)

The main point here, as I've been suggesting throughout this introduction, is that environmental expression is a global phenomenon, and while there are certainly important commonalties across cultures, it also seems important to recognize the rich local idiosyncrasies as well. As for ecocritical strategies and emphases, despite all efforts to develop what Turkish critic Serpil Oppermann half-jokingly calls "a universal field theory of ecocriticism," echoing similar efforts in the field of physics, pluralism remains the name of the game.

All of this must seem rather humorless and boring to people who just want to get a sense of what the environmental approach to literature is all about in order to teach or take a basic English class. There's actually plenty of melodrama in the field, with scholars taking each other to task for misdescribing fish (see Dana Phillips's *The Truth of Ecology*), writing in too celebratory a fashion about the beauty of environmental literature (see Michael Cohen's "Blues in the Green"), and seeming overly enamored with critical theory for some people's taste (see S. K. Robisch's "The Woodshed"). There is also humor—at least a little bit of it. Michael P. Branch gave a talk called "How Many Ecocritics Does It Take to Screw in a Light Bulb?" at a session on environmental humor at the June 2011 Association for the Study of Literature and Environment Conference in Bloomington, Indiana. His answer: ten. Branch's ten ecocritics contemplating the need for artificial light range from the gender-sensitized scholar concerned about the phallic shape of a light bulb to the energy-conscious critic who wonders if we should instead be *un*screwing light bulbs! The final two ecocritics, according to this list, don't accomplish much screwing-in or unscrewing at all, but instead "argue about whether the light emitted by the bulb is first, second, or third-wave."

What's all this talk about waves? I'd like to conclude my overview by talking briefly about the recent history of ecocriticism. For a fuller discussion, you can track down my 2009 article on "The Third Wave of Ecocriticism." Lawrence Buell started the use of the wave metaphor to describe the progression of ecocritical approaches in his 2005 book; this approach follows the description of feminist scholarship as a series of waves. Buell wrote:

No definitive map of environmental criticism in literary studies can . . . be drawn. Still, one can identify several trend-lines marking an evolution from a "first wave" of ecocriticism to a "second" or newer revisionist wave or waves increasingly evident today. This first-second wave distinction should not, however, be taken as implying a tidy, distinct succession. Most currents set in motion by early ecocriticism continue to run strong, and most forms of second-wave revisionism involve building on as well as quarreling with precursors. In this sense, "palimpsest" would be a better metaphor than "wave." (17)

I certainly agree with the idea that a palimpsest would make a better metaphor here, as it suggests the reality that early approaches to the field continue to be active and important even in the present; they don't disappear as actual waves in the sea vanish when replaced by newer waves. Still, the notion of a recognizable sequence of trends in the field does make sense.

Here's a thumbnail summary of the major sequences I've noticed in my quarter-century working in the field:

- Starting around 1980, but continuing to the present, we had an initial surge (a "first wave") of ecocritical work, even before people were generally using the term *ecocriticism*. This ground-breaking work tended to focus on literary nonfiction (so-called nature writing); there was a strong emphasis on nonhuman nature (or *wilderness*), as represented in literature; initially the field was oriented toward American and British literature; and discursive ecofeminism was one of the most politically engaged submovements within the field.

- We can date the second wave to approximately the mid-1990s (continuing to the present), when the field began to expand to encompass multiple genres and even popular culture—some would call this "green cultural studies"; the works and authors being studied became increasingly multicultural; we saw an increasing interest in local environmental literatures around the world; environmental justice ecocriticism began to emerge at this time; and the scope of ecocriticism expanded to include urban and suburban contexts in addition to rural and wild locations.

- Joni Adamson and I began using the term "third-wave ecocriticism" in our introduction to the summer 2009 special issue of *MELUS: Multiethnic Literatures of the United States*. Initially, we focused on the comparatist tendency in new ecocriticism, dating back to approximately 2000 (comparisons across national cultures and across ethnic cultures). But later I began to describe other notable trends: the melding and tension between global concepts of place ("eco-cosmopolitanism" à la Ursula Heise) and neo-bioregionalism (as in Tom Lynch's discussion of "nested" bioregions); a rising emphasis on *material* ecofeminism and multiple gendered approaches (including ecomasculinism and green queer theory); a strong interest in animality (evolutionary ecocriticism, animal subjectivity/agency, vegetarianism, justice for nonhuman species, and posthumanism); the critiques from within the field (such as those by Phillips and Cohen, mentioned above) that have contributed to the growing maturity of ecocriticism; and various new forms of ecocriticist activism (such as John Felstiner's use of poetry as a means of environmental engagement).

All of this might seem like more than you need to know if you're just dipping your toes into the ocean of ecocritical scholarship. Don't worry—the water's warm. (Some, such as Alaskan author Marybeth Holleman, who writes about endangered polar bears in the Arctic, might say *too* warm—but that's another story!)

The goal of this book is to offer a welcoming, informative initiation into one of the most energetic and socially urgent branches of research and creative activity in the humanities, a field of inquiry that offers certain trends and traditions of its own but also porously absorbs vocabulary and ideas from many other disciplines and kinds of literary analysis. Read the articles that follow and try to figure out what these authors imagine ecocriticism to be. Then give it a try yourself!

Works Cited

Adamson, Joni, and Scott Slovic. "Guest Editors' Introduction: The Shoulders We Stand On; An Introduction to Ethnicity and Ecocriticism." *MELUS* 34.2 (Summer 2009): 5–24.

Adelson, Glenn, and John Elder. "Robert Frost's Ecosystem of Meanings in 'Spring Pools'." *ISLE: Interdisciplinary Studies in Literature and Environment* 13.2 (Summer 2006): 1–17.

Agosín, Marjorie. *Of Earth and Sea: A Chilean Memoir*. Tucson: U of Arizona P, 2008.

Aridjis, Homero. *Eyes to See Otherwise/Ojos de otro mirar: Selected Poems*. Ed. George McWhirter and Betty Aridjis. New York: New Directions, 1998.

Barry, Peter. "Ecocriticism." *Beginning Theory: An Introduction to Literary and Cultural Theory*. 2nd ed. Manchester: Manchester UP, 2002.

Bashō, Matsuo. *The Narrow Road to the Deep North and Other Travel Sketches*. Trans. Nobuyuki Yuasa. New York: Penguin, 1966.

Branch, Michael P. "How Many Ecocritics Does It Take to Screw In a Light Bulb?" The Biennial Conference of the Association for the Study of Literature and Environment (ASLE). Indiana University, Bloomington, Indiana. June 2011. Presentation.

Bruchac, Joseph. "The Circle Is the Way to See." *Literature and the Environment: A Reader on Nature and Culture*. Ed. Lorraine Anderson, John P. O'Grady, and Scott Slovic. New York: Longman, 1999. 492–98.

Buell, Lawrence. *The Future of Environmental Criticism*. Malden: Blackwell, 2005.

Carpentier, Alejo. *The Lost Steps*. Minneapolis: U of Minnesota P, 2001.

Cohen, Michael P. "Blues in the Green: Ecocriticism under Critique." *Environmental History* 9.1 (January 2004): 9–36.

Ekman, Kerstin. *Blackwater*. New York: Picador, 1997.

Estok, Simon C. "Theorizing in a Space of Ambivalent Openness: Ecocriticism and Ecophobia." *ISLE: Interdisciplinary Studies in Literature and Environment* 16.2 (Spring 2009): 203–25.

Felstiner, John. *Can Poetry Save the Earth?: A Field Guide to Nature Poems*. New Haven: Yale UP, 2009.

Glotfelty, Cheryll. Introduction. *The Ecocriticism Reader*. Ed. Cheryll Glotfelty and Harold Fromm. Athens: U of Georgia P, 1996. xv–xxxvii.

Gomides, Camilo. "Putting a New Definition of Ecocriticism to the Test: The Case of *The Burning Season*, a Film (Mal)Adaptation." *ISLE: Interdisciplinary Studies in Literature and Environment* 13.1 (Winter 2006): 13–23.

Hay, Peter. *Main Currents in Western Environmental Thought*. Bloomington: Indiana UP, 2002.

Haynes, Roslynn D. *Seeking the Centre: The Australian Desert in Literature, Art and Film*. Cambridge: Cambridge UP, 1998.

Heise, Ursula K. *Sense of Place and Sense of Planet*. New York: Oxford UP, 2008.

Hoeg, Peter. *The Woman and the Ape*. New York: Penguin, 1997.

Holleman, Marybeth. "What Happens When Polar Bears Leave?" *ISLE: Interdisciplinary Studies in Literature and Environment* 14.2 (Summer 2007): 183–94.

Ihimaera, Witi. *The Whale Rider*. 1987. Orlando: Harcourt, 2003.

Le Clézio, J. M. G. *The Prospector*. Boston: Godine, 1993.
_____. *The Round and Other Cold Hard Facts*. Lincoln: U of Nebraska P, 2002.
Lu, Shuyuan. *The Space for Ecocriticism*. Shanghai: East China Normal UP, 2006.
Lynch, Tom. *Xerophilia: Ecocritical Explorations of Southwestern Literature*. Lubbock: Texas Tech UP, 2008.
Mazel, David. *A Century of Early Ecocriticism*. Athens: U of Georgia P, 2001.
_____. *American Literary Environmentalism*. Athens: U of Georgia P, 2000.
Mda, Zakes. *The Whale Caller*. New York: Picador, 2006.
Murphy, Patrick D. *Farther Afield in the Study of Nature-Oriented Literature*. Charlottesville: U of Virginia P, 2000.
Pamuk, Orhan. *Istanbul: Memories and the City*. New York: Vintage, 2004.
Phillips, Dana. *The Truth of Ecology: Nature, Culture, and Literature in America*. New York: Oxford UP, 2003.
Robisch, S. K. "The Woodshed: A Response to 'Ecocriticism and Ecophobia.'" *ISLE: Interdisciplinary Studies in Literature and Environment* 16.4 (Fall 2009): 697–708.
Rueckert, William H. "Literature and Ecology: An Experiment in Ecocriticism." *Iowa Review* 9.1 (1978): 71–86.
Russell, Sharman Apt. *Hunger: An Unnatural History*. New York: Basic Books, 2005.
Selvamony, Nirmal. "tiNai in Primal and Stratified Societies." *The Indian Journal of Ecocriticism* 1 (August 2008): 38–48.
Slovic, Scott, ed. "A Booklist of International Environmental Literature." *World Literature Today* (January 2009): 53–55.
_____. "Teaching United States Environmental Literature in a World Comparatist Context." *Teaching North American Environmental Literature*. Ed. Laird Christensen, Mark C. Long, and Frederick O. Waage. New York: MLA, 2008. 203–14.
_____. "The Third Wave of Ecocriticism: North American Reflections on the Current Phase of the Discipline." *Ecozon@* 1.1 (April 2010): 4–10. Web. 17 Jan. 2012.
Tredinnick, Mark. *The Land's Wild Music: Encounters with Barry Lopez, Peter Matthiessen, Terry Tempest Williams, and James Galvin*. San Antonio: Trinity UP, 2005.
Westphal, Bertrand. *La Geocritique: Reel, Fiction, Espace*. Paris: Minuit, 2007.
White, Curtis. "The Ecology of Work." *Orion* (May/June 2007): n. pag. Web. 17 Jan. 2012.
Wilson, Edward O. *Biophilia*. Cambridge: Harvard UP, 1984.
Winton, Tim. *Breath*. New York: Picador, 2008.
_____. *Dirt Music*. New York: Scribner, 2002.
Wylie, Dan. "//Kabbo's Challenge: Transculturation and the Question of a South African Ecocriticism." *Journal of Literary Studies* 23.3 (September 2007): 252–70.
Xingjian, Gao. *Soul Mountain*. 1990. Trans. Mabel Lee. New York: Perennial, 2000.
Zapf, Hubert. *Kulturökologie und Literatur: Beiträge zu einem Tranzdisziplinären Paradigma der Literaturwissenschaft*. Heidelberg: Universitätsverlag Winter, 2008.

CRITICAL
CONTEXTS

Thoreau and American Environmentalism: A Study in Critical Reception_____

Richard J. Schneider

America has always been "nature's nation."[1] Early settlers such as Captain John Smith extolled the natural wonders of the New World to lure others to immigrate to America. Early naturalists and explorers such as William Bartram and Lewis and Clark would later chronicle those wonders in detail. Thomas Jefferson would describe Virginia's natural bridge as an example of America's exceptional landscape.[2] It would not be until the mid-nineteenth century, however, that an environmentalist sense of the need to protect nature would begin to develop.

For the beginnings of American environmentalism in the nineteenth century one might at first look to George Catlin or Ralph Waldo Emerson. Catlin was the first to propose, as early as 1836, a national park where Native Americans and buffalo might preserve their endangered way of life. Catlin, however, was primarily a portrait painter, who focused more on preserving the humanity of Native American culture through his art than preserving the natural environment. Emerson's book *Nature*, published in 1836, offered a seminal philosophical and literary argument for the centrality of nature in American culture. But while Emerson's focus on nature as symbol inspired countless literary disciples, its impact on specific environmentalist concerns seems indirect at best. It would be Emerson's younger Concord townsman, Henry David Thoreau, who would become the acknowledged father of American environmentalism.

Henry David Thoreau and his most famous book *Walden* (1854) have always been seen through the lens of a specific historical time. His first biographer, his friend William Ellery Channing, saw Thoreau in 1873 as a "poet-naturalist," with the emphasis on poet. This view of him as a prose-poet of nature's beauty persisted into the early twentieth century, when his pastoral vision seemed useful to counteract rapid urbanization. To popular critics during the Great Depression of the 1930s, Thoreau's emphasis on simplicity seemed like a guide to weathering economic scarcity, while in 1941 F. O. Matthiessen's book of literary criticism, *American Renaissance*, shifted the emphasis from Thoreau's social philosophy to his literary craftsmanship. During World War II, Thoreau fell into disrepute for what was perceived as his unpatriotic political pacifism. But after the war, in the 1950s, critics returned to an emphasis on his literary art, especially the elements of myth and symbolism in *Walden*.

The 1960s were watershed years for Thoreau's reputation. He first became radicalized as an antiwar protester and advocate of passive resistance because of his essay "Civil Disobedience" (1848) and its pertinence to the Vietnam War. But later in the decade, the view of the radical environmentalist "green" Thoreau began to emerge with historian Roderick Nash's book *Wilderness and the American Mind* (1967). Nash cites Thoreau's now-famous statement in "Walking" (1862)—"in Wildness is the preservation of the World"—as a major shift in American attitudes toward nature. Thoreau, he argues, "cut the channels in which a large portion of thought about wilderness subsequently flowed" (84). Unfortunately, Nash's emphasis on the passage from "Walking" is misleading, because Nash conflates Thoreau's word "Wildness," a word that Thoreau uses to denote a state of mind, with "wilderness," a word that denotes a specific kind of place. Nonetheless, Nash's book presented Thoreau as a champion of the environment, and the Sierra Club picked up Thoreau's words and immortalized them as a motto for posters advocating wilderness preservation.

In 1977 another historian, Donald Worster, offered a more complex view of Thoreau's environmentalism. In his history of ecology, *Nature's Economy: A History of Ecological Ideas* (1977), Worster devotes several chapters to Thoreau's "Romantic ecology." Worster accurately notes ambivalence in Thoreau's attitude toward nature. On the one hand, "Thoreau's transcendental idealism"—derived in large part from Emerson and expressed eloquently in *Walden*—"directed human attention away from the present natural order and society's affairs, and toward an Eden-like, perfectionist utopia" (101). On the other hand, Worster shifts the emphasis to the years after Thoreau's stay at Walden Pond, when "the main thrust of Thoreau's scientific studies was ecological" (65). During these years, Thoreau spent much of his time exploring and recording in his journal the physical phenomena—the ponds and rivers, the plants, and the animals—in the woods around Concord, Massachusetts. Thus, in "the daily fabric of his life" and "in his ramblings about Concord, Thoreau came as close as any individual has to embodying the arcadian ideal" (110). "Imperfect as it may have been, and inconsistent as he was in its execution," Worster adds, "Thoreau's subversive ecological philosophy provided later generations with an example by which they might test their own lives" (110).

Nash and Worster established the centrality of Thoreau in environmental politics and ecological science, but it was not until the 1990s that Thoreau became important as a "nature writer," and that "nature writing" in general became respectable as part of mainstream American literature. Literary critics such as Peter Fritzell (*Nature Writing and America*, 1990) and Scott Slovic (*Seeking Awareness in American Nature Writing*, 1992) began to focus on the green Thoreau, emphasizing his ecological vision as a literary strategy. Lawrence Buell's *The Environmental Imagination: Thoreau, Nature Writing, and the Formation of American Culture* (1995) eventually dubbed Thoreau as "the patron saint of American environmental writing" (115), and that assessment has stuck until the present time.

What earns Thoreau that saintly position, Buell observes, is the complexity, and sometimes the ambivalence, of his approach to nature. Although Buell correctly notes that "*Walden* does not contain Thoreau's most self-consciously environmentalist statements, nor his most close-grained nature observations" (125), he nonetheless sees *Walden* as a seminal environmentalist literary text because

> *Walden* reflects Thoreau's commitment to not one but a cluster of distinct approaches to nature, none of which was wholly original or unique to him

and thus all of which may be found widely pursued throughout American environmental prose, though reinforced by his example. (126)

He focuses on *Walden* "not only because *Walden* remains Thoreau's most enduring work," but also because it "embeds much of the history of his thinking about the natural environment as it unfolded from his apprentice years to his full maturity" (118). Buell is right: Thoreau's *Walden* is still the best text with which to begin an exploration of the environmental tradition in American literature. That is true not only because of what it reveals about Thoreau, but also because it exemplifies a range of issues central to environmentalism and ecocriticism.

One of the most basic ecocritical issues is whether a writer is essentially anthropocentric (homocentric), focused on the human uses of nature, or biocentric (ecocentric), focused on nature as an entity with value apart from any human use. In *Walden*, Thoreau exhibits both attitudes, but his anthropocentric vision dominates the book. He begins not with a chapter about nature, but with a chapter on "economy," a word with the same root as "ecology" but with a decidedly human emphasis: Economy is the *management* of one's house or habitat, while ecology is the *study* of one's house or habitat. It is not until after this long introductory chapter that we get a description of his cabin by the pond, where in nature Thoreau lived, and what he lived for. Other chapters such as "Reading," "The Village," and "Former Inhabitants; and Winter Visitors" also focus on human activity. The most explicitly anthropocentric chapter, however, is "Higher Laws," in which he depicts our natural impulses as ones that are "reptile and sensual, and cannot be wholly expelled" (219). "Nature is hard to be overcome," he says, "but she must be overcome" (221).

As a transcendentalist, Thoreau conveys his vision through symbolism, a literary tool for finding human meaning in nonhuman objects. The book's iconic image is, of course, Walden Pond, which Thoreau develops as a complex symbol. It is "earth's eye," its clear water a symbol of the clarity of vision that he seeks. It also serves as a symbol of purity in human ethics, the "crystalline purity" of its water offering a symbolic purity against which the observer can "measure the depth of his own nature" (186). Its water, neither air nor solid, also symbolizes humanity's spiritual position between heaven (the sky) and earth. And when spring arrives the pond symbolizes spiritual resurrection: "Walden was dead and is alive again" (311).

Animals too are often depicted symbolically in *Walden*: They are "beasts of burden" that "carry some portion of our thoughts" (225). In the ironically titled "Brute Neighbors" chapter, Thoreau offers examples of these symbolic animals. The eyes of young partridges suggest "the purity of infancy" (227), and a "winged cat" that is said to roam the Walden Woods becomes a symbol for Thoreau's own soaring poetic aspirations. At the end of the chapter, Thoreau describes "a game of checkers" that he plays with a loon while he rows his boat on the pond. When the loon dives, Thoreau tries to guess where he will surface by rowing his boat to that spot, but he finds that the loon always outsmarts him. The loon represents to Thoreau the ability to explore the depths of the pond, which many of his neighbors consider to be bottomless, but also his own inability to fathom fully the mysterious ways of nature.

Thoreau's symbolism, however, is not as abstract as Emerson's. For Emerson a natural object can essentially be discarded once its symbolic meaning has been discerned, but for Thoreau the natural object remains as something beautiful and interesting beyond its symbolism. Despite his seeming rejection of nature in "Higher Laws," in that same chapter he also acknowledges that "I found in myself, and still find, an instinct toward a higher, or, as it is named, spiritual life, as do most men, and another toward a primitive rank and savage one, and I reverence them both" (210).

This biocentric respect for "primitive" nature for its own sake is best seen in the "Winter Animals" chapter, where Thoreau describes various animals with a naturalist's eye and ear. He listens to the "Hoo hoo hoo" of the owls (272), the barking of foxes in the distance (273), and the "discordant screams" of the blue jays (275). Thoreau watches the red squirrels play, which, he says, "afforded me much entertainment by their manoeuvres" (273); he feeds the squirrels, rabbits, and chickadees from the door of his cabin; and he observes the partridges coming to feed near his woodpile. Thoreau is also interested to hear hunters describe the behavior of a fox as it tries to outsmart a pack of hounds. Although a small part of *Walden*, this biocentric interest in and respect for nature as a source of value in its own right can be seen throughout Thoreau's complete works, especially in his journal and his notes on wild fruits and seeds.

Another central issue of ecocriticism is the tension between environmentalists, who are concerned with protecting nature, and agriculturalists, who actually work the land and depend on nature for their livelihoods. Robert Cummings, in his article "Thoreau's Divide" (published in *Nineteenth-Century Prose* in 2004), describes the issue this way: "To the many people who work the land, professional environmentalists often seem at best, out of touch, and at worst, a threat to their livelihood" (206–07). "In any given situation," he continues, "the environmentalists tend to see a land use issue, whereas the farmer sees a home and a job" (207). On this issue Thoreau again expresses both sides.

Several years before starting to live at Walden Pond, Thoreau expressed in his journal his concern that farming was not a psychologically healthy occupation: "I must not lose any of my freedom by being a farmer and landholder" (*Writings of Henry David Thoreau* 291). The farmer's life is too constricted: "He can do one thing long not many well" (191). The farmer can also easily become too devoted to financial profit. In *Walden* Thoreau complains that because of our habit of "regarding the soil as property, or the means of acquiring property chiefly, the landscape is deformed" and "husbandry is degraded with us, and the farmer leads the meanest of lives" (165).

In "The Ponds," the central chapter of *Walden*, Thoreau extols the beauty and symbolic significance of Walden Pond, but he also contrasts it to nearby Flint's Pond, named after a farmer for whom Thoreau feels only disgust. He spends a long paragraph expressing his environmentalist rage at how farmer Flint has desecrated the land around the pond that bears his name: "What right had the unclean and stupid farmer, whose farm abutted on this sky water, whose shores he has ruthlessly laid bare, to give his name to it?" (195). Flint, Thoreau virtually shouts from the page, "thought only of its money value; whose presence perchance cursed all the shore; who exhausted the land around it, and would fain have exhausted the waters within it" (196). Flint's fields "bear no crops . . . but dollars" (196). This reduction of nature to mere monetary value by modern industrial farming continues to be a key environmentalist concern even today.

On the other hand, Thoreau says on the same page, "Farmers are respectable and interesting to me in proportion as they are poor,—poor farmers" (196). Thoreau himself sometimes did genuinely have ambitions to be a farmer. At one point he considered becoming a cranberry farmer, and in the second chapter of *Walden* he recounts how he actually bought a farm, the Hollowell Place, although before he could get the deed the farmer asked to buy the farm back, and Thoreau gladly obliged. The attractions of the Hollowell Place for him were the opposite of what might have attracted others to the property: He liked "its complete retirement, being about two miles from the village," "the gray color and ruinous state of the house and barn, and the dilapidated fences," and "the hollow and lichen-covered apple trees, gnawed by rabbits" (83)—in short, it was a suitable site for a "poor farmer."

Eventually he did try farming on a small scale near his cabin at Walden Pond. While living at the pond, Thoreau planted beans, potatoes, and peas, and diligently hoed them throughout the summer as an experiment in getting to know the earth and his bean crop especially. He expresses an agriculturalist's concern for the best methods of farming. He reads books about farming and follows their advice regarding the value of frequent hoeing as a substitute for manure (162), and he gives his reader a full account of his farming methods: when to plant ("about the first of June"), what pests to watch out for (worms and woodchucks), and when to harvest (as early as possible to avoid frost) (163). He also gives a full account of his finances, which yielded a profit of $8.71 1/2 (163). As a transcendentalist, Thoreau eventually attaches symbolic meaning to the beans—"Why concern ourselves so much about beans for seed, and not be concerned at all about a new generation of men?" (164)—but he clearly appreciates the agriculturalist's attachment to the physicality of tilling the earth.

The environmentalist versus agriculturalist tension is also related to the literary tension between the pastoral and georgic traditions, both rooted in the works of the Roman poet Virgil. The pastoral tradition, expressed in Virgil's *Eclogues*, describes the peaceful life of a shepherd isolated from the busy life of the town, a "(re)turn to a less urbanized, more 'natural' state of existence" (Buell, *Environmental Imagination* 31). In this tradition, nature becomes an idealized symbol of the simple life that implicitly criticizes more complex urban life. On the other hand, the georgic tradition, expressed in Virgil's *Georgics*, involves "didactic writing about the natural world as apprehended through human labor practices" (Ziser 191) and focuses on a more realistic, agriculturalist view of country life.

According to formalist critic Leo Marx (*The Machine in the Garden*, 1964), Thoreau represents an American pastoral tradition in which the idealized life in nature becomes a means of removing meaning from nature itself, as well as from society, and moving meaning into the symbols created in the mind of the writer:

> In *Walden* Thoreau is clear, as Emerson was, about the location of meaning and value. He is saying that it does not reside in the natural facts or in social institutions or in anything "out there," but in consciousness. (264)

In Marx's view, Thoreau converts the simple life in nature into a complex set of symbols, thereby separating nature from consciousness and locating it in the symbol-making mind of the writer. On the other hand, as an ecocritic Lawrence Buell emphasizes that the pastoral does include a relation between natural fact and society in Thoreau's writing: "The move to Walden is both a frontal assault on mainstream values like the protestant work ethic and a ritual reenactment of the pioneer experience, New England-style, with which the average American do-it-yourselfer can identify" (52). Timothy Sweet (*American Georgics*, 2002) and Michael Ziser, however, find that the agriculturalist, do-it-yourself mode of Thoreau's writing actually puts Thoreau more in the georgic tradition. Once again Thoreau can be shown to be on both sides of the issue, and it would be a mistake to try to put him into only one literary camp or the other.

Thoreau can also be shown to be on both sides of perhaps the most persistent debate in ecocriticism: conservationists versus preservationists. Conservationists tend to be anthropocentric in their belief that it is humanity's duty to use the land, but to use it well and without waste, and that true waste would be not to use it at all. Preservationists, on the other hand, take the more biocentric view that some parts of nature deserve to exist for their own sake and should be preserved and unaltered by humans as much as possible. Today conservationists are undoubtedly the majority, but there is also a vocal minority of strict preservationists. Many environmentalists are inevitably a mixture of both, as is Thoreau.

There is little in *Walden* explicitly about either of these issues, but one passage in the "Spring" chapter does seem to address them. He expresses concern that

> our village life would stagnate if it were not for the unexplored forests and meadows which surround it. We need the tonic of wildness,—to wade sometimes in marshes where the bittern and the meadow-hen lurk, and hear the booming of the snipe; to smell the whispering sedge where only some wilder and more solitary fowl builds her nest, and the mink crawls with its belly close to the ground. (317)

This sounds at first like a preservationist call to protect nature, and to some extent it is, but it is also clear that Thoreau wants to preserve nature primarily for human use as a source of physical and psychological refreshment (a "tonic"), not for its own sake. His comment on wildness here is consistent with his more famously misinterpreted comment in "Walking"—more a call for conserving nature as a psychological resource for humans than a strictly biocentric call for preserving the natural environment around towns.

To understand Thoreau's stance on conservation and preservation more fully, however, we need to follow him beyond *Walden*. In *The Maine Woods* (1864) he bemoans the destruction of Maine's forests by the logging industry: "The mission of men there seems to be, like so many busy demons, to drive the forest all out of the country, from every solitary beaver swamp, and mountain side, as soon as possible" (5). Later in the book, his excursion into the Maine wilderness prompts him to call for nature preserves. Recalling the English tradition of "king's forest," he wonders:

> Why should not we, who have renounced the king's authority, have our national preserves, where no villages need be destroyed, in which the bear and panther, and some even of the hunter race, may still exist, and not be "civilized off the face of the earth,"—our forests, not to hold the king's game merely, but to hold and preserve the king himself also, the lord of creation,—not for idle sport or food, but for inspiration and our own true recreation? or shall we, like villains, grub them all up, poaching on our own national domains? (156)

This call for preservation, echoing George Catlin's earlier call, would eventually help to persuade congress to establish Yellowstone, the first national park. Implicit in it is America's ongoing tension between the preservation of nature and the use of nature. Thoreau was not a purely biocentric preservationist; although today there are still relatively few absolute preservationists, the impulse to protect the natural environment that Thoreau expresses continues to be an important part of our national consciousness.

Ironically, Thoreau was also a professional surveyor who often was asked to survey the woodlots on the farms around Concord so that farmers could estimate how much money they might make by cutting the trees down to sell as firewood. In the course of his work, farmers often asked him why, when one species of tree was cut down, a different species would grow up in its place. Thoreau had a ready answer, which he gave in a speech to farmers at the annual Cattle Show that has been posthumously published as "An Address on the Succession of Forest Trees" (1860). He reminds his audience that seeds can be transported by various means: "chiefly by the agency of the wind, water, and animals" (167). Thus seeds of one species can be transported to succeed a different species that might have exhausted the soil of the nutrients it needs or that might have blocked the new species from thriving. The result is that

> when you cut down an oak wood, a pine wood will not *at once* spring up there unless there are, or have been, quite recently, seed-bearing pines near enough for the seeds to be blown from them. But, adjacent to a forest of pines, if you prevent other crops from growing there, you will surely have an extension of your pine forest, provided the soil is suitable. (168)

As ecologist David Foster points out, Thoreau's principle of the succession of tree species is the source of the concept of succession in modern ecology (134). Foster observes that Thoreau "recorded in great detail [in his Journal] many of the processes that gave rise to the forests that we have today" and that "we can apply this information in interpreting the development and current functions of our modern landscape" (12). Elsewhere in his late notes on plants (published posthumously as *Faith in a Seed* and *Wild Fruits*), Thoreau also describes species that are the first to develop in a new habitat as "pioneers," and the term "pioneer species" has since become part of the vocabulary of ecological science (Foster 136).

Although Thoreau is in many ways a quintessentially American writer whose observations of the American landscape might be hard for non-Americans to envision, we should not forget that there is also an international dimension to his writing. *Walden* begins not with a description of nature but with a comparison of his townsmen to "the Chinese and Sandwich Islanders" (4). As he watches the railroad race by the pond, his thoughts wander far beyond the Concord woods:

> I am refreshed and expanded when the freight train rattles past me, and I smell the stores which go dispensing their odors all the way from Long Wharf to Lake Champlain, reminding me of foreign parts of coral reefs, and Indian oceans, and tropical climes, and the extent of the globe. I feel more like a citizen of the world at the sight of the palm-leaf which will cover so many flaxen New England heads the next summer. (119)

Even the water of Walden Pond takes him to the far reaches of the globe in his imagination. As the pond's water evaporates, he can imagine that eventually

> the pure Walden water is mingled with the sacred water of the Ganges. With favoring winds it is wafted past the site of the fabulous islands of Atlantis and the Hesperides, makes the periplus of Hanno, and, floating by Ternate and Tidore and the mouth of the Persian Gulf, melts in the tropic gales of the Indian seas, and is landed in ports of which Alexander never heard the names. (298)

As Lawrence Buell has observed, "Thoreau cannot think locally without bringing in the rest of the world" ("Ecoglobalist Affects" 238). The environmental issues that Thoreau raises are not only local and national, but global. The same can be said of many of the writers who would come after him.

In 1864, two years after Thoreau's death, an American polymath scholar named George Perkins Marsh published *Man and Nature*, which historian Lewis Mumford has called "the fountainhead of the conservation movement" (78). Less philosophical and more pointedly conservationist than Thoreau's writing, Marsh's book was the first to catalog extensively how humans were destroying nature on a global scale and to recommend specific steps to solve the problem. It was, one might say, a nineteenth-century version of Al Gore's *An Inconvenient Truth* (2006). Marsh's goal was to return human culture to "the command of religion and of practical wisdom, to use this world as not abusing it" (13). Although Marsh seems not to have read Thoreau, he shares with Thoreau a concern for "humankind's proper relation to the material environment" (Sweet 168).

The cause of preservation expressed by Thoreau, on the other hand, was next championed by John Muir. Thoreau became one of Muir's heroes after Muir read *The Maine Woods*.[3] Muir fell in love with the Sierra Nevada mountain range as a young man, and he would successfully fight for the preservation of the Yosemite Valley as part of the national park system, found the Sierra Club, and fight unsuccessfully to stop California's Hetch Hetchy Valley from being flooded. But Muir was also a world traveler, having traveled around the world and visited most of the seven continents by the time he died in 1914, making his concern for preserving nature global as well as intensely local.

Early in the twentieth century, a young naturalist named Gifford Pinchot shared Thoreau's interest in forests and traveled to Europe to study forest management in France, Germany, and Switzerland. Returning to America, he advocated for wiser forest management practices on the European model and for the concept of "wise use"—the idea that nature *should* be used, but used wisely to benefit humanity. Pinchot's writings about wise use made him an influential voice for conservation, and his anthropocentric view of conservation influenced our first conservationist president, Theodore Roosevelt, who appointed Pinchot to head the new U.S. Forest Service.

Another forester, Aldo Leopold, began his career accepting Pinchot's wise use philosophy but eventually became one of the strongest voices for a more biocentric approach to nature. Leopold eventually came to believe that nature has an inherent right to exist for its own sake, not just for human use, and that some parts of nature are simply best left alone. In his most famous work, *A Sand County Almanac* (published posthumously in 1949), he argues that we need an "ecological conscience" that views nature as an intricate biological system with a much broader value than as mere commodity. He describes American attitudes toward the environment as "the A-B cleavage": "One group (A) regards the land as soil, and its function as commodity-production; another group (B) regards the land as a biota, and its function as something broader" (258–59). Leopold also knew and quoted from Thoreau's writing, and his concept of "home range" (the limited area in which an animal conducts its daily life) echoes Thoreau's close observation of animals.

After World War II, views such as Leopold's began to gain more traction in the public consciousness. Donald Worster has argued that the "age of ecology" began with the detonation of the first atomic bomb in 1945, an explosion that made humans realize for the first time that we actually had enough destructive power to destroy our planet. But if a bomb shocked us into ecological consciousness, a literary bombshell, Rachel Carson's *Silent Spring* (1962), prodded society into ecological action. Carson provided powerful evidence that pesticides were causing possibly irreversible damage to plants and animals, a price too high to pay for eliminating insect pests. Her book led to the banning of the insecticide DDT and to a reassessment of how our attempts to control nature might be hurting us more than helping us.

Several years after *Silent Spring*, another advocate for environmental activism emerged. Edward Abbey, an aspiring fiction writer urged by his publisher to write about what he knew best, published *Desert Solitaire* (1968), a collection of personal essays about his experience as a fire lookout and park ranger in Arches National Park. As a park ranger, Abbey feels that it is his duty to protect all of the park's living things without exception. His philosophy, he remarks ironically, is that "I prefer not to kill animals. I'm a humanist; I'd rather kill a *man* than a snake" (17). His view of nature is staunchly preservationist; he believes that "wilderness is a necessary part of civilization and that it is the primary responsibility of the national park system to preserve *intact and undiminished* what little still remains" (47).

Abbey returned to fiction in 1975 with his novel *The Monkey Wrench Gang*, which depicted a fictional ragtag group of friends who decide to sabotage construction sites of companies that are destroying the environment. They pull such pranks as pouring sand into the gas tanks of the crew's equipment. This novel and Abbey's popularity as a speaker for environmental causes led to the founding by some of his admirers of EarthFirst!, an informal group of activists who continued the tradition of "monkey-wrenching" to interfere with projects that destroy the environment. Since then other groups dedicated to ecosabotage, such as People for the Ethical Treatment of Animals (PETA) and the Earth Liberation Front (ELF), have emerged, often advocating more radical and violent methods than did Abbey, whose motto was "nobody gets hurt." Abbey himself remained somewhat aloof from these more radical organizations until his death in 1996.

Abbey explicitly acknowledges his debt to Thoreau in his essay "Down the River with Henry Thoreau" (from *Down the River*, 1982), in which he carries on a mental dialogue with Thoreau as he and his friends descend the Green River in Utah. Although Thoreau is most famous for the passive resistance expressed in "Civil Disobedience," he could also advocate a more active role against environmental destruction. Even as early as *A Week on the Concord and Merrimack Rivers* (1849), Thoreau speculates, "What may avail a crow-bar against that Billerica dam?" (37).

One of Abbey's contemporaries, Wendell Berry, has opted for a more agriculturalist approach to environmental activism. With deep family roots in Kentucky farming, he lives on a small farm in rural

Kentucky and writes passionately about the importance of small farms to American culture and the negative economic effects of large industrial farms. In his book *The Unsettling of America: Culture and Agriculture* (1977), Berry makes a distinction, similar to Leopold's "A-B cleavage," between the "exploiter," whose goal for nature is monetary profit, and the "nurturer," whose goal for nature is health for the land, his family, and himself (7). Berry began as a preservationist and has sometimes been a member of the Sierra Club, but he believes that it is at least as important to preserve our use of the soil that grows our food as it is to preserve the wilderness. In the early years of the twenty-first century, Berry has also been an activist against the damage done to the environment by coal mining. As a cultural critic and writer of essays, fiction, and poetry, Berry continues to be one of our most eloquent defenders of nature.

Less individualistic and more focused on community action than Thoreau, Berry nonetheless shares Thoreau's emphasis on local environments and the connection between nature and spirit.[4] Basic to Thoreau's transcendentalism is the assumption that nature is a spiritual resource leading to a better relationship with God. In almost every study of Thoreau, this assumption is axiomatic. Two recent studies that focus specifically on Thoreau's spiritual connection with nature are Alan Hodder's *Thoreau's Ecstatic Witness* (2001) and David Robinson's *Natural Life: Thoreau's Worldly Transcendentalism* (2004).

As a lifelong Baptist, Wendell Berry is also concerned about the role of religion in environmental issues, but he is not the first to raise that issue. In 1967, historian Lynn T. White published an essay titled "The Historical Roots of Our Ecologic Crisis," which provided a compelling argument that the medieval Christian church, with its emphasis on the biblical injunction to "subdue the earth," was the source of our continuing exploitation of nature. In his book *The Gift of Good Land: Further Essays Cultural and Agricultural* (1981), Berry counters White by pointing out that Christianity need not be an environmental villain, because the Bible also contains admonitions to be good stewards of the land. This issue has prompted various Christian denominations in America to issue official positions about their stance on the environment; see, for instance, "Sufficient, Sustainable Livelihood for All" by the Evangelical Lutheran Church in America (1999). It has also prompted an interest in how other religions, both in America and worldwide, relate to nature; see, for example, "Religion and Ecology: Can the Climate Change?," a special issue of *Daedalus: Journal of the American Academy of Arts and Sciences* from 2001.

Another eloquent environmental voice that emerged in the 1970s was that of Annie Dillard, whose book *Pilgrim at Tinker Creek* appeared in 1974. At the beginning of her writing career, Dillard lived in a small cabin on Tinker Creek in the Blue Ridge Mountains of Virginia, where she observed nature with a poet's eye. Readers understandably view Dillard's attempt to find truth in nature as a modern female version of Thoreau. Dillard, however, is less certain than Thoreau about finding absolute answers in nature (in *Walden* he writes, "hard bottom and rocks in place, which we can call *reality*," 98). Dillard is more intrigued by the mystery of nature:

> We don't know. Our life is a faint tracing on the surface of mystery. . . . We must somehow take a wider view, look at the whole landscape, really see it, and describe what's going on here. Then we can at least wail the right question into the swaddling band of darkness, or, if it comes to that, choir the proper praise. (9)

Her experience in nature is, however, similar to Thoreau's in that she is always attempting to "return to my senses" (34).

But Dillard and Carson are not the first female environmentalist writers. We can look back to the nineteenth century to find Susan Fenimore Cooper, a contemporary of Thoreau, whose book *Rural Hours* (1850) was more popular than *Walden* in its day. There is also the fiction of Sarah Orne Jewett that features the Maine landscape, or the observations of the desert in Mary Austin's essays. A strong contingent of female environmentalist writers has emerged since Dillard; see, for instance, the essays of Terry Tempest Williams, Anne LaBastille, Gretel Ehrlich, Ann Zwinger, and Alison Hawthorne Deming, or the essays and fiction of Barbara Kingsolver and Ursula K. Le Guin.

Implicit in the literature of these writers is the basic question of ecofeminism: Is there a significant difference between the way men and women respond to nature? Thoreau, a bit of a misogynist himself, would probably have answered no. It is a commonplace observation that *Walden* contains no sympathetic female characters, unless we include "Mother Nature," but some female readers of *Walden* see no problem with that and can even see the book as a "feminist manifesto"; see Laura Dassow Walls's "*Walden* as Feminist Manifesto" (1993) and Sarah Ann Wider's "'And What Became of Your Philosophy Then?': Women Reading *Walden*" (2004). On the other hand, some ecofeminist critics see the male vision of nature—as "a womb of generation and a provider of sustenance" (Kolodny 176), but also as a body to be dominated and violated—as dangerous to the environment.

Since the 1970s, environmental writing—nature writing, if you will—has exploded as a major genre. Thoreau would be interested to note that some of the strongest voices have been those of minorities with their own unique perspective on nature. Thoreau read avidly and took extensive notes about Native American culture, and he went to the Maine woods several times to learn woodcraft from his Native American guides, convinced that they knew nature in a unique way.[5] Today, Native American writers such as N. Scott Momaday, Leslie Marmon Silko, Louise Erdrich, and Joseph Bruchac offer a view of oneness with nature that sometimes seems an antidote to the European American exploitation. Latino writers (Alberto Ríos, Jimmy Santiago Baca, Rudolfo Anaya), African American writers (Alice Walker, Eddy L. Harris, Jamaica Kincaid), and Asian American writers (Maxine Hong Kingston, Diane Wakatsuki Houston) all add perspectives on nature that offer alternatives to the dominant culture's view.

Minority writers also raise issues of environmental justice caused by the exploitation of resources on the lands of indigenous people both in America and elsewhere, and by the disproportionate placement of polluting industries in minority neighborhoods. Thoreau could not have foreseen the latter issue, but he was aware of the former issue regarding Native Americans. Like many otherwise enlightened thinkers of his day, however, Thoreau chose to ignore obvious injustices, such as the removal of the Cherokees to Oklahoma, and to assume that Native Americans were doomed to lose their land to progress.[6]

Environmentalist voices today also come from various backgrounds and genres. Some, such as Loren Eiseley, Gary Paul Nabhan, and E. O. Wilson, have roots in the sciences. Thoreau, who lived during a time when science was still part of the broader unified study of natural history, would undoubtedly be pleased to see these writers reconnecting science to broader philosophical and social issues. Recent studies by Laura Dassow Walls (*Seeing New Worlds*, 1995), William Rossi ("Thoreau's Transcendental Ecocentrism," 2000), and Michael Berger (*Thoreau's Late Career*, 2000) have shown how Thoreau participated in the history of science as it was splitting off from the humanities into a separate intellectual culture.

Although Thoreau's writing includes sharp observations of nature worthy of the sciences, many of his works were first published in popular periodicals of the time, such as *Sartain's Union Magazine* (*The Maine Woods*) and *Atlantic Monthly* ("Walking"). Thus it is appropriate that some environmentalist writers, such as Barry Lopez and Bill McKibben, began in magazine writing and continue to use the popular media to convey their messages. As Thoreau also tried his hand at poetry early in his career (with little success), he would likely enjoy the visions of nature in the poetry of contemporary nature poets Mary Oliver and Gary Snyder.

Other environmentalist voices, such as Al Gore, Neil Everndon, and Yi-Fu Tuan, have connections to the social sciences. In recent years there has also been renewed interest in the links between Thoreau's interest in nature and his interest in the social sciences and social reform; see, for instance, Lance Newman's *Our Common Dwelling* (2005), Shawn Bingham's *Thoreau and the Sociological Imagination* (2007), Richard Schneider's "Thoreau's Human Ecology" (2008), or two edited volumes: William Cain's *A Historical Guide to Henry David Thoreau* (2000) and Jack Turner's *A Political Companion to Henry David Thoreau* (2009).

The range of nature writing today is too diverse to allow all of the significant writers to be included here, but for connections among Thoreau and modern nature writers see the following: John Elder's *Imagining the Earth: Poetry and the Vision of Nature* (1985), Scott Slovic's *Seeking Awareness in American Nature Writing* (1992), John P. O'Grady's *Pilgrims to the Wild* (1993), Richard J. Schneider's *Thoreau's Sense of Place* (2000), or Bill McKibben's anthology *American Earth: Environmental Writing Since Thoreau* (2008).

The issues that contemporary nature writers raise are crucial to our understanding of our humanity and our relation to the world around us. While some postmodern thinkers prefer to see "nature" as a social construction of the human imagination, with no reality beyond what we give it, environmental writers insist on the reality of the external world and on the necessity of understanding it. They believe, along with Thoreau, that we must value both the knowledge and the mystery of nature: "At the same time that we are earnest to explore and learn all things, we require that all things be mysterious and unexplorable, that land and sea be infinitely wild, unsurveyed and unfathomed by us because unfathomable" (*Walden* 317–18). Their goal is also Thoreau's: "We can never have enough of Nature" (318).

Notes

1. See Perry Miller, *Nature's Nation* (1967).
2. For examples of environmental writing prior to the nineteenth century, see Branch, *Reading the Roots* (2004).
3. See Buell, *The Environmental Imagination,* 136.

4. See Buell, *The Environmental Imagination*, 445, note 27.
5. See Sayre, *Thoreau and the American Indians*.
6. See Schneider, "Thoreau's Human Ecology" and Bellin, "In the Company of Savagists."

Works Cited

Abbey, Edward. *Desert Solitaire: A Season in the Wilderness*. New York: Simon, 1968.

_____. *Down the River*. New York: Dutton, 1982.

_____. *The Monkey Wrench Gang*. Philadelphia: Lippincott, 1975.

Bellin, Joshua David. "In the Company of Savagists: Thoreau's Indian Books and Antebellum Ethnology." *The Concord Saunterer: A Journal of Thoreau Studies* New Series 16 (2008): 1–32.

Berger, Michael Benjamin. *Thoreau's Late Career and "The Dispersion of Seeds": The Saunterer's Synoptic Vision*. Rochester: Camden, 2000.

Berry, Wendell. *The Gift of Good Land: Further Essays Cultural and Agricultural*. San Francisco: North Point, 1981.

_____. *The Unsettling of America: Culture and Agriculture*. San Francisco: Sierra Club, 1977.

Bingham, Shawn Chandler. *Thoreau and the Sociological Imagination: The Wilds of Society*. Lanham, MD: Rowman, 2007.

Branch, Michael P., ed. *Reading the Roots: American Nature Writing Before* Walden. Athens: U of Georgia P, 2004.

Buell, Lawrence. "Ecoglobalist Affects: The Emergence of U.S. Environmental Imagination on a Planetary Scale." *Shades of the Planet: American Literature as World Literature*. Ed. Wai Chee Dimock and Lawrence Buell. Princeton: Princeton UP, 2007. 227–48.

_____. *The Environmental Imagination: Thoreau, Nature Writing, and the Formation of American Culture*. Cambridge: Belknap of Harvard UP, 1995.

Cain, William E., ed. *A Historical Guide to Henry David Thoreau*. New York: Oxford UP, 2000.

Carson, Rachel. *Silent Spring*. Boston: Houghton, 1962.

Cooper, Susan Fenimore. *Rural Hours*. 1850. Ed. Rochelle Johnson and Daniel Patterson. Athens: U of Georgia P, 1998.

Cummings, Robert. "Thoreau's Divide: Rediscovering the Environmentalist/Agriculturalist Debate in *Walden*'s 'Baker Farm.'" *Nineteenth-Century Prose* 31.2 (Fall 2004): 206–29.

Dillard, Annie. *Pilgrim at Tinker Creek*. New York: Bantam, 1974.

Elder, John. *Imagining the Earth: Poetry and the Vision of Nature*. Urbana: U of Illinois P, 1985.

Emerson, Ralph Waldo. *Emerson's "Nature": Origin, Growth, Meaning*. Ed. Merton M. Sealts and Alfred R. Ferguson. New York: Dodd, 1969.

Foster, David R. *Thoreau's Country: Journey through a Transformed Landscape*. Cambridge: Harvard UP, 1999.

Fritzell, Peter A. *Nature Writing and America: Essays upon a Cultural Type*. Ames: Iowa State UP, 1990.

Gore, Al. *An Inconvenient Truth: The Planetary Emergency of Global Warming and What We Can Do about It*. New York: Rodale, 2006.

Hodder, Alan D. *Thoreau's Ecstatic Witness*. New Haven: Yale UP, 2001.

Kolodny, Annette. "Unearthing Herstory: An Introduction." *The Ecocriticism Reader: Landmarks in Literary Ecology*. Ed. Cheryll Glotfelty and Harold Fromm. Athens: U of Georgia P, 1996. 170–81.

Leopold, Aldo. *A Sand County Almanac with Essays on Conservation from Round River*. New York: Ballantine, 1970.

Marsh, George Perkins. *Man and Nature: Or, Physical Geography as Modified by Human Action*. 1864. Ed. David Lowenthal. Cambridge: Belknap of Harvard UP, 1965.

Marx, Leo. *The Machine in the Garden: Technology and the Pastoral Ideal in America*. New York: Oxford UP, 1964.

Matthiessen, F. O. *American Renaissance*. New York: Oxford UP, 1941.

McKibben, Bill, ed. *American Earth: Environmental Writing Since Thoreau*. New York: Library of America, 2008.

Miller, Perry. *Nature's Nation*. Cambridge: Belknap of Harvard UP, 1967.

Mumford, Lewis. *The Brown Decades: A Study of the Arts in America, 1865-1895*. New York: Harcourt, Brace and Company, 1931.

Nash, Roderick. *Wilderness and the American Mind*. New Haven: Yale UP, 1967.

Newman, Lance. *Our Common Dwelling: Henry Thoreau, Transcendentalism, and the Class Politics of Nature*. New York: Palgrave Macmillan, 2005.

O'Grady, John P. *Pilgrims to the Wild: Everett Ruess, Henry David Thoreau, John Muir, Clarence King, Mary Austin*. Salt Lake City: U of Utah P, 1993.

Religion and Ecology: Can the Climate Change? Spec. issue of *Daedalus: Journal of the American Academy of Arts and Sciences* 130.4 (Fall 2001): 1–306.

Robinson, David M. *Natural Life: Thoreau's Worldly Transcendentalism*. Ithaca: Cornell UP, 2004.

Rossi, William. "Thoreau's Transcendental Ecocentrism." *Thoreau's Sense of Place: Essays in American Environmental Writing*. Ed. Richard J. Schneider. Iowa City: U of Iowa P, 2000. 28–43.

Sayre, Robert F. *Thoreau and the American Indians*. Princeton: Princeton UP, 1977.

Schneider, Richard J. "Thoreau's Human Ecology." *Nineteenth-Century Prose* 35.2 (Fall 2008): 1–74.

_____, ed. *Thoreau's Sense of Place: Essays in American Environmental Writing*. Iowa City: U of Iowa P, 2000.

Slovic, Scott. *Seeking Awareness in American Nature Writing: Henry Thoreau, Annie Dillard, Edward Abbey, Wendell Berry, Barry Lopez*. Salt Lake City: U of Utah P, 1992.

Sweet, Timothy. *American Georgics: Economy and Environment in Early American Literature*. Philadelphia: U of Pennsylvania P, 2002.

Thoreau, Henry David. "An Address on the Succession of Forest Trees." *Excursions.* Princeton: Princeton UP, 2007.

_____. "Civil Disobedience" ("Resistance to Civil Government"). *Reform Papers.* Ed. Wendell Glick. Princeton: Princeton UP, 1973.

_____. *Faith in a Seed: The Dispersion of Seeds and Other Late Natural History Writings.* Ed. Bradley P. Dean. Washington, DC: Island, 1993.

_____. *The Maine Woods.* Princeton: Princeton UP, 1972.

_____. *Walden.* Ed. J. Lyndon Shanley. Princeton: Princeton UP, 1971.

_____. *A Week on the Concord and Merrimack Rivers.* Ed. Carl F. Hovde, William Howarth, and Elizabeth Hall Witherell. Princeton: Princeton UP, 1980.

_____. *Wild Fruits: Thoreau's Rediscovered Last Manuscript.* Ed. Bradley P. Dean. New York: Norton, 2000.

_____. *The Writings of Henry David Thoreau: Journal Volume 1; 1837–1844.* Ed. Elizabeth Hall Witherell, William L. Howarth, Robert Sattelmeyer, Thomas Blanding. Princeton: Princeton UP, 1981.

Turner, Jack, ed. *A Political Companion to Henry David Thoreau.* Lexington: U of Kentucky P, 2009.

Walls, Laura Dassow. *Seeing New Worlds: Henry David Thoreau and Nineteenth-Century Natural Science.* Madison: U of Wisconsin P, 1995.

_____. "Walden as Feminist Manifesto." *Interdisciplinary Studies in Literature and the Environment* 1.1 (Spring 1993): 137–44.

Wider, Sarah Ann. " 'And What Became of Your Philosophy Then?': Women Reading *Walden.*" *Nineteenth-Century Prose* 31.2 (Fall 2004): 152–71.

Worster, Donald. *Nature's Economy: A History of Ecological Ideas.* Cambridge: Cambridge UP, 1977.

Ziser, Michael G. "*Walden* and the Georgic Mode." *Nineteenth-Century Prose* 31.2 (Fall 2004): 186–205.

Pastoral, Antipastoral, and Postpastoral as Reading Strategies_____

Terry Gifford

The Pull of the Pastoral: A Story from England

When we have arrived home from work after the start of another school year, my wife Gill and I, both teachers, have taken to driving out of the big industrial city where we live in Sheffield, England, past the last houses of our suburb, and up over heather moorland to park on a hilltop. Fifteen minutes from our house and we have passed a sign into the Peak District National Park. We walk along the hill's crest to the start of the rocks called Stanage Edge that look out far to the west. We're in the very last of the daylight and we don't go far. Darkening gales and rain blow us back to the car quite quickly. But on at least one day a week we've escaped briefly from the shackles of work and preparing the evening meal. Then we coast back down into town feeling slightly pleased with ourselves and quietly better within ourselves. Why?

Is it because we've snatched, against the odds, a forbidden midweek aftertaste of, say, "Flying Buttress," our rock climbing on Stanage Edge the weekend before? Not really. Our short dusk walk is a rather different thing. It's more to do with soaking up the place itself. Up on that exposed cliff top, facing west into the fading light and feeling the full force of the elements coming at us over Sir William Hill and Eyam Moor, we simply look left down the length of the Derwent Valley toward the majestic Chatsworth House, or in the other direction, up to the peaty Kinder Scout plateau. We take in a whole topography. At our feet a farm nestles under the road below us, apparently pegged down by its stone walls that enclose smooth lawns descending to rough sheep-grazed pasture dipping toward the hidden village of Hathersage. The western sky at dusk is part of it, as are the brooding rocks of the emerging, upthrust, gritstone edge that dips back toward impenetrable bogs and, beyond, the twinkling city lights. I suspect that we take this horizontal walk so that we can look out more, take in that space, say again to each other, "Aren't we lucky to be living next to this?" Then we return to our student suburb, which visiting American friends find to be a city neighborhood of suffocating, overcrowded row housing and narrow streets. Actually, of course, we didn't choose to be living here. We've ended up with what we could afford in our economic circumstances, like everyone else. Secretly we'd like to live, if not actually in Robin Hood's Cave on Stanage Edge, then maybe in the farm below it.

Perhaps I'm giving too much away. You'll have guessed by now that we are aging hippies and fans of pastoral writing—writing about nature, wilderness, or what in England we call "the countryside." We're pastoralists, a sadly typical, modern urban subspecies of the breed. No, of course we don't herd sheep, in the original meaning of being a "pastor" or shepherd, although I've admitted that, secretly and unrealistically, we'd like to escape the city to that little farm and do just that. But what we've been subconsciously enacting on these evening jaunts and our weekend walks and climbs is the ancient pastoral impulse of retreat to a rural landscape and return to the city. This is what Shakespeare's pastoral dramas *The Winter's Tale* (1623) and *As You Like It* (1623) are about, and this is why we have popular weekend hikers' buses out of Sheffield to visit our local "Bohemia," "the blasted heath," or "the Forest of Arden." Indeed, this is why the Peak District National Park, right on the shoulder of Sheffield, is the second most visited national park in the world, serving as the "lungs," or breathing spaces, for the big crowded industrial cities of Sheffield, Manchester, Leicester, and Birmingham, and even drawing weekend rock climbers condemned to live in London. This is why the Scot John Muir invented national parks (after he emigrated to America from Scotland with his parents at the age of eleven), preserving Yosemite National Park in 1892 "for public use, resort and recreation"—the kind of recreation that would result from any retreat to a national park, followed by one's return to the city feeling somehow renewed, changed a little, and, most importantly for Muir, changed in the direction of wanting to preserve the national park from commercial exploitation and the destruction of its ecosystems. Muir was not to know in his time that the strength of the pastoral impulse was eventually to threaten the very source of renewal itself: queues of cars clog both Yosemite and the Peak District national parks on the weekends.

If the pastoral experience of retreat—from the tensions of the court, work, and the city, and into the country for raw contact with nature—is still a social need, is pastoral writing still alive? Some English academics do not think so, arguing that the separation of town and country is now defunct; even rural living is urbanized in so many ways. The Internet, for example, has turned many rural retreaters into workers in the global marketplace, their work directed from offices in urban tower blocks. So, any writing about the English countryside, or rural landscapes in other regions of the world, must now be tainted by urbanization or even globalism of different kinds, as villages have become suburbs and wild land has become domesticated and populated with urban hikers.

When, in the third century BCE, Theocritus wrote the first pastoral text for the Greek court in Alexandria about the shepherds that he remembered from his youth in Sicily, he idealized the country for his urban audience. His book was called *The Idylls*. Two centuries later, Virgil set his Latin pastorals in Arcadia, a real part of Greece, which has come to represent the idealized location of pastoral literature, which for Shakespeare was Bohemia and the Forest of Arden. So there has always been something suspect about pastoral writing, something nostalgic, escapist, comfortingly timeless, and stable: in a word, Arcadian.

Well, is that how I described our view from Stanage? How can I celebrate a valued place and its impact upon me without idealizing or prettifying it? Take another look at my opening paragraphs.

I really love this wild place, and I want to communicate that feeling in my writing. Is "nestling" prettifying? Perhaps it is. And I'm sorry about the alliteration. I just can't help it when I want you to enjoy, through my expression in language, what I enjoy about "feeling the full force of the elements." How can I avoid the traps of pastoralization—an idealizing tone—when I come to use language to evoke my feeling for my special place? How can a reader recognize that tone? Can a reader tell self-indulgent idealization from genuine insights brought back by the writer on return from a rural retreat?

Well, I could have mentioned in my opening paragraphs the Hope Valley Cement Works on the horizon, the scars made by quarries that I can see being dug daily in the National Park, the urban pay-and-display machine at the Stanage Edge Car Park, the nineteenth-century industrial grime on the grit, the current economic predicament of the struggling hill farmer, and the urbanization of the road beyond Ringinglow by the series of road signs warning of lambs, bends, walkers, parking restrictions, etc. This would have turned my writing into antipastoral. An English antipastoral poet of the eighteenth-century life of cottagers, George Crabbe, wrote in *The Village*, "I paint the Cot, / As Truth will paint it, and as Bards will not" (lines 53–54). He sought to draw attention to the difference between "the poet's rapture and the peasant's care." Indeed, he might have been addressing the modern Stanage hill farmer when he wrote, "Can poets soothe you, when you pine for bread, / By winding myrtles round your ruin'd shed?' (lines 59–60). Modern English shepherds, like their counterparts throughout Europe, are having as tough a time as they always have, despite subsidies from the European Union.

Perhaps modern writers like me, writing about delightful walks through the agricultural crisis of English hill farms, should take advice from George Crabbe. If they did, and they did not want to simply focus on an antipastoral corrective to idealization of the countryside, what third way is left open to them? Well, without wishing to sound prescriptive, I could offer suggestions for features of what I call "postpastoral" writing about the countryside: awe leading to humility in the face of the creative and destructive forces of nature; awareness of the culturally loaded language we use about the country; accepting responsibility for our relationship with nature and its dilemmas; and recognition that the exploitation of nature is often accompanied by the exploitation of the less powerful people who work with it, visit it, or less obviously depend upon its resources. It is the difference between reading a pastoral text, an antipastoral text, and a postpastoral text that this chapter will try to clarify.

What Is Pastoral Literature?

The pastoral is an ancient cultural tool. It has been a major way in which we, in Western culture, have mediated and negotiated our relationship with the land upon which we depend and the forces of nature at work in "outer nature," as we have simultaneously mediated and negotiated our relationships with each other and what we think of as our "inner nature." The very first pastoral texts from ancient Greece described shepherds' song competitions. These textual mediations are still the songs that we sing to each other as writers and as readers, and never have these songs, and the debate about their interpretation, been more important to our culture. Today the very survival of our species depends upon not just this debate, but our ability to find the right images to represent our way of living with, and within, what we variously characterize as nature, earth, land, place, and our global environment.

The earliest origins of the pastoral in ancient Greece established the characteristic mode of retreat and return that remains today—a retreat into living nature/countryside/wilderness, and a return with insights for those living in the court/city/computerized world. The first Greek and Roman pastoral texts also established the characteristic qualities of the pastoral: the idealizing of Theocritus's *Idylls*, and the Arcadian nostalgia for a past golden age in the later *Eclogues* of Virgil. American literature has continued this European tradition, from the writings of the eighteenth-century farmer Crèvecoeur to Thoreau's *Walden* (1854) and contemporary nature writing. The features of pastoral literature can be summed up under the following headings.

Idealized

Seeing nature through "rose-tinted spectacles" is the old-fashioned way of expressing the idealization found in pastoral writing. Another might be to say that an idealized text often emphasizes fertility, resilience, beauty, and unthreatened stability in nature. These are complacent and comforting representations of nature that strategically omit any sense of elements that might be counter to this positive image. Indeed, we have the word "idyllic" from Theocritus's original *Idylls*. What could be more idyllic than this?

> We lay stretched out in plenty, pears at our feet,
> Apples at our sides and plumtrees reaching down,
> Branches pulled earthward by the weight of fruit.
> (fifth stanza, lines 17–19)

No sweat is needed in harvesting for Theocritus, as everything is within easy reach, with even the fruit itself reaching down to be plucked. The key idyllic word for this uncertain subsistence agriculture is "plenty," a notion made visible in the heavy hanging "weight of fruit." It is a word used by eighteenth-century English poet Alexander Pope at the end of his idealization of the royal forest in his long poem *Windsor Forest*, in which Pope also employs the idealized image of corn bending to tempt the hand of the harvester:

> Here *Ceres'* gifts in waving prospect stand,
> And nodding tempt the joyful reaper's hand;
> Rich Industry sit smiling on the Plains
> And peace and plenty tells a STUART reigns. (lines 39–42)

The "joyful" worker is coyly "tempted" by the seductively "nodding" corn, the "gift" of Ceres, the goddess of agriculture and fertility. But Pope's pastoral obviously has the political purpose of endorsing for

---

his readers the "peace and plenty" brought by the reign of his patron, the Stuart king.

In nineteenth-century America, John Muir delighted in conjuring an idealized diary entry for July 11, 1869, celebrating his first view down into Yosemite Valley in California from his camp beside the Merced River:

> All the Merced streams are wonderful singers, and Yosemite is the centre where the main tributaries meet. From a point about half a mile from our camp we can see into the lower end of the famous valley, with its wonderful cliffs and groves, a grand page of mountain manuscript that I would gladly give my life to be able to read. . . . Some of the external beauty is always in sight, enough to keep every fibre of us tingling, and this we are able to gloriously enjoy though the methods of its creation may lie beyond our ken. (227)

This passage is full of Muir's most enthusiastic embellishments. The words "wonderful" (twice), "grand," and "glorious," taken together, might seem to be idealizations, but actually every time I have arrived at the rim to see again one of the wonders of the world, something like a "tingling in every fibre" does take place in the face of its breathtaking beauty. The metaphor of streams as "singers" might seem fanciful, but actually Muir would come to read the "manuscript" of the rock to discover, contrary to the scientific opinion of his time, that the glacial "method of its creation" was a huge ("grand") ice-carved trough. So despite Muir's tendency to gloriously idealize this landscape in pastoral writing, this actually inspired his scientific and later conservation writings, which took a quite different tone.

Nostalgic

In *The Idylls*, written in the third century BCE, Theocritus looks back to his childhood in Sicily; a nostalgic look back at the past is often a feature of pastoral texts. When childhood itself is not the focus of memories of innocent engagement with a more wild form of nature, the focus might be the past that only disappeared a few years ago. English critic Raymond Williams, when he started looking into this aspect of writing about the English countryside in *The Country and the City* (1975), detected that there was a kind of backwards moving escalator (60). A text might suggest that life was better in the countryside only ten years before, while the texts written at *that* time suggested that, only ten years before that, life lived in the same place was really better. The texts written at that time also echoed this backward-looking idealization of nature, and so on. The Scottish poet and story writer George Mackay Brown lived on the Hebridean island of Orkney, which he left only twice in his life. He almost never wrote about the present, but instead wrote about a mythical past, when life was at times tough but was rooted in the security of the seasons and without modern globalizing technologies like the radio. (He wrote an amusing short story about the arrival of a radio on the island.) The island summer practice of digging out brick-shaped lumps of peat from the bog (to put on the home fire when dried) is back-breaking work. "Peat Cutting," Mackay Brown's poem about this ancient activity, ends with a typical myth-making gesture toward a vague geological past:

> And a lark flashed a needle across the west
> And we spread a thousand peats
> Between one summer star
> And the black chaos of fire at the earth's centre. (lines 20–23)

The contemporary American farmer-poet Wendell Berry also chooses a life without modern technologies, preferring horse to tractor, for example. In his long poem "The Handing Down," he refers to a dialogue between a farmer (actually his grandfather) and a fern, in which the farmer has learned from the fern what to do with his hands—a lesson that he, in turn, has handed on:

> In his handing it has come down
> until now—a living

that has survived
all successions and sheddings. ("The Fern," lines 11–14)

Here is a pastoral evaluation of an idealized past to be set against the trials and uncertainties of the present.

Unproblematic

Against the turbulence and confusion of the present and the future, a pastoral past evoked in literature often provides imagery of order, stability, and agreed values—a stable "living," in Berry's terms. Thoreau went to live in his cabin at Walden Pond to simplify his life by escaping the tensions of so-called civilization in cities. He wrote, "I went to the woods because I wished to live deliberately, to front only the essential facts of life, and see if I could not learn what it had to teach" (135). Most people, argued Thoreau, are uncertain about the purpose of life and "live meanly, like ants" in busy cities, their lives "frittered away by detail" in building careers, homes, and wealth. For Alexander Pope, the idyllic idea of Windsor Forest is a place where variety and difference can be acknowledged while ultimately achieving a stable coexistence: "Where order in variety we see, / And where, tho' all things differ, all agree" (lines 15–16). Just like that! Perhaps the sudden glibness of this last line betrays its oversimplification of the difficulties of its achievement. In the title essay of her book *Teaching a Stone to Talk* (1982), American writer Annie Dillard evokes this sense of unproblematic unity by "witnessing" the "silence of nature": "There is a vibrancy to the silence, a suppression, as if someone were gagging the world. But you wait, you give your life's length to listening, and nothing happens. The ice rolls up, the ice rolls back, and still that single note obtains. The tension, or lack of it, is intolerable. The silence is not actually suppression; instead, it is all there is" (90). Pastoral literature can offer a reductive space in which the writer might encourage the reader to contemplate what the transcendentalist Thoreau calls "higher living."

Golden age

In the classical European story of creation, the earliest age of human life on the earth was an idyllic one:

> Men had no need of weapons.
> Nations loved one another.
> And the earth, unbroken by plough or hoe,
> Piled the table high. Mankind
> Was content to gather the abundance
> Of whatever ripened. (lines 186–191)

This passage comes from "Creation; Four Ages; Flood; Lycaon," translated from the Latin by Ted Hughes in *Tales from Ovid* (1997). Hughes was an environmentalist English poet, and he made this translation for a modern audience facing a global environmental crisis:

> And the first age was Gold.
> Without laws, without law's enforcers,
> This age understood and obeyed
> What had created it.
> Listening deeply, man kept faith with the source.
> (lines 160–164)

Here, listening represents what we might now call ecology, or the Intergovernmental Panel on Climate Change, or, as we shall see, postpastoral literature. Indeed, it might be argued that what we now urgently need from the pastoral tradition are images of how we might "keep faith with the source."

Of course, pastoral writing that refers to a golden age does not have to be set in the past, as William Morris's utopian novel *News from Nowhere* (1891) demonstrates. Although set in an imaginary future, Morris's novel does idealize a return to medieval peasant village agriculture. Perhaps I might dare to suggest that the modern equivalent might be the romantic notion of the golden age of the "ecological Indian" that can be detected in some of the writings of the Native American poet, novelist, and essayist Linda Hogan.

Retreat and return

At the end of Shakespeare's pastoral plays, the characters who have retreated from the turmoil of the court into an apparently simpler life in nature must inevitably return to the court. Marriages and reconciliations follow because lessons have been brought back that now make these possible. Thoreau seeks to "see if I could not learn what [the woods] had to teach" and his desire to publish the book *Walden* is his delivery of the results (135). In this he was following the pattern of what his mentor Emerson called "the chant," in which an experience of more elevated living in contact with nature carries with it the responsibility to communicate it upon return to ordinary life. The chant, song, poem, or story delivers the insights gained from the retreat. This common pattern to the pastoral impulse suggests that the best travel writing, and even the best mountaineering and adventure literature, serves a pastoral function. Does it make a difference if readers are aware of this? The question is one to test out on, say, John Krakauer's *Into the Wild* (1996).

Arcadian

Today you can visit Walden Pond and walk around its shoreline and into the woods to find the site of Thoreau's cabin. When I went, it was raining, and if I had written about getting cold and wet in those unimpressive thin woods beside the bleak chilly lake, what I would have written would hardly have been an idealization of the place. In other words, it would not have been Arcadian writing. The idealization of the pastoral is a literary construct that transforms an actual place, with its real mixture of positive and negative qualities, into a glowing Arcadia. This literary term derives from Virgil's famous pastoral verses, *The Eclogues*, set in the real Arcadia in Italy; Virgil's literary representation of that place as a haven from wars and land disputes has come to be know as Arcadian. Of course, in biblical terms the first Arcadia was the Garden of Eden, so we might also call an idealized description of a real place Edenic. For Pope, Windsor Forest could be turned into a green Eden by the heightened description of his song: "The Groves of Eden, vanish'd now so long, / Live in description, and look green in song" (lines 7–8). When I talked about the European pastoral tradition to scholars in a university in Nepal, I realized that European travellers had idealized a mythical hidden mountain village in Nepal as Shangri-la. This was an elusive Himalayan Arcadia invented by early travellers. In Alex Garland's novel *The Beach* (1996), is the hidden cove in Thailand a Shangri-la? Is Edward Abbey's version of Arches National Monument in *Desert Solitaire* (1967) an Arcadia?

Sentimental or complex pastoral?

Most of the features of pastoral literature listed so far have been about the idealizing distortion of the literary construct of the pastoral. But what of the lessons delivered on return from the retreat into nature? Could it not be the case that what had been expected as a delightfully simplified experience of the harmony, peace, and repose of nature had actually turned out to be more complicated than that? Might the literature of return contain insights into the complexity of our relationship with nature and affect our inner nature, with implications for the personal and social justice of our relationships with each other? In 1964, American literary critic Leo Marx offered, in his landmark book *The Machine in the Garden*, a distinction between what he called "sentimental pastoral" and "complex pastoral" (25). The former delivers no insights, but merely indulges in complacent escapism in its celebration of retreat into nature; however, the complex pastoral offers lessons, often implicit or delivered with ironic disguise. Marx's great example is Shakespeare's *The Tempest*, at the end of which, Marx argues, Prospero's renewal comes as a result of "an effort of mind and spirit" from inner resources gained during his island retreat from the court

(70). But Marx also includes comments on an American tradition of complex pastoral, from *Moby-Dick* (1851) through *Walden*, *Huckleberry Finn* (1884), and *The Great Gatsby* (1925). The challenge for contemporary readers is to distinguish between sentimental and complex pastorals today.

What Is Antipastoral Literature?

Some writers have wanted to correct the idealization of the pastoral by presenting counter evidence that emphasizes the opposite features in a gritty realism. George Crabbe has already been mentioned as an antipastoral poet of the eighteenth century, but it was the farm worker Stephen Duck who considered Pope on his own terms and style. Telling it how it was, with sweat "in briny streams" running down his face, in *The Thresher's Labour* (1736) Duck directly countered Pope's version with the agricultural reality:

> No Fountains murmur here, no Lamkins play,
> No Linnets warble, and no Fields look gay;
> 'Tis all a gloomy, melancholy Scene,
> Fit only to provoke the Muse's Spleen. (lines 58–61)

Duck attacks the idealized verbs of Pope's type of pastoral: "murmur," "play," "warble." Pope's classical Muse would be sent into a melancholy mood by the reality of the labour that actually maintains the countryside.

As long as there have been idealized pastoral texts, there have been elements of the antipastoral in literature, the features of which can be summed up as the opposite of those of the pastoral. Elements of the antipastoral are corrective of the pastoral, often explicitly so. They are not in any way idealized; in fact, they are often harsh and and unattractive. Further, the antipastoral emphasizes realism, is problematic, showing tension, disorder, and inequalities. The antipastoral challenges literary constructs as false distortions and parses the mythologies from such settings as Arcadia, Eden, Shangri-La.

Sometimes writers of mainly pastoral texts will introduce elements of the antipastoral to give their texts authenticity. Even Theocritus's *Idylls* carries a health warning for peasants going barefoot on idyllic Mediterranean hills: "You shouldn't go barefoot on the hillside, Battus. / Wherever you tread, the ground's one thorny ambush" ("The Herdsmen," lines 58–59). Even Thoreau complained that his bean field was under attack from first worms and then woodchucks. But perhaps the most common contemporary antipastoral texts are dystopian novels, which often depict a future in which humans have devastated the environment to such an extent that their own survival is threatened. Cormac McCarthy's *The Road* (2006) would be an extreme example. In this novel the last birds have already flown, and the novel's final paragraph reminds readers that the future of the brook trout and, indeed, pure water itself lies in their hands. The apocalyptic, antipastoral novel can act as a warning about the very future of nature itself, but such a stance by a writer, hoping not just to frighten and threaten but to engage with the complex questions for our species, might better be described as postpastoral.

What Is Postpastoral Literature?

While the English literary critics John Barrell and John Bull, editors of *The Penguin Book of English Pastoral Verse* (1974), were declaring the pastoral to be dead, the American critics Leo Marx and Lawrence Buell were suggesting that the pastoral was so important that we could expect to see it reinventing and reinvigorating itself into the future. Indeed, Buell's confidence in the radical role of the pastoral in America to offer critiques that then would become institutionally accepted and acceptable ("dissent becoming consensus") led him to suggest that this was a continuing pattern: "So American pastoral has simultaneously been counterinstitutional and institutionally sponsored" (50). But Williams, in *The Country and the City*, finally put the last nail in the coffin

---

of the critical use of the term "pastoral." He exposed the politically conservative function of English pastoral literature in its distortions and omissions, emphasizing only idealization, and he saw no evidence since Shakespeare of the complex pastoral in literature. Since 1964, no critics seem to have taken up Leo Marx's distinction between the sentimental and complex pastoral. The term "pastoral" has come to be associated only with idealization, as in the verb "to pastoralize" the representation of a landscape. What was clearly needed was a term for writing about nature that outflanked the closed circle of the pastoral and its opposite, the antipastoral. In 1994, I offered the notion of the postpastoral in relation to the poetry of Ted Hughes, and I later developed the idea to apply to different kinds of literature. In some senses this is an alternative term for Marx's "complex pastoral." Postpastoral texts, I now suggest, are texts that raise for readers some or all of the following six questions, illustrated with examples from British and American poetry.

1. *Can awe in the face of nature (e.g., landscapes) lead to humility in our species, reducing our hubris?* Much pastoral poetry begins with awe but leans toward comfort and complacency. In the poetry of Gerard Manley Hopkins, awe at "God's Grandeur," in the poem of that title, leads to humility. This is essential if the hubris of our species' treatment of its environment is to be recognized. The Scottish poet Sorley MacLean, in a Gaelic praise-song for the deserted township of Screapadal on his native island of Raasay, laments the brutal clearances of 1852, but concludes his poem "Screapadal" by transforming the image of a basking shark into the back of a nuclear submarine, representing a hubris "that would leave Screapadal without beauty / just as it was left without people" (309). Pope's pastoral celebrated the human exploitation of the gift of nature, but postpastoral poetry recognizes the dangers of a complacent view of our fragile relationship with nature, seeking to avoid hubris. The contemporary American poet Gary Snyder provides plenty of evidence for all six questions in his book of selected poems *No Nature* (1992). Snyder's awe for nature leads to the

humility of seeking a purified form of attention to it by close contact, as is evident in the following passage from Snyder's "Cold Mountain Poems": "I'll sleep by the creek and purify my ears" (twelfth stanza, line 8).

2. What are the implications of recognizing that we are part of nature's creative-destructive processes? The awe at the heart of Blake's famous poem "The Tyger" is for the circular dynamic of its "fearful symmetry": its very vitality is sustained by destructive power. It is not a paradox that both tiger and lamb are necessary; it is simply the awesome mystery that a biocentric vision offers. The perspective of the pastoral is static and anthropocentric. A biocentric view accepts that what grows decays, which in turn feeds growth, but neither growth nor decay is dominant. The early poetry of Ted Hughes satirizes the cultural protections that we erect to avoid confronting and celebrating the death process. Blake's major project in *The Marriage of Heaven and Hell* (1790–93) is an exploration of how we might view ourselves in a destructive-creative universe "if the doors of perception were cleans'd" and we could break our own "mind-forg'd manacles," such as the pastoral. For Blake, what the pastoral suppresses then creates an actual hell out of what should be a heaven, a heaven of both bees and worms in which the tiger and the lamb live their deaths. In his poem "Ripples on the Surface," Snyder evokes salmon ripples in the birthing and dying stream as an image of vitality in nature and its erasure, "Ever-fresh events / scraped out, rubbed out, and used, used again" (lines 10–11) as an image of what we learn from nature: "the little house in the wild, / the wild in the house" (lines 16–17).

3. If our inner nature echoes outer nature, how can the latter help us understand the former? The result of such recognition is that the destructive and creative processes in the natural world can provide images for understanding our own inner processes. Indeed, our inner processes have a continuum with the outer world, as singers of folk songs have always known (the folk song "The Seeds of Love" goes, "But I oftentimes have snatched at the red rose-bud / And gained but the willow tree"—Lloyd 184, lines 3–4). In the twentieth century, Peter Redgrove's poetry, for example, explored the way in which we are influenced by external natural forces of which we have lost our understanding. We respond to atmospheric pressure, natural electricity, and the seasons and phases of the moon in our sensuous apprehension of the world, but it is in our dreams that we often formulate our understanding of this relationship. Redgrove's poem "The Big Sleep" suggests that maybe women who live by the sea have a pregnancy that is related to the tides, and that their dreams are also influenced also by rhythms of the sea. Snyder takes a more simple view: "creek music, heart music" ("For All," line 12).

4. If nature is culture, is culture nature? In an obvious way, making this connection is what poetry has always done, even before it was written down. The oral tradition largely consists of images by which our inner nature can be understood in terms of cultural constructs that define external nature, as the singer of the folksong quoted above clearly understood. Thus, natural images in poetry only work because nature is culture, and poetry in particular plays upon the instability or variability of our constructs. One person's "sowing" of the seeds of love is another person's sexual harassment.

But the realization that culture itself is natural provides a vital opportunity for the poetic imagination. At the climax of "Home at Grasmere," William Wordsworth struggles at the limits of language to articulate what Andrew Marvell had hinted at a century and a half earlier in "The Garden." Wordsworth says he is

> Speaking of nothing more than what we are—
> How exquisitely the individual Mind
> (And the progressive powers perhaps no less
> Of the whole species) to the external world
> Is fitted; and how exquisitely too—
> Theme this but little heard of among men—
> The external world is fitted to the mind. (lines 1005–11)

If, as Snyder says, the writing of poetry is "the practice of the wild mind," then poetry is not thinking about nature, but nature thinking. If "the external world is fitted to the mind," then our thinking is leading to either our own natural extinction as a species or our adaptation to our environment. As Snyder says in "By Frazier Creek Falls," "We *are* it / it sings through us" (lines 16–17).

5. How can consciousness, through conscience, help us heal our alienation from our home? The revolutionary degree of Wordsworth's discovery can be seen in light of the Enlightenment notion that consciousness was what separated us, and indeed elevated us, from the rest of nature. But for those who, like Wordsworth, sought a connectedness with nature, consciousness remained a source of alienation from the rest of nature. With consciousness comes conscience and the exercise of choosing to reverse some of our alienating conceptions, such as those D. H. Lawrence refers to as "the voice of my education" in the poem "Snake." A "petty" attitude toward the possibility of threatening the otherness of nature's underworld is actually, he points out, a demeaning of humanity. The logic of such an idea can lead down the road of a poetry that can reminds us of a taken-for-granted exploitation of "natural resources." As Snyder puts it in "Little Songs for Gaia": "The log trucks remind us, / as we think, dream and play / of the world that is carried away" (eighth stanza, lines 4–6).

6. Is the exploitation of our planet aligned with our exploitation of ethnic minorities? Ecofeminists such as Carolyn Merchant have pointed out that the exploitation of women has derived from the same mindset that has been exploiting the planet for centuries under the guise of science. Ecofeminists argue that we need to counteract both at the same time; otherwise there will be no uncontaminated environment in which emancipated women, and others, can live in the future.

The treatment of the environment in the poetry of Black and Asian women poets writing in Great Britain today is often found to be parallel to considerations of the treatment of people. Guyanese poet Grace Nichols, in her sequence *I Is a Long Memoried Woman* (1983), assumes that a woman's ease or anger about her own treatment is echoed by that of the landscape in which she lives. This is not so much metaphorical as sensuously linked within the poetry. In a sense, a woman's life in Guyana, the poetry suggests, is lived through the environment. Crimes against nature are crimes against women in this case, as in so many others around the globe.

Such holistic thinking embedded in Indian mythology is contributing to contemporary British culture through poems such as Debjani Chatterjee's "Ganapati." After telling the story of the elephant god marrying the banana tree, the poem's concluding line suggests that by embodying in myth such an unusual marriage, "We stretched our notions of humanity" (line 6). It is an expanding of humanity to conceive of marrying the animal and the vegetable in a natural as well as cultural sense. Thus the poem claims to have challenged "swamps of intolerance." Intolerant attitudes can obscure our conceptions of nature and of cultures that challenge those conceptions. Snyder thought of North America as Turtle Island, colonized internally and externally in "Mother Earth: Her Whales": "North America, Turtle Island, taken by invaders / who wage war around the world" (lines 43–44).

Pastoral as a Reading Strategy

If our "art itself is nature," postpastoral literature might be seen as nature's way of offering us imaginative challenges to conceptions that are leading to our extinction. Each of the six features of postpastoral literature urgently needs exploration and raises key questions also engaged by contemporary science, environmental ethics, and cultural geography. Postpastoral writing provides a mode for integrating and questioning these inquiries in a holistic "stretching of our notions of humanity." Such writing might be able to nudge us into some ways of answering the most crucial question of our time: by what kind of relationship can people and planet live together?

But first, the obvious challenge to the contemporary reader of literature, especially literature that refers to nature, is to distinguish between the pastoral, the antipastoral, and the postpastoral. Such a reading strategy will help the reader to consider the works that are likely to raise the most useful questions for our time.

Works Cited

Barrell, John, and John Bull, eds. *The Penguin Book of English Pastoral Verse*. Harmondsworth: Penguin, 1974.

Berry, Wendell. "The Handing Down." *The Collected Poems of Wendell Berry, 1957–1982*. San Francisco: North Point, 1984. 47.

Buell, Lawrence. *The Environmental Imagination*. Cambridge: Harvard UP, 1995.

Chatterjee, Debjani. "Ganapati." *I Was That Woman*. Frome: Hippopotomus Press, 1989. 51.

Crabbe, George. "The Village." *The Penguin Book of English Pastoral Verse*. Eds. John Barrell and John Bull. Harmondsworth: Penguin, 1974. 399–412.

Dillard, Annie. *Teaching a Stone to Talk*. New York: HarperCollins, 1982.

Duck, Stephen. "The Thresher's Labour." *The Penguin Book of English Pastoral Verse*. Eds. John Barrell and John Bull. Harmondsworth: Penguin, 1974. 385–90.

Gifford, Terry. *Pastoral*. New York: Routledge, 1999.

Hughes, Ted. *Tales from Ovid*. London: Faber, 1997.

Lloyd, A. L. *Folksong in England*. London: Lawrence, 1967.

Mackay Brown, George. "Peat Cutting." *Fishermen with Ploughs*. London: Chatto, 1971. 40.

MacLean, Sorley. *From Wood to Ridge: Collected Poems in Gaelic and English*. Manchester: Carcanet, 1989.

Marx, Leo. *The Machine in the Garden*. New York: Oxford UP, 1964.

Muir, John. *John Muir: The Eight Wilderness-Discovery Books*. Seattle: Mountaineers Press, 1992.

Pope, Alexander. "Windsor Forest." *The Penguin Book of English Pastoral Verse*. Eds. John Barrell and John Bull. Harmondsworth: Penguin, 1974. 275–76.

Redgrove, Peter. "The Big Sleep." *Poems 1954-1987*. London: Penguin. 1989. 227–28.

Snyder, Gary. *No Nature: New and Selected Poems*. New York: Pantheon, 1992.

Theocritus. *The Idylls*. Trans. Robert Wells. London: Penguin, 1989.

Thoreau, Henry David. *Walden*. 1854. New York: Penguin, 1983.

Williams, Raymond. *The Country and the City*. London: Chatto, 1973.

Wordsworth, William. "Home at Grasmere." *William Wordsworth: The Major Works*. Ed. Stephen Gill. Oxford: Oxford UP. 1984. 174–99.

Environmental Wisdom in Two Mexican American Novels: An Ecocritical Reading of . . . *And the Earth Did Not Devour Him* and *Bless Me, Ultima*_____

Priscilla Solis Ybarra

The aspirations and challenges concerning each central character in the two novels . . . *And the Earth Did Not Devour Him* (1971) and *Bless Me, Ultima* (1972) can be summarized in the following brief sentences, respectively. A boy wants to grow up to become a telephone operator, but must first endure a childhood of difficult farm labor. Another boy tries to decide whether to become a farmer or a cowboy when he grows up, and along the way he learns to channel magical powers. Both novels feature young protagonists who mature as a result of harrowing experiences. Most readers consider these novels a window into Mexican American experience and culture. In addition, readers can put the approach of ecocriticism to use with these texts to gain valuable new perspectives. While . . . *And the Earth Did Not Devour Him* seems a novel of endless suffering and the loss of all but a mere glimmer of hope, the ecocritical lens shows optimism in the way a minority and oppressed culture survives with its positive relationship to the land intact. As the issue of indigenous identity plays a role in Mexican American ethnicity, viewing *Bless Me, Ultima* through an ecocritical lens helps to show that Mexican American culture fosters a link to the land that predates and trumps the power of Christianity.

Ecocriticism—also known as environmental literary criticism— offers a way to understand a text that takes into account the natural environment. Ecocriticism includes a variety of thematic concerns and approaches. What role does the natural environment play in the human story? How does the novel or story represent the natural environment? What relationships do the human characters maintain with the natural environment? Is the natural environment an important character in the text that makes things happen in the story? These are just a few of the questions that ecocriticism introduces. The ecocritical approach opens new ways to interpret the events and lessons of any novel, story, or poem. For example, many works refer to nature as "Mother." Why do we choose to make nature feminine? This reference can be seen as positive when we care for and respect nature, but how do things change when we exploit and abuse nature? Literary critic Annette Kolodny asks these and other questions as she interprets the way Americans understand nature as female.

Another example involves the word "landscape." We often talk about a beautiful landscape as a vista of nature in a painting, or an open expanse of land that we view from afar. Where does this word come from, and how might our ideas about nature change if we did not use this word? Writer Leslie Marmon Silko tells us that among her people's stories, in Laguna Pueblo culture, the word "landscape" does not exist, because her people do not separate themselves from the natural environment. In Laguna traditions, nature is never "over there," but is always part of the Laguna people's stories, integral to their survival. The above are just two examples of the ways in which ecocritics ask why we use certain words and see nature in certain ways and examine what impact such practices have on how we understand and relate to our environment.

This essay employs the above-described ecocritical approach in readings of the major novels by Mexican American authors Tomás Rivera and Rudolfo Anaya. I will focus in particular on the fact that both novels centrally feature agricultural experience. Agriculture, of course, is a major way that humans relate to the natural environment—agriculture is the means by which we feed ourselves and work with natural elements such as land, climate, and our own bodies' labor to gain sustenance. . . . *And the Earth Did Not Devour Him*, which was published in 1971, offers a narratively inventive representation of migrant farmworkers' lives in the 1950s. Rivera challenges readers to walk in the workers' shoes, especially those of a young boy. Yet so much in this novel moves beyond the tragedy of deplorable working conditions—what really stands out is that this community maintains a positive relationship to the natural environment despite the way their life's work exposes them to the harshest aspects of nature. Anaya's novel, published in 1972 and set in northern New Mexico during and after World War II, shows that the Mexican American community's relationship with the natural environment is, in part, preserved through indigenous traditions, stories, and herbal remedies. That this narrative is set during a time and in a place where homeopathy and organic agriculture were widely appreciated only shows that Mexican American culture preserves traditions vital to the survival of all communities. The fact that these novels are two of the best known works to emerge from the very productive and politically engaged period of Chicano literature during the 1970s makes an environmental reading of them all the more urgent.

. . . And the Earth Did Not Devour Him: Rejecting Alienation from the Land

Tomás Rivera's novel depicts the stark and barren lives of migrant farmworkers traveling between Texas and the Midwest during the early 1950s. The hard-working characters in Rivera's novel struggle to maintain a positive relationship with nature. The fact that the characters succeed in this becomes a telling triumph in light of the cruel treatment that they continuously endure from others. Ironically, they suffer proximity to harsh elements of nature—hot sun, dirt, thorny plants, pests, hard-to-reach vines, limited and sometimes contaminated water sources—in order to provide food for the very people who reject them. For their part, the migrant farmworkers refuse to reject nature, taking into account both its harsh and nurturing elements, choosing instead to appreciate that nature gives them a way to provide for their needs. Still, their labor in the fields that feed the nation goes unrecognized: They live in deplorable conditions, with most families sleeping in tents, old barns, and former chicken coops. They receive low pay, work in unpredictable seasons, with children often missing school days, and the communities into which they arrive treat them with suspicion and contempt.

It is curious that a novel written and published in 1971, during the vibrant Mexican American civil rights movement, dwells on the haunting past of the 1950s instead of painting a vivid portrait of the present or future. Indeed, readers often complain of the novel's relentless pessimism. But this novel offers a unique opportunity to honor the difficulty of life prior to the civil rights movement while also providing a direct critique of Mexican American responsibility for their own plight. Although it might not seem like it from the outset, this novel is steeped in the lessons of the civil rights movement, especially in regard to collective community action. . . . *And the Earth Did Not Devour Him* directs the community to reject superstitions—especially Christianity—that keep the people powerless and insists they work together to voice their rights. Hope glimmers, albeit faintly, when the farmworkers refuse to allow religion and oppressive communities to determine their relationship with nature. Only with this wisdom does the community emerge from its powerlessness. The narrative leads to insight about the people rejecting Christianity and helping themselves via an organic approach of storytelling. They piece together home, healing, and comfort from the nature that surrounds them, inherently rejecting consumerist aspirations. In this manner they move away from exploitation of themselves, and the land, and toward empowerment. The fact that Rivera wrote the novel in a colloquial Spanish (later translated into English; both versions are readily available in print) that is unique to Mexican Americans of Texas makes even clearer the idea that the novel aims to offer the community concrete strategies.

By no means, however, does the novel present these messages in a didactic or simple manner. The characters in *Earth* constantly find themselves on the road looking for employment, and in a narrative sense readers wander alongside them. By definition, migrant farmworkers follow seasonal crops around the country, settling in one place only for short periods at a time, and often not knowing where they will land next. Rivera lets readers experience this mobility and uncertainty by employing a unique narrative style. The book consists of many short vignettes, some only a few lines long, others simply dialogues with no concrete indication of who speaks the lines. No central protagonist links all the stories, although readers do tend to rely on the inconsistently recurring perspective of a young boy as a general orientation to the novel's events, such as a fight at school, working in the fields with other young siblings, taking his first communion, and questioning the existence of the Christian God. Readers must piece together the narrative from these disparate pieces much the way the characters themselves create a life from a constant variation of places and experiences. For more on the novel's unique form, see the critic Ralph F. Grajeda's 1979 article.

The very evocative title . . . *And the Earth Did Not Devour Him* makes reference to the earth that sustains the community and upon which they survive merely by not quite getting devoured by their labors. The title takes on an additional meaning midway through the novel, when a young boy challenges the devil in a vignette titled "A Silvery Night." Curiosity driven, he visits an empty wood at midnight and summons the devil. When the devil does not appear, he experiences relief at first. But then his thoughts wander to the next logical conclusion: If the devil does not exist, then neither does God. He cannot quite bring himself to say aloud that God does not exist, but he does declare to himself the following: "There is no devil, there is nothing" (106). A child raised in strict Christianity and in harsh living conditions fears the devil more than he sustains a relationship with God; on this moonlit night, the boy discovers that "there is nothing" to scare him, but there is also no more sanctified protection for him either. The novel does not regret the loss of God. The vignette immediately following belies a deep cynicism about Christianity—it concerns a carpenter and a minister's wife who use their presence together "helping" the farmworker community as a cover for their extramarital affair; they do nothing to help the migrants. Together, these two vignettes clearly condemn religion, but the novel includes a third section with the eponymous title to seal the deal. The vignette "And the Earth Did Not Devour Him" unites the boy's loss of faith with the community's exposure to environmental extremes through their labor and the cruelty of their bosses. Far from devouring him, the earth reassures the boy, as evidenced in the next vignette, and we can see how this community resists alienation from the natural world.

"And the Earth Did Not Devour Him" concerns a young boy whose father suffers heatstroke while picking crops. The boy observes his mother's practice of candlelit prayer, but he does not see his father improving. At this point, the boy explodes at his mother: "How come we're like this, like we're buried alive? Either the germs eat us alive or the sun burns us up. . . . All the time feeding the earth and the sun, only to one day, just like that, get struck down by the sun. And there you are helpless . . . why, God doesn't care about us . . . I don't think there even is" (109). With this outburst, the boy condemns his mother's faith in God as useless, and he almost reveals to her his new knowledge of God's falseness. The next morning, instead of staying home to care for his father, the boy is compelled by the family's need to venture back into the fields with his younger siblings. His nine-year-old brother soon succumbs to the heat and sun that originally took their father. The weight of his young brother, passed out in his arms, drives the boy to an extreme: He curses God. Strangely, as with the devil, the unexpected occurs: "For a second he saw the earth opening up to devour him. Then he felt his footsteps against the earth, compact, more solid than ever. Then his anger swelled up again and he vented it by cursing God. He looked at his brother, he no longer looked sick" (111).

Instead of experiencing the wrath of God at his curse, the boy finds the situation improving immediately. The earth does not serve God's will; it stands firm under his feet. The next morning his father feels better and the boy takes joy in "the freshness of the morning" (111) and feels "for the first time . . . capable of doing and undoing anything he pleased" (112). His rejection of God inspires him to renew his commitment to his family's endeavor with a fresh spirit no longer weighed down by feeling intimidation and impotence in the shadow of God.

Importantly—especially from an ecocritical perspective—the boy and the earth become allies. He finds strength in treading upon the earth, and this strength helps him fight against hardship. His growing alliance with nature is foreshadowed when he first discovers the devil's—and therefore God's—absence. His last thoughts of the day concern these absences, and he falls "asleep gazing at the moon as it jumped through the clouds and the trees, as if it were extremely content about something" (106). The moon celebrates the boy's awakening to nature, even as he falls into his earthbound sleep.

Still, rejection of God and Christianity does not automatically lead to collective action against oppressive labor conditions. The boy voices his frustrations and gains a sense of power, but he does this alone, even alienating himself from his mother. The novel suggests a possible strategy for collective emancipation by showing the importance of oral culture—storytelling, songwriting, poetry—in Mexican American migrant farmworker communities. On the one hand, this oral culture results from a deeply regrettable circumstance: The farmworkers of the 1950s are often illiterate, attending very few days of school due to their destitute circumstances, child labor, and migratory ways. But another side exists to this orality. Although illiteracy leaves the community vulnerable to exploitation, oral culture emphasizes not only their reliance upon one another but also an intimacy with the natural environment. Indeed, in his book *The Spell of the Sensuous*, philosopher David Abram argues that human literacy and its resulting perception of separateness between the mind and the body, the human and the natural, plays a major role in our current environmental crisis. Abram shows how literacy convinces humans to retreat into individualistic identities and exaggerates their perception that they can dominate or control nature. In . . . *And the Earth Did Not Devour Him*, the oral culture emerges as a potential way for the farmworker community to unite against exploitation (rejecting individuality) at the same time that it shows how the farmworkers can offer their unique understanding of the human relationship to the natural environment. Far from collapsing the

Mexican American farmworker into the same category of nature, the novel shows the community preserving an intimacy with nature that does not require human domination over it. The farmworker community benefits from working with nature and not against it.

Orality appears in many forms throughout the novel, including many instances of dialogues with no speaker or setting indicated. At other times, the narrative addresses the reader in second person, as if involved in a personal conversation. Still other examples show how tales pass from one person to another, with the speaker shifting as the tale changes to his or her particular version. A good example of stories passing among different people occurs with the tale of the thwarted lover; the vignette is titled "The Night the Lights Went Out." It tells the story of a love triangle from many different perspectives, allowing the characters themselves a voice in the telling too. One voice says, "That Ramón, he loved his girlfriend a lot. . . . They say it was the first time in four months that he had seen her," and later another voice says, "They say she danced the whole night with Ramiro," while yet another pitches in, "Well, they say Juanita asked her parents for permission to leave early for the dance" (126). Each of these narrators declares from the outset that he or she heard the story repeated by others: "they say." The tale ends badly, with Ramón killing himself because Juanita succumbs to the charms of newcomer Ramiro.

One might interpret this story as a misogynistic judgment against women's whims, while another might see it as a critique of gossip within a community. Yet what really stands out is the manner in which the story is told—why include so many different voices if not making a point about the power of passing around stories? No one explicitly faults the woman for her role; the story simply shows the tragedy of lost love in the context of hard work. The new boyfriend Ramiro dressed well and did not join the former boyfriend Ramón on the migrant trail; his access to more stability and money overshadowed the hardworking Ramón. More than anything, the community circulates the story to show how an individual who tries to elevate himself alone above the rest only causes tragedy. They comment about Ramiro: "He was nothing but a show off and he was always all duded up. They say he wore orange shoes and real long coats and always had his collar turned up" (125). The community must cultivate more collective strategies, via an oral tradition, in order to improve its lot. After all, they already have an oral tradition, and now they must use it to work toward a better life together in social action.

The most poignant tale concerning the oral tradition comes at a key point, the next to last story in the novel, and provides one of the few respites in the otherwise harrowing narrative. It is a five-sentence vignette that tells of Bartolo the composer and reader of poems. He visits various communities and composes poems on the spot for whoever pays him, including their names in the poetry much to their delight: "And when he read them aloud it was something emotional and serious" (147). Enjoying very little agency in their lives, the farmworkers take joy in hearing poetry in which they play an active role. Indeed, the story ends with the valuable insight that "the spoken word was the seed of love in the darkness" (147). Although achieving literacy for all will go a long way to help this community, they cannot wait for that day to arrive before they take action. Tell your stories to one another now, the novel admonishes, and work together to create change. Otherwise, neither God nor anyone will help you in your silence. That the metaphor of a "seed" is used to describe the "spoken word," and that both the seed and the spoken word create "love," which they will need in abundance in order to create change, shows how this community understands its most important lessons via an organic worldview.

Given that humans gain environmental knowledge about a place over long periods of time, one would expect migrant farmworkers to harbor a very superficial relationship with nature. But characters in this novel display a kinship with nature that belies their constant exposure to harsh environments and their temporary, migratory relationship to various places. They reject individualistic consumerism and honor hard work, indicating that their voices can be the most useful weapon against oppression. Standing in alliance with the earth that does not devour but instead serves as a source of strength; they can work together toward change.

Bless Me, Ultima: Healing the Conflict between Farmers and Herdsmen via Indigeneity

Rivera's and Anaya's novels both focus on an agricultural context, and therefore give us an excellent opportunity to read their works environmentally. The centrality of agriculture in Anaya's text becomes obvious as the young protagonist Antonio (Tony) Márez struggles to decide which of his parents' traditions he will follow: his father's way of ranching or his mother's family's practice of farming. We meet Tony when he is on the brink of his seventh birthday, during the summer before he begins attending school. Tony's youth allows readers to observe the development of a young boy whose home life still makes a great impact on him and whose identity also begins to shift as a result of his experiences at school. Wanting Tony to carry on his or her respective family traditions, each parent competes to influence Tony, the youngest of five siblings. The difficulty for Tony lies in the fact that his parents' hopes for him differ so much.

His father explains why his *vaquero* ("cowboy") tradition excels—in part because he did not need school as a boy, preferring instead his special relationship with *el llano* ("the plains"): "Me, my father gave me a saddle blanket and a wild pony when I was ten. There is your life, he said, and he pointed to the llano. So the llano was my school, it was my teacher, it was my first love—" (51). Throughout the novel, Tony's father repeats his belief that the life of a vaquero teaches everything a man needs to know and that the nomadic style offers the deepest satisfaction. Even his surname, Márez, means oceans, and Tony speculates that the name describes "an exuberant, restless people, wandering across the ocean of the plain" (5). Still, Márez married a woman from a farming family, the Lunas, and she desires her youngest child to emulate her family's quiet ways and their deeply rooted cultivation of the land.

The contrast between tilling soil and herding animals in *Bless Me, Ultima* resonates with a familiar story from the Bible: the conflict between Cain and Abel. Cain was the firstborn son of Adam and Eve, and he chose to farm fruits and vegetables while his younger brother Abel opted for sheep herding. Their vocations were complementary and they only experienced discord after God asked them to make him an offering. Cain put his best fruits and vegetables on the altar, and Abel chose a beautiful lamb for sacrifice. God expressed a preference for Abel's offering of flesh, which resulted in Cain's harboring a deep jealousy toward his brother. Cain eventually murdered his brother Abel. When God inquired after Abel's whereabouts, Cain famously replied, "Am I my brother's keeper?" With this, God banished Cain to wander the world alone. Parents often invoke this story to help siblings cultivate better relations.

Tony, however, gets along well with his siblings, so the Cain and Abel story must indicate a different lesson in the context of northern New Mexico during the 1940s. Certainly, Tony's parental heritage pulls him in two different directions: vaquero or farmer. His community also struggles in choosing between the preservation of indigenous cultural and spiritual practices and the institution of Christianity alone. The lessons that Tony learns on the llano predate the domination of Anglo-Americans there, and the lessons show readers the way that the preservation of cultural heritage goes together with the protection and appreciation of the natural environment. Tony realizes that "the dreams of my mother were opposite the wishes of my father. She wanted a priest to watch over the farmers of the valley, he wanted a son to travel with him" (69). Throughout the novel Tony wonders if he even possesses the abilities that could fulfill his mother's ambitions for him: He recognizes that priesthood is a very special calling. He longs to know his future, and this unknown element drives the narrative; readers also want to know which path he will choose. Tony suspects that

Ultima, the elderly healing woman who joins his family's home at the novel's beginning, and whose name means "last one," possesses this knowledge. He knows that she was midwife at his birth; he shares a deep connection with her, and he even presumes that "she held the secret of [his] destiny" (11). Interestingly, it is he who holds the key to Ultima's life—if he takes up her healing ways, she need not be "the last one," but his continuance of her practices involves his cultivation of the earth's healing remedies.

Tony's parents want him to choose between two different vocations related to cultivation of the earth's bounty, but the arrival of Ultima gives Tony a third alternative that did not exist for Cain and Abel, and that his parents do not even imagine for their son. Ultima's calling as a *curandera*, a healing woman, seems to fit Tony's affinities, demeanor, and abilities; he could very well become a curandero, a healing man. From the first paragraph of the novel, readers see Tony's world change as a result of Ultima's mentorship:

> When she came the beauty of the llano unfolded before my eyes, and the gurgling waters of the river sang to the hum of the turning earth. . . . She took my hand, and the silent, magic powers she possessed made beauty from the raw, sun-baked llano, the green river valley. . . . My bare feet felt the throbbing earth and my body trembled with excitement. (1)

Ultima's practices bring Tony close to the natural environment, and he feels wisdom and peace as a result. With Ultima's arrival he still longs to know his future vocation, but spending time with her gives Tony a way to bring together the disparate worlds of his parents. When reflecting on the interdependence of the earth, moon, and sun, Tony reasons, "The sun was good. The men of the llano were men of the sun. The men of the farms along the river were men of the moon. But we were all children of the white sun" (25). He begins to see connections rather than differences. The story of Cain and Abel appeared in the New World with the Christianity of the European colonizers, and this story details a separation between two agricultural practices that do not necessarily compete with one another. The wisdom of *curanderismo*, or folk healing, gives Tony a better way to understand his parents' backgrounds. Curanderismo dates back to pre-Columbian times, to the traditions and knowledge of many different indigenous tribes. Tony's alternative choice, the possibility to become a curandero, indicates the indigenous connection to the natural environment maintained by his people in northern New Mexico, even after centuries of influence from European Christianity.

The story of the golden carp shows just how this novel resolves Tony's vocational conflict by letting him connect to an indigenous relationship with his local environment, a relationship that even predates the ancient competition between herdsmen and farmers. When Tony celebrates the end of his first year of school, he goes fishing with his friend Samuel, who takes the opportunity to tell Tony the reason why people of the village avoid catching and eating the carp in their local river. Tony observes the practice, but he has never known why the carp are prohibited. Samuel offers an explanation by way of an indigenous creation story, complete with "the people" wandering homeless until the gods let them dwell in the river valley (73). The gods give the people all they need and desire, with the exception of the carp in the river. The people abide by the gods' wishes until they suffer a forty-year drought. Finally, the people cannot resist catching and eating the carp, and the gods become angry. Before the gods follow through with their punishment of the people, one god pleads on their behalf and prevents their murder. He pleads with the gods to punish the people only by turning them into carp. In return, he volunteers to become a carp alongside them. The gods relent, turn the people into carp and the god as well, but they make the god larger and more beautiful, with golden, shimmering scales in honor of his status; the merciful god becomes the golden carp.

The story thrills and alarms Tony. On the one hand, he accepts the story intuitively—"I could not disbelieve Samuel" (75). Still, his years of Catholic indoctrination resist Samuel's story: "The roots of everything I had ever believed in seemed shaken. . . . If the golden carp was a god, who was the man on the cross? The Virgin? Was my mother praying to the wrong God?" (75). Slowly, Tony's experiences repeatedly show him the Christian God's power overshadowed by the indigenous way of harnessing the power of nature. Critic Alex Hunt offers a detailed analysis of the golden carp in this novel, and in northern New Mexico culture in general. An ecocritical approach adds another layer of understanding to Tony's experiences and the lessons he learns as a boy. His choice of profession involves not simply a choice between competing spiritualities, for his choice can ultimately determine whether or not a valuable cooperation between humans and nature survives beyond Ultima's generation.

Tony sees God's power diminishing in light of indigenous practices, and he learns to value the role that nature plays in indigenous medicine. One example of this is Ultima's rescue of his uncle from certain death. Her herbal remedies and rituals, dating back to Aztec times, keep his uncle from dying. When an evil man threatens Ultima, her owl plucks out one of his eyes and protects her from him. Only Ultima and the other boys who know the story of the carp feel the same presence from the river as Tony does, as if the river were a conscious entity. Even when Tony imitates the way Ultima walks, he gets closer to nature: "There was a nobility to her walk that lent a grace to the small figure. I watched her carefully and imitated her walk, and when I did I found that I was no longer lost in the enormous landscape of hills and sky. I was a very important part of the teeming life of the llano and the river" (37).

Looking at this novel through an ecocritical lens brings out a new understanding of what Tony's choice of profession means in the long struggle for survival of indigenous cultures and practices. Despite his parents' best efforts, Tony discovers among his peers and with Ultima's assistance a possible life wherein he can resolve conflicts, heal his people's illnesses, and maintain a connection to his pre-Columbian, indigenous roots, all the while making sure that a cooperative relationship with nature survives beyond Ultima. Tony hears Ultima explain that her remedies emerge from a deep past: "She spoke to me of the common herbs and medicines we shared with the Indians of the Rio del Norte. She spoke of the ancient medicines of other tribes, the Aztecas, Mayas, and even of those in the old, old country, the Moors" (39). More than simply a story about a boy growing up and choosing a profession, *Bless Me, Ultima* symbolizes the recovery of an indigenous identity and the way this identity preserves a positive relationship with the natural environment.

Conclusion

Both these novels evince perspectives from a unique Mexican American relationship with nature that conventional environmentalism does not always take into account: working class and indigenous worldviews from a culture that struggles to survive assimilation. As discussed above, Rivera's characters reject an oppressive Christianity that keeps them inert and choose instead to forge an alliance with the natural environment and with one another, to voice their rights and gather strength and courage. Doing so makes the moon dance in this impressionistic gathering of tales. Anaya's character Tony Márez develops an increasingly positive relationship with the natural environment via his growing knowledge of indigenous practices, showing how cultural preservation and harmony with nature work together. The telling of the golden carp's tale echoes the oral culture that Rivera's text encourages. Hearing the tale makes Tony take his first steps toward doubting the power of a Christian God.

An ecocritical reading of these novels offers a new dimension to texts already taught and analyzed for many years. Agriculture, and therefore nature, plays a big role in Mexican American literature and culture; these two novels give us an idea of how important as well as disparate this role can be. Many people still toil in the fields for low wages and in deplorable conditions. In this sense, Rivera's battle rages on, but his favored strategies of voicing the community's concerns and alliance with nature have won a few skirmishes, especially with the formation and continued growth of the United Farm Workers organization in California. Skepticism concerning "folk medicine" continues, but more and more people around the world appreciate the ancient wisdom found in natural remedies. Orientations regarding the treatment of illness have begun a slow shift from attempting control over nature toward working with nature to solve the mysteries of infirmity and disease. Both these novels offer insight not only into Mexican American culture, but also into the plight that greets us all as humans dwelling in an environment in crisis.

Works Cited

Abram, David. *The Spell of the Sensuous: Perception and Language in a More-Than-Human World*. New York: Vintage, 1997.

Anaya, Rudolfo A. *Bless Me, Ultima*. Berkeley: TQS, 1972.

Grajeda, Ralph F. ". . . *Y no se lo tragó la tierra: Discovery and Appropriation of the Chicano Past*." *Hispania* 62.1 (1979): 71–81.

Hunt, Alex. "In Search of Anaya's Carp: Mapping Ecological Consciousness and Chicano Myth." *ISLE: Interdisciplinary Studies in Literature and Environment* 12.2 (2005): 179–206.

Kolodny, Annette. *The Lay of the Land: Metaphor as Experience and History in American Life and Letters*. Chapel Hill: U of North Carolina P, 1984.

Rivera, Tomás. . . . *And the Earth Did Not Devour Him*. 1971. 3rd ed. Houston: Arte Público, 1995.

Silko, Leslie Marmon. "Landscape, History, and the Pueblo Imagination." *Antaeus* 57 (Autumn 1986): 83–94.

Original Nature: Buddhism and American Nature Writing_____

David Landis Barnhill

> In the morning I bathe my intellect in the stupendous and cosmogonal philosophy of the Bhagvat-Geeta . . . in comparison with which our modern world and its literature seem puny and trivial. . . . [1]
> —"The Pond in Winter," from Henry David Thoreau's *Walden* (1854)

Henry David Thoreau (1817–62), whose words begin this chapter, cultivated a deep and intimate connection with nature while drawing on Asian religions. For Thoreau and his fellow transcendentalist Ralph Waldo Emerson (1803–82), Asian religions such as Buddhism became a cultural lens for communing with nature and contemplating life's mysteries. Today Buddhism is perhaps the greatest non-Western influence on not only nature writing, but environmental philosophy as well.[2] An odd feature of the history of American nature writing is that with the death of Emerson, Asian religions lost their significance in this genre until the 1940s, when Kenneth Rexroth (1905–82) began to write nature poetry that displayed a sophisticated understanding of East Asian Buddhism.[3]

Rexroth was the leader of what was called the San Francisco literary Renaissance in the 1940s and 1950s, and he became a mentor to a young nature poet from the Pacific Northwest named Gary Snyder (b. 1930), one of the subjects of this chapter. Snyder went beyond Rexroth by taking the unprecedented step in 1956 of moving to Japan to practice Zen in Japanese monasteries. Snyder spent the greater part of the next twelve years there, and with his return to the West Coast in 1968, and the rise of the counterculture in the late 1960s, Snyder's poetry and essays became popular in the United States. In the ensuing decades his work has become the most celebrated example of American Buddhist environmental literature.

78 Critical Insights

Peter Matthiessen (b. 1927), the other focus of this chapter, is a prolific writer of novels, travel literature, and nature studies. Raised in the New York area, he became involved in Zen in the late 1960s and is now an officially recognized Zen teacher and priest, leading a Zen practice community from his home in Long Island, New York.[4] His autobiographical account of a pilgrimage to the Himalayas, *The Snow Leopard* (1978), remains the most eloquent articulation of an American wrestling in personal ways with the complexities of Buddhist experience. Snyder and Matthiessen offer just two examples of how Buddhism, and Asian religions more generally, play a substantial role in contemporary environmental literature, providing a distinctive cultural lens for understanding our experience of nature.[5]

Buddhism, of course, presents a challenge to writers and readers of environmental literature. To begin with, it is a religion from a very different culture (actually several cultures, as Buddhism arose in India and then spread to China, Japan, and other Asian countries). Scholars divide Buddhism into two main branches, Theravada in South and Southeast Asia, and Mahayana in East Asia, with Mahayana having many different sects, such as Zen.[6] In addition, Buddhism, at least the kind that has been important in nature writing, is a largely mystical religion whose teachings diverge radically from Western thought. To understand Buddhist nature writing, then, we need to delve into views and values that are foreign to our conventional notions of nature and culture, the mind and the self.

Gary Snyder

Gary Snyder has become a distinctive force in American nature writing as well as environmental philosophy and American Buddhist literature.[7] We can see two general ways in which he differs from other nature writers. First, Snyder is not a nature or environmental writer, but rather an *ecological* writer. His writings do not deal primarily with expressing nature's power, beauty, and mystery. He is concerned more with understanding, through his Buddhist perspective, nature's processes and fundamental characteristics and how they relate to human society.

Second, unlike much nature writing, including Matthiessen's *The Snow Leopard*, Snyder's writings do not reflect a personal spiritual quest. For Snyder, the fundamental question is, how does one *live* Buddhism? What Katsunori Yamazato noted about Snyder's *Turtle Island* is true of much of Snyder's writing: "The merging of Buddhism and ecology has become an essential element in Snyder's exploratory poems on *Turtle Island*, and, beyond enriching the poetic world, these poems are didactic, directing poet and reader to answers for the question 'how to be'" (245). And in exploring that question, another question is implicit: How do we reconceive politics, society, economics, history, and domestic life in terms of Buddhist insights? This makes Snyder more of a *social* writer than many other nature writers. One way to name these two qualities is to talk of Snyder as an *ecosocial* writer.

With these two general points in mind, we can turn to Snyder's philosophy of nature. Perhaps the most fundamental insight in ecology is the interrelatedness of all phenomena, captured memorably by John Muir: "When we try to pick out anything by itself, we find it hitched to everything else in the universe" (157). Snyder characteristically develops this point in a Buddhistic way. "Emptiness" is a traditional Buddhist term that affirms the radical interpenetration of phenomena: Reality is empty in the sense of lacking "thingness"; that is, independent existence. In *Riprap and Cold Mountain Poems* (1959), Snyder asserts that the universe is "interconnected, interpenetrating, mutually reflecting, and mutually embracing" (65–66). Here Snyder's chief influence is the Chinese Buddhist school of Huayan and its image of Indra's net, to which Snyder refers on several occasions:

It's a way of describing the totality of phenomena. You imagine the world and all its beings as a three dimensional net of clear-crystal beads. At all points in the structure, all beads reflect all other beads. They all appear, each one of them, to contain the whole net. Indeed, if you put a dot on one bead, every bead in the net shows the dot. This is one of many images that people in the past have come up with in trying to describe the realism of interconnection. (Plant and Plant 17)

Snyder emphasizes the paradoxical nature of this insight: "All is one and at the same time all is many" (*Place in Space* 47), and "any single thing or complex of things *literally* [is] as great as the whole" (*Earth* 31). Such a view resonates with an ecological view of interrelatedness, and the distinctive niches that species fill in an integrated ecosystem, a similarity that Snyder makes explicit (*Place* 67). Indeed, one can say that Snyder gives an ecological reading of Buddhism and a Buddhistic interpretation of ecology. He celebrates this interdependence in his poem "For All," adapting the Pledge of Allegiance to his notion of Turtle Island, a name for North America that is derived from American Indian creation myths.[8] In that poem, Snyder pledges allegiance to the soil of Turtle Island and all its beings:

> one ecosystem
> in diversity
> under the sun
> With joyful interpenetration for all. (lines 18–21)

One limitation of Indra's net as an image of interrelatedness is that it is static. Huayan also emphasizes the ongoing transformation of phenomena, and thus speaks in terms of mutual coarising. Every moment each thing is transformed, shaping and being shaped by all other things. Snyder also highlights this characteristic of reality. As Patrick D. Murphy has phrased it, "there is no nature as an entity but only *naturing*, a process of interaction and mutual transformation. Solidity consists of energy transformations in an apparent, but only apparent, period of stasis" (151). Once again Snyder combines his understanding of ecology with Buddhism. Nature, he tells us, is a "vast and delicate pyramid of energy transformations" (*Place* 38). Building on and spiritualizing the ecological insight that the food web is a way that energy is transformed in an ecosystem, he presents the food web as a "sacramental energy-exchange, evolutionary mutual-sharing aspect of life" (*Real Work* 89).

An important inflection that Snyder gives to his view of nature's energy is his notion of the wild. The wild has been a key term in environmental literature ever since Henry David Thoreau's proclamation in the essay "Walking" (1862) that "in Wildness is the preservation of the world." Among the many essays in which Snyder discusses the notion of the wild, "The Etiquette of Freedom," the opening chapter of *The Practice of the Wild*, is particularly striking because in it he explains the term along the lines of the Chinese religion of Daoism instead of Buddhism.[9] He first distinguishes between two notions of nature, one that refers to anything that is not created or controlled by humans—a dualistic notion that opposes nature and culture—and another that refers to the totality of the physical world—a monistic notion in which everything is natural, including toxic waste (*Practice* 8–9). Then he proposes his notion of the wild, which centers on the idea of living things spontaneously flourishing according to innate qualities (10). Snyder notes how his notion of the wild comes "very close to being how the Chinese define the term *Dao*, the *way* of Great Nature: eluding analysis, beyond categories, self-organizing, self-informing, playful, surprising, impermanent, insubstantial, independent, complete, orderly, unmediated, freely manifesting, self-authenticating, self-willed, complex, quite simple" (10). The term "wild," then, functions almost like an adverb, indicating a free, self-organizing quality of living.

While our notion of wilderness contrasts with civilization, the wild is everywhere for Snyder. In the poem "Ripples on the Surface," he associates wild with the term "house":

> The vast wild
> the house, alone.
> The little house in the wild,
> the wild in the house. (lines 14–17)

"House" in the poem has two meanings: the entire ecosphere of the planet ("eco" derives from the Greek word for "house"), and civilization, that which humans build. The wild is vast because it encompasses all of life, and it is the one house we live in, and thus "alone." Civilization is the house we have constructed. It is small in comparison with the essentially wild ecosphere, and wildness can be found in civilization, a point he stresses in "Etiquette of Freedom."

Snyder also uses a Buddhist lens to explicate his notion of the self and its relation to the rest of reality. Buddhism holds that our belief that there is an "I" that is separate from an external reality is false. It is, in fact, the fundamental delusion that gives rise to craving, fear, attachment, and thus suffering; likewise, it leads to our tendency to consume and destroy that which we believe is outside of our self. Snyder cites a famous teaching of the Japanese Zen Buddhist master Dōgen (1200–53): "We study the self to forget the self . . . when you forget yourself you become one with the ten thousand things" (*Practice* 150). The only true sense of the self is nothing less than the totality of the universe. With hyphenations suggesting interrelatedness, and with a touch of whimsy, Snyder tells us that the "jeweled-net-interpenetration-ecological-systems-emptiness-consciousness tells us no self-realization without the Whole Self, and the whole self is the whole thing" (*Place* 188–89). This is his Buddhist perspective on the ecological view of humans as fully a part of nature. As he puts it in the poem "By Frazier Creek Falls,"

> This living flowing land
> is all there is, forever
>
> We *are* it
> it sings through us– (lines 14–17)

Snyder explains this unity with nature in another Buddhist way—this one more psychological—in which one experiences such complete absorption in observed phenomena that one loses the sense of a self separate from the supposedly outside world. In his explanation, Snyder once again quotes Dōgen: "Whoever told people that 'mind' means thoughts, opinions, ideas, and concepts? Mind means trees, fence posts, tiles, and grasses" (*Practice* 19–20). This idea is clearly of great significance to nature writing. It is a way of talking about a kind of experience that many nature writers have felt, but which makes little sense in terms of the Western view of subject and object. I like to relate an experience that I had when discussing this point with students. My wife and I had just hiked several thousand feet up the Cascade Mountains, and I was sitting at White Pass, gazing at ridge after ridge of beauty while the sun was slowly setting. I thought to myself, "this is the most exquisite scene I have ever beheld," and my mind continued to chatter like that for a while. Then it calmed and cleared as I become totally rapt in the moment, until there was no longer an "I" looking out. There were only mountains. The Western tradition would relegate this experience to a peculiar (and deluded) subjective consciousness of objective reality. Buddhism, however, would say that my delusions of consciousness separate from reality had fallen away. There clearly were mountains, and there clearly was consciousness, but there was no self that was conscious of the mountains. There was only Mind.[10] Of course, we find this kind of consciousness, more deeply experienced and more eloquently expressed, in Snyder's writings as well as in Matthiessen's *The Snow Leopard*.

Such a view emphasizes not only our unity with but also the unqualified value of the natural world. Snyder, in fact, often gives the notion of our oneness with the world an ecological and moral inflection. We should, he claims, "take ourselves as no more and no less than another being in the Big Watershed. We can accept each other all as barefoot equals sleeping on the same ground" (*Practice* 24). The result, for Snyder, is an affirmation of solidarity with all beings, as he exclaims in the poem "Mother Earth: Her Whales":

Solidarity. The People.
Standing Tree People!
Flying Birds People!
Swimming Sea People!
Four-legged, two-legged, people! (lines 48–52)

The term "solidarity" has political overtones, and in fact Snyder uses Buddhism to develop in a distinctive way the kind of radical politics that was part of his upbringing in Washington state.[11] He builds this Buddhist version of politics, in part, on the idea of original Buddha nature. In his important essay "Buddhism and the Possibilities of Planetary Culture," Snyder states that

> Buddhism holds that the universe and all creatures in it are intrinsically in a state of complete wisdom, love and compassion, acting in natural response and mutual interdependence. The personal realization of this from-the-beginning state cannot be had for and by one-'self' because it is not fully realized unless one has given the self up and away. (*Reader* 41)[12]

As an ecosocial writer, Snyder applies this notion to the social and political level:

> There is nothing in human nature or the requirements of human social organization that requires a society to be contradictory, repressive, and productive of violent and frustrated personalities. . . . One can prove it for himself by taking a good look at Original Nature through meditation. Once a person has this much faith and insight, one will be led to a deep concern for the need for radical social change through a variety of non-violent means. (*Reader* 42)

Radical social change involves radical political critique, and Snyder voices rage in his poem "Front Lines." This intense verse opens with "the edge of the cancer" (1) swelling up against the hill, land seekers

---

telling the land "Spread your legs" (13), as bulldozers grind and slobber on top of the "skinned-up bodies of still-live bushes" (20) and the "rot at the heart / In the sick fat veins of Amerika" (15–16) pushes closer.[13]

His critique aims beyond America's corporate and consumer society to the nation-state itself, and beyond that to civilization as a whole. He analyzes these in terms of the Buddhist notion of the deluded and desiring ego: "Civilization itself is ego gone to seed and institutionalized in the form of the State, both Eastern and Western. It is not nature-as-chaos which threatens us, but the State's presumption that *it* has created order" (*Practice* 92). His critique even extends to traditional Buddhism, which he claims has "failed to analyze out the degree to which ignorance and suffering are caused or encouraged by social factors," and thus "has been conspicuously ready to accept or ignore the inequalities and tyrannies of whatever political system it found itself under" (*Reader* 41).

Snyder explicates the drive for political activism in terms of the ideal of the Bodhisattva. A Bodhisattva is the embodiment of the Mahayana fusion of wisdom and compassion, in which the goal is not one's own enlightenment, but rather the well-being of all. While in traditional Buddhism this has meant helping others enter the Buddhist path toward enlightenment, Snyder argues for a direct engagement in the pain and loss that mark our world, including social injustice and environmental devastation: "To be true to Mahayana, you have to act in the world. To act responsibly in the world doesn't mean that you always stand back and let things happen: you play an active part. . . . That's what the Bodhisattva ideal is all about" (*Real Work* 106–07). Part of engagement is resistance to unnecessary pain and loss. He portrays this vividly in the final stanza of "Front Lines." The narrator of the poem describes a forest that stretches all the way to the Arctic and a desert that still belongs to the Piute Indians. Then he draws his readers into the struggle by the plural pronoun: "here we must draw / Our line" (25–26).[14]

Snyder's most engaging and idiosyncratic call for a defense of the natural world is his "Smokey the Bear Sutra," a long poem that adapts the structure of a Buddhist scripture. As Patrick D. Murphy explains, "Snyder here both seriously and playfully adapts and updates the Buddhist mantra to emphasize the interrelationship of the spiritual and social dimensions of his vision for a new way of life" (108). Showing the combination of radical politics, environmental conservation, and Buddhism, Smokey the Bear is described as follows:

> Wearing the blue work overalls symbolic of slaves and laborers, the countless men oppressed by a civilization that claims to save but only destroys;
> Wearing the broad-brimmed hat of the West, symbolic of the forces that guard the Wilderness, which is the Natural State of the Dharma and the True Path of beings on Earth[15]

This Buddha bear, "Wrathful but Calm, Austere but Comic," is known for "trampling underfoot wasteful freeways and needless suburbs; smashing the worms of capitalism and totalitarianism" (*Reader* 242).

Yet Snyder's Buddhism leads him to be more concerned with working toward a positive alternative. What we need, he asserts, is

> the kind of societies that would follow on a new understanding of that relatively recent institution, the national state, an understanding that might enable us to leave it behind. The state is greed made legal, with a monopoly on violence; a natural society is familial and cautionary. A natural society is one that "follows the way," imperfectly but authentically. (*Reader* 43)

Such a society will have the characteristics of anarchism not in the sense of violent chaos, but in the ideal of a nonhierarchical and nonauthoritarian society. Snyder points to the idea of an anarchist community in his depiction of societies that exemplify wildness, societies whose order has grown from within and is maintained by the force of consensus and custom rather than explicit legislation. Primary cultures, which consider themselves the original and eternal inhabitants of their territory. Societies which resist economic and political domination by civilization. Societies whose economic system is in a close and sustainable relation to the local ecosystem. (*Practice* 10)

One of his first essays was titled "Buddhist Anarchism" (1962), and in a 1990 interview he emphasized the link he continues to make between Buddhism and anarchism.

If you keep in touch with the Buddhist or Taoist insight, you're constantly reminded that, no matter what your cultural regenerative exercises are, they're not in the direction of revalidating hierarchy, or revalidating structures of dominance, or reconstructing the state. We are anarchists; we must never forget that. And the proof of anarchism is self-government. Without hierarchy. (Plant and Plant 16)

Such a natural society Snyder also discusses in terms of *bioregionalism*, an ideal of small societies living in harmony with the local landscape. "The aim of bioregionalism," Snyder has stated, "is to help our human cultural, political and social structures harmonize with natural systems. Human systems should be informed by, be aware of, be corrected by, natural systems" (Plant and Plant 13). Snyder extends the traditional notion of the Buddhist community, or *sangha*, which originally referred to the monastic community, to the entire biotic community. The local bioregion, including plants, animals, streams, and soil, is one's sangha. And the bioregion is one part of what he calls, in the poem "O Waters,"

> great
> earth
> sangha. (lines 14–16)[16]

Peter Matthiessen

The practice of Buddhism is not the only characteristic that Peter Matthiessen shares with Snyder. Like Snyder, he has displayed a deep kinship with wilderness, and both are keenly interested in Native American culture, seeing it as a source of wisdom for the modern world. Matthiessen, like Snyder, is politically engaged, not only advocating for conservation efforts, but also sharply criticizing the oppression of indigenous societies, the destruction wrought by global capitalism, and the waste of consumer society. But Matthiessen is a very different writer than Snyder. He has written many books about the majesty and perils of endangered wildlife. His first book, *Wildlife in America* (1959), might be considered "conservation literature," as it chronicles the struggles of wildlife in the face of rapacious development in our country.[17] Matthiessen is also acutely sensitive to the dignity of indigenous societies and the beauty and mystery of the natural worlds they live within, portrayed exquisitely in *The Tree Where Man Was Born* (1972). Indeed, Matthiessen is one of our finest contemporary travel writers.[18] He has a particular interest in the struggles of traditional cultures to maintain their ways and fight against injustice.[19] Such books are characterized by a profound, elegiac tone, lamenting the loss of what is precious.

Matthiessen is also a renowned novelist, and his fiction includes richly described scenes of nature and portrayals of people attempting to live in it, often destructively.[20] But Matthiessen is still perhaps best known for his autobiographical account of a pilgrimage to the Himalayas, *The Snow Leopard* (1978). The journey took place in 1973, as he accompanied the famous field biologist George Schaller, who was investigating the bharal sheep of those mountains. Matthiessen's chief motivations for joining the expedition were to visit the famous Crystal monastery of Tibetan Buddhism and hopefully see the elusive snow leopard. The journey was also a spiritual pilgrimage, as it was a means for him to cultivate his understanding of Zen Buddhism while dealing with the grief of his wife Deborah's death the previous year. It was an arduous and dangerous trek, replete with spectacular scenery. In *The Snow Leopard*, the journey is presented in the literary style Matthiessen is famous for—what McKay Jenkins has called "his unequaled powers of observation and the remarkable clarity with which he transmits this to the page" (xv), and what Mark Tredinnick has summarized as "restrained celebration, hard-headed mysticism, elegy, all articulated in long, undulant sentences" (115).

Buddhist mysticism shapes Matthiessen's experience of nature. Central to that experience is the notion of Oneness, which diverges from Snyder's stress on the interpenetration of the many. "In the mystical vision, the universe, its center, and its origins are simultaneous, all around us, all within us, and all One" (*Snow Leopard* 66).[21] Matthiessen also refers to emptiness, although he uses the term in a different way than Snyder: "There is only a pearly radiance of Emptiness, the Uncreated, without beginning, therefore without end" (94). What then is the relationship between the ultimate reality of Emptiness and the world of forms? Matthiessen cites the famous Buddhist scripture, the Heart Sūtra,[22] which affirms that ultimate reality is in fact the world of phenomena, and this world is itself ultimate reality: "Though I am blind to it, the Truth is near, in the reality of what I sit on—rocks. These hard rocks instruct my bones in what my brain could never grasp in the Heart Sutra, that 'form is emptiness, and emptiness is form'" (217). As with Snyder, ultimate reality is not separate from this world of wind and waterfalls; nature is the sacred.

For Matthiessen, this Buddhist perspective leads to an unqualified affirmation of the phenomena of this world, "a declaration of being, of Is-ness . . . *It* is! *It* exists! All that is or was or will ever be is right here in this moment! *Now!*" (108–9), the exclamation points capturing what Matthiessen calls the "implacable being" (179) of mountain and sky. Matthiessen puts this in terms of meaning: "The secret of the mountains is that the mountains simply exist, as I do myself: the mountains exist simply, which I do not. The mountains have no 'meaning,' they *are* meaning; the mountains *are*" (218). The conventional notion of meaning takes us away from pure reality. The true meaning of a mountain is the simple but infinite reality of that mountain, not some abstract idea or a connection to a transcendental realm.

In *The Snow Leopard*, Buddhism also acts as a cultural lens for Matthiessen's philosophy of human nature, our essential relationship to the natural world, and the existential dilemmas involved in both. Like Snyder, he sees human nature in terms of our original Buddha nature. We are all Buddhas, right now, and Matthiessen uses the term "the divine within" twice to suggest our inherent Buddha nature (107, 311). The problem is that our Buddha nature is covered over by our desires and delusions, in particular our notion of a separate self. Matthiessen states that this fundamental misapprehension is

> often likened to a sealed glass vessel that separates the air within from the clear and unconfined air all around, or water from the all-encompassing sea. Yet the vessel itself is not different from the sea, and to shatter or dissolve it brings about the reunion with all universal life that mystics seek, the homegoing, the return to the lost paradise of our "true nature." (67–68)

Taking up this line of thought later in the book, he expands poetically on the experience of a mystical search: "To glimpse one's own true nature is a kind of homegoing . . . the homegoing that needs no home, like that waterfall on the upper Suli Gad that turns to mist before touching the earth and rises once again into the sky" (238–39). Why does the homegoing need no home? Why is it like a mist dissolving? The notion of original nature not only describes our own nature, but also our relationship to nature. We are the world, not in the sense of aggrandizing it into our self but in the sense of dissolving into it. When you are the world, where is there to go? When you are always and already a Buddha, what is there to achieve? Matthiessen quotes the Tibetan Buddhist teacher Lama Govinda: "The pilgrim abandons himself to the breath of the greater life that . . . leads him beyond the farthest horizons to an aim which is already present within him, though yet hidden from his sight" (9).

Why is that goal hidden from sight? Why can't we find the home we are always in? The principal problem is the delusion that we are cut off from the rest of reality. Matthiessen claims that children naturally feel a unity with the world, as he recalls seeing his son rapt in the beauty of nature: "The child was not observing; he was at rest in the very center of the universe, a part of things . . . still in unison with the primordial nature of creation, letting all light and phenomena pour though. Ecstasy is identity with all existence" (41–42). As intensely as he experiences nature in the Himalayas, he usually finds that the feeling of separation remains, but he does have moments of full clarity, as in this experience late in his pilgrimage:

> The ground whirls with its own energy . . . [and] that energy pours through me, joining my body with the sun until small silver breaths of cold, clear air, no longer mine, are lost in the mineral breathing of the mountain. A white down feather, sun-filled, dances before me on the wind: alighting nowhere, it balances on a shining thorn, goes spinning on. Between this white feather, sheep dung, light, and the fleeting aggregate of atoms that is "I," there is no particle of difference. There is a mountain opposite, but this "I" is opposite nothing, opposed to nothing. (238)

Matthiessen's true goal is not to see the snow leopard, but to experience "that vital present in which we do not stand apart from life, we *are* life, our being fills us" (257).

In such an experience, the focus is wholly on the Present, which I capitalize because we are not talking about the present moment in the conventional sense. Consciousness is so absorbed in the fullness of the present that there is no sense of a past or future. Everything that matters is "right here now," all truths are Now (57, 112, 138, 310). Here is where the One is experienced: "In a landscape without past or future time—in this instant, in all instants, transience and eternity, death and life are one" (137).

Another key aspect of the ideal consciousness is the experience of "acceptance," the calm acceptance of whatever comes (117, 164, 292, 311), including the failures of the journey, most notably not seeing the snow leopard. The goal is tranquility in the face of the journey's vicissitudes and difficulties, an abiding contentment. "To be whole," American Buddhist Stephen Levine has said, "we must deny nothing" (11). Put more positively, we need to embrace everything, even what is repugnant (*Snow Leopard* 96). But embracing all also requires that we "let everything go" (210) and rid oneself of attachments. "I am trying to let go," he recounts, "to blow away, like that white down feather on the mountain" (240). But as in so many other of his ideals, the effort is difficult: "Between clinging and letting go," he admits, "I feel a terrific struggle" (154). Still, *The Snow Leopard* conveys the ideal of an open embrace of the world, with expansive receptivity and clarity undistorted by expectations and judgment, qualities that are certainly important to a nature writer.

The Snow Leopard is an account of a spiritual quest following a personal tragedy. Missing in the book is serious consideration of social justice or environmental degradation. The Buddha, Matthiessen notes, "never involved himself in social justice, far less government; his way holds that self-realization is the greatest contribution one can make to one's fellow man" (19). But this limitation is not true of Matthiessen's writings as a whole. As noted before, his books about conservation detail the human causes of the loss of wildlife, and he has also written powerful works on social advocacy. But in his explicitly Buddhist writings, *The Snow Leopard* and *Nine-Headed Dragon River*, he has not articulated a Buddhist perspective on social justice. His Buddhist perspective is largely invisible in his other books, though Buddhism surely helped to shape and sharpen his compassion for other beings and his exquisite presentations of nature's beauty. In interviews, Matthiessen has admitted that his conservation literature and his fiction do not explicitly present a Buddhist perspective.[23] It is easy to lament these points as a limitation in his oeuvre, in contrast to Snyder, for whom Buddhism is the principal lens for virtually all of his writings, from his poetry to his political advocacy. One could suggest, however, that in the case of Matthiessen, spiritual humility may be involved, and perhaps his writings exhibit the Zen tradition of despising spiritual pretension and eliminating all "extras" (including Zen itself) that cloud the simple and total awareness of the present.

Conclusion

For Snyder and Matthiessen, Buddhism has provided a distinctive cultural lens for understanding the natural world, our relationship to it, the social context of our lives, and our responsibilities to the Great Earth Sangha, the sacred community of life. For Matthiessen, especially in *The Snow Leopard*, that lens is largely personal and mystical. William Dowie has remarked that "Matthiessen's basic orientation toward the world is one of watchfulness" (104). But it is important to recognize that this watchfulness is Buddhist, aiming for the pure, total experience of nature in the present moment. As Matthiessen put it in one of his interviews, he could give Buddhist sermons "for a hundred years and all I'm ever teaching, in the end, is moment-by-moment awakening of mind. Again: Pay attention to this moment. Right here! Now!" (Shainberg 45).

For Snyder, the lens is ecological, as he traces nature's processes and interconnections and our place within the diverse and integrated flow of life. But Snyder's complex vision gives us reason to reexamine the notion of cultural lens. Rather than say that Buddhism is the lens though which Snyder experiences nature, we could say that Buddhism, ecology, and radical politics were each a lens through which the others are seen—the image of Indra's net transformed from mirror-like jewels to lenses. Snyder does understand ecology and politics through a Buddhist lens, but he also understands Buddhism and politics through an ecological lens, and understands Buddhism and ecology through the lens of radical politics. Put in terms of the Buddhist notion of mutual coarising, in Snyder's writings ecology, radical politics, and Buddhism arise together and shape each other.

As noted in the beginning of this article, other nature writers draw on Buddhism in their experience of nature and their writing about the natural world. No doubt the influence of Buddhism on nature writing will continue in the coming generations. It will be fascinating to see how those writers will adopt and adapt Buddhism in new and distinctive ways, and how nature writing and Buddhism will continue to coarise.

Notes

1. *The Bhagvat-Geeta* is one of the seminal texts in the Indian religion of Hinduism.

2. Among the many books on Buddhism and environmental thought, see Mary Evelyn Tucker and Duncan Ryūken Williams, eds., *Buddhism and Ecology: The Interconnection of Dharma and Deeds* (Cambridge: Harvard UP, 1998). For a recent article by an environmental philosopher, see J. Baird Callicott, "The New New (Buddhist?) Ecology" *Journal for the Study of Religion, Nature, and Culture* 2.2 (2008): 166–82.

3. For Rexroth's poetry, see *The Complete Poems of Kenneth Rexroth* (Port Townsend: Copper Canyon, 2003), especially his long poem written in Japan, "The Heart's Garden, The Garden's Heart." *The Complete Poems*, however, does not include most of his translations of fine Chinese and Japanese verse, which have been influential in American literature and nature writing. He also published several volumes of essays on literature and culture.

4. Matthiessen chronicles his study of Zen in his autobiographical book *Nine-Headed Dragon River: Zen Journals 1969-1982* (Boston: Shambhala, 1987).

5. For a more general overview of the influence of East Asian culture on American nature writing, see David Barnhill, "East Asian Influence on Recent North American Nature Writing," *Teaching North American Environmental Literature*, ed. Laird Christensen, Mark C. Long, and Frederick O. Waage (New York: Modern Language Association, 2008) 277–93. For an outline of spirituality in general in American nature writing, see Barnhill, "The Spiritual Dimension of North American Nature Writing," *Oxford Handbook on Religion and Ecology*, ed. Roger S. Gottlieb (New York: Oxford UP, 2006) 419–45.

6. Theravada is actually the only surviving sect of the first branch of Buddhism, often termed Hinayana, though that is a derogatory word ("lesser vehicle") used in Mahayana ("greater vehicle"). Some scholars and Buddhists consider esoteric or tantric Buddhism, most fully developed in Tibetan Buddhism, to be a third branch, Vajrayana, while others consider it part of Mahayana.

7. For succinct and useful overviews of Snyder's work, see Scott Slovic, "Gary Snyder," *Encyclopedia of Environmental Ethics and Philosophy* (Detroit: Macmillan, 2009), vol. 2, 247–49, and Bron Taylor, "Snyder, Gary (1930–) and the Invention of Bioregional Spirituality and Politics," *Encyclopedia of Religion and Nature* (London: Continuum, 2005) 1562–67.

8. For one of his statements about Turtle Island, see the introductory note to *Turtle Island* (n.p.)

9. Daoism (formerly written Taoism), which began to develop in China around the same time as Buddhism in India, emphasizes harmony with nature. When Mahayana Buddhism came to China, it was strongly influenced by Daoism, the Zen sect most of all.

10. As such, our fundamental distinction between mind and reality dissolves, and Buddhism speaks of reality both in terms of "things in themselves" and as Mind.

11. In an interview, Snyder recalled that "our family tradition was radical politics on both sides, particularly on my father's side because my grandfather was an active IWW and socialist speaker and thinker" (Martin 148). The IWW is the International Workers of the World, an anarchist-inclined labor organization.

12. This article first appeared with the title "Buddhist Anarchism" in the *Journal for the Protection of All Beings* 1 (1961): 10–12, and was revised slightly and retitled "Buddhism and the Coming Revolution" in *Earth House Hold* (New York: New Directions, 1969), then revised slightly once again and retitled as "Buddhism and the Possibilities of Planetary Culture" in *The Gary Snyder Reader* (Washington, DC: Counterpoint, 1999).

13. For an even more vehement verse, see "A Curse on the Men in Washington, Pentagon," which Snyder does not include in any of his collections of poetry.

14. The Piute (or Paiute) are an American Indian people native to California and surrounding areas. For an analysis of the Buddhist ecosocial dimensions of Snyder's works, see Barnhill, "Gary Snyder's Ecosocial Buddhism," *How Much Is Enough?: Buddhism, Consumerism, and the Human Environment*, ed. Richard Payne (Somerville: Wisdom, 2010), 83–119.

15. Dharma can refer to Buddhist truths and to the true character of reality.

16. For an analysis of Snyder's notion of Buddhist community, see Barnhill, "Great Earth *Sangha*: Gary Snyder's View of Nature as Community," *Buddhism and Ecology: The Interconnection of Dharma and Deeds*, ed. Mary Evelyn Tucker and Duncan Ryūken Williams (Cambridge: Harvard UP, 1998), 187–218.

17. For other books on wildlife, see *Birds of Heaven* (New York: North Point, 2001) and *Tigers in the Snow* (New York: North Point, 2000).

18. For example, he ventures into the Amazon jungle in *The Cloud Forest* (New York: Viking, 1961) and to New Guinea in *Under the Mountain Wall* (New York: Viking, 1962).

19. For his social advocacy, see *Sal Si Puedes*, about Cesar Chavez's migrant farmworker movement, and *In the Spirit of Crazy Horse* (1983), where he exposes the abuse of Native Americans and a flawed legal system in the prosecution of

Leonard Peltier, an Indian serving a life sentence for a crime Matthiessen insists he did not commit.

20. His two greatest novels may be *Far Tortuga* (New York: Random House, 1975), about the last of the traditional Caribbean sea turtle hunters, and *Shadow Country* (New York: Modern Library, 2008), about a man who sought power and fortune in the untamed regions of southwestern Florida over one hundred years ago.

21. All the following quotations are from *The Snow Leopard*, unless otherwise noted.

22. The Heart Sūtra is a very brief (one page) scripture that has been extremely influential in East Asian Buddhism. For the text and an analysis, see Donald S. Lopez, *The Heart Sūtra Explained* (Albany: SUNY P, 1987).

23. See, for example, his interview with Lawrence Shainberg, "Emptying the Bell: An Interview with Peter Matthiessen," *Tricycle* 3 (Fall 1993), 42–47.

Works Cited

Armbruster, Karla, Cheryll Glotfelty, and Tom Lynch, eds. *The Bioregional Imagination: New Perspectives on Literature, Ecology, and Place.* Athens: U of Georgia P, 2012.

Barnhill, David Landis. "East Asian Influence on Recent North American Nature Writing." *Teaching North American Environmental Literature.* Ed. Laird Christensen, Mark C. Long, and Frederick O. Waage. New York: Modern Language Association, 2008. 277–93.

_____. "Gary Snyder's Ecosocial Buddhism." *How Much Is Enough?: Buddhism, Consumerism, and the Human Environment.* Ed. Richard Payne. Somerville: Wisdom, 2010. 83–119.

_____. "Great Earth *Sangha*: Gary Snyder's View of Nature as Community." *Buddhism and Ecology: The Interconnection of Dharma and Deeds.* Ed. Mary Evelyn Tucker and Duncan Ryūken Williams. Cambridge: Harvard UP, 1998. 187–218.

_____. "The Spiritual Dimension of North American Nature Writing." *Oxford Handbook on Religion and Ecology.* Ed. Roger S. Gottlieb. New York: Oxford UP, 2006. 419–45.

_____. "Surveying the Landscape: A New Approach to Nature Writing." *ISLE: Interdisciplinary Studies in Literature and the Environment* 17.2 (Spring 2010): 1–18.

Callicott, J. Baird. "The New New (Buddhist?) Ecology." *Journal for the Study of Religion, Nature and Culture* 2.2 (2008): 166–82.

Dowie, William. *Peter Matthiessen.* Boston: Twayne, 1991.

Jenkins, McKay. Introduction. *The Peter Matthiessen Reader.* New York: Vintage, 2000.

Levine, Stephen. *Who Dies?: An Investigation of Conscious Living and Conscious Dying.* Garden City: Anchor, 1982.

Lopez, Donald S. *The Heart Sūtra Explained.* Albany: SUNY P, 1987.

Martin, Julia. "Coyote-Mind: An Interview with Gary Snyder." *Triquarterly* 79 (Fall 1990): 148–72.

Matthiessen, Peter. *Birds of Heaven: Travels with Cranes*. New York: North Point, 2001.

_____. *The Cloud Forest: A Chronicle of the South American Wilderness*. New York: Viking, 1961.

_____. *Far Tortuga*. New York: Random House, 1975.

_____. *In the Spirit of Crazy Horse*. New York: Viking, 1983.

_____. *Nine-Headed Dragon River: Zen Journals 1969-1982*. Boston: Shambhala, 1987.

_____. *Sal Si Puedes (Escape If You Can): Cesar Chavez and the New American Revolution*. New York: Random House, 1971.

_____. *Shadow Country: A New Rendering of the Watson Legend*. New York: Modern Library, 2008.

_____. *The Snow Leopard*. 1978. New York: Bantam, 1979.

_____. *Tigers in the Snow*. New York: North Point, 2000.

_____. *The Tree Where Man Was Born*. New York: Dutton, 1972.

_____. *Under the Mountain Wall: A Chronicle of Two Seasons in the Stone Age*. New York: Viking, 1962.

_____. *Wildlife in America*. New York: Viking, 1959.

Muir, John. *My First Summer in the Sierras*. Boston: Houghton, 1916.

Murphy, Patrick D. *A Place for Wayfaring: The Poetry and Prose of Gary Snyder*. Corvallis: Oregon State UP, 2000.

Plant, Judith, and Christopher Plant. "Regenerate Culture!" Interview with Gary Snyder. *Turtle Talk: Voices For a Sustainable Future*. Ed. Christopher Plant and Judith Plant. Philadelphia: New Society, 1990. 12–21.

Rexroth, Kenneth. *The Complete Poems of Kenneth Rexroth*. Port Townsend: Copper Canyon, 2003.

Shainberg, Lawrence. "Emptying the Bell: An Interview with Peter Matthiessen." *Tricycle* 3 (Fall 1993): 42–47.

Slovic, Scott. "Gary Snyder." *Encyclopedia of Environmental Ethics and Philosophy*. Ed. J. Baird Callicott and Robert Frodeman. Vol. 2. Detroit: Macmillan, 2009. 247–49.

Snyder, Gary. "By Frazier Creek Falls." *The Gary Snyder Reader: Prose, Poetry, and Translations, 1952–1998*. Washington, DC: Counterpoint, 1999. 477.

_____. "A Curse on the Men in Washington, Pentagon." *War Poems*. Ed. Diane di Prima. New York: Poets, 1968. 78–79.

_____. *Earth House Hold: Technical Notes & Queries to Fellow Dharma Revolutionaries*. New York: New Directions, 1969.

_____. "For All." *The Gary Snyder Reader: Prose, Poetry, and Translations, 1952-1998*. Washington, DC: Counterpoint, 1999. 504.

_____. *The Gary Snyder Reader: Prose, Poetry, and Translations, 1952-1998*. Washington, DC: Counterpoint, 1999.

_____. "Mother Earth: Her Whales." *The Gary Snyder Reader: Prose, Poetry, and Translations, 1952-1998*. Washington, DC: Counterpoint, 1999. 478–80.

_____. "O Waters." *The Gary Snyder Reader: Prose, Poetry, and Translations, 1952-1998*. Washington, DC: Counterpoint, 1999. 483.

_____. *A Place in Space: Ethics, Aesthetics, and Watersheds*. Washington, DC: Counterpoint, 1995.

_____. *The Practice of the Wild*. San Francisco: North Point, 1990.

_____. *The Real Work: Interviews and Talks, 1964–1979*. New York: New Directions, 1980.

_____. "Ripples on the Surface." *The Gary Snyder Reader: Prose, Poetry, and Translations, 1952-1998*. Washington, DC: Counterpoint, 1999. 568.

_____. *Riprap and Cold Mountain Poems*. 1959. 50th Anniversary Edition. Berkeley: Counterpoint, 2009.

_____. *Turtle Island*. New York: New Directions, 1974.

Taylor, Bron. "Snyder, Gary (1930–) and the Invention of Bioregional Spirituality and Politics." *Encyclopedia of Religion and Nature*. London: Continuum, 2005.1562–67.

Thoreau, Henry D. *Walden: A Fully Annotated Edition*. New Haven: Yale UP, 2004. 287–88.

Tredinnick, Mark. *The Land's Wild Music: Encounters with Barry Lopez, Peter Matthiessen, Terry Tempest Williams, & James Galvin*. San Antonio: Trinity UP, 2005.

Tucker, Mary Evelyn, and Duncan Ryūken Williams, eds. *Buddhism and Ecology: The Interconnection of Dharma and Deeds*. Cambridge: Harvard UP, 1998.

Whalen-Bridge, John, and Gary Storhoff, eds. *The Emergence of Buddhist American Literature*. Albany: SUNY P, 2009.

Yamazato, Katsunori. "How to Be in This Crisis: Gary Snyder's Cross-Cultural Vision in *Turtle Island*." *Critical Essays on Gary Snyder*. Ed. Patrick D. Murphy. Boston: G.K. Hall, 1990. 230–47.

Yu, Beongcheon. *The Great Circle: American Writers and the Orient*. Detroit: Wayne State UP, 1983.

Wordsworth as Environmental "Nature" Writer_____

Ashton Nichols

William Wordsworth is perhaps the romantic poet most often described as a "nature" writer. From his earliest poems describing places in the 1780s to his final poems (written when he was almost eighty years old), Wordsworth paid careful attention to the details of the nonhuman world in almost all of his poems and prose writings. What the word "nature" meant to Wordsworth, however, is not a simple matter. Wordsworth was a careful naturalist, always paying close attention to the physical environment that surrounded him: animals, plants, landscape, and weather. At the same time, he was a thoughtful literary artist, who described the "mind of Man" as "My haunt, and the main region of my song" ("Home at Grasmere," lines 989–90; later, "Prospectus" to *The Excursion*, lines 40–41).[1] So, does the poet objectively describe the details of his natural environment, or does he subjectively shape those sensory experiences into a unity in his mind? He does both, since the human mind, in Wordsworth's view, is "creator and receiver both" (*Prelude* [1850] Book 2, line 258), taking in the details of the world around him, but then shaping those details into his own mental creations. This helps to explain how he has played such an important role in recent years in the development of "environmental literature." In Wordsworth's masterful language, a simple poem about daffodils can become a significant lesson about the operations of memory and the powers of the human mind. His long poems *The Prelude* and *The Excursion* trace the growth of the mind amid the powerful influences of the natural world—mountains, lakes, forests, and sky—and suggest how the operations of the mind in nature produce many of the most valuable aspects of each person: memory, imagination, and sympathy. His career as a poet also came to embody the nature writer as a wider cultural influence, much like Henry David Thoreau would do later in America.

In his autobiographical poem *The Prelude*, Wordsworth records those moments—he calls them "spots of time"—when the interaction between his growing awareness and a natural scene had a particularly powerful impact on his own development. In "Tintern Abbey," he warns his younger sister Dorothy that she should retain her close connection to the natural world, a connection that will be threatened as she grows into adult consciousness. Many times in his work, nature speaks to the poet—the boy of Winander literally has a conversation with owls—but the poet then ends up speaking for the natural world, praising its value, revealing its beauty, and cautioning humans about their ability to harm its wonders. Wordsworth lived at a time before the Industrial Revolution had a widespread negative effect on the landscapes of England, a time before serious pollution and significant environmental preservation. At the same time, however, he saw what was coming. In the 1830s, Wordsworth spoke out forcefully against the idea of bringing the railroad line deeper into his beloved Lake District. Wordsworth's "environmental" poems helped to establish the value of a naturalistic form of writing that reaches from the poets James Thomson and William Cowper in the eighteenth century to Derek Walcott and Seamus Heaney in the twenty-first century. Although it would not technically be correct to call Wordsworth an "environmentalist"—the term did not even exist when he was writing—his poetic flowers, birds, and emotionally affecting landscapes prepared the way for the powerful sense of an essential connection between human beings and the natural world.

William Wordsworth was the second child of John Wordsworth and Ann Cookson, born in Cockermouth, Cumbria, on April 7, 1770. His sister Dorothy was born a year later, and the two remained extremely close throughout their lives, with Dorothy's *Journals* eventually providing naturalistic imagery and precise details (daffodils, storm clouds, and their Grasmere neighbors) for some of her brother's most famous poems. Although his childhood was marred by the early deaths of both parents—his mother when he was eight, his father when he was twelve—Wordsworth's memories of growing up, as recounted in his poetry, included powerful moments of fear and excitement, anticipation and enthusiasm, almost always connected with the "sublime" landscapes and countless smaller natural phenomena around him. His childhood included constant attention to the plants, animals, and countryside of the Lake District; he was often a natural historian in poetry, writing lyrics to yew trees, thorn bushes, rivers, sparrows, butterflies, a daisy, a cuckoo, a lesser celandine, and, of course, daffodils. At Hawkshead Grammar School, he received a thorough classical education, fostered by three Cambridge-educated headmasters, one of whom was the brother of Fletcher Christian, famous for the mutiny on the HMS *Bounty* (Wu 162–63).

His poem "The Boy of Winander" records a clearly autobiographical moment when the young naturalist tried to communicate with Lake District owls with surprising results:

> There was a Boy: ye knew him well, ye cliffs
> And islands of Winander!—many a time,
> At evening, when the earliest stars began
> To move along the edges of the hills,
> Rising or setting, would he stand alone
> Beneath the trees or by the glimmering lake,
> And there, with fingers interwoven, both hands
> Pressed closely palm to palm, and to his mouth
> Uplifted, he, as through an instrument,
> Blew mimic hootings to the silent owls,
> That they might answer him; and they would shout
> Across the watery vale, and shout again,
> Responsive to his call, with quivering peals,
> And long halloos and screams, and echoes loud,
> Redoubled and redoubled, concourse wild
> Of jocund din; and, when a lengthened pause
> Of silence came and baffled his best skill,

Then sometimes, in that silence while he hung
Listening, a gentle shock of mild surprise
Has carried far into his heart the voice
Of mountain torrents; or the visible scene
Would enter unawares into his mind,
With all its solemn imagery, its rocks,
Its woods, and that uncertain heaven, received
Into the bosom of the steady lake. (*Prelude* [1850] Book 5,
lines 364–88)

The boy's attempt to communicate with wild creatures is immediately successful. Once the owls answer his calls, he has made a direct and immediate connection across the species boundary that prepares the way for the poem's most important moment. In the silence that follows the owls' response, the young nature-lover learns the way memories are made; the sound of waterfalls, the rocks and forests, and the sky reflected in "the steady lake" all make their way into the poet's mind with a force that causes their images to last for decades in the mind.

Wordsworth's earliest major poems, begun while he was still a student at St. John's College, Cambridge, indicate the influence of an earlier neoclassical poetic tradition, but they also reveal a unique emerging voice that would come to identify him as a founder of the romantic movement in English literature. As early as "An Evening Walk" (1787–89) and "Descriptive Sketches" (1791–92) he is already paying close attention to the details of the nonhuman world around him: plants and animals, streams and sky, geography and weather. At the same time, he is also deeply interested in the operations of the human mind. He complicates issues for all readers and critics who want to see him primarily as a nature poet when he says, "the mind of Man— / My haunt, and the main region of my song." If the human mind is the main region of his song, however, he still needs the natural world as the source of the countless objects and creatures on which the mind operates, a world that gives him his subject matter as a poet: "On Man, on Nature, and on human Life, / Thinking in solitude, from time to time" ("Home at Grasmere," lines 959–60; *The Excursion*, lines 1–3). Poetic images rise up in his mind but never without corresponding emotions: "I feel sweet passions traversing my Soul / Like music" (lines 961–62); and they rise not only from grand, majestic, or sublime circumstances, but also typically from the simple details of daily life and ordinary events.

The poem "Tintern Abbey" (actually titled "Lines written a few miles above Tintern Abbey on revisiting the banks of the Wye during a tour, July 13, 1798") is the poem that, more than any other, defines a new way of conceiving poetry, the poet, and the relationship between the mind of the author and the world of nature. In this poem, Wordsworth describes his sister Dorothy, just one year younger, beside him, and he sees her developing mind as the key to the lesson he wants to teach. He tells her to make sure and remember the powerful natural scene they see before them in the Wye Valley. Memory is the capacity that helps to create a vision of the self, a psychological capacity that preserves the past but, more importantly, enshrines that same past "for future renovation":

> . . . And I have felt
> A presence that disturbs me with the joy
> Of elevated thoughts; a sense sublime
> Of something far more deeply interfused,
> Whose dwelling is the light of setting suns,
> And the round ocean, and the living air,
> And the blue sky, and in the mind of man,
> A motion and a spirit, that impels
> All thinking things, all objects of all thought,
> And rolls through all things. Therefore am I still
> A lover of the meadows and the woods,
> And mountains; and of all that we behold
> From this green earth . . . (lines 94–106)

"Tintern Abbey" is notable for the way it presents particular places as especially valuable in terms of their ability to trigger remembrance, enhance the present, and provide "life and food / For future years" (lines 65–66). The two metaphors, "life" and "food," are not insignificant. Each person's experience of nature provides "life" because each human is an organic being, connected by a powerful *élan vital* (a life-force) to all other living things. No longer trapped in a mechanistic model of the physical universe first proposed by Enlightenment science, Wordsworth draws on his friend Coleridge's view that both life and art derive from organic principles; romantic human beings are more like plants and animals than machines. The metaphor of "food" is equally important; the nonhuman world provides spiritual nourishment for the emotions ("the passions") just as organic food provides sustenance for the body.

Here is a forerunner of the green movement in modern ecological criticism, emerging by way of Wordsworth's belief in a force that pervades all living things, an organic unity that links the world of human beings to the wider living world around them. The discrete and isolated objects of eighteenth-century rationalist thinking are replaced by a force ("And I have felt / A presence," lines 94–95) that is spiritual without being religious, influential without being deterministic, always able to connect the fragmentary elements of human experience together into a unified identity, a personal self. In the rural world of nature, not the urban world of cities (Blake's "Satanic mills"?), Wordsworth finds just those affecting scenes that are most likely to achieve this result in his mind: waterfalls ("The sounding cataract / Haunted me like a passion," lines 77–78), hillsides ("the tall rock, / The mountain," lines 78–79), and forests ("The mountain, and the deep and gloomy wood, / Their colours and their forms, were then to me / An appetite: a feeling and a love," lines 79–81). This world of birds, flowers, and trees is not important simply for its beauty, but because it links the developing mind to the same wider world from which these natural objects come, the material world on which they depend. Wordsworth's ideas here lay a part of the groundwork for the environmental movement of the twentieth century. Percy Shelley may have been the first to call Wordsworth the "Poet of Nature" ("To Wordsworth," 1816), but modern criticism has asserted Wordsworth's role as a forerunner of environmentalism, as well as the recent movement in literary scholarship known as ecocriticism. In *Romantic Ecology*, Jonathan Bate writes, "Of course, Wordsworth's poem about the boy of Winander addresses itself to the workings of the mind and the power of imagination"—the typical subjects of romantic poetry—"but let us not forget that it is also about a boy alone by a lake at dusk blowing mimic hootings to unseen owls," and these owls, Bate concludes, "are there to answer him" (115). The potential value of the natural world to human beings is, in our modern sense, at once the subject and the object of such a poem.

Wordsworth began his great autobiographical poem, later known as *The Prelude*, in 1798. He had no idea that the childhood memories he began to recount in letters to his friend Coleridge during the freezing winter of 1798–99, when he was shut up in damp, icy rooms in the small Saxon town of Goslar, would become the origins of the greatest autobiographical long poem in English, and perhaps the last epic—an epic of the self—ever written in English literature. (The lyrical lines began: "Was it for this / That one, the fairest of all rivers, loved / To blend his murmurs with my nurse's song" [*Prelude* [1850] Book 1, lines 269–71].) This great poem began as small snippets of recollection—snare robbing, bird's egg- and boat-stealing, ice-skating, and waiting for horses to take him home for vacation—that formed the basis of the young poet's earliest memories of life in the Lake District. These memorable "spots of time," as he would call them, chronicle moments when the nonhuman elements of the growing child's world combine with powerful human influences in the mind—fear of the boat's owner, a woman struggling against the wind, youthful anticipation of a family holiday—to produce lasting lines of poetry. Whether he is robbing snares set by other hunters, waiting for the horses that would take him home not long before his father died, or ice-skating to the point of dizzying "transport," the young mind feels itself thinking and feeling, not alone but always amid powerful presences in the natural world.

The year 1798 also saw the publication of *Lyrical Ballads*, the volume of poetry that more than any other defined the new movement in poetry announced by Wordsworth and Coleridge. This volume would also become the occasion for the 1802 "Preface," in which Wordsworth would first describe poetry as "the spontaneous overflow of powerful feelings" that "takes its origin from emotion recollected in tranquillity" (preface to *Lyrical Ballads* 611). He also notes that it should be written in a "language really used by men" and should take its subject from "low and rustic life" since "in that condition, the passions of men are incorporated with the beautiful and permanent forms of nature" (Preface 597). This emphasis on rural life gets Wordsworth's contemporary readers, and many subsequent readers, closer to the natural world by emphasizing lives lived close to the land, to agriculture, and even to a wilder world devoid of human beings.

Many of Wordsworth's most powerful poetic insights were fully shaped by this time. "The Tables Turned" offers perhaps the first statement of Wordsworth's central naturalistic philosophy: "Come forth into the light of things, / Let Nature be your teacher" (lines 15–16). This view emerges from his belief that rational thinking needs to be balanced by an emotional response to one's surroundings. The mental capacity that had given its name to the entire age of reason is now described by Wordsworth as "our meddling intellect." This same capacity for rational thought "misshapes the beauteous forms of things" so that humans "murder to dissect" (lines 26–28). In the 1800 edition of *Lyrical Ballads*, the poem "Nutting" chronicles the sort of human destructiveness that would later come to be associated with assaults on the physical environment. A young boy, who heads off through the woods with the innocent goal of gathering hazelnuts, ends up virtually ravaging the peaceful, natural scene: "Then up I rose, / And dragged to earth both branch and bough, with crash / And merciless ravage" (lines 43–45). But this boy soon learns the lesson wrought by his own destructiveness: "I felt a sense of pain when I beheld / The silent trees, and saw the intruding sky" (lines 52–53), and so to his companion he says: "Then, Dearest Maiden, move along these shades / In gentleness of heart; with gentle hand / Touch—for there is a spirit in the woods" (lines 54–56). In such short and simple lyrics, Wordsworth develops a complex theory of the way human beings seek to control a natural world in which power is sensed or intuited; but this is always a power that cannot be fully understood by the rational intellect.

Such an expansive but vague natural power is sometimes associated with God, leading to claims that the early Wordsworth was a pantheist—or one who sees God *in* nature as the ancients did: "I'd rather be / A Pagan suckled in a creed outworn" ("The World Is Too Much with Us," lines 9–10). For fundamentalist Christian theology based on a literal reading of the Bible, God can never be found *in* the natural world, since all aspects of physical nature—birds, flowers, trees, sky, you and I—are only parts of a fallen world that was left to humans after Adam and Eve were cast out of the Garden of Eden. God is somewhere else, since divinity cannot inhabit a fallen world that was solely the result of human weakness. According to this strict, theological interpretation of Christian "nature," humans were given paradise, but they ended up in a fallen world of death, decay, and corruption. The issue of whether the power that created and controls the universe is to be found in (immanent, within, inherent) or beyond (supernatural, above, outside of) physical nature propels much of the debate that has occupied theologians since the time of Martin Luther. Indeed, the Protestant Reformation is a series of debates about precisely what form or forms of mediation—scripture, Eucharist, priest, prayer, bishops, the heart of the believer—may be required to bridge the gap that separates humans from a God that has left the natural world for the realm of "supernature": heaven. For the young Wordsworth, however, the issue is not so simple. For him, "Heaven lies about us in our infancy!" ("Immortality Ode," line 67), and the place we live in, the sublunary world we inhabit on a daily basis, is "the very world, which is the world / Of all of us,—the place where, in the end, / We find our happiness, or not at all!" (*Prelude* [1850] Book 10, lines 725–27; also in *The Friend*, 26 October 1809). The young Wordsworth posits a secular version of salvation that saves human beings in the material world they inhabit—rocks, lakes, trees, waterfalls, and mountains—not beyond this world in another.

By the time of the publication of *Poems in Two Volumes* in 1807, Wordsworth had completed most of the lyrics for which he is best known today, especially those associated with the powers of the natural world and the role of the human mind in creating a connection between human beings and their surroundings: "Resolution and Independence" (also known as "The Leech-Gatherer"), "My Heart Leaps Up," "The Solitary Reaper," "The World Is Too Much with Us," and "Ode: Intimations of Immortality from Recollections of Early Childhood." The latter poem contains a number of the most often-quoted Wordsworthian lines and phrases: "Whither is fled the visionary gleam? / Where is it now, the glory and the dream?" (lines 57–58); "Our birth is but a sleep and a forgetting" (line 59); "nothing can bring back the hour / Of splendor in the grass, of glory in the flower" (lines 182–83); "To me the meanest flower that blows can give / Thoughts that do often lie too deep for tears" (lines 207–8).

This is also the volume of poetry that includes a short lyric that is probably Wordsworth's best known to the general public over two hundred years later. Called "the daffodil poem" and formally titled by its first line, "I Wandered Lonely as a Cloud" begins:

> I wandered lonely as a Cloud
> That floats on high o'er Vales and Hills,
> When all at once I saw a crowd
> A host of dancing Daffodils;
> Along the Lake, beneath the trees,
> Ten thousand dancing in the breeze.

The waves beside them danced, but they
Outdid the sparkling waves in glee:—
A poet could not but be gay
In such a laughing company:
I gazed—and gazed—but little thought
What wealth the show to me had brought:

For oft when on my couch I lie
In vacant or in pensive mood,
They flash upon that inward eye
Which is the bliss of solitude,
And then my heart with pleasure fills,
And dances with the Daffodils. (lines 1–18)

This poem is more complex than it seems at first. While it appears to be a simple record of a field of bright yellow flowers on a spring day, it actually shows its readers how memories are made and preserved; it offers a profound meditation on the psychological powers of the human mind. The "wealth" of the memory of these daffodils is "little" known until long after the initial experience, and only then the mind acts to save these flowers for future "renovation" of the self.

By 1814, Wordsworth was a famous public figure as well as the representative of a new voice in poetry, a voice that would come to be called romantic. Wordsworth's version of this movement leaned toward a form of nature-worship and away from Coleridge's interest in the German focus on the mind, especially the heightened imagination and extreme psychological states. Wordsworth was interested in the imagination, but his version of this power was anchored firmly in ideas about memory and the power of youthful experience. Coleridge, by contrast, concentrated on the heightened mental states produced by the opium (laudanum) that he ingested daily for much of his adult life, and by other intense mental states such as melancholy, dejection, and nightmare. The poem Wordsworth published that year, *The Excursion*, became one of his best-selling poems, and although it is now often seen as limited in its power, the poem offered a view of the relationship between the mind and nature that has had a powerful impact for the past two centuries. In this poem, Wordsworth is very clear about his growing disdain for the rise of industry: "Here a huge town . . . Hiding the face of earth for leagues . . . wilderness erased" (lines 119–29). "I grieve," the poet concludes, "when on the darker side / Of this great change I look; and there behold / Such outrage done to nature" (lines 151–53). This poem was supposed to be the second part of his great three-part epic, a long poem about a poet much like the young Wordsworth: "a philosophical Poem, containing views of Man, Nature, and Society, and to be entitled the *Recluse*; as having for its principal subject the sensations and opinions of a poet living in retirement," as he would say in his 1850 introduction to *The Prelude*, which had originally been intended as an appendix to the planned but never written epic.

By middle age, Wordsworth settled into the life of the "smiling public man," as W. B. Yeats would describe his own role as a famous poet a century later ("Among School Children," line 8). In 1813, the financially strapped poet accepted a salary that was to be derived from his work as a distributor of stamps in Westmoreland. He had earlier received a small bequest as a result of caring for his dying friend Raisley Calvert. Wordsworth continued to write poetry, much of which now fell into traditional categories: poems on places, celebrations of public events, sonnets on people and memorable dates in English history. The standard view is that Wordsworth's poetic powers failed as he aged, and that the earlier revolutionary, pantheistic liberal became an aging, hidebound, Anglican (Episcopalian) conservative. This view seems overly harsh if we consider poems like the River Duddon sonnets "Scorn Not the Sonnet," "Yarrow Revisited," "On the Projected Kendal and Windermere Railway," and "Extempore Effusion upon the Death of James Hogg," among other important examples of Wordsworth's later poems. Wordsworth retained elements of his poetic powers until he gave up writing for good upon the death of his daughter Dora in

1847. What faded with age were his philosophical curiosity, radical politics, and willingness to challenge received wisdom for the sake of intellectual consistency. Like many aging authors—Alfred, Lord Tennyson and Yeats are notable exceptions—the future poet laureate became more predictable and a good deal more complacent as he aged.

Many of the second generation of romantic poets died early deaths: Lord Byron succumbed to "a fever" at age thirty-six while fighting with the Greeks in their war for independence; Shelley drowned off the coast of Italy at age twenty-nine; and John Keats died of tuberculosis in Rome when he was only twenty-five. Such early deaths came to be associated with the other-worldly literary styles of these authors, and even the excessively romantic styles of their lives; as Wordsworth had written: "the good die first, / And they whose hearts are dry as summer dust / Burn to the socket" *(The Excursion,* lines 500–2). Wordsworth, however, went on to live a long life surrounded by friends and family, suffering the early loss of one brother at sea and the deaths of three of his children. His life as a public figure was enhanced with the publication of the fifth edition of his *Guide to the Lakes* in 1835. The guide first appeared in 1810 as a money-making effort by a struggling young family man. Wordsworth's expanded descriptions of the beauties of these landscapes in a later version of the book led readers to argue for the need to preserve such places for the benefit of future generations. The poet also objected forcefully, in letters to the newspaper and in poetry, to the proposal to bring the Lakeland railroad line as far as Ambleside: "Is then no nook of English ground secure / From rash assault?" ("On the Projected Kendal and Windermere Railway," lines 1–2). In this poem, Wordsworth laments the "false utilitarian lure" of such a scheme, the coming "blight" of industrialization that needs the very natural "winds" and "torrents" of water themselves to "protest against this wrong." By this point Wordsworth has become the voice of an early environmental preservationist; the railway, however, came to the Lake District despite the poet's vociferous protests.

Queen Victoria named Wordsworth poet laureate in 1843, just seven years before his death. This honor, the most prestigious public recognition available to a British poet at this point in history, came to an author who had not written his long-promised epic, *The Recluse*, nor had he published *The Prelude*, the poem "on his own life," which was not even named until after Wordsworth's death. He and the family had always known *The Prelude* as the "poem to Coleridge," since it had been dedicated to his best friend in its earliest drafts. In retrospect, it is clearly this poem that gives the most complete version of Wordsworth's developing consciousness, as well as the most thorough analysis of his own life in nature: "Ye Presences of Nature in the sky / And on the earth! Ye Visions of the hills! / And Souls of lonely places!" (lines 464–66). It is not just places that matter, however, since these natural presences "impressed upon all forms the characters [images] / Of danger or desire; and thus did make / The surface of the universal earth . . . Work like a sea" (Book 1, lines 471–75). The earth works like a sea in the mind of the young poet, sending out waves of imagery, stirring rising and falling tides of poetry, stimulating the imagination, and providing the raw materials for art. This is also the poem that will reveal how "[n]ature by extrinsic passion first / Peopled the mind with forms sublime or fair / And made me love them" (Book 1, lines 545–47).

In the century and a half since the publication of *The Prelude*, scholars have come to see this autobiographical epic as Wordsworth's masterwork, a major poem that sets forth his most complete and coherent philosophy of the interaction between nature and culture, while also providing a prototype for modern writing about the self. Recent critical work reveals just how influential Wordsworth has been as a prophet of natural preservation and a protoenvironmental author. As early as 1964, the historian of science Philip C. Ritterbush noted, "Wordsworth's notion of natural harmony anticipated the conclusions of modern science" (203). Jonathan Bate cites Karl Kroeber as the first critic to offer an "ecological reading of Wordsworth," in Kroeber's 1974 essay on "Home at Grasmere," Wordsworth's earliest poetic attempt to describe and understand the power of this place in his own imagination (*Ecology* 125). Kroeber is also important for *Ecological Literary Criticism: Romantic Imagining and the Biology of Mind* (1994), a book that relies on Wordsworth as a central example of a literary artist whose works, in poetry and prose, were crucial texts for the development of early ecological awareness. Bate's own *Romantic Ecology* likewise sees Wordsworth as the originator of a new role for "nature" (and the link between nature and mind) in English literature. He compares Wordsworth to Thoreau, noting that while Thoreau produced the "romantic ecology" (*Ecology* 39) by which the vast geographic expanses of America might be considered worthy of preservation, it was Wordsworth who became the voice for saving smaller spaces: domestic settings and gentler landscapes like those found in his own beloved Lake District.

Not until Bate's own *Song of the Earth* (2000) did Wordsworth come in for a full treatment as the practitioner of a new ecopoetics, a form of environmental writing as revolutionary, in its own way, as all of the critical descriptions of Wordsworth's early version of romanticism. In this view, the specific geographic places and spaces of Wordsworth's poems are as important as these poems' language, politics, and role as autobiographical documents. Of course, Wordsworth praises not only those gentler landscapes around his village home of Grasmere but also the sublime High Peaks of Westmoreland (Helvellyn and Snowdon), as well as the European Alps (Mont Blanc and Gondo Gorge). In recent years, an expanding body of critical opinion has placed Wordsworth among those English authors now being discussed in terms of the critical approach known as ecocriticism. Recent literary critics who have argued persuasively for the central role of the British romantic tradition in the development of ecological awareness, and an increased sensitivity to the natural world, include Kevin Hutchings, James McKusick, Kurt Fosso, and Timothy Morton, among others. Indeed, this line of research has become a major aspect of ecocritical ways of reading, emphasizing the key importance of literature that links humans and the nonhuman world. Wordsworth, as much as any earlier author, gives modern readers and writers good reasons to praise natural places and work toward preserving those landscapes increasingly threatened by the actions of modern technology and industry.

A rarely quoted fragment of Wordsworth's early philosophical verse (1798)—later incorporated into *The Excursion*—includes lines that embody the central principle of almost all of Wordsworth's writing about the natural world:

> There is an active principle alive in all things;
> In all things, in all natures, in the flowers
> And in the trees, in every pebbly stone
> That paves the brooks, the stationary rocks,
> The moving waters and the invisible air.
> All beings share their properties which spread
> Beyond themselves, a power by which they make
> Some other being conscious of their life,
> Spirit that knows no insulated spot,
> No chasm, no solitude, from link to link
> It circulates the soul of all the worlds.
> This is the freedom of the universe . . . (lines 1–12)

This passage, as much as any in Wordsworth's body of work, reveals the central premise of his protoecological poetry. The natural world is pervaded by a "principle." It might be made of matter, and it might be spiritual, but whatever composes this nonhuman world, a force—as in "may the Force be with you"—pervades every living, and even non-living, thing; the very rocks, stones, and falling waters share in the power that links all things together. All living beings also share in this power; there is one world that unifies creation into a single ecological home. The prefix "eco-" literally means "house" or "home." So there is no solitude, chasm, or separation among the countless parts of the natural world. We are all here together in nature—in Wordsworth's beautiful phrasing, circulating with "the soul of all the worlds"—and our freedom is granted not by Thomas Jefferson's Declaration of Independence or the "creator" mentioned there; our freedom combines the full freedom of the human mind with the natural freedom of the nonhuman universe. A powerful vision of our life in nature lies at the heart of Wordsworth's writing.

Notes

1. Unless otherwise noted, all quotations of Wordsworth can be found in *William Wordsworth: The Oxford Authors*, edited by Stephen Gill (1984).

Works Cited

Bate, Jonathan. *Romantic Ecology: Wordsworth and the Environmental Tradition.* London: Routledge, 1991.

_____. *The Song of the Earth.* Cambridge: Harvard UP, 2000.

Coupe, Laurence, ed. *The Green Studies Reader: From Romanticism to Ecocriticism.* London: Routledge, 2000.

Fosso, Kurt. *Buried Communities: Wordsworth and the Bonds of Mourning.* Albany: SUNY P, 2004.

Gill, Stephen. Preface. *Guide to the Lakes.* By William Wordsworth. Ed. Ernest de Selincourt. London: Frances Lincoln, 2004.

_____. *William Wordsworth: A Life.* Oxford: Oxford UP, 1989.

Hutchings, Kevin. *Imagining Nature: Blake's Environmental Poetics.* Montreal: McGill-Queen's UP, 2002.

Kroeber, Karl. *Ecological Literary Criticism: Romantic Imagining and the Biology of Mind.* New York: Columbia UP, 1994.

_____. "'Home at Grasmere': Ecological Holiness." *PMLA* 89 (1974): 132–41.

McKusick, James. *Green Writing: Romanticism and Ecology.* New York: Palgrave, 2000.

_____. "Introduction: Romanticism and Ecology." *Romantic Circles Praxis Series* (November 2001): n. pag. Web. 25 June 2011.

_____. "Romanticism and Ecology." *Wordsworth Circle* 28 (Summer 1997): 121–200.

Morton, Timothy. *The Ecological Thought.* Cambridge: Harvard UP, 2010.

_____. *Ecology Without Nature.* Cambridge: Harvard UP, 2007.

Nichols, Ashton. *The Revolutionary "I": Wordsworth and the Politics of Self-Presentation.* London: Macmillan, 1987.

_____. *Romantic Natural Histories: William Wordsworth, Charles Darwin, and Others.* Boston: Houghton, 2004.

Ritterbush, Philip C. *Overtures to Biology: The Speculations of Eighteenth-Century Naturalists*. New Haven: Yale UP, 1964.

Wordsworth, Dorothy. *The Grasmere Journals*. Ed. Pamela Woof. Oxford: Oxford UP, 1991.

Wordsworth, William. *The Friend: A Literary, Moral, and Political Weekly Paper*, 26 Oct. 1809.

_____. *Guide to the Lakes*. 1835. Ed. Ernest de Selincourt. London: Frances Lincoln, 2004.

_____. *The Prelude: 1799, 1805, 1850*. Ed. Jonathan Wordsworth, M H. Abrams, and Stephen Gill. New York: Norton, 1979.

_____. *William Wordsworth: The Oxford Authors*. Ed. Stephen Gill. Oxford: Oxford UP, 1984.

Wu, Duncan. *Wordsworth's Reading, 1770-1799*. Cambridge: Cambridge UP, 1993.

Yeats, W. B. *The Collected Poems of W. B. Yeats*. Ed. Richard J. Finneran. New York: Scribner's, 1996.

CRITICAL
READINGS

Walt Whitman, *the* Ecological Poet_____

M. Jimmie Killingsworth

All American poetry written in the nineteenth century was to some extent nature poetry. It emerged from a nation of farmers and frontier people, a settler culture in regular contact with a host of indigenous tribes, and it was influenced by philosophies concerned with how culture relates to nature and the ways that human and natural history intersect—German idealism, British romanticism, and American transcendentalism. But Walt Whitman's *Leaves of Grass* (1855) is the one major poetical work of the period that might lay claim to the category of ecological poetry. True, the book had passed through four editions before the German scientist Ernst Haeckel coined the term "ecology" in 1866, to describe the study of how an organism interacts with its environment. Even so, Whitman's poetry can be distinguished from the standard nature poetry of his day because it more fully anticipates the science, the politics, and the cultural perspective that people today call ecology.

In poems like "Song of Myself," "Spontaneous Me," and "Calamus," Whitman's "poetry of the body" anticipates the *new materialism* of our time by affirming and celebrating the actual physical connection of human, animal, vegetable, and mineral existence—a topic once considered too mundane or earthy for the elevated language of poetry. As equally "the poet of the soul," Whitman uses Christian imagery and concepts such as resurrection and miracle—refitted with a scientific update—to promote a protoecological outlook in "This Compost." And in poems like "Song of the Redwood-Tree," he anticipates the late-twentieth-century revival of animism, the worldview associated with indigenous peoples, which grants the full status of life, both body and soul, to animals, plants, and even "inanimate" objects like rocks and soil. Anticipating twenty-first-century "animal studies," Whitman connects his ecological views to his project of radical democracy. In questioning the separation of human and animal into different categories, he offers

---

insights into the political misuses of the categories, most especially the dehumanizing effects of slavery and other forms of exploitation. The very category of the animal, the poet suggests, provides the basis for treating some classes of human beings as animals, or bodies without souls. In connecting ecology and democracy, Whitman foretells the movement for environmental justice in our own time. Environmental justice holds that people are equally entitled to a share of the common riches of the earth, and that the costs of environmental degradation should be equally distributed as well (see Bullard; also Martinez-Alier).

This chapter traces the body, soul, and politics of ecology as topics in *Leaves of Grass*, while also honoring Whitman's insistence on the deep connections between the three areas of interest. "[If] the body were not the soul," he asks in "I Sing the Body Electric," "what is the soul?" (lines 7–8). In that poem, he uses the intertwining of body with soul for a political purpose, to protest the trafficking of human bodies in slavery and prostitution. Whitman did not entirely transcend the prejudices of his time. He was inclined to accept the doctrine of manifest destiny, for example—the attitude of racial superiority by which Euro-Americans justified not only the destruction of forests and other misuses of the land, but also the near genocide of Native Americans in the westward migration of settlement. In offering new prospects for the growth of nature poetry into an ecological and democratic literature, however, Whitman pointed the way for the American imagination to attain new levels of awareness and envisage new ways of life.

The Body of Ecology

Three of the most striking features of *Leaves of Grass* are its free verse, which Whitman developed and exploited more thoroughly than any poet writing in English before him (see Killingsworth, *Cambridge* 26–28); its wide-ranging diction, language from the streets as well as the parlor and lecture hall, from various dialects, regions, and ethnic groups (see Warren; also Folsom); and its frank treatment of sex and the human body, which shocked many readers in his time and continues to raise eyebrows even now (see Killingsworth, *Whitman's Poetry of the Body*; also Moon). All of these features relate to the ecological trends embodied in Whitman's poetic art. The verse form and diction were part of an effort to make the poetry less artificial-seeming and formal than the poetry commonly written and admired in Whitman's time, a product of the classroom and bookish learning. Whitman wanted a poetry that gave the feeling of rhapsodic singing in the open air. *Leaves of Grass* was modeled on conversation, oratory, and music, using the breath as the measure of the line rather than syllable-counting and meter first developed for Latin poetry. Instead of rhyme and strict metrics, Whitman wanted a more organic form, one fitted to the various moods and tones of life spent mainly in the city streets, in the woods and prairies, and on the open road, among teeming populations of people from varied backgrounds and ways of life. In the preface to the first edition of *Leaves* in 1855, the poet instructed readers to take the book outdoors and read the poems aloud.

At times he seems even to want to do without words and feel only the vibrations and contact of the elements and other bodies: "Not words, not music or rhyme I want, not even the best," he writes in "Song of Myself," "Only the lull I like, the hum of your valvèd voice" (lines 85–86). He reinforces the meaning of the lines with the repetition of the liquid *l* sounds and the hum of *m*'s and *v*'s, as if the sounds themselves were striving to overcome the limits of language. In "Song of the Rolling Earth," Whitman says that real words are not those "upright lines . . . those curves, angles, dots" we find on printed pages: "No, those are not the [real] words, the substantial words are in the ground and sea, / They are in the air, they are in you" (lines 2–4). Indeed, "Human bodies are words" (line 7). As for poetry, "In the best poems re-appears the body, man's or woman's, well-shaped, natural, gay, / Every part able, active, receptive, without shame or the need of shame" (lines 8–9). In an effort to write "the best poems" in this sense, Whitman deploys long breath-absorbing lines, alternately flowing and pounding irregular rhythms, and provocative diction—such as the celebration in "Spontaneous Me"

---

of "Love-thoughts, love-juice, love-odor, love-yielding, love-climbers, and the climbing sap / Arms and hands of love, lips of love, phallic thumb of love, breasts of love, bellies press'd together and glued together with love" (lines 11–12). Again with alliteration for emphasis (especially with the *l*'s) and also with the forthright reference to the parts of the body given literally ("Arms and hands of love") and figuratively ("phallic thumb" as a metaphor for penis, "climbing sap" as a metaphor for semen and blood, "lips" as a double entendre referring both to mouth and vagina), the poet strives to engage the reader's body even as he aims to change minds and shift attitudes about how we live in the world and how we engage others. (See Holcomb and Killingsworth, chapter eight, on the engagement of the reader's body through an image-rich style.)

Whitman's use of the word "gay" in describing the body as "well-shaped, natural, gay" will likely suggest homosexuality to twenty-first-century readers, although his usage appears over a hundred years before the wide acceptance of the slang term. Even the word "homosexual" was not coined till the 1890s, just after Whitman died. And yet, some scholars have argued that "gay" may have been used as an underground code term among men who loved other men in Whitman's time (see Shively)—possibly another instance of street language in *Leaves of Grass*. Other poems suggest strongly that, in Whitman's view, the human sexual desire was highly volatile and, if followed, could lead a person in many directions. Homoerotic attraction was certainly one such direction and was a theme in many poems. In the notorious "Calamus" section of *Leaves*, Whitman uses the first-person persona to recount episodes of what he calls "manly love" among "comrades." Against the prevailing notion that same-sex love is unnatural, "Calamus" reinforces the naturalness of such desire through the use of outdoor settings and imagery drawn from the processes and sensations of the natural world. In "When I Heard at the Close of the Day," for example, the speaker tells of lying in the arms of his lover on the beach and hearing "the hissing rustle of the liquid and sands . . . whispering to congratulate me" (line 10). Enwrapped and "congratulated" by the setting, which the reader is encouraged to envision clearly and even to hear in the onomatopoeia of the hissing *s* sounds, the speaker feels at one with the environment, his desire fulfilled and his body stilled by the calm of the moonlit night and the rhythms of the sea washing the shore. The return to the seashore—the scene of Whitman's boyhood on Long Island, New York—often represents the search for completion and fulfillment in *Leaves of Grass* (see Killingsworth, *Walt*, chapter three; also Loving).

In another "Calamus" poem, "Earth, My Likeness," we see an earlier stage of desire, the aching hunger for completion, again figured in images drawn from natural processes. The speaker's still unspoken and yet insistent desire is volcanic in its power. Like the crust of the earth, which seems placid and solid but may hide eruptive powers of untold dimension, the speaker says, "an athlete is enamour'd of me, and I of him, / But toward him there is something fierce and terrible in me eligible to burst forth" (lines 5–6). (See also the treatment of Whitman's "perturbations" in Killingsworth, "The Case"; and for more on the intersections of sexuality studies and ecopoetics, see Mortimer-Sandilands and Erickson's *Queer Ecologies*.)

Leaves of Grass is replete with images and scenes of vibrant active bodies, gay and otherwise, consumed with the desire to connect with others and complete the circle of life. In the infamous section eleven of "Song of Myself," Whitman tells the story of a lonely woman who "owns the fine house by the rise of the bank" and "hides handsome and richly drest aft the blinds of the window" (lines 202–3), watching twenty-eight young men swimming by the shore. In her fantasy, she gives way to her desire and becomes the "twenty-ninth bather," "Dancing and laughing along the beach" (line 208). The young men are oblivious as she imagines swimming among them and touching their bodies and wet hair, and more: "They do not know who puffs and declines with pendant and bending arch, / They do not think whom they souse with spray" (lines 215–16). The power that attracts the woman to the water's edge is represented in the double meaning of "souse with spray"—the ability of both the foaming ocean and the men with their "love juice" to relieve tension and refresh the staleness of life. The language suggests the ultimate unity of human actions with the motion and rhythms of the material world. In human sexuality as in the ocean with its tides, the elements yield to the pull of nature.

In "Spontaneous Me," the poet even more forcefully depicts the strong demands of desire upon the body of the healthy human being. Against the views of the conventional moralists of his day—remember that Whitman wrote his poems in the middle of what is now known as the Victorian Era, with its reputation for super politeness and modest restraint—the poem's premise is that the most spontaneous uprising of energy and pleasure is the sensation most likely to connect the human being with the forces of the natural world. Again, he returns to the theme of the body as the real poem, this time with a phallic emphasis. The things we call poems, he says, are "merely pictures" (line 8). "The real poems," he says, with metaphoric expansiveness, are "poems of the privacy of the night, and of men like me, / The poems drooping shy and unseen that I always carry, and that all men carry" (lines 9–10). He finds "likenesses" (homologies, analogies, similes, metaphors) everywhere in nature: the "hairy wild-bee," for example, "gripes the full-grown lady-flower, curves upon her with amorous firm legs, takes his will of her, and holds himself tremulous and tight till he is satisfied" (line 17). The imagery of sustenance, desire, fulfillment, and fertility—the sensuous "wet of the woods through the early hours" (line 18) and "aromas from crush'd sage-plant, mint, birch-bark" (line 20)—correlates with the sensuous experience of human beings. "Two sleepers at night" (line 19), for example, and the boy who confides in the poet what amounts to a wet dream or masturbation fantasy: "The curious roamer the hand roaming all over the body, the bashful withdrawing of the flesh where the fingers soothingly pause and edge themselves, / The limpid liquid within the young man . . . / The torment, the irritable tide that will not be at rest" (lines 26–28). The drive within the "young man that flushes and flushes, and the young / woman that flushes and flushes" (the pun on *flush* indicating both blushing and purging—before the age of flush toilets, however) mimics the regularity and certainty of the tides and the movement of waters through the world (line 31).

In short, sexual desire teaches that the world and the person are one. We are not divided into culture and nature, matter and life. The boundaries of social categories like gender divisions are also transgressed (or queered) by the poet's wild and transformative imagination, one thing merging and melding with the next, categories collapsing like the banks of a river in flood. Everything is joined in a powerful process of movement and fruition, which Whitman calls "the merge." For him, sexual desire is as constant and strong as the force of gravity. "Urge and urge and urge," he writes in "Song of Myself," "Always the procreant urge of the world" (lines 43–44).

For all its drama, sex is only one of many experiences in life that Whitman draws upon to impress the reader with the radical connectivity of material existence, which ecological thinkers in more recent times have called the "web of life" (see Leopold; also Capra). As ecocritic Timothy Morton puts it, "The ecological crisis we face"—which was not as obvious in Whitman's time, but was coming into awareness with the heating up of the industrial revolution and rampant urbanization— "is so obvious that it becomes easy . . . to join the dots and see that everything is interconnected. This is *the ecological thought*. And the more we consider it, the more our world opens up" (1). Instead of the web of life as the key to ecological interconnection, Morton prefers the term "mesh," the very sound of which feels right for the squishy, messy, merging interconnectivity found in Whitman's poetry. Echoing Whitman, Morton writes, "In the mesh, sexuality is all over the map" (84), meaning that sex is both everywhere apparent and not easily located according to a heterosexual norm or center. "Really thinking the mesh," says Morton, "means letting go of an idea that it has a center"; the mesh "permits no distance . . . dissolving the barrier between 'over here' and 'over there'" and denying "the metaphysical illusion of rigid, narrow boundaries between inside and outside" (38–39). In the same mood, Whitman challenges the reader to open up to new sensations and identities: "Unscrew the locks from the doors! / Unscrew the doors themselves from their jambs!" says the poet, who had once earned a living as a carpenter (lines 501–2).

As Morton suggests, once we begin to think about the meaning of true ecological interconnectedness everything changes, and we are faced with a new poetics, a new ethics, a new politics, a new way of being and imagining the world. The intellectual world was certainly opening up in the mid-nineteenth century, and Whitman was right in the middle of the fray. Five years before Darwin published his *Origin of Species* in 1859, the treatise that changed our understanding of the interconnections of human history and natural history, Whitman was among a number of other contemporaries, including the anonymous author of a book that Whitman reviewed, called *Vestiges of Creation*, who were already thinking about evolutionary connections among people and other beings. "I find I incorporate gneiss, coal, long-threaded moss, fruits, / grains, esculent roots," the poet writes in "Song of Myself" (first published in 1855), "And am stucco'd with quadrupeds and birds all over" (lines 670–71). Through eating, drinking, and being in the world, as well as through heredity and history, Whitman could see and celebrate that we are joined with the earth through our bodies and all our actions. The gene had not been discovered in Whitman's time, so he could not know scientifically that "every single form of life is literally familiar: we're genetically descended from them" (Morton 29). But he could nevertheless understand that he was "stucco'd with quadrupeds and birds all over." At least in a rudimentary and poetic form, Whitman anticipated not only the theories of evolution and genetics, but also the thinking of ecocritics like Stacy Alaimo, who speaks of our "trans-corporeal" relationship with the earth (4), and political theorists like Jane Bennett, who questions the age-old distinction of life and matter in her book *Vibrant Matter* (2010).

But Whitman's revolutionary prefiguring of ecopoetics and ecological thinking as a breaking down of traditional categories has not always been received with open arms by ecocritics. Dana Phillips argues, for example, that Whitman's kind of nature writing, like that of the whole transcendental tradition from Emerson down to Annie Dillard, is *"too selfish"* (195). Phillips complains that "the landscape in Whitman always turns out to be an inscape" (200). In other words, Whitman is too quick to override important differences between the self and the other, whether a human other or an entirely other life-form. He finds it too easy to speak for others—"Through me many long dumb voices" are channeled, as he says in "Song of Myself" (line 508)—and to transpose his own inner feelings onto the outer world.

To appreciate Whitman fully, you must be willing to accept his claim that "every atom belonging to me as good belongs to you" ("Song of Myself," line 3) and suspend, if not overcome, the desire to maintain your distance and difference. If you are unable to resist the demands of your ego or your own special identity while reading *Leaves of Grass*, or accept the "myself" of the poem not as a single individual (who happens to be male, white, Euro-American, and gay), you are likely to feel put upon, or even colonized, by the expansive identity of Whitman's "I," despite his frequent encouragement of "you" to find your own way of being in the world. His goal, he says in many places, is to show the way for all of us to become better individuals. But in the process he seems at times to undercut the possibility, speaking for us and for all of nature. There is no escaping *him*. Considering his acceptance of the doctrine of manifest destiny in poems like "Passage to India" and "Song of the Redwood-Tree" (discussed below), we may be looking at what was a blind spot for the poet—his acceptance of an imperial, colonial, or settler mentality about the land and about people different from himself. (For a critique similar to Phillips's, but from a Native American perspective, see Gannon. For a more positive, but still critical treatment of the transcendentalist tradition of nature writing, see Buell; also McMurry.)

The Spirit of Ecology

Whitman could never rest satisfied with a fully materialist worldview. "I am the poet of the Body and I am the poet of the Soul," he insisted from the start ("Song of Myself," line 422). He experimented with several versions of spirituality throughout the four decades during which he composed and revised *Leaves of Grass*. From his Quaker background and close reading of the Bible, he drew language and concepts associated with the Judeo-Christian tradition, though he was never a practicing or conventional Christian. He was also attracted by the worldview of animism, which he encountered in Egyptian, Greco-Roman, northern European, Native American, and other mythic systems. The idea that the earth is enchanted and teeming with living spirits appealed strongly to his poetic imagination and intense sympathy for all the life forms of the earth. Animism (from the Latin word *anima*, meaning soul, also the root word for "animal") would also prove attractive to the practitioners of what came to be known as deep ecology in the late twentieth century. With something like prophetic anticipation, Whitman once again looked forward to this cultural development (see Killingsworth, "As If"; also Gibson; and Manes).

To get a sense of the range of Whitman's ecospirituality, consider two poems, separated by roughly twenty years. In my book *Walt Whitman and the Earth: A Study in Ecopoetics*, I treated this pair—"This Compost" and "Song of the Redwood-Tree"—as the opposing poles in the spectrum of Whitman's shifting and conflicted ecopolitical views over the six editions of *Leaves of Grass* (see also Rasula). "This Compost," the first version of which appeared in the 1856 or second edition, is arguably the most ecologically enlightened English-language poem of the nineteenth century. By understanding death as the compost of life, the poet shows that the things we find most offensive—the repulsive smells and disgusting decay of an animal's corpse or rotting plant matter or any kind of swampy putrefaction—actually provide the foundation for the continuation of life's cycles. "Song of the Redwood-Tree," first published as a magazine piece in 1873, then added to *Leaves of Grass* in 1881, is among the most sadly conventional celebrations of environmental devastation in the name of progress to be found in English and American poetry. The poem celebrates the cutting of the great forests and the westward march of civilization, the remaking of the western wilderness and the peoples living there in the image of the citified east and the settler culture of Euro-Americans.

If the two poems are considered in light of ecospirituality, a somewhat different picture emerges. The earlier poem, "This Compost," employs figurative language derived from Christianity, the theological terminology of religious conversion and faith—death, resurrection, and belief—reinterpreted by science. Earth substitutes for the awe-inspiring Creator of the Judeo-Christian tradition: "Now I am terrified at the Earth," Whitman writes, "it is that calm and patient, / It grows such sweet things out of such corruptions . . . It gives such divine materials to men, and accepts such leavings from them at last" (lines 42–43, 47). The first version of "This Compost" was awkwardly but revealingly titled "Poem of Wonder at The Resurrection of the Wheat"—an allusion to the words of Jesus: "Unless a grain of wheat falls into the earth and dies, it remains a single grain; but if it dies, it bears much fruit" (John 12:24, New Revised Standard Version). In the dramatic situation recounted in "This Compost," the speaker confronts a disgustingly putrid object (probably a corpse, but never named, as if it were unspeakably disgusting), but finally realizes that "summer growth is innocent and disdainful above all those strata of sour dead" (line 30). At the point of his conversion to the new view, he turns from religion to science as he begins a series of celebratory exclamations by saying "What chemistry!" (line 31).

In "Song of the Redwood-Tree," Whitman replaces imagery derived from soil chemistry and Christianity with figures from animism—dryads and hamadryads, the spirits of the forest. The poet imagines listening to their voices as they resign themselves to the axes of a new race of creatures, the human pioneers who harvest their wood to build and fuel a new civilization. The poet pointedly remarks that the lumbermen do not hear what he hears: the voices of the spirits leaving the wood, which are reproduced (and italicized for emphasis) so that the reader can listen with the poet. The poet and reader are thus distanced from the agents of progress, who are deafened by the sound of their own axes. In thus identifying with the forest spirits, Whitman sounds a note of resignation in the face of industry and modernity, creating an elegiac mood that undercuts the conventional praise of western expansion. The poem dramatizes not only the literal disenchantment of the old-growth forest, the driving out of ancient spirits, but also the poet's personal disenchantment with the material progress of the nation.

So it is that, between the publication of "Compost" in 1856 and "Redwood-Tree" in 1873, Whitman more or less abandons science and religion for animistic mythology as the source of his imagery and inspiration. In the movement from one to the other, Whitman enacts what would become a division in twentieth-century environmentalism between *reform environmentalism*, based on faith in science and conventional religious ideas like stewardship, on the one hand, and on the other hand *deep ecology*, with its more mystical approach to both science and the natural environment (see Killingsworth and Palmer; also Garrard).

The Politics of the Animal

Whitman's communion with nonhuman creatures—the forest in "Song of the Redwood-Tree," as well as the mockingbird in "Out of the Cradle Endlessly Rocking" and the hermit thrush in "When Lilacs Last in the Dooryard Bloom'd," whose dramatized voices are also ventriloquized by the poet and italicized in the print text—creates some curious political affinities. In "Song of Myself," the speaker—who calls himself "Walt Whitman, a kosmos" and the "friendly and flowing savage" (lines 497, 976)—insists on an identity with the animals as a corrective to the processes of civilization that threaten to block the flow of physical and spiritual energy to humankind. He has possession, he says, of "the pass-word primeval" (line 506) and brings forth "forbidden voices, / Voices of sexes and lusts" and "Voices indecent

. . . clarified and transfigur'd" by his poetry (lines 516–18); he aims to "remove the veil" from "voices veiled" by cultural conventions and genteel manners: "Voices of the interminable generations of prisoners and slaves / . . . Of the deform'd, trivial, flat, foolish, despised, / Fog in the air, beetles rolling balls of dung" (lines 509, 514–15). Once considered sacred in the animistic culture of ancient Egypt, the dung beetle was consigned to the lower echelons of "the Great Chain of Being" in the poet's time, with God at the top, humans just below, and insects grubbing along at the last step between animals and plants (see Lovejoy). Whitman flattens the hierarchy. He also implies that once devaluation of the animals begins, human beings themselves are not safe. The mention of slaves in these lines reminds us that in Whitman's day, slaves were not considered fully human. They were herded and sold like domestic beasts. Whitman suggests that animality is a category in which people place living beings that they want to master in some way. By putting himself in that category, Whitman questions the universal difference between humans and animals, and exposes the political motives of animalizing others. With this move, he aligns his interest with the twenty-first-century perspective known as animal studies, sometimes called posthumanism (see Wolfe; Haraway).

In "Song of Myself," the articulate voice indicates the presence of the soul that has been neglected in slaves and denied in animals. Sounds that most people would find disturbing or inconsequential— sounds filtered out as noise in the flow of information—admit a plentitude of meaning for the poet, a world of newfound sympathies, and a path to a restored kinship with nature and with humanity broadly defined. He hears, for example, the "wild gander" that "leads his flock through the cool night":

> Ya-honk he says, and sounds it down to me like an invitation,
> The pert may suppose it meaningless, but I listening close,
> Find its purpose and place up there toward the wintry sky. (lines 246–48)

He represents the language of the goose roughly as he hears it, "*Ya-honk.*" The utterance has no equivalent in English. At the end of the poem, he insists that "I too am not a bit tamed, I too am untranslatable," as another great bird on high, the "spotted hawk swoops by" and speaks to him, complaining of his "gab" and "loitering" (lines 1,331–32).

A slang term for the steady flow of impressive conversation, "gab" is considered a gift in human society, but a phrase like "the gift of gab" undercuts the very eloquence it ostensibly praises. It is meaningless banter, the special province of the street hustler or the "loitering" criminal. For Whitman, the phrase *denotes* a power of linguistic performance, but *connotes* the art of the snake-oil salesman and the con game. As if in response to the hawk's calling accusation, the poet says, "I sound my barbaric yawp over the roofs of the world" (line 1,333). The Whitmanian yawp resonates with the "ya-honk" of the goose, the wild call of animal being that will not be refined into language or debased into cheap or cheating speech. Yawp and ya-honk serve no purpose other than singing the song of oneself—expressing the soul, that is—and calling out to companions. The gander, remember, "leads his flock through the cool night" (line 245); his ya-honk sounds to Whitman "like an invitation" (line 246). A poet like Whitman's old friend on the New York newspaper scene, William Cullen Bryant, would see in the flight of the goose an invitation to think of God's goodness in leading His creatures home. In Whitman, not God but the gander leads the flock. Bryant's "To a Waterfowl" suggests that as animals have their instincts, humans have their rational relationship to the Higher Power, their ability to reason out their salvation. Whitman says only that "I see in them and myself the same old law," refusing to go further and reinforce the Great Chain of Being (line 252). He places humans within nature rather than above it, one step closer to God.

Indeed, for Whitman listening to the animals reveals the unhappiness and discontentedness of modern humanity. By contrast, he says, the animals are "placid and self-contained" (line 684). The very silence of animals seems eloquent to him:

> They do not sweat and whine about their condition,
> They do not lie awake in the dark and weep for their sins,
> They do not make me sick discussing their duty to God,
> Not one is dissatisfied, not one is demented with the mania of owning things,
> Not one kneels to another, nor to his kind that lived thousands of years ago,
> Not one is respectable or unhappy over the whole earth. (lines 686–91)

The great accomplishments of civilization—religion, material success, and government—are shown here to have their downsides: sweaty and whining guilt, maniacal greed, and groveling submission to others. The animals present alternatives to the speaker; they "show their relations to me" and bring "tokens of myself" (lines 692–93). These tokens indicate elements of the self left behind or buried deep by the forces of civilization. As "the razor-bill'd auk" that "sails far north to Labrador," says the poet, "I ascend to the nest in the fissure in the cliff" (lines 682–83). Poetry provides the imaginative means to "follow" the animal, of course, but so does science as Whitman reads it: The scientific imagination brings the mastodon back to life when it "retreats beneath its own powder'd bones" (line 676).

"Song of Myself" is a poem of recovery, a poem about gathering energy from animal life. It is a poem about ascent rather than descent—about arising from the bed of depression where people lie awake in the dark and weep for their sins, arising from the knee bent to oppressive government, and arising from the spiritual poverty of consumerism, the mania for owning things, which leaves people perpetually unsatisfied and unhappy. It is about allowing the senses to awaken and spark the imagination that hears and responds to the voices of the beasts, within and without.

The New Ecological Poetry

Whitman's concern with the science, spirituality, and bodily experience of ecology would later deeply engage such American poets as Robinson Jeffers, Gary Snyder, Mary Oliver, Linda Hogan, and Joy Harjo. Whitman also puts further items on the agenda for the future of ecopoetics:

- As America's first urban poet, Whitman provides a model for nature poetry that looks beyond the tradition of the romantic rural or pastoral poem to reaffirm the needs of city people for clean water and good air, and to urge his readers to a deeper awareness of bodily health and natural beauty, wherever one might find it (see Killingsworth, *Walt*, chapter five).

- As the poet of the northeastern seashore and the island cities of New York, Whitman prefigured the tropes and themes of literary bioregionalism in current writing, including the ceremonial treatment of sacred sites and ancestral places (see Killingsworth, *Walt*, chapter four).

- As the author of significant prose writings on nature, such as his memoir *Specimen Days*, Whitman participated with his contemporaries Henry David Thoreau and John Burroughs in the development of an ecopoetical form of creative nonfiction (see Killingsworth, *Walt*, chapter six).

- As the best-known poet of the Civil War, with such works as *Drum-Taps* (1865) and *Memoranda During the War* (1876), Whitman anticipated post-World-War literary environmentalism in considering the dire effects of war on land, kinship, and connections of all kinds (see Killingsworth, *Walt*, chapter five; see also Rasula on Whitman and the later ecopoetic tradition).

Above all, reading Whitman's work urges the modern reader not to lose touch with the forces of life that thrive beyond (as well as within) the walls of our climate-controlled, locked-door, electronically mediated existence. One of the last poems he ever wrote, "To the Sun-Set Breeze," tells how the old poet's body—immobilized by age and illness and confined to his room on a sweltering summer day, "sick, weak-down, melted-worn with sweat" (line 4)—is graced by a refreshing gust of wind from the open window at the end of the day. A companion "better than talk, book, art" (line 5), the sunset breeze comes over him like a spirit that momentarily revives his creative soul. It brings the large and living world back to the poet: "I feel the sky, the prairies vast—I feel the mighty northern lakes, / I feel the ocean and the forest—somehow I feel the globe itself swift-swimming in space" (lines 10–11). He can only conclude that the wind is indeed "spiritual, Godly," and all the more valuable for being "known to my sense" (line 13). Thus, to the end of his life, Whitman remained true to his vision of the unity of body and spirit, the twining of the mortal and the Godly. The truth of the matter comes home clearly in this poem, which plays upon the etymology of the word "spirit," from the Latin *spiritus*, meaning breath or wind.

Works Cited

Alaimo, Stacy. *Bodily Natures: Science, Environment, and the Material Self.* Bloomington: Indiana UP, 2010.

Bennett, Jane. *Vibrant Matter: A Political Ecology of Things.* Durham: Duke UP, 2010.

Bryant, William Cullen. "To a Waterfowl." *The Oxford Book of American Poetry.* Ed. David Lehman and John Brehm. New York: Oxford UP, 2006. 26.

Buell, Lawrence. *The Environmental Imagination: Thoreau, Nature Writing, and the Formation of American Culture.* Cambridge: Harvard UP, 1995.

Bullard, Robert, ed. *Confronting Environmental Racism: Voices from the Grassroots.* Boston: South End, 1993.

_____. *Dumping in Dixie: Race, Class, and Environmental Quality.* Boulder: Westview, 1990.

Capra, Fritjof. *The Web of Life: A New Scientific Understanding of Living Systems.* New York: Anchor, 1997.

Folsom, Ed. *Walt Whitman's Native Representations*. Cambridge: Cambridge UP, 1994.

Gannon, Thomas C. "Complaints from the Spotted Hawk: Flights and Feathers in Whitman's 1855 *Leaves of Grass*." *Leaves of Grass: The Sesquicentennial Essays*. Ed. Susan Belasco, Ed Folsom, and Kenneth M. Price. Lincoln: U of Nebraska P, 2007. 141–75.

Garrard, Greg. *Ecocriticism*. London: Routledge, 2004.

Gibson, James William. *A Reenchanted World: The Quest for a New Kinship with Nature*. New York: Holt, 2009.

Haraway, Donna. *Primate Visions: Gender, Race, and Nature in the World of Modern Science*. London: Routledge, 1989.

_____. *When Species Meet*. Minneapolis: U of Minnesota P, 2008.

Holcomb, Chris, and M. Jimmie Killingsworth. *Performing Prose: The Study and Practice of Style in Composition*. Carbondale: Southern Illinois UP, 2010.

Killingsworth, M. Jimmie. "'As If the Beasts Spoke': The Animal/Animist/Animated Walt Whitman." *Walt Whitman Quarterly Review* 28.1 (2010): 19–35.

_____. *The Cambridge Introduction to Walt Whitman*. Cambridge: Cambridge UP, 2007.

_____. "The Case of Cotton Mather's Dog: Reflection and Resonance in American Ecopoetics." *College English* 73.5 (2011): 498–517.

_____. *Walt Whitman and the Earth: A Study in Ecopoetics*. Iowa City: U of Iowa P, 2004.

_____. *Whitman's Poetry of the Body: Sexuality, Politics, and the Text*. Chapel Hill: U of North Carolina P, 1989.

Killingsworth, M. Jimmie, and Jacqueline S. Palmer. *Ecospeak: Rhetoric and Environmental Politics in America*. Carbondale: Southern Illinois UP, 1992.

Leopold, Aldo. *A Sand County Almanac*. 1949. New York: Ballantine, 1966.

Lovejoy, Arthur O. *The Great Chain of Being: A Study of the History of an Idea*. Cambridge: Harvard UP, 1936.

Loving, Jerome. *Walt Whitman: The Song of Himself*. Berkeley: U of California P, 1999.

Manes, Christopher. "Nature and Silence." *The Ecocriticism Reader: Landmarks in Literary Ecology*. Ed. Cheryll Glotfelty and Harold Fromm. Athens: U of Georgia P, 1996. 15–29.

Martinez-Alier, Joan. *The Environmentalism of the Poor: A Study of Ecological Conflicts and Valuation*. Cheltenham: Edward Elgar, 2002.

McMurry, Andrew. *Environmental Renaissance: Emerson, Thoreau, and the Systems of Nature*. Athens: U of Georgia P, 2003.

Moon, Michael. *Disseminating Whitman: Revision and Corporeality in* Leaves of Grass. Cambridge: Harvard UP, 1991.

Mortimer-Sandilands, Catriona, and Bruce Erickson, eds. *Queer Ecologies: Sex, Nature, Politics, Desire*. Bloomington: Indiana UP, 2010.

Morton, Timothy. *The Ecological Thought*. Cambridge: Harvard UP, 2010.

Phillips, Dana. *The Truth of Ecology: Nature, Culture, and Literature in America*. New York: Oxford UP, 2003.

Rasula, Jed. *This Compost: Ecological Imperatives in American Poetry.* Athens: U of Georgia P, 2002.

Shively, Charley, ed. *Calamus Lovers: Walt Whitman's Working Class Camerados.* San Francisco: Gay Sunshine, 1987.

Warren, James Perrin. *Walt Whitman's Language Experiment.* University Park: Pennsylvania State UP, 1990.

Whitman, Walt. *Leaves of Grass: Norton Critical Edition.* Ed. Sculley Bradley and Harold W. Blodgett. New York: Norton, 1973.

Wolfe, Cary. *Animal Rites: American Culture, the Discourse of Species, and Posthumanist Theory.* Chicago: U of Chicago P, 2003.

Wolfe, Cary, ed. *Zoontologies: The Question of the Animal.* Minneapolis: U of Minnesota P, 2003.

The Return to the Primitive: Evolution, Atavism, and Socialism in Jack London's *The Call of the Wild*_____

Tina Gianquitto

On July 25, 1897, twenty-one-year-old Jack London (1876–1916) boarded a steamer and headed to the "new" frontier wilderness of Alaska in search of gold. A scant four years before, in 1893, and just before scores of would-be millionaires rushed north seeking fortune and adventure, American historian Frederick Jackson Turner declared the American frontier, the cornerstone of American exceptionalism and the source of the rugged individualism of the national character, closed. As Turner argues in "The Problem of the West" (1896): "Out of [the frontiersman's] wilderness experience, out of the freedom of his opportunities, he fashioned a formula for social regeneration—the freedom of the individual to seek his own" (213). As Roderick Nash explains in his monumental *Wilderness and the American Mind*, Turner believed that living "in the wilderness, 'the return to primitive conditions,' fostered individualism, independence, and confidence in the common man that encouraged self-government" (146). Of course, Turner is building off—yet modifying significantly—an idea of the frontier popularized over one hundred years earlier, in J. Hector St. John de Crèvecoeur's *Letters from an American Farmer*. In the essay "What Is an American?" Crèvecoeur credits the settlers' contact with the wild frontier as imbuing the national consciousness with viciousness and savagery. "By living in or near the woods, their actions are regulated by the wildness of the neighbourhood. . . . The chase renders them ferocious, gloomy, and unsocial. . . . the worst of them are those who have degenerated altogether into the hunting state" (76). Turner, and later Jack London, redeemed the frontier space, and transformed the wild frontier landscape into a "clean slate to which idealists could bring their dreams for a better life" (Nash 146).

Turner's great contribution, however, came in his recognition of the closing of the American frontier, and with it the end of an epoch marked by vital contact with the wild: "The first rough conquest of the wilderness is accomplished, and that great supply of free lands which year after year has served to reinforce the democratic influences in the United States is exhausted. . . . The free lands that made the American pioneer have gone" (244–45). The closing of the American frontier undoubtedly affected America's conception of its self and its destiny, which is perhaps why the discovery of gold in the vast and largely inaccessible Alaskan wilderness prompted the opening of a new chapter of America's "frontier" history. London's articulation of the savage confrontation with the wilderness of the frozen North both continued and broke with the frontier narratives of earlier generations. Certainly, the movements of his Arctic inhabitants and interlopers conform to those of earlier generations of settlers; they follow the same paths—"the arteries made by geology," as Turner puts it—and penetrate the wilderness with "lines of civilization growing ever more numerous" (14–15). At the same time, the human and nonhuman animals that populate London's stories narrate not a national narrative, but rather a more elemental one of an individual's struggle to survive and thrive in a hostile world.

Although Jack London has long been "contemptuously dismissed" by many American literary critics, many of whom deem his writing "hack work," irredeemably racist (especially his South Seas stories), or simplistically political, a new critical appraisal of his work is under way (Tavernier-Courbin 2). His writings are of special interest in the context of studies of literature and the environment. London's seemingly simple tales provide ample opportunity to examine the broad set of questions that generally inform "environmental" readings of texts. Following the "rough checklist" of "ingredients" often found in environmentally oriented literature, as outlined by Lawrence Buell, we can ask of London's texts: To what extent is the nonhuman environment present not merely as a passive backdrop for the affairs of dog and man, but rather as a palpable force that plays an active role in determining the success or failure of those affairs? To what extent is

---

"the environment" understood as a process, not as a static construct? Finally, to what extent are the interests of nonhuman animals granted legitimacy, "a habitat, a history, a story of [their] own" (7–8)? In other words, to what extent are Jack London's dogs "dogs"?

Beyond these basic questions we can ask more specific ones of London's texts. To what extent are the actions of human and nonhuman animals governed by the logic of evolution? What are the conditions under which community develops? If, as London writes, the white and motionless "wild aims to destroy movement," how can readers comprehend the red, raw forces, the "irresistible impulses" and "blood-longing" that seize Buck, driving him away from human campfires and into the company of wolves (*White Fang* 77, 80)? Finally what does "the wild" mean to Jack London—or, for that matter, to his readers? Clearly, London's Arctic saga remains relevant even to a contemporary generation. "Jack London is King" and "All Hail the Dominant Primordial Beast!" read graffiti left behind by Christopher McCandless, who died alone in 1992 in Alaska during an ill-fated attempt to live out a wilderness fantasy (Krakauer 9, 38). What accounts for the enduring popularity of London's vision of the natural world?

London purposefully cultivated an image of himself as an author of the "wild." Indeed, not only was his well-known, well-publicized personal life something of a walk on the wild side—from his early years spent oyster-pirating, hoboing, and gold-prospecting to his later life as a hard-drinking, sea-voyaging, best-selling author—his spare yet evocative stories detail hard lives lived in unforgiving climates. While London may have been dismissed by the critical set, he was embraced by the public one, long remaining a best-selling author both at home and abroad. Although London explored a variety of landscapes in his work, from the gold trails of the Arctic to the slums of London and the sun-soaked waters of the South Pacific, his most enduringly famous tales depict, in often brutal detail, the confrontation of the individual (human, canine, or other) with the "savage, frozen-hearted" wild of the Klondike and Yukon territories.

London was a consummate professional when it came to his writing career. He was keenly aware of the market value of his words, and his correspondence and publishing contracts detail the author's careful negotiation with editors over both storyline and length, as well as the price he would earn per word written. He capitalized on popular conventions such as naturalism—the effort to apply scientific principles to human (and nonhuman) action in order to represent the real and unmediated experiences of the individual in the environment—in framing his narratives. He also knew that audiences were longing for the kind of "surrogate tourism" that came from reading narratives rich in local detail (Auerbach 50), and he crafted his novels and short stories to take advantage of the Arctic landscapes of the new frontier to meet this desire. As a writer, London understood that establishing a sense of place was critical to the success of the literary endeavor. In a letter written to aspiring writer Ethel Jennings in 1915, London criticized a piece Jennings had sent him, saying "Your story . . . had no locality. Your story had no place as being distinctively different from any other place of the earth's surface. . . . Develop your locality. Get in your local color" (*No Mentor* 152). Yet despite the seeming attention London pays to "local color," his Arctic landscapes are surprisingly monochromatic. Sounds predominate in this world of white, sounds of water running under ice, ice cracking underfoot, and breath freezing in the air. We hear the dialects of the polyglot miners and mail carriers, and the half-wild "sobs" of their sled dogs. But we do not see much beyond the "weary mile of trail and toil" (*Call of the Wild* 25).

It is this very lack of detail, however, that paradoxically accounts for much of the enduring power of a book like *The Call of the Wild* (1903). Landscape functions as much as a mythic construct as an actual place, and London deployed the landscape of the frozen North to expound upon a hybrid philosophy comprising individualism and mutual aid, a scatter-shot mixture of evolutionary theory, biological determinism, radical socialism, and a touch of American transcendentalism. Here, the details of London's autobiography, often so important for understanding the philosophical and political trajectories of many of his works, come into play. London brought with him to the Alaskan frontier a small but influential library: Charles Darwin's *On the Origin of Species* (1859), John Milton's *Paradise Lost* (1667), Ernst Haeckel's *The Riddle of the Universe* (1901), Karl Marx's *Das Kapital* (1867, 1885, 1894), and Herbert Spencer's *Philosophy of Style* (1852). Each had a profound effect on London's conception of the "wild" and his articulation of it. The frozen Arctic confirmed London's belief in biological determinism and the evolutionary dictates of "fitness" and "adaptation" learned from Darwin, Haeckel, and Spencer. It taught him, as he wrote in the grim tale "To Build a Fire," that man's "frailty as a creature of temperature . . . able only to live within certain narrow limits of heat and cold" limits his ability to survive in a hostile landscape (463). At the same time, Milton and Marx showed him the dangers of radical individualism and the promise of socialism, and he saw reflected in the communities that inhabit the Arctic landscape the importance of cooperation, community, and mutual aid.

Into the Primitive: London and the "Pitiless Struggle for Existence"

Jack London is often recalled, especially by those who read *The Call of the Wild* as schoolchildren, as a children's writer, a perception cemented early in the twentieth century with the inclusion of many of his books in a series called the "Every Boy's Library," selected by and published under the auspices of the Boy Scouts of America. The most obvious reason for the persistence of this perception, despite the fact that a great many of London's stories are filled with scenes of unrelenting (and often gory) violence and death, is undoubtedly that London's most revered tales are dog stories. Buck stars as the canine protagonist of London's best-selling *The Call of the Wild*, while other famous dog heroes include White Fang, Bâtard, Brown Wolf, and That Spot. People are also found in these tales, of course, but something about these dogs has spoken to readers' minds and hearts for over a century, as through them readers are able to tap into the "primordial" wild. The dogs of London's stories—half-wolf, yet only half-wild—connect readers to a mythic past, to that moment when wild wolves came into the human home and became our domestic dogs.

At the same time, London's dogs remind us that all living creatures, not just humans, are subject to the unceasing violence of the natural world. Even to readers in a modern world where the graphic details of crime and war provide regular fodder for evening news programs, London's account of the brutal treatment of his canine protagonists is often breathtaking. Take Buck. Stolen with a violent twist of a rope around his neck from his comfortable, "sun-kissed" home—where he was the privileged dog of a wealthy family—Buck is carried to Alaska and bludgeoned into obedience (though not submission) by the man wearing the red sweater and, perhaps more to the point, wielding the club. He is sold and put to hard labor, pulling the mail train along the frozen courses of gold field trails. He and his teammates are overworked, starved, and brutalized by human masters, while rival dogs terrorize him into fighting for his life. Dog and human inhabit a landscape hostile to their very existence; as London elaborates in *White Fang*, the wild "was the masterful and incommunicable wisdom of eternity laughing at the futility of life and the effort of life" (91). All individuals face the pitiless "struggle for existence" described by the evolutionist Charles Darwin and popularized by the philosopher Herbert Spencer, and all must endure a world whose commands are brutally simple: "Kill or be killed, eat or be eaten, this is the law" (62).

Certainly, London fashions "nature" in *The Call of the Wild* according to the tenets of Darwinian evolutionary theory, a biological theory with which most of his readers would have been familiar. In *On the Origin of Species*, Darwin argues that species adapt over time to their environment and, moreover, that those adaptations involve a struggle for existence. Darwin reminds his readers "never to forget that every single organic being . . . lives by a struggle at some period of its life" (49). As Herbert Spencer famously put it in his influential *Principles of Biology* (1864), evolution amounts to the "survival of the fittest," whereby through the ongoing process of natural selection those that are most "perfectly adapted" to their environment multiply, while the "unfittest" suffer "continual destruction" (311, 444). As London explained in a letter to his friend Cloudsley Johns, "Natural selection, undeviating, pitiless, careless alike of the individual or the species, destroyed or allowed to perpetuate, as the case might be, such breeds as were unfittest or fittest to survive" (Labor, Leitz, and Shepard 101). Suffering and death are ever present in the Northland Wilds, which London describes in the opening of his novel *White Fang*: "It is not the way of the Wild to like movement . . . and the Wild aims always to destroy movement. It freezes the water to prevent it running to the sea; it drives the sap out of the trees till they are frozen to their mighty hearts; and most ferociously and terribly of all does the Wild harry and crush into submission man" (92). Throughout these tales, humans and nonhumans alike submit to the constant threat of predators, famine, cold, fear, greed, and viciousness. In *The Call of the Wild*, Buck's new life as an Arctic sled dog initiates him into this struggle. His first day on Dyea beach teaches him the "law of club and fang," and he adapts accordingly; after several brutal days on the trail, Buck learns to fight as "the wolfish creatures fought," with a quick snap of the jaws and a leap away (15). He learns to bed down under the snow and steal to supplement his meager rations, actions London describes using Darwinian language. Buck's first theft

> marked [him] as fit to survive in the hostile Northland environment. It marked his adaptability, his capacity to adjust himself to changing conditions, the lack of which would have meant swift and terrible death. It marked, further, the decay or going to pieces of his moral nature, a vain thing and a handicap in the ruthless struggle for existence. It was all well enough in the Southland, under the law of love and fellowship, to respect private property and personal feelings; but in the Northland, under the law of club and fang, whoso took such things into account was a fool, and so far as he observed them he would fail to prosper. (21)

Weakness equals death, a law he discovers as he watches Curly, "the good-natured Newfoundland," torn to pieces before his very eyes by Spitz, who would soon fight Buck to the death for mastership of the sled-team. "So that was the way," Buck muses. "No fair play. Once down, that was the end of you" (16).

By the end of the book, Buck has been transformed into a "killer, a thing that preyed, living on the things that lived, unaided, alone, by virtue of his own strength and prowess, surviving triumphantly in a hostile environment where only the strong survived" (77). This triumphant moment comes when, "guided by that instinct which came from the old hunting days of the primordial world," he mercilessly culls a venerable bull from a herd of migrating moose. Over the course of four long days, during which Buck "clung to the flank of the herd" with the "patience of the wild—dogged, tireless, persistent as life itself," Buck forces the herd to abandon their harried leader (79). In the bull, wounded by an arrow in his side, he finds "as formidable an antagonist as even Buck could desire" (79). In the terrible closing scenes of this passage, the once-great beast, now transformed into an "old bull . . . with lowered head," watches as "his mates—the cows he had known, the calves he had fathered, the bulls he had mastered" shamble off, leaving him to face the "merciless fanged terror" alone (80). London writes with both passion and pathos of the contest:

> From then on, night and day, Buck never left his prey, never gave it a moment's rest, never permitted it to browse the leaves of trees or the shoots of the young birch and willow. Nor did he give the wounded bull opportunity to slake his burning thirst in the slender trickling streams they crossed. . . .
>
> The great head drooped more and more under its tree of horns, and the shambling trot grew weak and weaker. He took to standing for long periods, with nose to the ground and dejected ears dropped limply. . . .
>
> At last, at the end of the fourth day, he pulled the great moose down. (80–81)

This kill, even more than Buck's destruction of Spitz and mastery of the sled-team, proves absolutely his transformation into the "dominant primordial beast" (24).

London conceives of *The Call of the Wild* as a tale of devolution from a civilized state, and in writing of Buck's "retrogression," he collapses the long history of the wild wolf's evolution into the domestic dog, as he describes the physical and mental changes that accompany the animal's "decivilization" (Labor 454). His account draws not only on Darwinian evolutionary ideas, especially notions of biological and cultural atavism (the reappearance in a later generation of long-lost ancestral traits), but also on popular expositions of the process of evolution, such as Ernst Haeckel's notion of recapitulation (the repetition, during development, of past stages of evolutionary history). London pondered both during his winter stay in the Klondike.

For London, atavism was the "key" to *The Call of the Wild*, a point he expressed to John O'Hara, whose poem of that name opens the text: "Old longings nomadic leap / Chafing at custom's chain / Again from its brumal sleep / Wakens the ferine strain" (5). As Darwin explains, feral animals, those that have reverted to a wild condition, "invariably return to their primitive . . . type" and exhibit atavistic characteristics, or behavioral and structural attributes common to ancestral generations (*The Variation of Animals and Plants Under Domestication* 32). Buck's atavistic traits are awakened by his contact with the wild, with his half-wolf, half-wild teammates, and with the "law of club and fang." As Buck devolves, he passes backward through the stages of civilization and "the domesticated generations fell from him" (22). He transforms from a hyper-civilized dog that "could have died for a moral consideration, say the defense of Judge Miller's riding-whip" (21) into a "dominant primordial beast" whose body and soul stirred "instincts long dead" and memories of the "youth of the breed." As Buck adapts mentally to his new state, he adapts physically, as his "muscles became hard as iron" and "sight and scent became remarkably keen" (22). His feet, which had "softened during the many generations since the day his last wild ancestor was tamed by cave-dweller or river man," later "grew hard to the trail" (28). Gradually, even his soul responds to his new conditions of life, and as the aurora borealis flames overhead, Buck "delights" in joining the "weird and eerie chant" of his "wild wolf husky" companions (31). "His cadences," London explains, "were their cadences, the cadences which voiced their woe and what to them was the meaning of the stillness, the cold, and the dark" (22).

Notably, Buck's "retrogression" into the primitive state is delineated as a series of educational moments—cast out his own, Buck would have undoubtedly succumbed to the harsh conditions of his new life. He must unlearn his civilized ways and instead "learn to be wild" (Auerbach 91). As Jonathan Auerbach observes, *The Call of the Wild* refuses to follow the contours of a simple plot of effortless primordial atavism. "Instead," he writes, "attaining wildness entails disciplined education" (92). In his reversion to the wild state, Buck recapitulates—or experiences in reverse—the stages of his breed's development. And although Buck does not "reason it out," as London clearly and simply states, this dog-hero is hardly an automaton, acting only according to blind instinct (21). Buck exhibits consciousness in his apprehension of the world, easily identified in the verbs that London employs to describe Buck's mental actions (Auerbach 89). Buck "perceived and determined and responded" (78); he mused and "remembered" (73); he possessed "imagination" and understanding (35); he "wanted" and desired"; and finally, he "learned" (22).

Indeed, London believed fervently that dogs possessed simple reasoning skills; he is not merely humanizing his animals, but rather he grants them an independent consciousness. And as with his presentation of the survival of the fittest, he believes that his representation of that consciousness is "in line with the facts of evolution." He "hewed them to the mark set by scientific research" ("Other Animals" 200). Darwin is again London's source, although he also freely borrowed many of his canine characters and traits from other popular dog stories of the day, especially Egerton Young's *My Dogs in the Northland*

(1902), which was published shortly before London began writing *The Call of the Wild*. In the little-studied *The Expression of the Emotions in Man and Animals* (1872), Darwin devotes pages to describing the emotions and resulting actions of dogs. He talks of dogs "grinning" to exhibit excitement, licking and rubbing against humans to show affection, howling and writhing to reveal pain, and finally, biting a master's hand to show love—as Buck does with John Thornton (118–21). Darwin writes: "Animals may constantly be seen to pause, to deliberate, and resolve" (*Descent* 77). He credits dogs with the "power of imagination"; "there must be something special," he concludes, "which causes dogs to howl in the night, and especially during moonlight, in that remarkable and melancholy manner called baying" (77).

More importantly, however, London absorbed the theoretical underpinning of Darwin's work: the notion that "the difference in mind between man and the higher animals . . . [is] certainly one of degree and not of kind" (*Descent* 130). Cognition and consciousness are shared traits. As he explains in "The Other Animals" (1908), "these dogs-heroes of mine were [directed] by instinct, sensation, and emotion, and by simple reasoning" (199–200). London wrote this biting essay in response to sharp criticism leveled at him by none other than President Theodore Roosevelt, who accused London of being a "nature faker." In this famous controversy, Roosevelt, along with the distinguished nature writer John Burroughs, protested the so-called humanizing of animals in popular animal stories of the day and criticized writers for portraying all animals as reasoning beings. Roosevelt and Burroughs, as London charges in his essay, wrongly "assert that all animals below man are automatons and perform actions only of two sorts—mechanical and reflex—and that in such actions no reasoning enters at all. They believe that man is the only animal capable of reasoning and that ever does reason." London, never one to back down from a fight, takes aim at Roosevelt, the big-game hunter, calling him "an amateur" (200). Nevertheless, despite the darkly satirical tone of his essay, London feels passionately about the abilities of other animals to reason precisely because this capacity is yet another evolutionary trait that links humans to their nonhuman companions. London closes the essay with a passionate appeal:

> Let us be very humble. We who are so very human are very animal. . . .
> No . . . though you stand on the top of the ladder of life you must not kick out that ladder from under your feet. You must not deny your relatives, the other animals. Their history is your history, and if you kick them to the bottom of the abyss, to the bottom of the abyss you go yourself. By them you stand or fall. What you repudiate in them you repudiate in yourself. (210)

As Lilian Carswell notes, London's recognition of the "cognitive and emotional kinship between human beings and other animals . . . suggests the necessity of a reevaluation of how we treat these other animals." London, Carswell concludes, "suggests that we inflict morally significant harm on animals" when they are denied "the opportunity to express their capacities for 'direction, control, and reason,' and . . . 'choice'" (193). For London, then, the issue of animal consciousness is as much a political position as it is a literary one. These dogs enable London to think more broadly about the ties that link human and nonhuman, home and wild, organism and environment, and individual and community.

"For the Love of a Man": London, Socialism, and "Mutual Aid" in the Wild

The image of the abyss with which London ends his essay "The Other Animals" is a recurrent symbol in his writings, especially his political works dealing with the ravages that the capitalist economic system inflicts on the poor and working classes. It is worth stressing in this context that London's Arctic wanderers are first and foremost laborers, a detail that is often overlooked in critical accounts of the story. Yet that fact is crucial to understanding the critique of both individualism and the competitive market system that runs throughout the text. Human laborers (mail carriers and others) suffer as they work to support that fundamental aspect of capitalist enterprises, the extraction of the earth's resources for personal profit. Dogs also performed essential work functions in the Arctic. Without them, transportation and communication would have been impossible, as they were employed delivering supplies and mail into the wilderness and carrying precious gold out of it. Long used by Native American tribes to pull sleds, dogs were in general far more suited to the icy environment than the horses that were brought to the North only to suffer cruel and violent deaths as they fought to navigate the treacherous mountain and river passages.

Of course, Buck's experiences with the man in the red sweater, Spitz, the dark, and the cold confirm that life in the North is marked by the constant struggle of the individual against both the environment and other organisms. But Buck's adventures with John Thornton, and, later, his integration into the wild wolf pack, demonstrate another dimension of London's philosophical orientation: his "socialist consciousness" (Berliner 56). As Jonathan Berliner explains, in the author's "recurrent praise of primordial supermen"—übercanines like Buck, for instance—"London presents nature as a brutal force but crucially one that could be harnessed for socialistic purposes" (56). This political dimension—that of exposing the cruel dimensions of the labor market and presenting alternative options based in communal action—plays a prominent role in the text. Although London is primarily remembered for his wilderness stories, a great many of his novels, essays, short stories, and political tracts deal with the harsh conditions of the working classes. Here again, London's autobiography plays a pivotal role in understanding his political and philosophical orientation.

As a young man London joined the Socialist ranks: His initiation came about when he hoboed his way across the country with ranks of unemployed workers heading to Washington to protest the plight of the poor. Already London saw himself, with others of the working classes, at "the bottom of the [Social] Pit . . . hanging onto the slippery wall by main strength and sweat" (*War of the Classes* 274–75). While many critics read Buck as a confirmation of triumphant individualism, in fact his story represents the utter necessity of community over individualism as a means of surviving a hostile landscape. Solidarity equals success while individualism spells destruction, a fact many of London's characters ignore at their peril.

In *Origin*, Darwin imagines the struggle for existence in a "large and metaphorical sense including dependence of one being on another" (16). The Russian anarchist Peter Kropotkin expanded on this notion of interdependence, arguing, in *Mutual Aid: A Factor of Evolution*, that "in the animal world we have seen that the vast majority of species live in societies, and that they find in association the best arms for the struggle for life" (246). London employs the relationship between Buck and Thornton to inquire into other kinds of relationships that can form in the midst of the pitiless struggle for existence. Although all life is marked by constant warfare, survival ultimately depends upon the interaction of individuals across communities. Thus, Darwin writes in *Origin*:

> How have all those exquisite adaptations of one part of the organisation to another part, and to the conditions of life, and of one distinct organic being to another being been perfected? We see these beautiful co-adaptations most plainly in the woodpecker and mistletoe; and only a little less plainly in the humblest parasite which clings to the hairs of a quadruped or feathers of a bird . . . in short, we see beautiful adaptation everywhere and in every part of the organic world. (45)

Even that blind force natural selection, Darwin argues, acts in "social animals" to "adapt the structure of each individual for the benefit of the community" (87). Such adaptation gradually leads to the development of the social instincts, a point Darwin makes in *The Descent of Man* (1871) when he argues that these social instincts "give the impulse to act for the good of the community" (72). Darwin meditates on the role that sympathy plays both in the development of the social instincts and in their role in the community. He writes: "As sympathy is thus directed [toward beloved objects], the mutual love of the members of the same community will extend its limits" (82). Thus, the sympathy inspired by the social instincts eventually enabled humans to expand the bounds of community to include nonhuman animals, especially dogs. It accounts for humankind's "strong love for the dog," as well as for that love "which the dog returns with interest" (74).

Sympathy is likewise the means by which London extends the bounds of community across both class and species in the frozen North, and it is in many ways the foundation of cooperation, as London articulated in a brief socialist tract in 1899. In this essay, "What Communities Lose by the Competitive System," London writes that man's "strength lay in numbers, in the unity of interests, in solidarity of effort—in short, in combination against the hostile elements of his environment" (Foner 419). Perhaps, also, London's vision of solidarity against the hostile forces of the Arctic environment derived from Kropotkin's bemused exclamation: "But how many human settlers will perish in new countries simply for not having understood the necessity of combining their efforts!" (38).

Such a vision of labor undergirds all of the cross-species relationships in the text. François and Perrault tend to the dogs before they prepare their own meals; Hal, Charles, and Mercedes fail to do so. Indeed, Kropotkin's observation seems particularly relevant to the ultimately fatal journey of these three Arctic novices. Arrogant in their ignorance of the ways of the wild, all three are doomed to failure largely because of their resistance to uniting with other more experienced members of the community. Nor can they sympathize with the dying and haggard dogs at their command. Since that party views the sled dogs only as property—"It's my dog," Hal replies, when Thornton beats him away from Buck's prone body (57)—whatever sympathy might be extended to the animals (and notably only by the sole female character in the book, the weepy and shallow Mercedes) is rendered "uninformed and hollow" (Carswell 199). The dogs are still required to work despite their misery and suffering. As the outfit of starved dogs and miserable humans pull into John Thornton's camp far up the trail at the mouth of the White River, they betray their foolishness and their adherence to unsuitable modes of individualism. When Thornton reluctantly advises the trio "to take no more chances on the rotten ice," Hal mocks and defies him, and then brutally whips and clubs the skeletal dog team to force them back onto the thinning ice of the trail. In their single-minded pursuit of wealth, the three humans—and their innocent dogs—are consumed by the abyss; they "disappear" into the "yawning hole" that opens in the ice when the bottom drops out of the trail (58).

Meanwhile, Thornton undergoes a significant transformation in his encounter with Hal and company: When he intervenes in what will surely be the scene of Buck's death, his sympathy for that poor laborer transforms him into an enraged and "inarticulate . . . animal" (57). His "humanity" (often a troublesomely violent trait in London's stories) is erased, and along with it the hierarchical distinctions between human (master) and dog (slave). Similarly, Buck evolves "into a new existence," as Thornton nurses him back to vibrant health (59). Or perhaps it is that Buck further "devolves," for in this moment London imagines Buck reliving the single crucial evolutionary moment in the history of the domestic dog—that moment when the original wolf ancestors abandoned the wild and came into the human home. Through Buck's narrative, London investigates the ambiguous moment of domestication, that point at which the protodog abandoned the solitary yet free life of the wild for the companionable chains of domestication. Love, "genuine passionate love, was his for the first time . . . love that was feverish and burning, that was adoration, that was madness," and it compels Buck to give himself wholeheartedly to Thornton, even going so far as to put his own life in peril to save the man (60).

There is a kind of freedom in this relationship, though, in that it enables Buck to connect with his distant, ancestral past. As the frozen wastelands of the Arctic warm in the spring sunshine, Thornton and his dogs press deeper into the wilderness and pass through "weird," "melancholy," and "silent" landscapes. Buck, in quiet company with Thornton, "spent long hours musing by the fire," dreaming of "other," older fires and "different" men (73, 41). As he blinked into the fire, he felt "the call still sounding in the depths of the forest. It filled him with a great unrest and strange desires. It caused him to feel a vague, sweet gladness, and he was aware of wild yearnings and stirrings for he knew not what" (74). As he dreams, Buck travels back to the dawn of the breed and wanders through dimly remembered worlds and landscapes—beaches, forests, and jungles—with a hairy, primitive companion.

Of course, Buck's story cannot end by Thornton's fire. "Irresistible impulses" seized the dog, compelling him deep into the forest wilderness. Significantly, as Buck kills the moose and is transformed into "a thing that preyed," Thornton, Buck's great love, has died at the hands of the (fictional) Yehat tribe. Sated and satisfied, Buck returns to Thornton's camp only to find it desolated, and his bitter rage prompts him to destroy the celebrating Yehats. Thematically, London has no choice but to kill off Thornton: He is the last "tie" to "man and the claims of man." Buck could never be completely free while Thornton lived. But, in avenging his death and in killing man—"the noblest game of all"—Buck breaks the final taboo of the domesticated dog (83). He is finally free to respond with whole heart to the wild's call.

The Sleeping Wolf: London's Dog Gets Away

London uncharacteristically struggled with the title of his dog novel. When his story was first serialized, he wrote to his publisher George Brett that he "did not like the title, *The Call of the Wild*, and neither did *The Saturday Evening Post*." London explained: "I racked my brains for a better title, and suggested *The Sleeping Wolf*. They, however, if in the meantime they do not hit upon a better title, are going to publish it in the *Post* under *The Wolf*. This I do not like so well as *The Sleeping Wolf*, which I do not like very much either." London concludes: "There is a good title somewhere, if only we can lay hold of it" (Labor 351).

London could no more "lay hold of" a better title for the book than he could of the story itself. As an author, he was known for his discipline and his "stint," writing one thousand words a day, recording the word count of each story, and hewing carefully to word-count specifications of the most popular (and well-paying) magazines. But some inexplicable element of Buck's story compelled the author to abandon his word-count discipline. London initially conceived his dog story as a four-thousand-word companion piece to the "Bâtard," a short tale in which London examines the causes and consequences of the "exceeding bitter hate" between a brutal man and his equally brutal dog (387). But in letters, he marvels to George Brett and Anna Strunsky about his inability to call his story to a "halt." As he explains to Brett, his editor and publisher, he "sat down to write [the story] into a 4,000 word yarn, but it *got away from me* & I was *forced to expand it* to its present length" (Labor 351). To Strunsky he added, "It got away from me . . . ran to 32,000 words before I could call a halt" (Labor 352).

Clearly, London, like the American transcendentalist Henry David Thoreau, imagined the wild past as something remarkable, something to be cherished. Contact with the wild was a necessary precursor to the settling of the frontier and the evolution of civilization. In his essay "Walking," Thoreau meditates on the nature of wildness, stating emphatically that "in Wildness is the Preservation of the world" (239). "Life consists *with* wildness," Thoreau declares. "The most alive is the wildest" (240). Like London, Thoreau locates the human kinship with wolves as a source of that wildness: "From the forest and wilderness come the tonics and barks which brace mankind. Our ancestors were savages. The story of Romulus and Remus [the mythic founders of Rome] being suckled by a wolf is not a meaningless fable. The founders of every state which has risen to eminence have drawn their nourishment and vigor from a similar wild source" (239).

By the end of *The Call of the Wild*, Buck becomes such a "founder" of a new state, a new breed. He joins the wild wolf pack and "ran with them, side by side with the wild brother" (85). In the end, Buck is fully consumed by the mythic valence of London's text. He is transformed into the Ghost Dog, the untamed wolf that has haunted the human imagination for centuries and still exerts its strange and often devastating power. More than that, Buck leaves generations of offspring marked by his contact with the wild: "The years were not many," London writes, "when the Yehats noted a change in the breed of timber wolves; for some were seen with splashes of brown on head and muzzle, and with a rift of white centering down the chest" (85).

Works Cited

Auerbach, Jonathan. *Male Call: Becoming Jack London*. Durham: Duke UP, 1996.

Berliner, Jonathan. "Jack London's Socialistic Social Darwinism." *American Literary Realism*. 41.1 (2008): 52–78.

Buell, Lawrence. *The Environmental Imagination: Thoreau, Nature Writing, and the Formation of American Culture*. Cambridge: Harvard UP, 1995.

Carswell, Lilian. "Telling the Truth about Animals: Epistemology, Ethics, and Animal Minds in Melville, Darwin, Saunders, and London." Diss. Columbia U, 2004. *ProQuest Dissertations and Theses*. Web. 29 June 2011.

Crèvecoeur, J. Hector St. John de. *Letters from an American Farmer and Sketches of Eighteenth Century America*. Ed. Albert E. Stone. New York: Penguin, 1986.

Darwin, Charles. *The Descent of Man and Selection in Relation to Sex*. Vol. 1. Princeton: Princeton UP, 1981.

_____. *The Expression of the Emotions in Man and Animals*. London: Murray, 1872.

_____. *On the Origin of Species By Means of Natural Selection, or the Preservation of the Favoured Races in the Struggle for Life*. Ed. Paul Barrett and R. B. Freeman. New York: New York UP, 1988.

_____. *The Variation of Animals and Plants Under Domestication*. London: John Murray, 1868.

Foner, Philip. *Jack London: American Rebel*. New York: Citadel, 1964.

Krakauer, Jon. *Into the Wild*. New York: Random, 1997.

Kropotkin, Peter. *Mutual Aid: A Factor in Evolution*. Ed. Paul Avrich. New York: New York UP, 1972.

Labor, Earle, Robert C. Leitz, and I. Milo Shepard. *The Letters of Jack London*. Vol. 1. Stanford: Stanford UP, 1988.

London, Jack. *The Call of the Wild. Jack London: Novels and Stories*. New York: Library of America, 1982. 5–86.

_____. *No Mentor But Myself: Jack London on Writing and Writers*. Ed. Dale L. Walker and Jeanne Campbell Reesman. Stanford: Stanford UP, 1999.

_____. "The Other Animals," *The Wild Animal Story*. Ed. Ralph Lutts. Philadelphia: Temple UP, 1998. 199–210.

_____. "To Build a Fire." *Jack London: Novels and Stories*. New York: Library of America, 1982. 462–78.

_____. *War of the Classes*. New York: Macmillan, 1905.

_____. *White Fang. Jack London: Novels and Stories*. New York: Library of America, 1982. 87–284.

Nash, Roderick. *Wilderness and the American Mind*. New Haven: Yale UP, 1982.

Spencer, Herbert. *The Principles of Biology*. London: Williams, 1864.

Tavernier-Courbin, Jacqueline. "Jack London: A Professional." *Critical Essays on Jack London*. Ed. Jacqueline Tavernier-Courbin. Boston: G. K. Hall, 1983.

Thoreau, Henry David. "Walking." *Henry David Thoreau: Collected Essays and Poems*. Ed. Elizabeth Hall Witherell. New York: Library of America, 2001. 225–55.

Turner, Frederick Jackson. *The Frontier in American History*. 1896. New York: Holt, 1920.

Cultivation, Progress, or Conservation: Conflicting Impulses in Willa Cather's *O Pioneers!* and *A Lost Lady*

Matthias Schubnell

Anyone interested in Willa Cather as an environmentally conscious writer will find *Willa Cather's Ecological Imagination* (volume five of the *Cather Studies* series, 2003) an excellent point of departure. Edited by Susan Rosowski, it brings together a group of articles that shows the growing interest in and varying approaches to Cather's environmental writing. Cheryll Glotfelty's "A Guided Tour of Ecocriticism, with Excursions to Catherland" is particularly helpful, as it surveys the discipline of ecocritical study and then reviews a selection of articles that deal with Cather's treatment of nature, highlighting contrasting responses to her work, some of which "fault Cather for being *un*environmental" (31). Glotfelty also provides "a 'canon' of environmental scenes" (33), such as Jim Burden's communion with the universe in Grandmother Burden's pumpkin patch. One may add many more of these ecological scenes to her list: Anton Rosicky's sense of being disconnected from the earth in New York, and the moment in which Rosicky passes the country cemetery in Nebraska at the beginning of "Neighbour Rosicky"; or Thea Kronberg's experience of erasure and merging with nature in Panther Canyon in *The Song of the Lark* (1915); or the boys' exploration of the ever-changing riparian environment of the River Platte in "The Enchanted Bluff"; or Bishop Latour's sense of "sitting in the heart of a world made of dusty earth and moving air" (230) as he seeks shelter in Eusabio's Navajo hogan in *Death Comes for the Archbishop* (1927). These and many other scenes reveal Cather's conviction that there is a strong physical and spiritual relationship between the characters in her works of fiction and the places they inhabit or visit. Exposure to such places shapes and often redirects the course of the characters' lives, and this is a rich motif to analyze from an ecocritical point of view.

The following discussion of *O Pioneers!* (1913) and *A Lost Lady* (1923) reveals conflicting impulses in Cather's work, which celebrate the taming and improvement of nature on the one hand, and privilege leaving nature alone—or at least minimizing human interference—on the other. On the whole, I agree with critics like Joseph W. Meeker and Mary R. Ryder, who view Cather as essentially embracing a philosophy of cultivation that fundamentally alters the natural environment. As Meeker writes about *O Pioneers!,* "Wildness is 'unfriendly to man,'" and taming it for human benefit is the central story of the novel" (79). Referring to *One of Ours* (1923) and *A Lost Lady*, Ryder notes that "Cather uses a male protagonist to voice her [ecological] concerns, but their cries in the wilderness go unanswered, leaving them and the land ripe for destruction" (75). When Cather does articulate ideas of conservation or a land ethic, it is against the background of an already destroyed wilderness or tamed landscape, as if the growing scarcity of untouched places calls for an ecological consciousness. This is reinforced by the fact that the characters who voice the idea of stewardship are themselves marginalized, aging, or at odds with the new era in America that thrives on environmental destruction.

Willa Cather's *O Pioneers!* is her first novel set in Nebraska, the region where she lived from 1883 until her departure to Pittsburgh in 1896, and which would become the literary heartland of her writings. The novel celebrates the transformation of the wild prairie into rich agricultural land, emphasizing that the land only reaches its full potential through human labor. In this respect, Cather stands with wise-use conservationists like Gifford Pinchot, who considered undeveloped nature a waste. What makes this novel remarkable, however, is the character of Ivar, who embodies a biocentric philosophy that stands in sharp contrast to the anthropocentric attitude of the other pioneer farmers. Despite the fact that Cather emphasizes his inability to sustain his way of life outside the farming community, she draws in him a countercultural figure in tune with land and animals, and a moral voice for wilderness and the rights of all living creatures. Here Cather anticipates Aldo Leopold's articulation of a land ethic in *Sand County Almanac* (1949):

> A land ethic of course cannot prevent the alteration, management, and use of these "resources," but it does affirm their right to continued existence, and, at least in spots, their continued existence in a natural state. In short, a land ethic changes the role of Homo sapiens from conqueror of the land-community to plain member and citizen of it. It implies respect for his fellow-members, and also for the community as such. (240)

Ivar's respect for all life-forms is evident in his practice of non-violence and vegetarianism, his knowledge of herbs, his protection of wildlife in the midst of farmland, and his healing practices as a cow and horse whisperer. His peculiar habits of howling at night and walking barefoot underscore his proximity to wild animals and the soil, and his spells and visions suggest shamanic powers that allow him to communicate with nature, a gift that Alexandra Bergson acknowledges when she comments, "He understands animals" (*O Pioneers!* 26). He tells the local boys that he tolerates "no guns, no guns!" (30) on his property, a plea that opposes the killing of his animals, but also a call, had it been heeded, that could have prevented the tragic shooting of Emil and Marie later in the novel.

As a part-time veterinarian, Ivar tends to the livestock in the community. He takes care of the Berquists' panicking cow (26) and attends to the Crow Indians' horses, as when "he kept patting [the mare] and groaning as if he had the pain himself, and saying, 'There now, sister, that's easier, that's better'" (25). His ability to identify with the horse as his kin and share its pain and absorb it shows that the lines between human and animal life are more apparent than real. Ivar is certainly able to cross them because of his deep respect for life in all its manifestations. His conviction that "hogs do not like to be filthy" (34) grows from the same regard and results in Alexandra's changing the way in which she raises her hogs.

Cather frequently uses her fictional characters' setting as a way to reveal their true nature. Ivar's existence on the fringes of civilization shows his rootedness in the local ecology; his dwelling place is partially built into the earth, with a "door and a single window . . . set into the hillside" (27). The only drastic change in his environment is the dam that creates the pond, which attracts the wildlife he so jealously guards. His home is well camouflaged, and served in fact as an animal den. "But for the piece of rusty stovepipe sticking up through the sod, you could have walked over the roof of Ivar's dwelling without dreaming that you were near a human habitation. Ivar had lived for three years in the clay bank, without defiling the face of nature any more than a coyote that had lived there before him" (28). Despite the construction of the dam, it is apparent that Ivar's way of life seeks to minimize his ecological footprint and preserve the spiritual purity of God's creation:

> Ivar found contentment in the solitude he had sought out for himself. He disliked the litter of human dwellings. . . . He preferred the cleanliness and tidiness of the wild sod. . . . He best expressed his preference for his wild homestead by saying that his Bible seemed truer to him there. If one stood in the doorway of his cave, and looked off at the rough land, the smiling sky, the curly grass white in the hot sunlight; if one listened to the rapturous song of the lark, the drumming of the quail, the burr of the locust against that vast silence, one understood what Ivar meant. (28–29)

Cather evokes here a deeply desirable but ultimately doomed existence, for the forces of growth and development leave no room for Ivar's Edenic homestead. His biocentric, spiritual life is unsustainable because his opting out of the local economy finally forces him to take refuge on Alexandra's farm, where he chooses to live in her barn, still preferring the company of animals to that of humans.

Alexandra's empathy for Ivar suggests that she understands and values his philosophy, which resembles deep ecological thought in its egalitarian view of all forms of life. While her rise to wealth and prominence is the result of her taming the land and replacing native plants with monoculture, she remains keenly aware of the many local species that surround her. Her mother, Mrs. Bergson, cooks and preserves fox grapes, goose plums, and ground-cherries (22). Other plant and animal species abound in the novel, such as coreopsis (26), shoestring, iron-weed, snow-on-the-mountain (27), osage orange and mulberry hedges, scrub willow, walnut, wild rose, and bunch grass (63), as well as lark, quail, locust, ducks, snipe, and cranes (29–30). Alexandra's sense of place relies on these local specifics, and like Ivar she recognizes a profound spiritual presence that lies beyond them.

This spiritual awareness can best be understood in the context of Arne Naess's observation that "most people in deep ecology have had the feeling—usually, but not always, in nature—that they are connected with something greater than their ego, greater than their name, their family, or their special attributes as an individual—a feeling that is often called oceanic because many have had this feeling on the ocean" (30). Alexandra's oceanic feeling originates from the vastness of the prairie that envelopes her life and leads to this crucial epiphany:

> Alexandra [was] looking at the stars which glittered so keenly through the frosty autumn air. She always loved to watch them, to think of their vastness and distance, and of their ordered march. It fortified her to reflect upon the great operations of nature, and when she thought of the law that lay behind them, she felt a sense of personal security. That night she had a new consciousness of the country, felt almost a new relation to it. (53–54)

Despite this new spiritual consciousness of and relation to the land, as a practical matter Alexandra remains committed to her utilitarian approach to cultivating the earth's fertility and expanding her flourishing farm. Her character reflects the tension between the two stances. This much-quoted passage reveals Cather's conviction that ultimately the spirit of nature submits to human will, gives itself up to, and thus legitimizes, the human urge to "improve" and make useful what nature has to offer:

> For the first time, perhaps, since that land emerged from the waters of geologic ages, a human face was set toward it with love and yearning. It seemed beautiful to her, rich and strong and glorious. Her eyes drank in the breadth of it, until her tears blinded her. Then the Genius of the Divide, the great free spirit which breathes across it, must have bent lower than it ever bent to a human will before. The history of every country begins in the heart of a man or a woman. (50)

Alexandra, her brothers, and the other local farmers all share the common purpose to profit from the land. What makes Alexandra different is that she nurtures a spiritual connection to it, while the men view the land as an adversary to be conquered. What Cather seems to suggest here is that precisely because of Alexandra's deeper understanding of the land, she is rewarded with nature's riches. In two key passages, "the Genius of the Divide" visits Alexandra in dream-like, transcendental experiences, once as lover and once as death. In the first fanciful encounter, Alexandra elopes with a youthful figure who "was yellow like the sunlight, and there was the smell of ripe cornfields about him" (153). Given that Alexandra, at this point in the novel, is a mature, unmarried woman, the passage suggests a sexual fantasy that unites her with the land, bringing forth not children, but the bountiful harvests she enjoys. Alexandra's repressed sexuality is reflected in the cold bath she gives herself after her vision.

In the second visit, Alexandra calls the mythical youth "the mightiest of all lovers" (211), and her following comment suggests that she recognizes him as death, whom she is glad to follow: "She knew at last for whom she had waited, and where he would carry her. That, she told herself, was very well" (211). The full import of this statement does not become clear until later in the novel, when Cather spells out her idea of an ongoing life cycle of death and rebirth, a process of per-

---

petual recycling: "Fortunate country, that is one day to receive hearts like Alexandra's into its bosom, to give them out again in the yellow wheat, in the rustling corn, in the shining eyes of youth!" (230). Cather clearly suggests that human activity on the land will be its own reward so long as the land is treated with respect. Her conviction that humans and nature can fruitfully cooperate, despite the failures of some farmers or the occasional drought (as examined in her short story "Neighbour Rosicky"), ignores the real possibility of human-made ecological disasters, like the Dust Bowl of the 1930s, which would ravage American agriculture only twenty years after the publication of this novel.[1]

Another major novel that reveals Cather's conflicting impulses to celebrate progress and advocate conservation is *A Lost Lady*, published a year after "the world broke in two in 1922 or thereabouts" (*Not Under Forty* v), which already reflects the cultural pessimism that would only deepen in her later works. The novel contrasts Captain Forrester—who embodies the self-reliance, vision, and sense of noblesse oblige that characterized the pioneer aristocracy—with an aggressive new breed of men, represented by Ivy Peters, whose selfish impulses and actions signal the end of an era in American history when the pursuit of happiness and material wealth did not preclude communal responsibility. While Forrester absorbs the losses of his collapsed banking business, and ruins himself in the process, Ivy Peters lacks any social conscience because it would only get in the way of his ruthlessly efficient, morally corrupt activities. Yet they both share one thing: Their rise to wealth comes at the expense of the environment and native people. The reason this commonality is easily overlooked is that Niel Herbert, the first-person narrator, decries Peters's vices but remains largely blind to Forrester's role in the dispossession of American Indians and the destruction of American forests, because he idealizes the aging Captain's love for the remnants of wild nature on his property. Behind this contrast, however, lies the larger issue that Cather seeks to explore in this novel, namely that the health of a society relies on its ecological consciousness. In this argument Cather revives those values that Henry David Thoreau advocates in his essay "Walking" (1862).

Cather draws Captain Forrester as an embodiment of empire-building; his rank evokes the military conquest of the North American continent, while his profession as railroad contractor places him at the frontline of American expansionism and progress. Yet his family name links him to the great American wilderness, and his sympathy as an older man for the wild is reflected in his groves and the marsh that surrounds his house in Sweet Water. Cather's imagery also relates Forrester to nature in other ways; twice she likens him to a mountain (31, 39); later, as he is recuperating from his first stroke, "he looked like an old tree walking" (97); and his observation of the sun dial suggests an unconscious yearning for an older, cyclical time directly tied to the natural world.

His emotional affinity to nature and his professional association with the railroad are, of course, contradictory aspects of his character: His social standing and wealth originate from the conquest of the American wilderness, namely the clearing of forests to build the infrastructure for a modern society. Yet his sensibility toward the wild affords him the moral fiber that makes him, as Merrill Skaggs put it, an "honorable Robin Hood of the forest" (50) and sets him apart from his young contemporaries. The Robin Hood reference is problematic because it ignores that Forrester's wealth derives not from the rich, but from Indians who lost land and forests leveled to supply millions of railroad ties.[2]

As a builder of the infrastructure for civilization in his early years and an advocate of wilderness in his later ones, Forrester represents conflicting forces in American history, and his choice of rootedness and settlement over expansion ultimately brings him into conflict with the same aggressive forces of change and mobility of which he was himself once a part. Put another way, the old Captain Forrester unconsciously seeks to atone for his role in deforesting America's wilderness and opening up the continent for a mobile, rapidly expanding society by conserving remnants of ecologically intact nature on his property. As noble as this may be, it must be remembered that he can only afford this because of the wealth he accumulated from his earlier, destructive ventures, and when he loses his money, he succumbs to the nouveau riche much like Ivy Peters, who continues Forrester's earlier will to dominate the natural world. In short, Forrester only appears to be less harmful than Ivy because Cather remains essentially silent about the devastating impact of the railroad on America's landscape.

Cather is clearly interested in the tension between wilderness and civilization, or conservation and progress, in this novel, and she follows closely the ideas of Henry David Thoreau, who explains the cultural significance of the wilderness, and the consequences of its destruction, in his essay "Walking": "The West of which I speak is but another name for the Wild; and what I have been preparing to say is, that in Wildness is the preservation of the World. . . . The founders of every state which has risen to eminence have drawn their nourishment and vigor from a similar wild source" (112). Forrester clearly belongs to this category of founders, but because his part in the construction of a new society ultimately destroys nature and with it his own source of strength, Forrester's demise, and that of his generation of "dreamers [and] great-hearted adventurers" (89), is inevitable. Thoreau explains:

> The civilized nations—Greece, Rome, England—have been sustained by the primitive forests which anciently rotted where they stand. They survive as long as the soil is not exhausted. Alas for human culture! Little is to be expected of a nation, when the vegetable mould is exhausted, and it is compelled to make manure of the bones of its fathers. (117)

Cather specifically points to this causal connection between social decadence, caused by rapacious commercialism, and the systematic exploitation of nature. She conveys this historical theory in this key passage:

> [The pioneers had been] a courteous brotherhood, strong in attack but weak in defence, who could conquer but could not hold. Now all the vast territory they had won was to be at the mercy of men like Ivy Peters, who

had never dared anything, never risked anything. . . . The space, the co-lour, the princely carelessness of the pioneer they would destroy and cut up into profitable bits, as the match factory splinters the primeval forest. All the way from the Missouri to the mountains this generation of shrewd young men, trained to petty economies by hard times, would do exactly what Ivy Peters had done when he drained the Forrester marsh. (89–90)

It is important to recognize that it is Niel Herbert, the first-person narrator, who passes this judgment on the two men, drawing a moral distinction between the actions of founders like Forrester and those of men like Ivy Peters. Niel, of course, is in awe of the Captain and idol-izes Marian, his wife, dedicating much of his time to their well-being, too naïve or too sentimental to discern their true nature and background for much of the novel, and ending up thoroughly disillusioned at the end when he recognizes his misperception. Thus, he cannot see that the Captain's railroad building contributed as much to the splintering of the primeval forest as the match factory, which he associates with the younger generation.

The splintering of the forest and the destruction of the marsh sig-nify, in Cather's view, the deterioration of America's vitality and moral fortitude. Thoreau anticipates these negative changes in "Walking." He expresses his fear of those impending "degenerate days of my vil-lage" (117), when the forest has disappeared as a source of communal strength, for "in the very aspect of those primitive and rugged trees there was, methinks, a tanning principle which hardened and consoli-dated the fibres of men's thoughts" (117). Yet it is not only the loss of forests that concerns Thoreau. His impassionate voice for marsh lands as fountains of health indicates the extent to which Cather shares Tho-reau's definition of a well-founded American society.

Thoreau confesses his faith in the promise of wild nature in "Walk-ing": "Hope and the future for me are not in lawns and cultivated fields, not in towns and cities, but in the impervious and quaking swamps. . . . I derive more of my subsistence from the swamps that surround my native town than from the cultivated gardens in the village" (114–15). The swamp as a symbol of fertility and future growth is central to Thoreau's romantic vision of America:

> *Sanctum sanctorum.* There is the strength, the marrow, of Nature. The wildwood covers the virgin mould, and the same soil is good for men and for trees. . . . A town is saved, not more by the righteous men in it than by the woods and swamps that surround it. (116)

Thoreau reminds us that out of such fertile ground have grown great men like Homer and Confucius (116), and for this reason he encourages us to "bring [our] sills up to the very edge of the swamp" (115). The way Cather locates the Forresters' house satisfies these requirements for a fruitful proximity to nature.

Captain Forrester's house is fully integrated into its natural surroundings, passed by two streams, embraced by a cottonwood grove, and bordered by meadows, fields, and the marsh. Enchanted by its beauty, Forrester, unlike his neighbors, has resisted economic development and refused to turn the wetland into productive fields. He had no need to do so before his financial ruin. So he excludes his marsh from human use and keeps guns out of it to preserve the sacredness of untouched nature, the *sanctum sanctorum* of the swamp. In short, the former pioneer now has turned away from his earlier impulse to dominate the natural world. The configuration of the whole property, with its blend of wilderness and cultivated land, represents the ideal relationship between civilization and the wild that Thoreau celebrates in "Walking": "I would not have every man nor every part of a man cultivated, any more than I would have every acre of earth cultivated" (126).

The importance of the wild, of course, also figures prominently in some of Cather's earlier works, particularly "The Enchanted Bluff," where the freshness and fluidity of "the spumy mud banks" (92) represent the same creative powers associated with the marsh in *A Lost Lady*, and in *O Pioneers!*, where Ivar's wildlife refuge remains an island of wilderness in a rapidly transforming landscape, and where his ban on guns, like the Captain's, seeks to restrain human control over nature. For Ivy Peters, however, Forrester's marsh is not a source of spiritual and ecologic strength; he perceives it as an offensive example of the Captain's conspicuous wealth, which, paradoxically, he himself desires yet against which he directs all his destructive energy. Cather draws Peters as one of the new men bent on replacing the great pioneer figures, such as Captain Forrester, by beating them at their own game. Appropriately, Peters's first name, Ivy, suggests a climbing vine strangling the tree-like giant of the frontier, just as the Captain leveled the forests and helped decimate native peoples.

Given the novel's concern with historical and cultural change, it is not surprising that Cather establishes a connection between Captain Forrester and Native Americans that reveals both the Captain's link to an older America and a pattern in American history that Wendell Berry clearly outlined in *The Unsettling of America* (1977). Berry notes the persistent conflict in American history between those who established roots on the continent and built traditions and communities, and the forces of progress that, driven by an exploitative and disruptive mentality, "have fragmented and demolished traditional communities, the beginnings of domestic culture. . . . [which were considered] outdated, provincial, and contemptible" (4). That Forrester constructs his home on an Indian camp site is significant because he literally builds upon an older civilization closely in tune with nature. Cather depicts the Captain's claim to the land not as an act of appropriation, but rather as the land's acceptance of its new owner: "He cut down a young willow tree and drove the stake into the ground to mark the spot where he wished to build. He went away and did not come back for many years; he was helping to lay the first railroad across the plains" (42). When Forrester returns, he buys the site from the railroad company: "I found my willow stake,—it had rooted and grown into a tree,—and I planted three more to mark the corners of my house" (43). What remains unsaid here is, of course, the fact that the railroad company appropriated the land from native peoples, and that their right to the land, at least morally if not legally, is in question.

While this romantic passage glosses over Forrester's indirect involvement in the subjugation of native peoples—the railroad construction greatly accelerated the near extinction of the buffalo and the demise of Indian tribes on the Great Plains—Cather later associates Forrester and the American Indian in her reference to the Captain's empire-building: "'We dreamed the railroad across the mountains, just as I dreamed my place on the Sweet Water. All these things will be everyday facts to the coming generation, but to us—' Captain Forrester ended in a sort of grunt. Something forbidding had come into his voice, the lonely, defiant note that is so often heard in the voices of old Indians" (45). The last sentence suggests that the Captain experiences history and his own decline with the pathos of a displaced Indian, having himself been edged out by a new generation of purely utilitarian and rapacious men. As Berry puts it, "The members of any *established* people or group or community sooner or later become 'redskins'—that is, they become the designated victims of an utterly ruthless, officially sanctioned and subsidized exploitation" (4). Ivy Peters, of course, simply continues this history of colonization and dispossession, not only by fraudulently acquiring Indian land (104–5), but by treating Forrester in much the same way as he does the Indians, exploiting both their reduced circumstances and power for his own gain.

Peters exemplifies exactly those characteristics that Berry attributes to the antagonists of communal and sedentary culture: "The only escape from this destiny of victimization has been to 'succeed'—that is, to 'make it' into the class of exploiters, and then to remain so specialized and so 'mobile' as to become unconscious of the effects of one's life or livelihood" (5). Peters actually is worse than this description suggests, for he relishes the damage he causes to Captain Forrester and his land.

Ivy Peters is undoubtedly one of Cather's most unsavory characters. Merrill Skaggs has correctly called him a 'misogynist" and a "sexual conquistador, seducing in order to dominate a female force he resents and hates" (57). Yet it is important to note that his hostility is by no means limited to women. Peters displays a fundamental hatred of the chaotic but intrinsically creative and generative forces of nature. His sexual and moral conquest of Marian Forrester is paralleled by his acts of environmental vandalism. Approaching Peters from an ecofeminist perspective helps illuminate the motivations and characteristics of Cather's monstrous new American.

Ecofeminism asserts that nature and women are victimized by the patriarchal desire for conquest and control. As Judith Plant puts it, "Ecology speaks for the earth, for the 'other' in human/environmental relationships; and feminism speaks for the other in female/male relations. And ecofeminism, by speaking for the original others, seeks to understand the interconnected roots of all domination, and ways to resist and change" (Plant 101). From the beginning, Cather depicts Ivy Peters as a destructive phallic force by pointing to his "unnatural erectness, as if he had a steel rod down his back" (13). His predilection for guns signifies raw male sexuality and an obsession with dominance. Not only has he earned the reputation of a dog killer, but his blinding of a female woodpecker reflects a deep-seated contempt for wild creatures and foreshadows his moral blinding and sexual conquest of Marian Forrester, whom he views as a "stuck-up piece" (15).

The fact that he has succeeded in warping her moral vision is evident when she explains to Niel Herbert why Peters manages her financial matters: "He gets splendid land from the Indians some way, for next to nothing. Don't tell your uncle; I've no doubt it's crooked. But the Judge is like Mr. Forrester; his methods don't work nowadays. . . . I don't admire people who cheat Indians. Indeed I don't" (105–6). But these protestations sound hollow in light of her dealings with Peters.

Less evident is Ivy Peters's sexual conquest of Marian, which Cather only subtly implies. From the start, Ivy desires "to get inside the Forresters' house" (18), and his comment to Niel later in the novel carries sexual overtones: "You remember how the old man used to put it over us kids and not let us carry a gun in [the marsh]? I'm just mean enough to like to shoot along that creek a little better than anywhere else, now" (88). This comment suggests not only Peters's penetration and ecological desecration of forbidden territory, but also his desire for sexual dominance over Marian, given Cather's emphasis on phallic symbols, such as Ivy's gun and his "unnatural erectness." The following scene, on the occasion of Niel's final visit to Sweet Water after the Captain's death, leaves little doubt that Peters has satisfied his sexual appetite for Marian: "Ivy Peters came in at the kitchen door, walked up behind her, and unconcernedly put both arms around her, his hands meeting over her breast. She did not move, did not look up, but went on rolling out pastry" (145). Her submission to his sexual advances in front of Niel Herbert suggests that the rumors of scandal in Sweet Water over Peters's frequent visits to Marian Forrester's house are well-founded.

Ivy Peters's draining of the marsh represents the most dramatic act of environmental destruction in the novel. It is equivalent to the widespread cutting of cottonwood trees in Nebraska to which Cather objected in a 1921 interview. She declared the cottonwood an integral part of pioneer life and therefore worthy of preservation (Bohlke 40). Peters's action, then, represents the continuity of the will to destroy that leveled America's forests, wiped out Native American cultures, and drove animal species to extinction or near extinction: "By draining the marsh Ivy had obliterated a few acres of something he hated, though he could not name it, and had asserted his power over the people who had loved those unproductive meadows for their idleness and silvery beauty" (89). What Ivy Peters is unable to name is his aversion to *any* vital source of creativity outside of human control. Thus, he represents a fundamentally life-denying, destructive presence in modern America that justifies his nickname, Poison. In *A Lost Lady*, then, Cather asserts that disregard for nature reflects a crisis of character and culture, and like Thoreau before her she illustrates that the destruction of the wild precipitates a decline in American civilization. Just as in *O Pioneers!*, in *A Lost Lady* Cather explores the conflict between cultivation and progress, on the one hand, and conservation, on the other. In doing so, she has earned our appreciation as an early-twentieth-century voice on environmental issues.

Notes

1. For further discussions of these ideas regarding *O Pioneers!* see my articles "Religion and Ecology on the Great Divide: Ivar's Monasticism in Willa Cather's *O Pioneers!*" and "Willa Cather: An Ecocritical Approach," *TRANS: Internet-Zeitung fuer Kulturwissenschaften* 9 (Mai 2001), Web.
2. Richard White, in *Railroaded: The Transcontinentals and the Making of Modern America* (2011), notes that James Joy, president of the Chicago, Burlington, and Quincy railroad, paid $1 an acre to the Cherokee nation in Kansas, and bought eight million acres from the Osage for 25 cents (60).

Works Cited

Berry, Wendell. *The Unsettling of America: Culture and Agriculture.* 1977. San Francisco: Sierra Club Books, 1986.

Bohlke, L. Brent, ed. *Willa Cather in Person: Interviews, Speeches, and Letters.* Lincoln: U of Nebraska P, 1986.

Cather, Willa. *O Pioneers!* 1913. New York: Signet, 1989.

_____. *A Lost Lady.* 1923. New York: Vintage, 1990.

_____. *Not Under Forty.* 1936. New York: Knopf, 1988.

_____. "The Enchanted Bluff." *Great Short Works of Willa Cather.* Ed. Robert K. Miller. New York: Harper, 1989. 91–103.

Glotfelty, Cheryll. "A Guided Tour of Ecocriticism, with Excursions to Catherland." *Willa Cather's Ecological Imagination. Cather Studies.* Ed. Susan J. Rosowski. Vol. 5. Lincoln: U of Nebraska P, 2003. 28–43.

Leopold, Aldo. *A Sand County Almanac.* 1949. New York: Ballantine, 1978.

Meeker, Joseph W. "Willa Cather: The Plow and the Pen." *Willa Cather's Ecological Imagination. Cather Studies.* Ed. Susan J. Rosowski. Vol. 5. Lincoln: U of Nebraska P, 2003. 77–88.

Naess, Arne. *Ecology, Community, and Lifestyle.* Trans. David Rothenberg. New York: Cambridge UP, 1989.

Plant, Judith. "Ecofeminism." *The Green Reader: Essays toward a Sustainable Society.* Ed. Andrew Dobson. San Francisco: Mercury, 1991. 100–3.

Ryder, Mary R. "Willa Cather as Nature Writer: A Cry in the Wilderness." *Such News of the Land: U.S. Women Nature Writers.* Ed. Thomas S. Edwards and Elizabeth A. De Wolfe. Hanover: U of New England P, 2001. 75–84.

Schubnell, Matthias. "Religion and Ecology on the Great Divide: Ivar's Monasticism in Willa Cather's *O Pioneers!*" *Willa Cather and the Culture of Belief: a Collection of Essays.* Ed John J. Murphy. Provo: Brigham Young UP, 2002. 41–49.

_____. "Willa Cather: An Ecocritical Approach." *TRANS: Internet-Zeitung fuer Kulturwissenschaften* 9 (Mai 2001). Web. 1 Feb. 2012.

Skaggs, Merrill Maguire. *After the World Broke in Two: The Later Novels of Willa Cather*. Charlottesville: UP of Virginia, 1990.

Thoreau, Henry David. "Walking." *The Natural History Essays*. Salt Lake City: Gibbs Smith, 1984. 93–136.

White, Richard. *Railroaded: The Transcontinentals and the Making of Modern America*. New York: Norton, 2011.

The Need of Being Versed in Natural Things: Robert Frost and Nature

Robert Bernard Hass

In a 1952 interview, Robert Frost declared, "I'm not a nature poet. There's always something else in my poetry" (Lathem 26). To those who have read Frost well, such a disclaimer must seem just another case of Frost's famous inclination toward "in and outdoor" fooling ("It Takes All Sorts," line 1).[1] Even the most cursory glance at Frost's poems reveals a poet so deeply familiar with the myriad flowers, birds, insects, and trees of his beloved New England landscapes that one might easily regard Frost as *the* nature poet of American literature—the counterpart in poetry to what Thoreau is in prose. Why, then, the disclaimer? What does Frost mean by "nature poet"? And what could that "something else" be?

For some, Frost's posture might simply be an effort to protect himself against the charges of sentimentality often levied by other modernists against the nature poets of the late nineteenth century (Marshall 266). A careful examination of his poetry and prose, however, suggests that Frost had other motivations for refusing the title "nature poet." When Frost acknowledges "there must be a human foreground to supplement this background of nature" (Lathem 34), it is clear that he views nature not simply as place—what Emerson once defined as all that is "not me"—but as place shaped and given meaning by "something else," namely the power of projected human thought. Indebted to the philosophy of William James and Henri Bergson, Frost believes that as our native environment provides the material form for our perception, so too does the mind shape, color, interpret, and thus give meaning to those objects of our contemplation. For Frost, poetry—and more specifically the act of making metaphor—bridges the gulf between the material objects of nature and the mental processes of mind and allows us to negotiate the physical world in practical and beneficial ways. The supple mind, as it encounters the natural world, not only sees nature as a domain of competition, struggle, and survival, but also retains the power to transform that domain into a domesticated realm more compatible with our desires and needs. The lessons of both poetry and the natural world are thus not static universals or indelible truths, but "momentary stay[s] against confusion" ("Figure a Poem Makes" 777) that enable us to adapt to our ever-changing physical environments. As both material place and idea, nature for Frost is simultaneously elusive and malleable, neither hostile nor friendly, and its ultimate meaning remains eternally inaccessible.

Frost's attitude toward nature, with its emphasis on a strong dichotomy between mind and matter, is unmistakably indebted to the traditions of philosophical dualism. In basic terms, philosophical dualism argues that reality is composed of two separate ontological principles that correlate with one another in a complex relationship. Unlike materialists, who believe that reality consists only of matter and its constituent properties, and idealists, who believe that reality exists only in fixed abstract forms or mental processes, philosophical dualists such as Frost insist that mind and matter exist simultaneously, and interact with one another in any given moment of experience. As Peter Stanlis has argued, Frost objected to materialism and idealism because such reductions were inconsistent with our perceptions of actual lived experience. "There can be little doubt," Stanlis asserts, that the "'endless . . . things in pairs ordained in everlasting opposition' [Frost's phrase] was to Frost the universal, God-given condition of man's trial by existence" (3), and that humans were incapable of synthesizing these two principles into a harmonious unity.

Such a position marks a significant departure from the philosophical idealism informing American transcendentalism. Frost would undoubtedly agree with Emerson that humans are part of nature, but separated from it by consciousness. Frost would disagree, however, with Emerson's view that spirit, or more precisely mind, has ontological primacy over the material processes of nature. For Emerson, the concrete objects of nature are merely subordinate phenomena, accidental effects of mind that have no meaning in and of themselves unless the mind engages them. For Emerson, such engagement inevitably leads to greater knowledge of the self and to an intuited understanding of God, the "Universal Being," or the spirit that circulates through both the self and the natural world. For a post-Darwinian such as Frost, the objects and processes of nature are more than accidental phenomena. Natural processes and the physical structures of nature give rise to the very habits of mind that enable perception. Because we have evolved in nature to perceive the world as three-dimensional space, our minds are natural products and are thus limited in their capacity to know things fully in themselves. We can never be as confident as Emerson that our perception of nature will ultimately grant us a complete understanding of the self, or a more confident knowledge of divinity. Like William James, Frost believes that if we invest natural facts with greater meaning, we have no way of determining whether or not such meaning is ultimately true because we have no reliable standard of objectivity to arbitrate between illusion and truth. Belief in itself can be psychologically beneficial, but as Frost asserts in "The Secret Sits," we ultimately "dance round in a ring and suppose / But the secret sits in the middle and knows" (lines 1–2).

Frost demonstrates the problems associated with natural perception in two of his finest lyrics, "For Once, Then, Something" and "Design." Both poems explore the ways one's subjective prejudices distort "objective" experience (thus rendering complete objectivity impossible) and end with large questions that each speaker refuses to answer. Taking as its starting point Democritus's adage, "Of truth we know nothing, for truth lies at the bottom of the well," "For Once, Then, Something" shows us how mental and natural processes act upon one another in any given moment of perception:

Others taunt me with having knelt at well-curbs
Always wrong to the light, so never seeing
Deeper down in the well than where the water
Gives me back in a shining surface picture
Me myself in the summer heaven godlike
Looking out of a wreath of fern and cloud puffs.
Once, when trying with chin against a well-curb
I discerned as I thought beyond the picture
Through the picture, a something white, uncertain,
Something more of the depths—and then I lost it.
Water came to rebuke the too clear water.
One drop fell from a fern, and lo, a ripple
Shook whatever it was lay there at the bottom,
Blurred it, blotted it out. What was that whiteness?
Truth? A pebble of quartz? For once, then, something. (lines
1–15)

Frost's only poem in hendecasyllabics, "For Once, Then, Something" is structurally divided into two halves that sustain an extraordinary tension as they yoke the self-cancelling strengths of the mental and material realms. In the first half, the speaker cannot escape his own subjectivity as he transforms and shapes the picture according to his desires. "Always wrong to the light," the speaker, despite his best efforts to gain an unbiased perspective, sees only his godlike image staring back at him. No matter how hard he tries, he cannot penetrate the surface to recover a picture of nature that is not saturated in his own subjectivity.

Had Frost ended the poem here, readers might be inclined to align Frost more closely with Emerson, as the speaker occupies a position from which his central awareness subordinates nature and "conforms things to his thoughts" (Emerson, "Nature"). As several readers have noticed, however, Frost never concedes that physical processes are simply mental constructs. The poem's second half reveals that the material world and its forces—the fern, the raindrop, and the concentric ripples—combine to limit the projections of the speaker's shaping sub-jectivity. In this case, the poet is not merely the maker of the reality he perceives; he too is being shaped and acted upon by natural forces that exist externally beyond his control. This self-cancelling clash of the equally matched mental and material forces confirms, in the echoing final line, that of ultimate truth "we know nothing." Is the essence of our existence purely material—the pebble of quartz, as modern sci-ence might claim? Or is reality based in immaterial thought—in abid-ing "truth," as the transcendentalists claimed in the previous century? Frost refuses to answer the question, preferring instead to use the well as a metaphorical frame that suspends both material and mental ele-ments in the binding field of the poem. The indistinct "something" the speaker sees is far less important than the poet's acknowledgment that the fundamental nature of our relationship to the world is one in which natural forces are mitigated by thought and thought itself is in part de-termined, and therefore limited, by natural constraints. The poet's cre-ative, metaphorical play creates commerce between the two realms by uniting the material and the spiritual in perpetual equilibrium.

Perhaps Frost's most poignant demonstration of epistemological uncertainty occurs in "Design," one of Frost's most famous poems, and the poem that eminent critic Lionel Trilling once singled out as evidence of Frost's "Sophoclean" terror and darker tendencies ("A Speech on Robert Frost" 445–52). One of Frost's most inventive son-nets, "Design" conflates the structural elements of both the Italian and Elizabethan forms and manipulates the sonnet's traditional rhetorical strategies to propose that any large inference from the designs in na-ture is impossible. At first glance, the poem appears to be a synecdo-che, a tiny, tragic melodrama, which suggests that behind the intricate designs of nature lies a malevolent "designer." As in Blake's poetry (one should recall here Frost's indebtedness to "The Lamb" and "The Tyger"), "Design" also moves from innocence to experience, with Frost juxtaposing symbolically innocent motifs against Darwinian im-ages of competition, struggle, and survival. Its terrors heightened by the language of advertising slogans ("Mixed ready to begin the morning right"), the poem cascades into a stark vision of the universe that is perhaps more diabolical than one would suppose:

> I found a dimpled spider, fat and white,
> On a white heal-all, holding up a moth
> Like a white piece of rigid satin cloth—
> Assorted characters of death and blight
> Mixed ready to begin the morning right,
> Like the ingredients of a witches broth—
> A snow-drop spider, a flower like a froth,
> And dead wings carried like a paper kite. (lines 1–8)

This small scene of death and decay is a perfectly reasonable scenario, with a plausible scientific rationale informing it: A camouflaged white spider builds an intricate web on a white flower whose pollen will attract a variety of insects. The speaker's intensifying fear, however, indicates that Frost has other designs. To the speaker, this small scene seems a gross disruption of a harmonious cosmic order (even the usually violet-colored "heal-all" is white), and he begins to fear that the scene may be the work of a malevolent designer who has intentionally woven violence into the fabric of the universe. Even more appalling is the stark Darwinian possibility that no designer exists at all. Instead of being predestined by divine providence, the relationship between the spider and the moth may instead be the culmination of mindless, random processes in which weaker species fall prey to those better equipped by nature to survive in their environments. The poem's stumbling meter reflects the speaker's confusion about what he has seen, and like a good scientist he attempts to form large conclusions based upon the evidence. Unfortunately, finding answers proves difficult. He is left with a series of questions, implicit in which are several disturbing assumptions about one's larger relationship to the cosmos:

What had the flower to do with being white,
The wayside blue and innocent heal-all?
What brought the kindred spider to that height,
Then steered the white moth thither in the night?
What but design of darkness to appall?—
If design govern in a thing so small. (lines 9–14)

Although perhaps rhetorical, these questions yield no satisfying answers. The speaker refuses to commit the mistake of Ahab by ascribing evil to the spider, nor will he substantiate Emerson's belief in the "choral harmony of the whole" of nature's divine design ("The Relation of Man to the Globe" 49). The speaker understands that both conclusions are merely anthropomorphic gestures that may or may not have any legitimate basis in reality.

That Frost further questions the relationship between thought and nature is substantiated by his inversion in "Design" of the sonnet's traditional internal structure. In general, one of the sonnet's most important virtues is that it forces a poet to forge a quick resolution to a problem. Most sonnets begin by confronting an initial problem, usually some form of universal paradox that the writer extends and complicates in succeeding quatrains or penultimate lines of the octave. Not until the volta, the rhetorical turn (signified by the sestet in the Italian form and the couplet in the Elizabethan form), does the writer force a resolution. That resolution is generally a clear statement, approaching the laconic quality of aphorism, which solves the paradox in question. Rebuking that tradition, Frost flips "Design" on its head and ends his sonnet with a series of questions that simply restate the problem. This lack of resolution is not the fault of a poet who cannot come to grips with his subject, but rather a statement of belief that the evidence available to our senses is insufficient for us to deduce any definitive answers about the true meaning of the natural world.

Frost's philosophical skepticism and refusal to commit fully to either a naturalist or supernaturalist vision of nature—a stance that critic Yvor

Winters once condemned as Frost's "spiritual drifting" ("Robert Frost: Or, The Spiritual Drifter as Poet" 564–96)—has unfortunately led to a great deal of confusion over Frost's nature poetry. To those inclined to accept the tenets of twentieth-century materialism (reality reduced to matter and its constituents), the ample evidence of poems such as "The Most of It," "Desert Places," "Blue-Butterfly Day," "The Last Mowing," and "Once by the Pacific" confirms the belief that Frost's nature poetry reflects a godless universe, rife with competition and struggle, whose mechanisms and interactions are the product of random forces. To those more inclined toward supernaturalism (reality with a basis in a divine source), poems such as "Kitty Hawk," "Directive," "Skeptic," "Astrometaphysical," and "Accidentally on Purpose" imply that Frost rejects materialism and retains belief in the possibility of a shaping divinity whose true nature we can never fully comprehend. Part of our confusion may be a reflection of Frost's own personal struggles to come to terms with modernity. As a poet who lived a long life and witnessed the transition from the nineteenth to the twentieth century, Frost desired to retain the essence of his mother's religious teachings but was continually thwarted in those efforts by modern scientific conclusions, which made such beliefs more and more untenable. As the lessons from evolutionary biology and geology facilitated a widespread religious skepticism, many writers, including Robert Frost, were left groping for spiritual certainties, finding it necessary to modify religious belief to accommodate the conclusions of modern science. Whatever the reasons for Frost's "drifting," he addressed this problem by entertaining both material and spiritual possibilities, and, true to his belief in the essentially dualistic nature of our makeup, he never attended to one side of the equation without also attending to its opposite.

A good example of Frost's tendency to pair poems with opposing conclusions occurs in "Two Look at Two" and "The Most of It." Although written nearly thirty years apart, the poems reveal Frost's penchant for returning time and again to the same problem and investigating it—like a "dog gnawing a bone," as Lawrance Thompson once described Frost's habits—from a different point of view. In the first poem, two lovers ascend a mountain during a twilight hike, ostensibly in an effort to extend and express their love for one another. Like Adam and Eve figures trying to reenter the garden, the two lovers represent the incursion of civilization into the wilderness, and as they climb, encountering physical difficulties and braving the mountain's "alien entanglements" ("Constant Symbol" 787), they come to an impasse, a barb-wired wall that metaphorically symbolizes a boundary they cannot cross. Though "love and forgetting" (line 1) might have compelled them higher up the mountain, the two will not go farther. It is at this moment that they encounter the mystery of nature as "other" in the form of a doe and a buck, whose meaning the lovers attempt to comprehend. Silent and unmoving, the lovers imagine what "doe consciousness" must be like:

> She saw them in their field, they in hers.
> The difficulty of seeing what stood still,
> Like some upended boulder split in two,
> Was in her clouded eyes: they saw no fear there. (lines 17–20)

When the doe is satisfied that the lovers pose no threat, she moves on, giving way to a magnificent buck, which also pauses to ascertain the potential of a threat. Unlike the doe, whose eyes are "clouded," the buck appears to possess greater sentience, and the lovers imagine it is he who inverts the situation and perceives them as inanimate and incapable of rational thought:

> He viewed them quizzically with jerks of head,
> As if to ask, "Why don't you make some motion?
> Or give some sign of life? Because you can't.
> I doubt if you're as living as you look." (lines 31–34)

Although the words "as if" clearly signify that the creatures' imagined cognition is merely a projection of human thought, what captivates the lovers is an intuited and united recognition of the creatures' mutual effort toward comprehension. The distance between instinct and intelligence is momentarily diminished, and the lovers provisionally feel kinship with the deer, which, like humans, are mutually bound by natural law and the urge to protect themselves and their progeny. Although the two lovers are well aware that the depth of their sympathy can never be reciprocated, they are nevertheless genuinely fascinated by the mystery of their encounter with something greater than themselves, which reinforces and confirms their love for each other:

> "This must be all." It was all. Still they stood,
> A great wave from it going over them,
> As if the earth in one unlooked-for favor
> Had made them certain earth returned their love. (lines
> 39–42)

While it is perhaps easy for two lovers in the thrall of their affections to transform their emotions into a greater kinship with the earth, the case is not so clear when a solitary wanderer actively seeks from the universe a "counter-love, original response" that can assuage cosmic loneliness ("Most of It," line 8). Evident from the revised refrain of "Two Look at Two," the last phrase of "The Most of It"—"and that was all"—offers a clear rejoinder to the earlier poem and, by implication, the entire enterprise of romantic poetry. Unlike the solitary hermits of Wordsworth or Emerson, who often find evidence of God in sublime, natural forms, Frost's speaker, after his entreaty to the earth, hears only the "mocking echo of his own" (line 3) voice. Once again, a clear dichotomy between mind and matter prevails, with the word "thought" dominating the first ten lines and generating the despair the speaker feels over his solitary condition. As if in response, the word "embodiment" interrupts the speaker's gloomy reflection, rescues him from his self-indulgence, and shifts the poem's emphasis toward non-sentient nature in the form of a great buck that appears out of the forest. The extended sentence, anaphora, and hurtling rhythms create an onslaught of momentum that signifies a powerful presence, impervious to the speaker's solipsistic thought:

> Unless it was the embodiment that crashed
> In the cliff's talus on the other side,
> And then in the far-distant water splashed,
> But after a time allowed for it to swim,
> Instead of proving human when it neared
> And someone else additional to him,
> As a great buck it powerfully appeared,
> Pushing the crumpled water up ahead,
> And landed pouring like a waterfall,
> And stumbled through the rocks with horny tread,
> And forced the underbrush—and that was all. (lines 10–20)

The word "embodiment" also suggests that what the speaker encounters is not simply matter, but matter animated by an impelling force that denies the buck freedom of volition. Unlike a solitary human in thoughtful repose, the buck is both real and the figured "embodiment" of the great energy that animates ecological systems. As the buck disappears through the underbrush—instinctually driven by forces beyond its control—the entropy of the moment increases significantly until the water calms and all movement dissolves into an eerie quiet. The encounter with the natural "other" is just as magnificent as the moment in "Two Look at Two," but Frost has stripped the experience of any sentimental overtones, and as such the later poem stands as the perfect corollary to the other.

Not all of Frost's solitary wanderings lead to this stark vision of nature. As John Elder has convincingly argued, Frost often took great solace from his excursions into the woods, in part to settle the personal

---

storms that sometimes welled up as he was beset by loss, doubt, or the difficulties of attending to his children's mental illnesses (see Wertlieb). A keen amateur naturalist and botanist fluent in the flora of all seasons, Frost was well versed in natural things and found in the ecological systems of nature a stabilizing constancy. His excursions into the woods were integral to his daily routines, and like Wordsworth or Thoreau he found in nature an endless storehouse of metaphors that would eventually find their way into his work. Though usually stripped of Emersonian confidence, Frost's poems about the local birds, trees, and flowers that he encountered during his walks celebrate the mountains of home and inform the bulk of his verse, almost as if the landscape itself had inscribed his consciousness with the very subjects of his poetry.

An excellent example of Frost's compelling, recurring need to wander into the far field is the lovely and exuberant "The Quest of the Purple-Fringed." A poem rich in botanical accuracy and metaphorical possibility, "Quest" chronicles a speaker's day-long search for a rare, late-blooming flower, whose eventual discovery will prove enormously gratifying. One of Frost's many poems that attempt to glean meaning from an investigation of the natural world, "Quest" pays homage to the tradition of nineteenth-century nature writers,[2] even as its most conspicuous theme involves the maturation of individual artistic awareness:

> I felt the chill of the meadow underfoot,
> But the sun overhead;
> And snatches of verse and song of scenes like this
> I sung or said.
>
> I skirted the margin alders for miles and miles
> In a sweeping line.
> The day was the day by every flower that blooms,
> But I saw no sign.

Yet further I went to be before the scythe,
For the grass was high;
Till I saw the path where the slender fox had come
And gone panting by.

Then at last and following him I found—
In the very hour
When the color flushed to the petals it must have been—
The far-sought flower.

There stood the purple spires with no breath of air
Nor headlong bee
To disturb their perfect poise the livelong day
'Neath the alder tree.

I only knelt and putting the boughs aside
Looked, or at most
Counted them all to the buds in the copse's depth
That were pale as a ghost.

Then I arose and silently wandered home,
And I for one
Said that the fall might come and whirl of leaves,
For summer was done. (lines 1–28)

Frost originally published a variant of this poem in the *Independent* in 1901 under the title "The Quest of the Orchis," a fact that has unfortunately (but understandably) led Lawrance Thompson and others to misidentify the actual flower in the poem, the fringed gentian (*Gentiana crinite*), as the purple-fringed orchid, two separate species of which bloom in Vermont: *Platanthera grandiflora*, the greater purple-fringed orchid, and *Platanthera psycodes*, the lesser purple-fringed orchid.[3] Although George Monteiro, the first to notice this mistake, has suggested Frost himself misidentified the very subject of his poem, as Glenn Adelson and John Elder have argued, such an assertion seems unlikely in light of Frost's extensive knowledge of botany and habit of precisely recording the idiosyncrasies of individual species.

Frost's precision as a naturalist was in part fostered by his general fascination with science, and by the tutelage of his good friend Carl Burrell, who in 1889 introduced the teenaged Frost both to botany and to the writings of Darwin, Huxley, and Spencer. Although he had been warned by his devout mother not to heed the "blasphemous and shocking claims of the evolutionists" (Thompson, *Early Years* 90), Frost, finding the forbidden seductive, nevertheless responded quickly to Burrell's offer to read such novel thinkers. As all Frost biographers have noticed, Darwin and Huxley changed Frost's life immediately and dramatically, not only challenging his religious belief but also enabling him to think about nature in a way that framed and made sense of particular species and the systems in which those species thrived and reproduced. Burrell also provided Frost a copy of Mrs. W. S. Dana's *How to Know the Wildflowers: A Guide to the Names, Haunts, and Habits of Our Common Wildflowers* (Thompson 216–23). Frost often consulted this field guide, one of his most prized possessions, admiring its systematic classifications as well as its beautifully illustrated plates. Grateful for Burrell's gift, Frost would spend the rest of his life wandering far afield and investigating the flora of Vermont and New Hampshire. Perhaps the most important gift Burrell's friendship bestowed, however, was the gift of poetry. In a more ironic twist of fate, it was Burrell, the amateur naturalist who first introduced Frost to natural selection, who also first urged the young poet to record his observations in poetry.

That Frost carefully applied the lessons of his early training is evident in the precise natural context he articulates in "The Quest of the Purple-Fringed," which clearly reveals the poem's flower as the fringed gentian. Several important details provide some unmistakable clues. First, the speaker feels "the chill of the meadow underfoot" (line 1). He skirts "the margin alders for miles and miles" (line 5) in a long search to find the elusive flower. Frost describes the smaller buds as "pale as a ghost" (line 24) and petals that have only recently "flushed" (line 15) with color after "putting the boughs aside" (line 21). Even the fact that no "headlong bee" (line 18) will disturb the flower's "perfect poise" (line 19) suggests that the flower in question is the gentian. To the untrained eye such details may seem innocuous. Yet to Frost, who clearly knew this flower well, each detail points to the particular qualities that make the fringed gentian such a rare and prized flower, and reveals why Frost might exploit its description to help disclose the kind of American poet he might become.

Unlike the purple-fringed orchid, which is a perennial that grows in the wetlands and bogs of Vermont and persists in the same place year after year, the fringed gentian is an herbaceous biennial whose seeds scatter and disperse widely after the flower blooms in its second year. An endangered species in several eastern states, the fringed gentian is extremely rare. It does not often grow in the same location twice, a fact highlighted in Dana's book and the very characteristic that commences the speaker's long search in the poem. The fringed gentian, unlike the orchid (which blooms in late July and August), is also a very late-blooming flower that generally does not emerge in Frost's part of the country until October, before the last cut of hay when the "chill of the meadow" (line 1) is underfoot and the first frosts are imminent. To amateur botanists, the flower's late, transient beauty is indeed a prized discovery, because the flower becomes visible only when the sunlight shines directly upon the fringed, lacerated petals. The fact that the speaker puts "the boughs aside" to provide more direct light is thus a telling detail, for in parting the boughs he hopes to facilitate a "flushing" of the ghostly white buds (another telling feature) with the iridescent blue color that is characteristic of the plant. Finally, because the fringed gentian blooms so late, the flowers protect their nectar by remaining tightly closed in narrow spires and on cloudy days, when the potential for rain to wash away the pollen is greatest. In such cases, the bumblebee, the hardiest of nature's pollinators, will attempt to force its way into the petals to gather nectar, at times damaging the flower. Frost's mention of the bee is particularly significant because the pollinators of purple-fringed orchids are yellow swallowtails, skippers, and other nocturnal moths that have long proboscides capable of penetrating the flowers.

The great care that Frost takes in describing this elusive flower is clearly reminiscent of Thoreau, who in his *Journals* records the flora around Walden Pond with the precision of a scientist. Although it is impossible to know if Frost had access to all of Thoreau's *Journals* prior to 1906, it is clear that Frost became aware of his predecessor's fascination with the fringed gentian from Dana's field guide, which includes a quotation from Thoreau's October 10, 1858, entry:

> I find the fringed gentian abundantly open at three and four P.M. (in fact it must be all the afternoon), open to catch the cool October sun and air in its low position. Such a dark blue! surpassing that of a male bluebird's back. (Blake 94)

Frost's poem also clearly echoes Thoreau's natural precision in a journal entry from October 19, 1852. Characteristically, Thoreau invests the gentian's description with a greater spiritual significance, which serves to elevate one's reward for having found the flower:

> I found the fringed gentian now somewhat stale and touched with frost, being in the meadow toward Peter's. Probably on high, moist ground it is fresher. It may have been in bloom a month. It has been cut off by the mower and apparently has put out in consequence a mass of short branches full of flowers. This may make it later. I doubt if I can find one naturally grown. At this hour the blossoms are tightly rolled and twisted, and I see that the bees have gnawed round holes in their sides to come at the nectar. They have found them, though I had not. . . . It is too remarkable a flower not to be sought out and admired each year, however rare. It is one of the errands of the walker, as well as of the bees, for it yields him

a more celestial nectar still. It is a very singular and agreeable surprise to come upon this conspicuous and handsome and withal blue flower at this season, when flowers have passed out of our minds and memories. (Gleason 96)

Whether or not Frost "touched" this passage remains speculative. Frost did, however, have access to H. G. O. Blake's excerpted passages in *Autumn: From the Journals of Henry D. Thoreau* (1892), in which Thoreau mentions the fringed gentian three times. If Frost's only acquaintance with Thoreau was the Dana passage, the parallels are nevertheless striking. Such a correspondence is not surprising, since Frost knew *Walden* (1854) well and admired the writer who had "surpass[ed] everything we have had in America" (Thompson, *Selected Letters* 278). In composing "The Quest of the Purple-Fringed," Frost, despite the misnomer of his early title, clearly pays homage to Thoreau's legacy by recording the great joy he experienced while botanizing. More important, Frost metaphorically announces at this early stage in his career what kind of poet he will become. Like Thoreau, he will explore nature on the fringes of society, where he will gather poems as rare as the flowers he seeks. He will follow the teachings of the fox (one of Thoreau's favorite animals), a solitary creature that travels and hunts on its own yet moves easily on the margins between nature and civilization. Similarly, he will employ Thoreau's precision in describing the flora and fauna of local habitats even as he gleans rare and precious metaphorical lessons from the natural objects he observes. Finally, like Thoreau and Emerson, Frost will come to a greater understanding of himself, as he situates himself more perfectly in both the poetic tradition and the cosmos. Though Frost's postromantic sensibilities will not allow him to accept the easy consolations of a perceived divinity, the poem's epiphany nevertheless resonates with the gravitas of religious ritual. After the speaker discovers the elusive flower, he kneels and parts the boughs to provide the petals with more light. Frank Lentricchia describes this moment as the "purest celebratory moment in Frost's poetry" (86), and although Frost tempers his joy—closing his poem by lamenting summer's transience and the onset of a winter—the recorded memory of the experience will provide joy long after winter has buried the landscape in snow.

The theme of rueful transience is, of course, one of Frost's most frequent poetic obsessions, as he is keenly aware of the precarious circumstances of all who struggle to keep their "hold on the planet." Poems such as "Hyla Brook," "The Oven Bird," "The Onset," "Blue-Butterfly Day," "After Apple-Picking," "The Exposed Nest," and "Nothing Gold Can Stay" center on themes of fragility, mutability, and loss and express a profound empathy for the inevitable fate of all living things. Perhaps nowhere does Frost convey this theme more beautifully than in his stunning lyric "Spring Pools." At first glance a lamentation for the living things that succumb to seasonal processes, "Spring Pools" is not just a poem about transience, but a poem that also, as Glenn Adelson and John Elder have argued, "offers an opportunity to reflect about larger patterns and connections in a world of change" (3). Balancing the fleeting disappearance of spring flowers with enduring patterns, "Spring Pools" does not descend into a vision of despair but communicates a consoling affirmation that natural processes are immutable. The poem also celebrates Frost's awareness that what is visible is only the tangible surface of a vast matrix of organic forms and processes tied to a specific geographical place and climate. Always faithful to ecological accuracy, Frost opens his poem with a precise description of the vernal pool, a common feature in the springtime Appalachian woodlands and an important ecosystem that helps incubate a wide variety of flowers and animals before summer's onset:

> These pools that, though in forests, still reflect
> The total sky almost without defect,
> And like the flowers beside them, chill and shiver,
> Will like the flowers beside them still be gone,
> And yet not out by any brook or river,
> But up by roots to bring dark foliage on. (lines 1–6)

Still capable of reflecting the sky before the forest's trees have exfoliated, the spring pools provide water necessary for the "watery flowers" to grow. As Adelson and Elder have explained, most flower species that bloom near spring pools are perennials that extend and develop an intricate matrix of rhizomes that ensures the plant's subsistence (9). Though the blooming period is relatively short-lived among such species, the plants themselves persist long after their aboveground visible structures succumb to seasonal decay. Similarly, the pool, which will be taken up by the roots and eventually dissipate into the atmosphere through the process of transpiration, is more permanent than one would suspect. Since much of the water in the vernal pool is groundwater raised to its highest vertical level, once the trees exfoliate the water recedes to its below-ground levels. The water still remains; it is simply not visible to a woodland wanderer. In light of this information, the second half of the poem does not seem nearly as ominous or threatening as the tone suggests. While the speaker implies some poised conspiracy among the trees to destroy the vernal pool and its inhabitants, "Let them think twice" (line 9) indicates that what Frost really desires is simply a delay of seasonal activity so he can linger over the beauty of this springtime phenomenon:

> The trees that have it in their pent-up buds
> To darken nature and be summer woods—
> Let them think twice before they use their power
> To blot out and drink up and sweep away
> These flowery waters and these watery flowers
> From snow that melted only yesterday. (lines 7–12)

Frost was quite fond of the phrase "waste [is] of the essence of the scheme" ("Pod of the Milkweed," line 40), and used it often in his prose and poetry to remind us how the biological cycles of nature exact an enormous cost in the perpetuation of species. In an indifferent universe, the fate of individuals is always precarious and, for humans,

---

ameliorated only by the saving structures of community and civilization. Yet there is, in Frost, the recognition that the "scheme" is equally important. As Frost makes abundantly clear in "Spring Pools," there is a "grandeur" in the view of life that the "planet has gone cycling on" (Darwin 425) through its fixed laws and processes. Viewed from this perspective, nature is never wasteful. As the energy of natural systems is converted through various species and forms, nature's individuals live and die in patterns of decay and renewal that have existed, and will continue to exist, despite our awareness of them. The "snow that melted only yesterday" will descend as snow again, creating the potential for the vernal cycle to repeat itself again and again until the energy necessary to sustain these processes dissipates with the death of our sun.

Such a view of nature, however grand, also acknowledges that something precious has been lost. In "The Oven Bird," Frost asks what he should "make of a diminished thing" (line 14). Just what has been diminished, however, is not entirely clear. Perhaps Frost laments the encroachment of modernity upon traditional religious belief, and its convictions that at one time one might have heard in the oven bird's call evidence of the workings of God. Perhaps he is more ardently concerned that "the highway dust is over all" (line 10), and that the once pristine American wilderness will disappear as civilization, with its growing potential for destruction, penetrates deeper and deeper into Frost's favorite New England landscapes. Perhaps Frost simply recognizes that we have lost our stature as the "paragon of animals," and can no longer believe that the earth was created solely for our habitation and benefit. Whatever the case, it is clear that modernity has forever severed our perceptions of the past and that we can never regard nature in the same sense as our most recent ancestors. That being the case, Frost nevertheless celebrates the glories of both the human spirit and the natural world, and the inability of one to triumph fully over the other. What unites all of Frost's nature poems is his belief that stasis between nature and spirit endures. A fitting closing to this essay, then, is the untitled poem that Frost conspicuously places, as his own last word on the subject, at the end of *In the Clearing* (1962), his last book of poems:

> In winter in the woods alone
> Against the trees I go.
> I mark a maple for my own
> And lay the maple low.
>
> At four o'clock I shoulder ax
> And in the afterglow
> I link a line of shadowy tracks
> Across the tinted snow.
>
> I see for Nature no defeat
> In one tree's overthrow
> Or for myself in my retreat
> For yet another blow. (lines 1–12)

Notes

1. All quotations of Frost's poetry and prose are excerpted from Poirier and Richardson's edition of Frost's complete works, *Frost: Collected Poems, Prose, and Plays* (1995).

2. Frost's subject in "The Quest of the Purple-Fringed" is not the purple-fringed orchid, as many scholars have suggested, but the fringed gentian, the subject of Bryant's "To the Fringed Gentian" and Dickinson's "XLVIII. Fringed Gentian." The flower is also a frequent subject of Thoreau's *Journals*.

3. Thompson first identified the flower in question as the purple-fringed orchid, claiming in the *Early Years* that Susan Hayes Ward, editor of the *Independent*, delayed publication until "the moment in spring when the purple-fringed orchid should be in bloom" (*Early Years* 270). Monteiro, noticing some editorial discrepancies in *New Hampshire's Child: The Derry Journals of Lesley Frost*, argues that both Frost and Ward misidentified the poem's flower as the orchid and that Frost emended his mistake by coining a more ambiguous title when he collected the poem in *A Witness Tree* in 1942. Recognizing Frost's botanical acumen, West and Thomas defend Thompson, basing their arguments in part on parallels between Thoreau's journals and the poem. West and Thomas do not, how-

ever, account for Thoreau's equally provocative entries concerning the fringed gentian, nor do they consider the poem's ecological and natural context, which clearly reveals the poem in question as the fringed gentian. Perhaps a plausible explanation for the poem's original title is that as a young poet Frost may have wanted to deflect attention from the antecedent source of Bryant's poem.

Works Cited

Adelson, Glenn, and John Elder. "Robert Frost's Ecosystem of Meanings in 'Spring Pools.'" *ISLE: Interdisciplinary Studies in Literature and the Environment* 13.2 (Summer 2006): 1–17.

Blake, H. G. O., ed. *Autumn: From the Journals of Henry D. Thoreau*. Cambridge: Riverside, 1892.

Dana, Mrs. William Starr. *How to Know the Wildflowers: A Guide to the Names, Haunts, and Habits of Our Common Wildflowers*. New York: Scribner's, 1893.

Darwin, Charles. *On the Origin of Species by Means of Natural Selection or Preservation of Favored Races in the Struggle for Life*. New York: D. Appleton, 1869.

Emerson, Ralph Waldo. "Nature." *American Transcendentalism Web*. Psymon, 12 Jan. 2003. Web. 15 Aug. 2011.

_____. "The Relation of Man to the Globe." *Early Lectures of Ralph Waldo Emerson*. Ed. Stephen Whicher. Cambridge: Harvard UP, 1959. 27–49.

Frost, Robert. *Collected Poems, Prose, & Plays*. Ed. Richard Poirier and Mark Richardson. New York: Library of America, 1995.

Gleason, Herbert Wendell, ed. *Through the Year with Thoreau: Sketches from the Writings of Henry D. Thoreau*. Cambridge: Riverside, 1917.

Lathem, Edward Connery, ed. *Interviews with Robert Frost*. New York: Holt, 1966.

Lentricchia, Frank. *Robert Frost: Modern Poetics and the Landscapes of Self*. Durham: Duke UP, 1974.

Marshall, Ian. *Story Line: Exploring the Literature of the Appalachian Trail*. Charlottesville: U of Virginia, 1998.

Monteiro, George. "Frost's Quest for the 'Purple-Fringed.'" *English Language Notes* 13.3 (1976): 204–6.

Stanlis, Peter J. *Robert Frost: The Poet as Philosopher*. Wilmington: ISI, 2007.

Thomas, Ron. "Thoreau, William James, and Frost's 'Quest of the Purple-Fringed': A Contextual Reading." *American Literature* 60.3 (1988): 433–50.

Thompson, Lawrance. *Robert Frost: The Early Years*. New York: Holt, 1966.

_____, ed. *Selected Letters of Robert Frost*. New York: Holt, 1964.

Thompson, Lawrance, and Arnold Grade, eds. *New Hampshire's Child: The Derry Journals of Lesley Frost*. Albany: SUNY P, 1969.

Trilling, Lionel. "A Speech on Robert Frost: A Cultural Episode." *Partisan Review* 26 (Summer 1959): 445–52.

Wertlieb, Mitch. "Vermont Reads: Robert Frost—New England, a Sense of Place." *VPR News*. 16 Sept. 2008. n. pag. Web. 15 Aug. 2011.

West, Michael. "Versifying Thoreau: Frost's 'Quest of the Purple-Fringed' and 'Fire and Ice.'" *English Language Notes* 16 (1978): 40–47.

Whicher, Stephen E., ed. *Early Lectures of Ralph Waldo Emerson*. Cambridge: Harvard UP, 1959.

Winters, Yvor. "Robert Frost: or, the Spiritual Drifter as Poet." *Sewanee Review* 56.4 (1948): 564–96.

Natural History in Hemingway's *The Old Man and the Sea* and Other Works_____

Bert Bender

Shortly after finishing his definitive five-volume biography of Ernest Hemingway, Michael Reynolds summarized his subject's life and career by describing him as "a natural historian" who took us with him to Africa, whose dark heart beats deep within his writing in ways not always obvious. He studied trout streams in several countries, Gulf Stream marlin, Spanish bulls, and African game. He studied the flight of birds, the bends of rivers, and the flow of country. But what he studied first, last, and always was that strange animal, his fellow man, rampant in his natural setting (Reynolds 47–48).

It will help clarify Hemingway's views on nature and the environment to remember that he published his first stories in 1923, and that in 1926 he mocked William Jennings Bryan's anti-Darwinism at the Scopes trial in *The Sun Also Rises*, published in the same year. By that time American writers had been exploring human nature in light of Darwin's *The Descent of Man* (1871) for more than fifty years, interpreting Darwinism in a variety of ways, some distinctly anti-Darwinian, and from different social points of view.[1] But as F. Scott Fitzgerald suggested in *This Side of Paradise* (1920), many people still "shuddered when they found what Mr. Darwin was about" (151).

Hemingway fully accepted Darwin's definition of the human being's place within the community of common descent and the web of life that is governed by natural selection and sexual selection. His general method was to expose his characters to these forces in their own natural history—the true terms of our existence—and then leave them, alone, to define their own humanity. Typically, the characters he gives us as examples of the "strange animal . . . man" lose everything, especially their belief in "love" or their faith in some higher law. But, like Santiago in *The Old Man and the Sea* (1952), Hemingway's most attractive characters accept their existence in a meaningless universe of "nothing," or "nada," as he frequently termed it, and embrace life on its own terms. Finding the courage "to really live. Not just let . . . life pass" (*Green Hills of Africa* 285), they affirm not only life's beauty and magnificence, but its essential violence, and they do so with a measure of grace and dignity.

I. Hemingway's Views on Natural History during the 1920s and 1930s

With "Up in Michigan" (1923), Hemingway began his career by probing the key Darwinian problem that many other novelists had addressed: how sexual selection undercut the meaning of love. In this daring story (which Gertrude Stein advised him was not publishable—see Baker, 87), a young woman named Liz selects her first lover, largely because she had been attracted by his sexual beauty; Darwin had defined this beauty in terms of sexual ornaments such as mustaches or beards. But their loveless encounter is essentially a rape, leaving Liz "cold and miserable" and feeling that "everything [was] gone" (85).[2] Hemingway explored the implications of sexual selection more fully in his first novel, *The Sun Also Rises*. And here, writing at a time when Darwinian natural history was meeting with so much resistance— not only in the Scopes trial but even in debates within the scientific community, which remained unresolved until the early 1940s, when Mendelian genetics and natural selection were aligned in "the Modern Synthesis"—Hemingway began his habit of satirizing other writers for their transcendental (i.e., anti-Darwinian) natural history. Among his favorite targets was W. H. Hudson, whom he blames for the character Robert Cohn's belief in romantic love in *The Sun Also Rises*: "Cohn had read and reread [Hudson's] "The Purple Land," a "very sinister book" that presents the "splendid imaginary amorous adventures of a perfect English gentleman in an intensely romantic land" (9).

Hemingway's novel also features Jake Barnes, a would-be lover who lost his penis during the war but not his capacity for sexual desire, as well as the sexually uninhibited Brett Ashley. Although the two talk a great deal about love, they realize "there was nothing that they could do about it" (Baker, *Letters* 745), and Brett selects several lovers. Both Cohn and Brett exemplify male/female behavior in sexual selection: Cohn, a boxer, is combative and jealous, while Brett's eye for beauty eventually draws her to the matador Romero. At the same time, Hemingway suggests that Jake's inability to experience a higher kind of love in prayer is also a matter of natural history: When Jake leaves a cathedral after a failed attempt to pray, he steps out into the square, where he realizes that "the forefingers and the thumb of my right hand were still damp [from the holy water], and I felt them dry in the sun. The sunlight was hot and hard" (97). There is much more natural history in *The Sun Also Rises* than we can take up here (regarding the bulls, for example, and the famous sequence on trout fishing), but the novel is a milestone in Hemingway's life-long meditation on the emotional and spiritual loneliness that he felt mankind must endure in light of Darwinian natural history.[3]

The critic Joseph Wood Krutch immediately attacked Hemingway for his offensive natural history in *The Sun Also Rises*, denouncing the novel's emphasis on "the biological urge" and its "dehumanized" view of only "animal" life. Krutch ended his famous essay by claiming, "We should rather die as men than live as animals" (113, 249).[4] Hemingway fired back with "The Natural History of the Dead,"[5] a bitterly satiric story on death in war, because that subject "has been omitted as a field for the observations of the naturalist" (440). In his own war experience he had observed—in gory detail worthy of "a Goya"—that men "died like animals" (444). Although he had never observed the "noble" exit of a "self-called Humanist," he concludes that "most men die like animals, not men" (445, 444). His insult to Krutch is obvious enough, but he also refers to romantic naturalists such as W. H. Hudson, Reverend Gilbert White, Bishop Stanley, and Mungo Park—men whose works suggest that the proper function of natural history is to increase "that faith, love and hope" that we all "need in our journey through the wilderness of life" (440–41).

Similarly, in *Green Hills of Africa* (1935, based on his African safari in 1933), Hemingway justified his own approach to natural history by criticizing other naturalists, this time Thoreau and other unnamed writers for their devotion to "art," "economics," or "economic-religion" (21–22). His reference to "economic-religion" is broad enough to include both Thoreau (whose chapter "Economy" lays the groundwork for his transcendental natural history in *Walden*) and socialist writers of the 1930s, who believed in the theory of mutual aid rather than competition and natural selection. In the last pages of *Green Hills*, Hemingway's guide concludes that "we have very primitive emotions" and that "it's impossible not to be competitive," even though that "spoils everything" (293). Hemingway takes a closing shot at religion. On the way home from the safari, he finds himself "by the Sea of Galilee," where he notices "many grebes, making spreading wakes in the water as they swam" and then wonders why grebes are never "mentioned in the Bible. I decided that those people were not naturalists" (294).

There is much more to say about *Green Hills*, but two points are worth noting before we examine Hemingway's approach to natural history two decades later, in *The Old Man and the Sea*. First, in his soaring tribute to the Gulf Stream, Hemingway reveals how his own view of nature is, in at least one respect, sadly outdated. He had already written that "the sea is one of the last places left for a man to explore" ("Marlin off Cuba" 78). Defending his hunting and fishing as a "serious occupation" and an important subject in writing, Hemingway compares the feeling a writer has when "writing well and truly of something" with the feeling one has "alone" on the Gulf Stream—that the stream will go on forever, beyond mankind's power to disrupt it. Describing how the sea was "blue and unimpressed" as ever in spite of the garbage dumped into it each day off Havana, he concludes that "the palm fronds of our victories, the worn light bulbs of our discoveries, and the empty condoms of our great loves float with no significance against one single, lasting thing—the stream" (150). (Surely Hemingway would have changed his mind on this subject had he lived to see the *Exxon Valdez* and British Petroleum oil spills of 1989 and 2010, or the great swaths of plastic debris that now clutter the world's oceans.)

Secondly, in *Green Hills*, Hemingway's thoughts on what he called "a country" include observations on soil erosion much like those that Aldo Leopold would later develop more fully in his ecological treatise *A Sand County Almanac* (1949). Hemingway writes, "A continent ages quickly once we come. The natives live in harmony with it. But the foreigner destroys, cuts down the trees, drains the water, so that the water supply is altered and in a short time the soil, once the sod is turned under, is cropped out and, next, it starts to blow away as it has blown away in every old country" (284). Clearly, Hemingway was struck by this ecological problem, but he raises the issue not as Leopold would—in order to call for soil preservation—but to justify his African search for a kind of virgin country. My point in bringing up these two passages from *Green Hills* is not to criticize Hemingway's shortcomings as an environmentalist, but to help narrow our focus on his central concern in *The Old Man and the Sea*: Santiago's effort, *alone*, to comprehend and accept his part in life as a fisherman.

As an example of Hemingway's Darwinian natural history, *The Old Man and the Sea* makes sense only if we note that Hemingway simply excluded that part of Santiago's life in which he dealt with his reproductive needs. Santiago must deal with only the first of his biological drives, his need to kill and eat. During Hemingway's career, Freud also concluded that just two forces move the world, "hunger and love" (Freud 64);[6] like Freud, Hemingway spent most of his career emphasizing the nature of sex in narratives such as the posthumous work *The Garden of Eden* (1986). Although most of his narratives take in both biological drives, he first excluded the sex problem in "Big Two-Hearted River" (1925), where the single character Nick "felt he had left everything behind, the need for thinking, the need to write, other needs" (210). Reflecting much of Hemingway's own life history at that time (his recent shattering experiences in war and love, as many critics have surmised), Nick finds himself in a "burned-over country" (209);

but, alone in the natural setting, he eventually reorients and steadies himself. This burned landscape is created by a forest fire, but it also reflects Hemingway's response to T. S. Eliot's vision of modern life in *The Waste Land* (1922). Quite unlike the figures in Eliot's poem, however, Nick will find his bearings by taking in images of the natural world as "the good place" (215). As Nick makes his way toward his camp, he "kept his direction by the sun" and, eventually lying down and looking "up at the sky," he realizes that "the earth felt good against his back" (212–13). And, watching the trout, Nick sees how he must deal with his own shattered life: He "watched the trout keeping themselves steady in the current," "watched them holding themselves" in the current, until "a kingfisher flew up the stream" and causes them to scatter before settling again to face "up into the current" (209–10).

Nick renews his sense that survival is keyed to adaptation and natural selection. He notices that all the grasshoppers are black and "realized that they had all turned black from living in the burned-over land" (212). Similarly, Nick sees that the trouts' backs are "mottled the clear, water-over-gravel color" (suggesting their adaptive defense from the kingfisher), and he realizes that "animals that lived in swamps were built the way they were" in order to survive in that environment (225, 231). In part one of the story, having watched the trout rising to take insects, "feeding steadily all down the stream," Nick makes his camp, and Hemingway writes that "now he was hungry. . . . Nick was hungry. . . . He was very hungry" (214–15). Then, taking his first bite, Nick says "Chrise . . . Geezus Chrise" (216). The next morning (at the beginning of part two) Nick feels too excited and "too hurried to eat breakfast, but he knew he must" (221). Then, before Nick experiences the excitement of catching his first fish, Hemingway forces him to confront his own frightful violence as a fisherman. A bait fishermen (like all of Hemingway's fishermen), Nick accepts his own part in the bloody drama of life feeding on life: He takes a grasshopper "by the head and held him while he threaded the slim hook under his chin, down through his thorax and into the last segments of his abdomen.

The grasshopper took hold of the hook with his front feet, spitting tobacco juice on it" (224).

The year after he published "Big Two-Hearted River," Hemingway
began another Nick Adams story, "Now I Lay Me" (1927), in which
Nick finds that his thoughts on eating and hook-baiting undermine
his ability to pray. In this story as well, Nick is recovering from war
wounds and is tormented by memories of his parents' poisonous marriage, but Hemingway suggests that both the war and the bitter, loveless
marriage are only corollaries of the elemental life-function that haunts
Nick throughout the story—the sound of silk-worms eating in the
night. Lying awake, Nick "listened to the silk-worms eating"—"you
could hear them eating and a dropping sound in the leaves" (363). Nick
was afraid to sleep for fear that his "soul would go out of his body,"
as it had seemed to do briefly when he was wounded (363). Sometimes, waiting for daylight, he could keep himself awake by thinking
of trout-fishing, his need to find different kinds of bait, and his decision
never to use salamanders or crickets again, "because of the way they
acted about the hook" (364). But on nights when he "could not fish,"
he recalled scenes of his parents' marriage and would "pray for them
both" (364, 366). On some nights, Nick "could not remember [his]
prayers even," and was "absolutely unable to get past" the words "on
earth as it is in heaven" (366). In this excellent example of his famous
"ice-berg" technique, Hemingway leaves his readers to grasp his sub-
merged reference to the words from the Lord's Prayer that Nick cannot
face: "Give us this day our daily bread."[7] Instead, Nick remarks, "You
can hear silk-worms eating very clearly in the night and I lay with my
eyes open and listened to them" (367). As the story develops, Nick's
friend notices that something is worrying him and advises him "to get
married," for then he "wouldn't worry" (370). But Nick cannot avoid
listening "to the silk-worms eating" and defecating, and Hemingway
leaves him with the bitter irony of his friend's certainty that marriage
"would fix up everything" (371).

II. "It is enough to live on the sea and kill our true brothers."

Returning to the subject of hunger and eating in *The Old Man and the Sea*, Hemingway gave us another fisherman, Santiago, whose old age has freed him from the Darwinian "sexual struggle" but not from his loneliness and his elemental need to eat. Alone on the sea, Santiago will suffer before accepting his own part in the violent order, his need to kill and eat. And for his suffering, and for his behavior in dealing with it, Hemingway will present Santiago as a kind of saint for modern times. Santiago is named for Saint James, the fisherman whom Christ chose as one of his first apostles, and perhaps for this reason he believes "that [to be a fisherman] was the thing that I was born for" (36). But Hemingway's Santiago insists, "I am not religious" (47). Hemingway will not suggest that Santiago even heard of Darwin, but from his long experience Santiago knows a great deal about sea life; more importantly, he fully embraces the most troubling of Darwin's insights: that all life, including human beings, exists within the community of common descent.[8] Santiago has "no mysticism about turtles" and knows that "I have such a heart [as the turtles] . . . and my feet and hands are like theirs" (26). He thinks of porpoises as "our brothers like the flying fish" (35). He realizes that his hooked marlin is his "brother" (43). He believes that "man is not much beside the great birds and beasts," and that he "would rather be that beast down there in the darkness of the sea" (50); and, finally heading in with the great marlin lashed to the side of his boat, he thinks, "We sail like brothers" (73).

Hemingway begins to develop the old man's inner conflict in the opening scenes, when the boy repeatedly encourages the old man to eat. Santiago first pretends that he has plenty to eat and then tells the boy that he is "not very hungry" (13). When the boy tells him that "you can't fish and not eat," Santiago replies, "I have," and we soon see that Santiago resists eating not because he cannot afford food, but because "for a long time now eating had bored him"—to the point that

---

"he never carried a lunch" when he went fishing (13, 19). On the fishing grounds, however, Santiago knows that he needs to eat and tells himself repeatedly over the next several pages, "I must remember to eat the tuna before he spoils in order to keep strong" (34). Although Santiago relents at this point, chewing the piece of fish "slowly and conscientiously," Hemingway does not.

Again and again he shows Santiago's efforts to bring himself to eat, especially the dolphin fish or *dorado*, the taste of which Santiago finds nauseating. Even after Santiago "ate half of one of the dolphin fillets," Hemingway creates an odd scene in which the old man, grasping the line that holds the untiring marlin, is "pulled down tight into the bow and his face was in the cut slice of dolphin and he could not move" (61). Santiago tries to wash "the dolphin flesh off of his face" and later, realizing again that "he should chew some more of the dolphin," he worries that he will not be able to keep it down because his "face was in it," and he decides to "eat the other flying fish" instead (61–63). Before this long meditation on killing and eating is finished, Santiago will kill his great marlin, watch a Mako shark attack it with its "clicking, thrusting all-swallowing jaws," and then harpoon the shark "with resolution and complete malignancy" (75–76). He will remind himself that the Mako "lives on the live fish as you do," and that "besides . . . everything kills everything else in some way" (78–79). Leaning over the side, then, he takes a piece of the marlin, "chewed it and noted its quality and its good taste," and then began to prepare for what he knew would be "a very bad time" (79). The other sharks come, and although he manages to kill several of them, they strip the marlin clean, leaving Santiago with only the tail and the "long backbone of the great fish that was now just garbage" (94).

We are left to contemplate Hemingway's reasons for ending this drama of killing and eating with repeated suggestions that Santiago's suffering is comparable to Christ's on the cross. When the last sharks attacked, Santiago says only "*Ay*," a word for which "there is no translation," Hemingway tells us, but it is "a noise such as a man might make, involuntarily, feeling the nail go through his hands and into the wood" (79). When he reaches shore, Santiago "shouldered the mast," climbed the hill to his hut, and fell asleep "with his arms out straight and the palm of his hands up" (90–91). I have suggested that Santiago is a kind of saint for modern times; Hemingway was troubled by the same facts of natural history that other writers fixed upon in the years just before the *Origin of Species*. These writers felt their faith challenged not only by the emerging geological record, but also the image of "Nature, red in tooth and claw," as Tennyson put it. Similar visions were put forward by Melville, who refers to the "shocking sharkish business" of life, and Thoreau, who recalled his own impulse to "seize and devour [a woodchuck] raw" and realized that he had "fished from the same kind of necessity that the first fishers did."[9] But, writing before Darwin had located the human being within the community of common descent, each of these writers found ways to transcend life's elemental violence and defend his faith; Thoreau, for example, asserted, "He is blessed who is assured that the animal is dying out in him day by day, and the divine being established" (146).

By the time Hemingway wrote "Now I Lay Me," many writers had responded to the Darwinian revolution, attempting in their own ways to accept (or in some cases deny) T. H. Huxley's post-Darwinian view of *Man's Place* in *Nature* (1863, my emphasis). Most were troubled by the theory of sexual selection and its threat to the meaning of love, and many took note of the human's canine teeth, but none had explored man's place *in* nature's bloody arena as unrelentingly as Hemingway. If the sound of the silk-worms' steady eating kept Nick awake, disrupting (along with his war experience) his ability to pray, Santiago prays quite easily—though not for "my soul to keep." Instead, he is "not religious" and prays only "mechanically" or "automatically" that he should "catch this fish" (47). In the dark of night he sees but does "not know the name of Rigel" (the brightest star in Orion the Hunter); while accepting that he "must kill" his marlin, he wonders "how many people will he feed," and who could be "worthy of eating him from the manner of his behavior and his great dignity" (55). Admitting in this scene that he does not "understand these things," Santiago thinks, "It is enough to live on the sea and kill our true brothers" (55). This, I suggest, is the point of Hemingway's natural history in *The Old Man and the Sea*: to imagine a man who can accept and engage life on its own bloody terms, and do so with dignity.

Hemingway will not suggest that even Santiago can console himself absolutely in believing it enough to be alive in the sea of life. But he suggests that three of Santiago's experiences are especially helpful in leading him to accept his part in life, for all his loneliness and suffering. First, in his own hunt for fish he is guided by a primal scene of life feeding on life. Seeing "flying fish spurt out of the water," Santiago watches a bird following

> the flying fish. The old man could see the slight bulge in the water that the big dolphin raised as they followed the escaping fish. The dolphin were cutting through the water below the flight of the fish and would be in the water, driving at speed, when the fish dropped. It is a big school of dolphin, he thought. They are wide spread and the flying fish have little chance. The bird has no chance. The flying fish are too big for him and they go too fast. (24)

The element of chance in the life hunt underscores Hemingway's sense of human spiritual loneliness, but it also underscores Santiago's sense that he is *not* alone in life. In a later scene, a warbler finds its way to his skiff and lands there to rest. Wanting the company, and seeing that the bird is very tired from its flight, Santiago talks to it, asking how old it is and if this is its first trip. He thinks of

> the hawks . . . that come out to sea to meet them. But he said nothing of this to the bird who could not understand him anyway and who would learn about hawks soon enough.
>
> "Take a good rest, small bird," he said. "Then go in and take your chance like any man or bird or fish." (40)

After the bird flies off, Santiago looked around "because he would have liked him for company" (40–41).

Immediately after Santiago watches the dolphin chasing the flying fish, Hemingway introduces a second series of scenes that helps Santiago know his way. In this first instance, Santiago looks into "the dark water" and sees "the strange light the sun made now" (25). Hemingway repeats the point that this is "strange light," and then gives us the second of these sea light scenes just after Santiago tells himself, "Now is the time to think of only one thing. That which I was born for" (28). Santiago looks overboard, noting that "the sea was very dark and the light made prisms in the water. The myriad flecks of the plankton were annulled now by the high sun and it was only the great deep prisms in the blue water that the old man saw now" (29). Hemingway will go no further than this to articulate his post-Darwinian sense that life emerged in the sea, but it is for this reason that the traditional solar or celestial light, now refracted in the water, seems "strange." And he gives us the third of the sea light scenes immediately after Santiago brings himself to eat, "slowly and conscientiously . . . all of the wedge-shaped strips" of the bonito (43). This time Santiago "looked across the sea and knew how alone he was now."

> But he could see the prisms in the deep dark water and the line stretching ahead and the strange undulation of the calm. The clouds were building up now for the trade wind and he looked ahead and saw a flight of wild ducks etching themselves against the sky over the water, then blurring, then etching again and he knew no man was ever alone on the sea. (44)

Moments later, Hemingway introduces a third sequence of scenes that begins with Santiago watching as "the surface of the ocean bulged" and the great Marlin "came out unendingly and water poured from his sides" (45). Seeing the "wonderful" fish, the biggest he had ever seen or heard of, Santiago prays mechanically for its death. He is determined to kill the fish "in all his greatness and his glory," even though "it is unjust." It is for this reason, he knows, that he is "a strange old man" (48). After long hours of battling his fish, Santiago finally draws near it and casts his harpoon. Then he sees as "the fish came alive, with his death in him, and rose high out of the water showing all his great length and width and all his power and his beauty. He seemed to hang in the air above the old man in the skiff. Then he fell into the water with a crash that sent spray over the old man" (69).

To appreciate the "great strangeness" of Santiago's vision, it will help to compare his marlin with Melville's imagining of the whale. With "all his power and his beauty," the marlin is surely the most magnificent image of life that Hemingway can imagine. Santiago thinks the marlin is "more noble" even than the man who "will kill him," and Hemingway writes that the dead marlin's "eye looked as detached as . . . a saint in a procession" (46, 71). Yet he knows that even this most wonderful form of life can "hang motionless in the sky" for only a moment. By contrast, Melville proclaimed his belief in "the ungraspable phantom of life" and defended his Christian faith from the threat of mid-nineteenth-century science. While acknowledging that human beings had driven the bison to near extinction, Melville maintained that "the eternal whale" would survive even another "Noah's flood," and "rearing upon the topmost crest of the equatorial flood, spout his frothed defiance to the skies" (105).

In Hemingway's more hardened natural history, the harsh sunlight dries the holy water on Jake Barnes' fingertips; the young Nick cannot recall the Lord's Prayer beyond "on earth as it is in heaven"; and the old waiter in "A Clean, Well-lighted Place" can bring himself to recite only a blasphemous version of it. Having concluded that there is only "nothing and a man was nothing too," he prays to "our nada who art in nada . . . Hail nothing full of nothing, nothing is with thee" (383). Yet each of these three characters will face the spiritual void with a measure of dignity, as Santiago does throughout his ordeal; first in his humility and his belief that "man is not much beside the great birds and beasts," and second—like all of Hemingway's hunters, fishermen, or bull fighters—in killing his "brothers" in life as mercifully and quickly as possible. Bringing in the tuna that he will so reluctantly eat, "the old man hit him on the head for kindness" (27). When he finally brings his marlin to the boat, he wields the harpoon as effectively as the most artful bullfighter would use his sword, and he thinks, "I felt his heart. . . . When I pushed on the harpoon shaft the second time" (70). Although he later killed the Mako with "complete malignancy," he did so by driving the harpoon into its brain and thus knew he had "killed him well" (79). To kill "well" had long been a guiding principle for Hemingway, as it had been in his remarks regarding sport fishermen in 1935, in which he rejected the idea that fishing with light tackle gives "the fish a sporting chance." On the contrary, he insisted in "Marlin off Cuba" that the truly "sporting thing is to kill your fish . . . as quickly and as mercifully as possible" (70). But in *The Old Man and the Sea*, with its religious imagery and emphasis on the need to kill and eat one's brothers, Santiago's determination to kill mercifully is not mere sportsmanship; rather, it harkens back to the spiritual wounds that ancient humans felt in complying with this essential element in their own natural history—the need to kill and eat.

Finally, Santiago's dignity inheres in his power to endure "suffering," even in thinking—like the old waiter in "A Clean, Well-lighted Place"—that he was beaten by "Nothing" (89–90). Four hours after the hooked marlin had begun towing him out to sea, with the tow line cutting "across his back," Santiago "tried not to think but only to endure" (33); when, much later, the marlin still "swam steadily . . . through the dark water," he "took his suffering as it came" (47). Even when the marlin pulls him into the bow, Santiago thinks, "This is what we waited for. . . . So now let us take it" (61). Sailing toward his harbor with the knowledge that other sharks await him, Santiago tells himself, "Sail on this course and take it when it comes" (77). Toward the end, Santiago wonders whether his "brother" the marlin is bringing him in or whether he is bringing in the marlin, for they are bound together in the bloody economy of life. In this way, Santiago's insight about the marlin reflects his own reality as a fisherman who cannot understand why he was born to kill and eat: "The punishment of the hook is nothing. The punishment of hunger, and that he [the hooked marlin] is against something that he does not comprehend, is everything" (56).

In Hemingway's meditation on killing and eating, Santiago's sense that hunger is "everything" acknowledges the ancient wound that still troubles the human mind, long after Tennyson and Melville proclaimed their faith in the transcendent spirit. But even Santiago's assertion seems an act of faith, likewise his claim that even in the face of "nothing" "it is enough to live on the sea and kill our true brothers." Santiago must call upon his own courage and dignity to endure. In Hemingway's long study of natural history, *The Old Man and the Sea* was only one exemplifying work, and it was certainly not the last of his efforts to comprehend man's place in nature. In this fable, he could come to terms with the first of life's demands only by setting aside the second. But he continued to explore the natural history of love in the much darker manuscript *The Garden of Eden*, and to explore hunger and love in the equally dark African journal *True at First Light* (1999) and *Under Kilimanjaro* (2005).

Notes

1. The main studies of American writers' views on human nature after *The Descent of Man, and Selection in Relation to Sex* and Darwin's subsequent volume, *The Expression of the Emotions in Man and Animals* (1872), are by Bert Bender: *The Descent of Love: Darwin and the Theory of Sexual Selection in American Fiction, 1871–1926* (U of Penn P, 1996), and *Evolution and "the Sex Problem": American Narratives during the Eclipse of Darwinism* (Kent State UP, 2004). For a completely different (i.e., a distinctly non-Darwinian) interpretation of Hemingway's take on natural history, see Susan F. Beegel, "Eye and Heart: Hemingway's Education as a Naturalist," in Linda Wagner-Martin, ed., *A Historical Guide to Ernest Hemingway* (New York: Oxford UP, 2000), pp. 53–92. Also of possible interest is Robert E. Fleming's collection of essays in *Hemingway and the Natural World* (Moscow: U of Idaho P, 1999).

2. Subsequent references to Hemingway's short stories are cited parenthetically by page number from *The Short Stories of Ernest Hemingway*.

3. Writing that *The Sun Also Rises* "is a treatise on basic loneliness and the inadequacy of promiscuity," Hemingway extends his critique of romantic love to the tenet of then-popular Freudianism that presents promiscuity as the solution to mankind's psychic ills, the major cause of which was sexual repression (Baker, *Letters* 767–68, 545).

4. Krutch published his essay, "Love—or the Life and Death of a Value," in the *Atlantic Monthly* in 1927, and included it in his *The Modern Temper*, which is the version quoted here.

5. He began the story in the same year that *The Modern Temper* appeared (1929), but did not publish it until 1932, in *Death in the Afternoon*.

6. According to Frank Sulloway, "perhaps more than anyone else in the nineteenth century," Freud "singled out the biological importance of the instincts for survival and reproduction" (252).

7. Hemingway first articulated this principle in 1932 in *Death in the Afternoon*: "If a writer of prose knows enough about what he is writing about he may omit things that he knows and the reader . . . will have a feeling of those things as strongly as though the writer had stated them. The dignity of movement of an ice-berg is due to only one-eighth of its being above water" (192).

8. As historian of science Ernst Mayr notes, the Darwinian revolution was not limited to the theory of natural selection; "the first" of Darwin's great intellectual revolutions was to include "man in the phyletic tree of common descent." Doing so, Mayr writes, "Darwin took away from man his privileged position in nature assigned to him in the Bible and in the writings of virtually all philosophers" (508).

9. Tennyson, *In Memoriam A. H. H.*, sec. 56; Melville, *Moby-Dick*, ch. sixty-four, "Stubb's Supper"; Thoreau, "Higher Laws," *Walden*.

Works Cited

Baker, Carlos. *Ernest Hemingway: A Life Story*. New York: Scribner's, 1969.

_____, ed. *Ernest Hemingway: Selected Letters, 1917–1961*. New York: Scribner's, 1981.

Fitzgerald, F. Scott. *This Side of Paradise*. New York: Scribner's, 1970.

Freud, Sigmund. *Civilization and Its Discontents*. Trans. and ed. James Strachey. New York: Norton 1961.

Hemingway, Ernest. *Death in the Afternoon*. New York: Scribner's, 1932.

_____. *Green Hills of Africa*. New York: Macmillan, 1987.

_____. "Marlin off Cuba." *American Big Game Fishing*. Ed. Eugene V. Connett III. Lanham: Derrydale, 1993. 55–81.

_____. *The Old Man and the Sea*. New York: Scribner's, 1961.

_____. *The Short Stories of Ernest Hemingway*. New York: Scribner's, 1953.

_____. *The Sun Also Rises*. New York: Scribner's, 1970.

Krutch, Joseph Wood. *The Modern Temper: A Study and a Confession*. New York: Harcourt, 1929.

Mayr, Ernst. *The Growth of Biological Thought: Diversity, Evolution, and Inheritance*. Cambridge: Harvard UP, 1982.

Melville, Herman. *Moby-Dick, or the Whale*. New York: Penguin, 2001.

Reynolds, Michael. "Ernest Hemingway, 1899–1961: A Brief Biography." *A Historical Guide to Ernest Hemingway*. Ed. Linda Wagner-Martin. New York: Oxford UP, 2000. 15–50.

Sulloway, Frank. *Freud: Biologist of the Mind: Beyond the Psychoanalytic Legend*. New York: Basic, 1979.

Thoreau, Henry David. *Walden and Civil Disobedience*. Ed. Owen Thomas. Norton Critical Edition. New York: Norton, 1966.

John Steinbeck's Environmental Evolution_____

Brian Railsback

John Steinbeck wrote his best work from an environmental perspective before the word "ecocriticism" was coined. Alone among writers of his stature in the United States during the 1930s, 1940s, 1950s, and early 1960s, Steinbeck undertook to inspect, as he put it, "mankind as a species" (*America and Americans* 137). Inspired by Charles Darwin, early creative evolutionists, and Albert Einstein, Steinbeck sought to portray humans as a species among species, tied to all other creatures and inevitably subject to natural forces. He believed that this holistic understanding revealed our true place in the scheme of things. Steinbeck tried to work inductively and with objectivity in order to discover what was true. The attempt to break out of humanity's narrow theological/philosophical perspective and see *Homo sapiens* as a species is a difficult and dangerous ideal. The course for Steinbeck eventually moved beyond biology into physics, and the attempt to name the whole in a unified field theory. As he considered humanity's true place in the natural and physical universe, Steinbeck fully understood our species' responsibility to be good stewards of the planet and not to poison it or blow it up in a cascade of nuclear weapons. As a result of his solid scientific foundation, one could argue that Steinbeck became the first mainstream, intentionally famous, and ecologically minded fiction writer in the United States.

Steinbeck's Biological Perspective and *The Grapes of Wrath*

Steinbeck went directly to Charles Darwin as early as 1923, when the author was largely floundering in his studies at Stanford University. He bypassed the social Darwinists completely and went directly to *On the Origin of Species* (1859), *The Descent of Man* (1871), and the account of *The Voyage of the Beagle* (1839). *Origin of Species* illustrates the kind of thinking that Steinbeck made his ideal: It shows an attempt to find truth by abandoning preconceived notions, making observations firsthand, gathering the facts together, and achieving what Steinbeck called "the inductive leap" to discover a great principle (*Sweet Thursday* 126). At the heart of Steinbeck's philosophy—articulated most clearly in his 1951 nonfiction narrative *The Log from the Sea of Cortez* (reprinted from 1941's *Sea of Cortez*)—is what he considered nonteleological thinking, or "is" thinking, as Steinbeck and his marine biologist friend Edward F. Ricketts defined it. "Non-teleological ideas derive through 'is' thinking, associated with natural selection as Darwin seems to have understood it. . . . Non-teleological thinking concerns itself primarily not with what should be, or could be, or might be, but rather with what actually 'is'—attempting at most to answer the already sufficiently difficult questions *what* or *how*, instead of *why*" (*Log* 139). Steinbeck embraced a holistic view of nature, with humans a part of all interrelations. This concept denies traditionally theological or humanist notions, which exalt our species by setting it apart.

A study of Charles Darwin and the art of John Steinbeck must, like any expedition through the novelist's lifework, arrive at his masterpiece *The Grapes of Wrath* (1939). In no other book is Steinbeck's dramatization of Darwin's theory more clear; the novel resonates with the naturalist's ideas. Through Steinbeck's narrative technique, from the parts (i.e., the characters' perspectives in the Joad chapters) to the whole (the intercalary chapters, which present a more consistently omniscient viewpoint), we are presented with a holistic view of the migrant worker's plight. The novel encompasses much of Darwin's theory of evolution, including the struggle for existence and the process of natural selection. The migrant workers act as a kind of species, torn from one niche and forced to find another. As the landowners in California complicate the migrants' struggle for survival out of sheer greed, the surviving workers become much tougher. Because of their inability to see the whole picture, the bankers and members of the Farmers' Association diminish themselves by their oppressive tactics while the surviving migrant workers become increasingly tougher and more resourceful. Ultimately, recognizing Darwin's ideas in *The Grapes of Wrath* enables us to discern some hope for the Joads and others like them; here is Steinbeck's manifesto of progress, based on biological law rather than political ideology. Despite the dismal scene that concludes the book, we come to a better understanding of what Ma Joad already knows: The people will keep on coming.

Steinbeck embarked on an expedition from 1934 to 1938 to gather information that would ultimately lead to his great novel. Jackson J. Benson's biography *The True Adventures of John Steinbeck, Writer* (1984) provides a very complete account of the novelist's research. Robert DeMott's introduction and notes for Steinbeck's *Grapes of Wrath* journal *Working Days* (1989) provide further illumination and detail.

Benson writes that Steinbeck—who "seems to have remembered in detail nearly everything he saw or heard"—entered the world of migrant labor in California when he interviewed two starving, fugitive strike organizers in Seaside, California, in early 1934 (291). Steinbeck gathered more information from James Harkins, an organizer who helped in the Imperial Valley strike (1934) and the Salinas lettuce strike (1936). Eventually, strike organizers began to frequent Steinbeck's cottage in Pacific Grove, California. As early as the summer of 1934, the author went out to see the migrant labor camps in the Salinas area. All of the information he gathered, along with very detailed information from a union leader, Cicil McKiddy, eventually became a part of the strike novel *In Dubious Battle* (1936). Serious research for *Grapes of Wrath* began with Steinbeck's *San Francisco News* assignment to write a series of articles about migrant farm labor in California, which required observing conditions at various labor camps. As Benson and DeMott show, Steinbeck, as he prepared to write *Grapes of Wrath*, was greatly influenced by Tom Collins, the manager of "Weedpatch," the government sanitary camp at Arvin (he is the "Tom" that the book is partly dedicated to). Collins was something of a social scientist; he made meticulous reports and gathered statistics about the migrant's life that Steinbeck used extensively in *Grapes of Wrath* (Benson 343–44). In 1937 Steinbeck took another, longer tour of migrant camps with Collins, and in February 1938 Steinbeck went to the flooded areas of Visalia where, as he wrote to his agent, "Four thousand families, drowned out of their tents are really starving to death" (Benson 368). As DeMott writes, "What he witnessed there became the backdrop for the final scenes of *The Grapes of Wrath*" (*Working Days* 134).

Like Darwin's *Origin*, *Grapes of Wrath* is a gathering of observations fused by a hypothesis, in this case a biological consideration of cycles in land ownership. Of course, unlike *Origin*, it is fictionalized and, above all else, a work of art. Yet Steinbeck's method in putting together the novel resembles an inductive, scientific one.

From the first pages of *Grapes of Wrath*, Steinbeck's biological, holistic view is evident. The novel presents a large picture in which humans are only a small part; in the great natural scheme of sky, land, rain, wind, and dust, they suffer with the teams of horses and the dying corn—all life-forms are helpless in this huge canvas of natural machinations. People are further associated with the natural world by being rendered in animal metaphors, by either their own language or the narrator's. In chapter eight, we meet the Joad family and hear how Ma fears Tom will be like Pretty Boy Floyd ("They shot at him like a varmint . . . an' then they run him like a coyote, an' him a-snappin' an' a-snarlin', mean as a lobo"); Grampa tortured Granma "as children torture bugs"; Grampa had hoped the "jailbird" Tom would "come abustin' outa that jail like a bull through a corral fence"; and somewhere Al is "a-billy-goatin' aroun' the country. Tom cattin' hisself to death" (82–89).

The narrator's famous image of the land turtle is the most extensive metaphor for the migrant worker. In chapter three, the tough, wizened turtle navigates the road, pushing ahead with "hands" rather than front claws. Tom picks up the turtle and observes, "Nobody can't keep a turtle though. . . . at last one day they get out and away they go—off somewheres. It's like me" (21). When Tom releases it, a cat attacks it to no avail, and the turtle goes in the same direction that the Joads will, southwest. The connection is made even stronger when, in chapter sixteen, a description of the flight of the Joads and the Wilsons across the Texas Panhandle is juxtaposed with the image of the land turtles that "crawled through the dust" (178). Steinbeck's extensive use of personification and anthropomorphism underscores his view of *Homo sapiens* as just another species.

The world Steinbeck portrays in *Grapes of Wrath* demonstrates what he, Darwin, and Ricketts believed: Humans are subject to the laws of ecology. The Joads and Wilsons are part of a movement of migrants, acting as a species turned out of a niche by natural and unnatural forces. The migrants go to a richer niche that appears to have plenty of room for them, but many of them die, overwhelmed by competition and repression. The survivors display an astounding ability to adapt. They come to California as a vigorous new species quite terrifying to the natives who, despite the crushing power of a brutal economic system they control, act from a growing sense of insecurity. "They have weathered the thing," Steinbeck writes of the migrant workers, "and they can weather much more for their blood is strong. . . . This new race is here to stay and . . . heed must be taken of it" (*Gypsies* 22).

The process of evolution that leads to the creation of "this new race" is patently Darwinian. With drought upon the land and the dissolution of the tenant system, the farmer can no longer live in the region, forcing the migration west. From the first day of the Joads' migration, a process of selection begins, and those who can adapt to the new way of life survive. Although a tough man, Grampa proves too rooted in the old land to adapt to the new, and his death, as Casy knows, is inevitable. "Grampa didn' die tonight. He died the minute you took 'im off the place" (160). Muley cannot leave either, and his future is doubtful; ironically, Noah, who himself will wander off alone into oblivion, tells Muley, "You gonna die out in the fiel' some day" (121). Granma cannot recover from the death of Grampa and loses touch with reality and eventually life. The Wilsons also fail; Ivy lacks the essential mechanical knowledge of cars to succeed, and Sairy is too physically weak to survive.

Because of the migrants' relentless trek, during which they are driven by the harshness of the weather, poverty, and cruelty, the ones who arrive in California already are transformed. As intercalary chapter seventeen shows, the group has adapted to the new way of life on the road. "They were not farm men anymore, but migrant men" (215). The new breed pours into California and "the owners hated them because . . . the owners had heard from their grandfathers how easy it is to steal land from a soft man if you are fierce and hungry and armed" (256–57). Ma Joad typifies the strong blood that Steinbeck refers to, for she adapts to each new situation, meeting difficulties with whatever ferocity or compassion is needed, constantly working to keep the family together and push them forward. Toward the end of the novel, Ma gives her famous speech about the people, and certainly she has come to understand what survival of the fittest means: "We ain't gonna die out. People is goin' on—changin' a little, maybe, but goin' right on. . . . some die, but the rest is tougher" (467–68).

A Darwinian interpretation of *Grapes of Wrath* reveals the novel's most terrible irony—the owners' perversion of the natural process only hastens their own destruction. The Farmers' Association of California sends out handbills to attract a surplus of labor, intensifying the competition for jobs so that the migrant laborers will work for almost nothing. But the owners are unconscious of the other part of the equation, that increased competition only toughens the survivors; Darwin notes that "in the survival of favoured individuals and races, during the constantly recurrent Struggle for Existence, we see a powerful and ever-acting form of Selection" (*Origin* 115). The novel's omniscient narrator recalls "the little screaming fact," evident throughout history, of which the owners remain ignorant: "Repression works only to strengthen and knit the repressed" (262).

The narrator describes the sense of coming change in more ominous tones at the end of chapter twenty-five. "In the eyes of the hungry there is a growing wrath. In the souls of the people the grapes of wrath are filling and growing heavy, growing heavy for the vintage" (385).

The narrator presents the whole view, which characters like Casy and Tom eventually see but the owners remain blind to, as they continue to create a breed that will be their undoing. "For while California has been successful in its use of migrant labor," Steinbeck writes, "it is gradually building a human structure which will certainly change the State, and may, if handled with the inhumanity and stupidity that have characterized the past, destroy the present system of agricultural economics" (*Gypsies* 25).

The other great irony of the novel is that, through a Darwinian process of adaptation and evolution, the dehumanizing conditions created by the owners only make the migrant workers more human. This process can be seen in nearly every chapter, as migrants share money, food, transportation, work, and ultimately anger, as they briefly unite in a strike that is defeated by an influx of hungry workers who do not yet see the big picture. But as the suffering continues, and more Casys are martyred and more Toms created, the people will eventually move forward. "This you may say of man . . . [man] stumbles forward, painfully, mistakenly sometimes. Having stepped forward, he may slip back, but only a half step, never the full step back" (*Grapes* 164). While the comfortable and rich owners are frozen in their "I" mentality, the surviving migrants are dynamic and continue to evolve into their "we" mentality. This process is the essence of Steinbeck's scientific, Darwinian belief in a progression for humankind, based on biological principles in general, and struggle in particular. This is why, by the time he published *America and Americans* in 1966, Steinbeck worried most of all that the people of the United States had lost the survival drive.

In a work so full of apparently hopeless suffering, the Darwinian/biological view of *The Grapes of Wrath* explains why characters such as Ma or Tom have a sense of victory. The struggle for survival creates a new race that, if continuously oppressed, will become a powerful new force that will change the social and political landscape of California. Because of the struggle, people like the Joads become better human beings, cooperating with each other in every crisis. Thus, even when famished and facing death herself, Rose of Sharon begins to see past her own selfishness and offers her breast to a starving man. She has reason to smile mysteriously, understanding something larger and greater than her oppressors will ever know.

Steinbeck, Physics, and *Cannery Row*

Begun by his reading of Darwin and other naturalists/biologists, Steinbeck's path to "what 'is'" depends on inductive reasoning—thinking free of preconceptions—that leads one to greater vistas. As we seek to understand the whole, we can only hope to recognize what "is" in an infinitely expanding horizon. For Steinbeck, the quest is not to *understand* the whole, but rather to see, to embrace, as much of it as possible. From biology, Steinbeck followed these widening circles into physics, specifically relativity, quantum theory, and the attempt to reconcile the two in an overarching theory—the unified field, or what has been called the Ultimate Theory. We find Steinbeck's view of the whole well informed by the physics of his day, as described in *Sea of Cortez* and as playfully dramatized in one of his greatest novels, *Cannery Row* (1945).

Steinbeck owned or read three books that would have given him the macro (universal or cosmic) and micro (subatomic or quantum) views in physics for the layman of his day: Albert Einstein's *Relativity* (1920), Arthur S. Eddington's *The Nature of the Physical World* (1928), and *Quantum Mechanics* (1929), by Edward Condon and Phillip Morse (DeMott 28, 36, 37). Steinbeck was attracted to several aspects of physics in the early twentieth century, such as the ways in which Einstein's theory of relativity radically altered Newtonian or Classical physics (much in the same way Darwin's theory of evolution shook up nineteenth-century natural science); the notion that the measurement of space and time is relative to our position, that there are no absolutes; physics' admitting only to describe accurately *what* but not *why* at the quantum level; that there are probabilities but no absolutes at the quantum level, hinting at chaos in the nature of things; the great paradox that quantum theory and relativity do not agree, and that concepts can explain the subatomic universe but not apply to the cosmic; and finally that a unified field theory to contain all is needed but does not yet exist. In short, physics, as Steinbeck might have understood it, would have been very exciting, and his exuberance for these questions shows itself in *Cannery Row*.

Alone among the American writers of his time and stature, John Steinbeck wanted to teach us that the disorder and paradox that we perceive in our world is relative—a figment of our own peculiar warp. If we move beyond our own boundaries, as he believed Darwin first encouraged us to do, we might sense an unseen order in things and therefore stand before the universe without trembling in fear when we cannot discern an order to our liking. Enlightened by the science of his day, and through his unique perspective, Steinbeck made it clear that an order exists *outside of us*, existing even if the greatest scientific or philosophical minds cannot explain it.

The Log from the Sea of Cortez provides a great source for Steinbeck's consideration of physics in a nonfiction work, and *Cannery Row* proves the richest dramatization of the author's interpretation of physics in a novel. *Cannery Row* embraces the whole—in style, form, and content—attempting to contain the peculiar problems of "warp," micro and macro worlds, and grand paradoxes. Ultimately, the novel suggests that we may find sanity in an apparently chaotic universe by attaining some sense of the unified field and our place in it.

Cannery Row opens with a consideration of the problems of perception, "warp," and relative positions—subjects covered in *Sea of Cortez*. As in Einsteinian physics, much of our sense of reality depends upon where we are when we observe it. Steinbeck neatly sums up the problem in *Sea of Cortez* in a discussion of sea waves and how they are perceived as breaking at Point Sur. "And so on and on to the shore, and to the point where the last wave, if you think from the sea, and the first if you think from the shore, touches and breaks. And it is important where you are thinking from" (31). Of course, "where you are thinking from" is of great importance in *Cannery Row*, and readers are instructed to consider this as we look at the Row: "Its inhabitants are, as the man once said, 'whores, pimps, gamblers, and sons of bitches,' by which he meant Everybody. Had the man looked through another peephole he might have said, 'Saints and angels and martyrs and holy men,' and he would have meant the same thing" (5). So often with Steinbeck there is this balancing of the two peepholes, the small and personal, and the great and infinite. Parallel to this is the strong desire to relate the views of all, or, in his fiction, the view of the truth. His greatest dramatization of this desire is *Grapes of Wrath*, structured so that we see the micro-view of the Joads against the macro-panorama of migrants, California history, and the dispossession portrayed in the intercalary chapters. *Cannery Row*, in a less rigid structure, does the same thing, as we follow the story of Mack and the boys' attempt to pull off a party for Doc against the larger picture of Monterey, California, and its surroundings. The novel careens from a view as small as a gopher's attempt to make a home for itself (chapter thirty-one) to Doc's journey to collect marine specimens in La Jolla (chapters seventeen and eighteen).

A most interesting presentation of the micro and macro views occurs when the little boy Andy taunts a mysterious old Chinese man. The man turns, and his eyes spread out until the boy is engulfed by one single eye. The boy sees a fantastic world of "mountains shaped like cows' and dogs' heads and tents and mushrooms" (25). The moment is just as disorienting for the reader; has the boy been swept into the mind's eye of the Chinese man, into a tiny micro-universe? Or has the Chinese man's giant eye grown outward, so that the boy perceives a vision of a colossal universe in which he is but a tiny, lonely part? The old man has provided a glimpse of the chaotic universe, and, for a little boy not ready to look through that peephole, it is a terrifying experience.

What readies us for that particular view, for a consideration of the whole? *Cannery Row* suggests, more so than any of Steinbeck's other works, that the key is *embracing* the disorder, and especially the paradoxes that life and the universe present to us. Because of its wide scope, physics must do exactly that: comprehend the bewildering reality of quantum theory and relativity, and the fact that the two views—at least in Steinbeck's time—seemed irreconcilable. The grand paradox is the fact that explanations for the quantum universe do not work for the cosmic universe, and vice versa. Hence the need for the unified-field theory that Steinbeck refers to, which might contain this gigantic contradiction. Steinbeck not only embraces paradoxes, he delights in presenting them. The driving force of *Cannery Row*'s plot, humor, and theme is paradox.

The central plot of the novel is itself a paradox. When Mack and the boys plan a party, it is a disaster; however, when they do not plan it, the party succeeds. The novel's humor, satire, and even tragedy derive from paradox, and most of the characters are defined by paradox. Mack and the boys are content because they do not work for contentment, and those who do work for it are miserable. "What can it profit a man to gain the whole world and to come to his property with a gastric ulcer, a blown prostate, and bifocals?" (18). Dora Flood, a madam who runs a "stately whore house," lives in a paradox as well: "Being against the law, at least against its letter, she must be twice as law abiding as anyone else" (19–20). Hazel asks questions of Doc, but she never listens to or cares about the answers. Henri builds boats but is afraid to finish them because that would mean he would have to set them on the water, and Henri hates the water. Frankie is a boy with no one to love until he finds Doc, and falling in love with Doc is his undoing, as he breaks into a store to get his father figure a birthday present. Chapter twenty-five opens with the observation that people on the Row do not believe in superstitions, although they certainly act on them, including Doc, who "was a pure scientist and incapable of superstition and yet when he came in late one night and found a line of white flowers across the doorsill he had a bad time of it" (147). The paradoxical focuses on something as small as a gopher building a perfect home that he cannot live in for lack of a mate, but the paradoxical also makes sweeping statements about the world, such as Doc's observation that the "things we admire in men, kindness and generosity, openness, honesty, understanding and feeling are the concomitants of failure in our system," and "those traits we detest, sharpness, greed, acquisitiveness, meanness, egotism and self-interest, are the traits of success" (135).

Doc, the unconventional hero of *Cannery Row*, is himself a paradox who has learned to take in larger paradoxes and, indeed, more of the whole than anyone else in the book. He is described as a man whose "face is half Christ and half satyr," a man with a "cool warm mind" who "can kill anything for need but he could not even hurt a feeling for pleasure" (29). Doc is a scientist with superstitions, a center of Row society but also "a lonely and a set-apart man," a man who loves true things but knows that sometimes it is easier to lie—to give the expected explanation—to those who cannot understand. He is a man who makes his livelihood in tide pools but is deathly afraid of even a single drop of water on his head (96). Doc also has the ability to take in the widest possible view: "His mind had no horizon—and his sympathy had no warp" (30). In *Cannery Row*, Doc embodies the paradoxical and the sweep of the unified field. He possesses the ever-expanding mind of a scientist, transcending the micro and macro, the sensual and intellectual. More than any other character in the novel, he comes closest to comprehending all—the convergence of things. Beyond Doc, this convergence of everything, the unified field, manifests itself in the novel as sunrise and sunset, and as music. The Chinese man walks in and out of the between time, the small "quiet gray period" at dawn and sunset (24). These times of convergence—peace between the daylight and nighttime boundaries—are the only times the mysterious Chinese man appears. They are periods of "magic" on the Row, when the place "seems to hang suspended out of time in a silvery light" (81). For Doc such moments can be savored at other times, for he literally tunes into the whole through music. Throughout the novel, we know Doc appreciates music of all kinds, including Gregorian chants, fugues, and concertos.

In chapter eighteen, one of the novel's most striking sections, Doc keys into the whole through music that is inside his head and around him as well. Beginning work at dawn, Doc spends the morning collecting specimens at the tide pools of La Jolla, when, at the outer barrier and before the deep, he discovers a drowned girl wedged in the rock. She presents an immediate paradox for Doc, for there is the fearful tragedy of a drowned girl, and at the same time the scene is strikingly beautiful: "On [her] face was only comfort and rest" (105). Doc's reaction is a mixture of emotion; he shivers, his heart pounds, his eyes grow moist but are "wet the way they get in the focus of great beauty" (105). Sitting on the beach, he seems to go outside himself—in place and time—for the picture of the girl's face is "set for all time" (105). As he extends into the whole, he hears music, piercing flutes from "a melody he could never remember . . . against this, a pounding surf-like wood-wind section" (105). The microcosm of his mind tunes into the macrocosm of the sea, and the tragedy of death for a moment greatly enhances Doc's life. He taps out the rhythm of the sea with his hand, while the "terrifying flute" plays in his head (106). The next line is disembodied: "The eyes were gray and the mouth smiled a little or seemed to catch its breath in ecstasy"; this is the girl or Doc or both. In this crucial scene, Doc, a man after the whole, connects to the whole— and, in Steinbeck's language, this is a moment when Doc keys into the unified field. This is a time when, as Steinbeck writes in *Sea of Cortez*, "one has a feeling of fullness, of warm wholeness, wherein every sight and object and odor and experience seems to key into a gigantic whole" (101). Such a time, when one can see "that man is related to the whole thing" is what makes "a Jesus, a St. Augustine, a St. Francis, a Roger Bacon, a Charles Darwin, and an Einstein" (*Log* 178). It also makes a Doc. Steinbeck himself came close to expressing the same view, as he refers back to Einstein, Darwin, and others: "Each of them in his own tempo and his own voice discovered and reaffirmed with astonishment the knowledge that all things are one thing . . . plankton, a shimmering phosphorescence on the sea and the spinning planets and an expanding universe, all bound together by the elastic string of time" (*Log* 179).

John Steinbeck's Environmental Stance

Steinbeck, an earth-centered writer, tended to observe things more in terms of science than ideology. However, in the 1950s and into the 1960s, Steinbeck moved toward a moralistic consideration of reality. As a result, his environmental standpoint became more overt and political. As early as *Sea of Cortez*, the author commented on our mindless exploitation of natural resources: "We in the United States have done so much to destroy our own resources, our timber, our land, our fishes, that we should be taken as a horrible example" (252). The novel *Sweet Thursday* (1954) begins by discussing the complete destruction of a sardine fishery in California. His great road-trip memoir *Travels with Charley* (1962) includes several observations of American material waste and environmental degradation, discussing the environmental stress of the West Coast and Seattle, Washington, in particular. In the speech he gave upon accepting the 1962 Nobel Prize for Literature, Steinbeck expresses fear regarding the complete destruction of all life by nuclear weapons. If these pointed observations were missed, he continues to lecture about the perils of ecological ignorance in the last book he published in his lifetime, *America and Americans* (1966). Steinbeck's alarm over the destruction of the environment is clear, the subject of discussion throughout the chapter "Americans and the Land," in which he writes:

> Our rivers are poisoned by reckless dumping of sewage and toxic industrial wastes, the air of our cities is filthy and dangerous to breathe from the belching of uncontrolled products from combustion of coal, coke, oil, and gasoline. Our towns are girdled with wreckage and the debris of our toys—our automobiles and our packaged pleasures. Through uninhibited spraying against one enemy we have destroyed the natural balances our survival requires. All these evils can and must be overcome if America and Americans are to survive. (127)

His ecological voice is certainly strident here. What other American author of this stature—let alone a best-selling author and personal friend of President Lyndon Johnson—took this position in 1966? How did John Steinbeck come to this place before so many others? His journey began with Charles Darwin. Had it not been for the principles Darwin introduced to him—notions of inductive reasoning and holism—Steinbeck's work likely would have lacked his unique applications of science to the dilemmas of humanity. He would not have been inspired to venture into areas such as physics, and he would have had no reason to venture forth as the United States' first econovelist, the first mainstream literary voice to call a halt to our foolish experiments with the environment. Dying of heart failure on December 20, 1968, Steinbeck just missed the environmental movement in America. He would have been pleased to see people heed the environmental warnings he began issuing as early as the 1930s.

Works Cited

Benson, Jackson J. *The True Adventures of John Steinbeck, Writer*. New York: Viking, 1984.

Condon, Edward, and Phillip Morse. *Quantum Mechanics*. New York: McGraw-Hill, 1929.

Darwin, Charles. *The Autobiography of Charles Darwin and Selected Letters*. 1892. Ed. Francis Darwin. New York: Dover, 1958.

_____. *On the Origin of Species* and *The Descent of Man*. 1859/1871. New York: Modern Library, 1936.

_____. *The Voyage of the Beagle*. 1839. New York: Penguin, 1988.

DeMott, Robert. *Steinbeck's Reading: A Catalogue of Books Owned and Borrowed*. New York: Garland, 1984.

Eddington, Arthur S. *The Nature of the Physical World*. 1929. Ann Arbor: U of Michigan P, 1963.

Einstein, Albert. *Relativity*, New York: Holt, 1920.

Steinbeck, John. *America and Americans*. New York: Viking, 1966.

_____. *Cannery Row*. 1945. New York: Penguin, 1986.

_____. *In Dubious Battle*. 1936. New York: Penguin, 1983.

_____. *The Grapes of Wrath*. 1939. New York: Penguin, 1976.

_____. *The Harvest Gypsies*. Ed. Charles Wollenberg. Berkeley: Heyday, 1988.

_____. *The Log from the Sea of Cortez*. 1951. New York: Penguin, 1995.

_____. "Nobel Prize Speech." 1962. *America and Americans and Selected Non-fiction*. Ed. Susan Shillinglaw and Jackson J. Benson. New York: Viking, 2002. 172–74.

_____. *Sea of Cortez: A Leisurely Journal of Travel and Research*. New York: Viking, 1941.

_____. *Sweet Thursday*. 1954. New York: Penguin, 1986.

_____. *Travels with Charley in Search of America*. 1962. New York: Library of America, 2007.

_____. *Working Days: The Journal of* The Grapes of Wrath. Ed. Robert DeMott. New York: Viking, 1989.

Robinson Jeffers, Environmental Consciousness, and the Poetics of Nature_____

David J. Rothman

> Multitude stands in my mind but I think that the ocean in the bone
>   vault is only
> The bone vault's ocean: out there is the ocean's;
> The water is the water, the cliff is the rock, come shocks and flashes
>   of reality. The mind
> Passes, the eye closes, the spirit is a passage;
> The beauty of things was born before eyes and sufficient to itself; the
>   heart-breaking beauty
> Will remain when there is no heart to break for it.
>
> —Robinson Jeffers, "Credo" (lines 10–18)

I.

One function of literary criticism is to suggest how certain writers have not only described but actually transformed our understanding of a phenomenon in such a fundamental way that we have taken it for granted ever since. It is one thing to observe that the Italian poet Petrarch was a humanist; it is another to point out that he helped to define what we now understand as the humanities. It is one thing to argue that he wrote hundreds of sonnets about love, but another to argue that they are not merely love poems, but redefinitions of what romantic love (and the sonnet itself) could be. As Gabriel Harvey—the scholar, poet, and friend of Edmund Spenser—wrote in 1593, "Petrarckes Inuention is pure Loue it selfe, and Petrarckes Elocution pure Bewty it selfe" (259). Similarly, it is one thing to argue that Shakespeare's characters are powerfully convincing and lifelike, but quite another to argue, as Harold Bloom has, that Shakespeare invented the modern notion of what it means to be a human being. Bloom argues that Shakespeare's characters are the first dramatic representations of what we think of as modern people, because their thoughts and feelings are fluid, they hold internal dialogues with themselves, their motivations are often conflicting, even self-contradictory, and they appear to have what we might call a subconscious. Their lives, like ours, are often messy and confused (as are their relationships), covering the full range of the personal to the political. Bloom argues that no one had ever expressed that before, and that Shakespeare imagined what it might mean to be a human being so well that we have come to view his vision as the natural one, even though it is an invention.

The twentieth-century California poet Robinson Jeffers is one of those artists whose contribution to our collective imagination is as large as Petrarch's was to our notions of humanism and love, Shakespeare's to our notions of personality and politics. Jeffers was the first poet—indeed, perhaps the first artist—to build his poetics on an accurate, precise understanding of the natural world as articulated in modern physics, astronomy, geology, biology, and other disciplines. He did not merely reflect that scientific knowledge; rather, he construed it in a unified cosmology, thereby transforming such knowledge from fact and theory into art. He was the first to express the pure nonanthropocentric view of reality in art, the idea that, as he puts it in "Credo," "The beauty of things was born before eyes and sufficient to itself; the heart-breaking beauty / Will remain when there is no heart to break for it." This distinctly modern vision of the natural world finds its first artistically coherent representation in Jeffers, making the subsequent development of environmental writing possible—even if Jeffers's heirs do not always share his tragic vision, spiritual inclinations, or political ideas.

II.

Jeffers is not as well known today as he once was. He had one of the most fascinating and controversial careers of any American poet. Unlike high modernists such as Ezra Pound and T. S. Eliot, he did not wear his learning on his sleeve, but, as James Karman points out in *Robinson Jeffers: Poet of California*, the emphasis on learning in his childhood home was striking. His father, William Hamilton Jeffers, was a minister in the United Presbyterian Church and an academic at several institutions in the course of his career. When Jeffers was born, his father was professor of Old Testament Literature and Exegesis at Western Theological Seminary in Pittsburgh, where he pursued scholarly work in Greek, Latin, Hebrew, Aramaic, Syriac, Arabic, Babylonian, Assyrian, German, and French. When he was young, Jeffers was sent abroad to study in several European boarding schools. By the time he was in his early teens, he could work equally well in German, English, and French. He also studied Latin and Greek. He may well have been the most widely and deeply educated of the modern poets, with serious competition only from Eliot, whose training was actually far more narrow, as Jeffers pursued a wide variety of possibilities in graduate school before trying to become a writer. After graduating from Occidental College in Pasadena at the age of seventeen, Jeffers pursued work over the next several years in comparative literature and medicine (both at the University of Southern California), as well as forestry (University of Washington). He also had extensive contact with contemporary science, particularly astrophysics, through his younger brother Hamilton, who earned a PhD in astronomy from Berkeley, was hired by the Lick Observatory in San Jose, California, in 1924, and worked at the forefront of astronomy throughout the period, including collaborating with Edwin Hubble.

In the course of his studies, Jeffers met Una Call Kuster, and she eventually left her husband, Teddy Kuster, to marry him, creating a scandal among southern Californian social circles. The couple planned to move to England, but the outbreak of WWI put an end to that plan, and the Jeffers settled in Carmel, California, living primarily on Jeffers's small inheritance. Soon after they arrived, Una gave birth to twin sons, Donnan and Garth (an earlier child, Maeve, died a few days after birth), and Jeffers set about building Tor House and its accompanying Hawk Tower, both made from local stone (the tower was an homage to Yeats, one of the few contemporary poets Jeffers admired). Jeffers also began to write more seriously, and it seems apparent that some mixture of the harsh beauty of Carmel, a profound disillusionment caused by the spectacle of the war, perhaps the death of his first child, and the labor of working on the house triggered a climactic change in his poetry.

By the mid-1920s Jeffers was already in his late thirties and remained unknown. He had published two slim volumes of traditional poetry that do not seem to foreshadow his mature work in any significant way. When he produced *Roan Stallion, Tamar, and Other Poems* in 1925, major poets and critics—such as James Rorty, Mark Van Doren, Babette Deutsch, Harriet Monroe, and others—all wrote pieces in the national press that secured his reputation for some time. Over the next dozen years Jeffers went on a tear rarely seen in the poetry world, publishing seven thick volumes, each of which included a book-length narrative poem and a number of accompanying lyrics. He also wrote a substantial number of verse dramas, though they were intended primarily to be read and few if any were performed at the time. Many of the books became both critical successes and best-sellers that went through multiple printings. During this period, Jeffers was famous in a way that few poets are today and that, given the way he is currently ignored in the academy, few people realize. The only poets with comparable reputations at the time were Edna St. Vincent Millay (also rarely given her due), Carl Sandburg, Robert Frost, and Eliot. In 1932, Jeffers was so popular that when he published *Thurso's Landing and Other Poems* a photograph of him by Edward Weston appeared on the cover of the April 4th issue of *Time* magazine. The unsigned notice for that book referred to Jeffers as an author "whom a considerable public now considers the most impressive poet the U.S. has yet produced" (Everson, "Harrowed Marrow" 63).

Beginning in the mid-1930s, Jeffers's reputation began to sink quickly. This is the period when he received some of the most vicious reviews in the history of American poetry from some of the most prominent critics, many of them poets themselves: Yvor Winters,

Robert Fitzgerald, Kenneth Rexroth, Louise Bogan, and many others, including even some of his early supporters. These attacks have continued up to the present, notably in Helen Vendler's extraordinarily hostile 1988 review of the Jeffers anthology *Rock and Hawk*, edited by Robert Hass. Other groups, notably the New Critics, pretended Jeffers did not exist, especially when they were busy designing curricula in the image of Eliot and Pound. The causes for the hostility had much to do with Jeffers's continuing emphasis on social detachment and advocacy of isolationism during WWII, and likewise the prevailing opinion that these views were inappropriate during a time when many artists believed that art should be engaged directly with the issues of the day. There was also the judgment by some that Jeffers's poems were motivated by nihilistic ideas, and the aesthetic judgment that his poems were "hysterical" (a charge that seems to have been leveled first by Yvor Winters) and lacking in erudition, complexity, and craft.[1]

Although Jeffers published work of high quality in his later life (his version of Euripides's *Medea* became a Broadway hit after WWII), when he died in 1962 his poetic and critical foes seemed to have won the day, and he was all but ignored by many poets, critics, and scholars especially. Nevertheless, he has always somehow attracted readers, even when his books were not easily available. Those who understood the revolutionary quality of his approach to the natural world have always admired him. Today several famous lyrics (such as "Shine, Perishing Republic" and "The Purse-Seine") still appear in anthologies, and most who care about modern poetry have probably read at least "Roan Stallion." Yet, outside academic circles, Jeffers retains profound influence on a wide range of poets, demonstrating how much less influence such institutions have than those who work in them might imagine. Over the last fifty years, poets as diverse as William Everson, Czeslaw Milosz, and Horace Gregory have cited Jeffers's effect on them, and more recently Mark Jarman, Dave Mason, Dana Gioia, Robert McDowell, and many others have done the same. Jeffers's poetry also continues to sell well. In 2001, Stanford University Press published the final volume in

its five-volume *Collected Poetry of Robinson Jeffers*, the first fully annotated collection, edited by Tim Hunt and collecting all Jeffers's work
for the first time (including his prose). Stanford has also published a
substantial *Selected Poetry* (1938), edited by Hunt, and a shorter one,
The Wild God of the World (2003), edited by Albert Gelpi, both of
which are in print and continue to sell well. James Karman, after producing the best biography of Jeffers to date, is in the process of editing
the complete letters, of which one volume appeared in 2009, with two
more to follow. What all of this means is that for the first time since his
death almost fifty years ago, the public and the scholarly community
will soon see Jeffers's entire oeuvre.[2]

III.

Whenever we look closely enough at the past, no century appears particularly calm, but the twentieth century was particularly violent. In
an age characterized, in poetry, by the sublime disorder and spiritual
chaos of Eliot's *The Waste Land* (1922), Jeffers refused the ruptures
of modernism and founded a heretical, personal faith on the basis of
what he dubbed *inhumanism*, a mixture of postmonotheistic pantheism, scientific knowledge, and close attention to the fierce beauty of
nature. In 1948, in the preface to *The Double Axe and Other Poems*
(1977), he defined this "philosophical attitude" as "a shifting of emphasis and significance from man to not-man; the rejection of human
solipsism and recognition of the transhuman magnificence" (428). For
Jeffers, the natural world was not merely a subject for study or art; it
was a transcendent reality that grounded his creativity. As he wrote in
"The Answer":

> Integrity is wholeness, the greatest beauty is
> Organic wholeness, the wholeness of life and things, the divine
>   beauty of the universe. Love that, not man
> Apart from that, or else you will share man's pitiful confusions, or
>   drown in despair when his days darken. (lines 14–18)

Jeffers is often accused of misanthropy for his views, and in the passage above he at first appears to be denouncing human beings and encouraging us to "Love that [the divine beauty of the universe], not man," but of course Jeffers quickly corrects himself to encourage us to "Love that, not man / Apart from that," a vision that reimagines human beings in a new way—where we are far smaller than we used to imagine.

Jeffers's explicit diminution of man's place in the cosmos is crucial to our understanding of how and why he is one of the preeminent artists of environmentalism, specifically of the strain of environmentalism that takes up concepts of nature and scientific understanding of nature in the history of art. Other writers before Jeffers had imagined what we now call "nature" quite powerfully, but before the romantics the boundary between physical nature and other phenomena was nowhere near as clear as we often consider it. As political theorist Leo Strauss and others have argued, classical notions of political order were often explicitly tied to notions of appropriate human governance in light of ideas evident in the natural, divine, and supernatural worlds, with high levels of fluidity among them. Greeks such as Hesiod and Homer, and Romans such as Ovid, Virgil, and Lucretius, wrote in such a way that their entire poetic project depends on a vision of how the natural world functions. This vision is subject to a pagan supernaturalism in Hesiod, Homer, Ovid, and Virgil, and it is notably antisupernatural in the Epicurean Lucretius, who developed the idea of the atom to describe how matter works. The natural and divine worlds of Dante and Milton may not be simultaneously apprehensible, but they are contiguous.

Shakespeare was as important in articulating early modern ideas of natural order as he was in imagining the modern personality. As Hamlet's mother Gertrude says, trying to console him about his father's death, "All that lives must die, / Passing through nature to eternity" (*Hamlet* 1.2.72–73). One difference to note here regarding post-Einsteinian science is that "nature" and "eternity" are not the same;

eternity is something that nature touches but in which it plays no part, a distinction that relativity theory, quantum mechanics, and string theory now render more difficult to sustain. Later in the play, when Hamlet is instructing the players how to deliver their lines in the scene that he hopes will reveal Claudius as his father's murderer, there is another revealing use of the word:

> Be not too tame neither, but let your own discretion be your tutor: suit the action to the word, the word to the action; with this special observance, that you o'erstep not the modesty of nature: for any thing so overdone is from the purpose of playing, whose end, both at the first and now, was and is, to hold, as 'twere, the mirror up to nature. (3.2.17–23)

The notion of art imitating nature is, of course, as ancient as criticism and appears in Plato and Aristotle. In Hamlet's words the distinction is quite firm: Art and artifice are not part of nature (which here means human nature, not the world of physical matter), but separate from it, reflecting it. Human beings are, again, contiguous with the world of phenomena yet separate from it at the same time.

Romantic poets such as Goethe, Wordsworth, and Shelley reimagined the natural world more broadly, and as more psychologically internal and external. In concert with scientific advancement, they expanded the understanding of nature to account for more phenomena than the ancients or the Renaissance humanists. In a famous passage from "Tintern Abbey," Wordsworth uses the term as we might use it today in a colloquial sense, finding in the natural world some of that very eternity that Shakespeare presented as beyond nature, and placing it far closer to the core of his art than Hamlet would have it for the players. When speaking of what he, as an adult, finds in the natural world, Wordsworth describes

> a sense sublime
> Of something far more deeply interfused,
> Whose dwelling is the light of setting suns,
> And the round ocean and the living air,
> And the blue sky, and in the mind of man;
> A motion and a spirit, that impels
> All thinking things, all objects of all thought,
> And rolls through all things. (lines 95–102)

Wordsworth's vision of physical nature is more capacious than Shakespeare's, holding greater dominion in the universe. It does not stop at the edge of eternity—for eternity is part of "all things"—nor does it stop at the gateway of art, which is surely part of "all objects of all thought." Wordsworth finds nature "sublime" not only in its "motion," but also in its "spirit," a spirit that "impels" him as it does "all thinking things." Nature is still animated by something divine that appears to be separate from it, and that spirit still finds its noblest expression in human perception of it. But nature and spirit are now "far more deeply interfused" than in earlier literature, in which whatever realm transcends the natural world remains far greater.

The limited selections presented here suggest a broad generalization: From antiquity through the early modern period, human beings may have understood the power of the world outside themselves, but they always conceived of it in anthropomorphic terms. While the Copernican revolution, Lyell's demonstration of geological time, and Darwinian evolution forced serious artists and thinkers to reconceptualize and diminish the role of human will and consciousness in the larger scheme of nature, the human role remained dominant.

In the 125 years between the publication of "Tintern Abbey" in 1798 and when Jeffers began to publish his mature work ("Credo" was probably written in 1925), our knowledge of the physical world advanced in an unprecedented way. By the time Jeffers was writing, Einstein and others had been publishing papers on special and general relativity for several decades, and the theories were recognized by the well-educated general public. Also, beginning in the 1910s, several astronomers began to argue that some celestial objects believed to be nebulae up to that point (especially the Andromeda nebula) were in fact "island universes" or external galaxies. This debate was considered to be settled by Edwin Hubble in 1924–1925, when he was able to prove conclusively that Andromeda and other astral objects included what are known as Cepheid variable stars and were therefore not Milky Way nebulae but external galaxies. The importance of this discovery can hardly be overstated, as it transformed our notions of space, suggesting that the known universe was unimaginably larger than had been previously thought.

IV.

The new scientific material discussed above quickly found its way into Jeffers's work, not only because of his own awareness, but perhaps also because his brother Hamilton was involved with some of it. At a time when little if any of the contemporary scientific revolution was appearing in art, Jeffers not only seemed to be familiar with the material as it was published, but completely integrated it into his poetics, presenting a cosmology unheralded in the history of human imagination. Scientific understanding was essential in the emergence of Jeffers's mature poetic voice in the 1920s. And, as the physicist Ron Olowin has pointed out in a number of unpublished papers, Jeffers's facts are always accurate.

In one of the first examples of Jeffers's mature poetry, "Roan Stallion," science is at the heart of the poem's vision. In this midlength narrative from 1925, a woman named California who is in an abusive marriage has fallen in love with a stallion that her husband Johnny won in a poker game. Perhaps because her emotional misery is so intense, perhaps partly because she is mentally ill, California comes to believe the stallion is a god—to the point that she even imagines making love to it. As this happens in her mind, Jeffers suddenly turns away from his narrative and directly addresses the reader in the first of several such apostrophes:

> Humanity is the start of the
>   race; I say
> Humanity is the mould to break away from, the crust to break
>   through, the coal to break into fire,
> The atom to be split.
>   Tragedy that breaks man's face and a white fire
>   flies out of it; vision that fools him
> Out of his limits, desire that fools him out of his limits, unnatural
>   crime, inhuman science,
> Slit eyes in the mask; wild loves that leap over the walls of nature, the
>   wild fence-vaulter science,
> Useless intelligence of far stars, dim knowledge of the spinning
>   demons that make an atom,
> These break, these pierce, these deify, praising their God shrilly with
>   fierce voices: not in a man's shape
> He approves the praise, he that walks lightning-naked on the Pacific,
>   that laces the suns with planets,
> The heart of the atom with electrons: what is humanity in this
>   cosmos? For him the last
> Least taint of a trace in the dregs of the solution; for itself, the mould
>   to break away from, the coal
> To break into fire, the atom to be split. (lines 314–35)

Critics often focus on this passage as a philosophical or prophetic commentary on humanity, which can obscure the fact that the poem is first and foremost an ars poetica, its subject both grammatically and rhetorically a definition, or a redefinition, of "tragedy." At the same time Jeffers's project in "Roan Stallion" is not merely to exemplify the criteria for tragedy from Aristotle's *Poetics* in modern guise, but to transform them and rejuvenate them, fusing them with utterly accurate and contemporary science, psychology, philosophy, and aesthetics. One need not look far, for example, to find plentiful material to begin a fruitful discussion about Jeffers's ideas of *hamartia* (generally translated as "tragic flaw")[3] and *hubris* (generally translated as "blind arrogance"): "vision that fools him / Out of his limits, desire that fools him out of his limits, unnatural crime, inhuman science, / Slit eyes in the mask."

Jeffers was deeply aware that this resonates with Aristotle's characterization of tragic heroes in *The Poetics*, even though California may not be an exalted character who falls. Despite her humble origins, however, even her name indicates that she stands in for all of us. For Jeffers, our arrogance proceeds simply from being conscious and desiring something as simple as change for the better in our lives, something animals (such as the stallion) cannot imagine. The "slit eyes in the mask" are thus not only the literal holes in the masks of classical tragic actors, but also metaphorical apertures through which burn Jeffers's apocalyptic visions of the modern world: Einsteinian relativity, Freudian psychology, contemporary politics, nuclear explosions, bestial perversion, narcissistic madness, Nietzschean philosophy and aesthetics, Spenglerian social theory, and more. Jeffers touches on the same subject matter as Eliot and Pound, but his center holds; it is this quality that drove some of his critics wild, as they had come to believe it was not possible to represent the modern world in such a coherent manner, even if that coherence were tragic. His knowledge is modern, as is his language, but he integrates the two rather than shoring fragments against his ruins.

In terms of environmental consciousness, the crucial point is Jeffers's fusion of modern science and his tragic poetics. Humanity is not separate from nature but identical with it, right down to its accurately described atoms. There is no "spirit" brooding outside of it. Classical poetics fuses with the tradition of atomistic science, from Lucretius to Einstein, in an unheralded representation of reality. Divinity and the spirit are still present but are now unified with all other elements in a single, fierce creation, in which humanity is unimaginably small—"the last / Least taint of a trace in the dregs of the solution." As Frederic Carpenter has put it when discussing the same passage, "Man ceases to exist as an autonomous human individual, independent of nature or of God" (137). At the same time, and as Carpenter points out, Jeffers's poetry is paradoxical, because every poem that proclaims the insignificance of human beings in a postrelativity, post-Andromeda universe is nonetheless still about human beings, or at least one human being: Jeffers. The stage on which humans act, however, has been recalibrated in a way that could not have been imagined before. Jeffers himself reiterated his position again and again that "mankind is neither central nor important in the universe," and that to think so is "pathetic and ridiculous."[4]

Jeffers's scientifically based view of man's insignificance is a new cosmology, one that undergirds a new poetics, one that may seem utterly familiar to us now, where even the most popular of popular films encourages us to imagine it as taking place "a long time ago, in a galaxy far, far away." Yet in 1925 the knowledge of such vast time, space, and energy offered a radical departure in terms of how to view human life and art, especially in the way this knowledge transformed scientific understanding with tragic consciousness. The work still has the power to shock, for Jeffers's creation is not gentle or benign, and goes far beyond Tennyson's famous "nature red in tooth and claw," as described in *In Memoriam*—published in 1849, and one of the first literary works influenced by the theory of evolution. In light of that idea, Tennyson was troubled by the possibility of an indifferent God. In section fifty-five of the poem, Tennyson poses the question of whether, given new developments in biology, God and Nature must oppose each other:

> Are God and Nature then at strife,
> That Nature lends such evil dreams?
> So careful of the type she seems,
> So careless of the single life;

That I, considering everywhere
Her secret meaning in her deeds,
And finding that of fifty seeds
She often brings but one to bear,

I falter where I firmly trod,
And falling with my weight of cares
Upon the great world's altar-stairs
That slope thro' darkness up to God,

I stretch lame hands of faith, and grope,
And gather dust and chaff, and call
To what I feel is Lord of all,
And faintly trust the larger hope. (lines 5–20)

The difference between Jeffers and Tennyson is that Jeffers has no such qualms. For him, the universe is a fierce, fiery, and tragic natural order that is already the incarnation of God as a whole. Evolution and modern astrophysics in no way compromise his vision of God, but rather affirm it. His God is the totality of creation itself and is indifferent to man except insofar as man is one tiny part of that larger creation. All of terrestrial biology is merely a blip on a larger astrophysical screen, which is itself subject to greater forces.

In "The Ocean's Tribute," a lyric from the late 1950s only published posthumously, Jeffers describes seeing a pod of whales off the Carmel coast whose spouts are caught in the gleam of the setting sun:

Yesterday's sundown was very beautiful—I know it is out of fashion
   to say so, I think we are fools
To turn from the superhuman beauty of the world and dredge our own
   minds—it built itself up with ceremony
From the ocean horizon, smoked amber and tender green, pink and
   purple and vermilion, great ranks

Of purple cloud, and the pink rose-petals over all and through all; but
   the ocean itself, cold slate-color,
Refused the glory. Then I saw a pink fountain come up from it,
A whale-spout; there were ten or twelve whales quite near the deep
   shore, playing together, nuzzling each other,
Plunging and rising, lifting luminous pink pillars from the flat ocean
   to the flaming sky. (lines 1–13)

Jeffers here sounds a bit like Gerard Manley Hopkins in "The Wind-
hover," where the poet first accuses himself of overweening pride for
taking joy in the beauty of the small falcon riding the wind, then realizes that such admiration is acceptable to God as long as he also realizes
that the creation is just as holy even in something as low as "blue-bleak
embers" that "fall, gall themselves, and gash gold-vermilion." Jeffers's
poem is also an epiphany—literally "a shining forth of light"—but one
which requires no external deity as Hopkins does, for the light is itself
a manifestation of "the superhuman beauty of the world." At the same
time, like Hopkins, Jeffers is suspicious of his own apprehension of
such beauty, for perhaps it seems too gentle and sweet to him to be
real, given what appears to be the indifference of creation at large. He
initially resists such beauty as something that may be merely the creation of his own mind, an exaggeration of one property of reality at the
expense of the truth, which is more like the fire of the "flaming sky"
with which he ends. It is the aside near the beginning of the poem—
the moment where language turns on itself—that transforms this short
lyric from mere nature poetry into poetry, for the remark reveals a human mind fully engaged in contemplating the natural world and what
it means to be conscious and self-conscious in it. As Jeffers wrote in
an earlier lyric from 1930, "The Place for No Story," "No imaginable
/ Human presence here could do anything / but dilute the lonely self-
watchful passion" (lines 9–11). And yet, there is at least one human
presence here: the one who makes the observations, and without whom
we would not be able to contemplate such ideas in the first place. This

compelling, persuasive paradox is Jeffers's great contribution to environmental consciousness, indeed one of its foundational gestures—a negative capability that makes the entire conversation possible.

Environmentalism and environmental writing are human artifacts, and therefore filled with contradiction. On the one hand there is the move to regard human beings as part of nature, but on the other, an earnest attempt to discredit certain human activities as damaging to nature. Yet how can these activities contradict nature if everything that human beings do is by definition part of nature? On the one hand is skepticism of the destruction that technology has wrought, and on the other is the call for better technology. On the one hand, we may agree with Thoreau's notion in "Walking" that "in Wildness is the preservation of the world" (613), but on the other hand, to think of "Wildness" as something that preserves anything is already a contradiction: How might a preservation of wildness still be wild?

In "Roan Stallion," "The Place for No Story," "The Ocean's Tribute," and hundreds of other poems, Jeffers did not merely contribute to the complex conversation about what nature is, and what our relationship with nature might be. In his poetic conception of the universe, he gave utterance to the tangled, contradictory realities of what it meant to be conscious during his century's particular vision of time and space. His vision of the natural world maps out, as Edward Abbey understood it, both the bedrock and the paradoxes of modern environmental thinking. Among Jeffers's many achievements, his articulation of modern environmental thinking and poetics may eventually come to take pride of place. For just as Petrarch first described our notion of romantic love, and just as Shakespeare first described our personalities, so has the poetry of Robinson Jeffers articulated a powerful vision of the natural universe that we envision ourselves inhabiting, both literally and imaginatively.

Notes

1. Many of the reviews that trace responses to Jeffers's work can be found in S. S. Alberts, *A Bibliography of the Works of Robinson Jeffers* (1933); Alex A. Vardamis, *The Critical Reputation of Robinson Jeffers* (1972); and James Karman, *Critical Essays on Robinson Jeffers* (1990). There is also an online bibliography at www.robinsonjeffersassociation.com.

2. The question remains of what specific import Jeffers's scientific and tragic poetics has for the development of environmental consciousness. Jeffers is frequently held out as a harbinger of various ecological movements, especially deep ecology, through his obvious influence on figures such as Edward Abbey (whose *Desert Solitaire* quotes and responds to Jeffers dozens of times), Arne Naess, and many others. But Jeffers is, if anything, more fierce and far more politically detached or neutral than most of his followers. He is not a reformer. In much of his work, including the dramas, narratives, and lyric poems, nature burns with a ferocious, obliterating power that the poet asserts will eventually destroy everything in its path, even itself, and that is as it should be. At the same time, many have confused Jeffers's tragic vision of the universe and man's role in it for prophetic sermonizing, or pure misanthropy, rather than seeing it for what it is—poetry. William Everson practically ties himself in knots to insist that understanding Jeffers's poetics requires "a religious solution" (*Cawdor and Medea* xxi) and he therefore gives short shrift to both classical poetics and science. Without denying the crucial importance of Jeffers's religious background, or the profound spiritual intentions and implications of his art, this does a disservice to Jeffers. It is time to see him more clearly for what he was despite his often didactic and prophetic tone: a poet, not a religious figure. For it is as a poet—a poet often arguing with himself—that Jeffers returns us again and again to the world as we live in it, even if that life is now to be understood in a new way, as one tiny element of consciousness in a vast cosmos.

3. *Hamartia* does not have one clear or obvious meaning in English. In its various contexts it suggests a major mistake and gives a sense ranging from a profound error in judgment to sinfulness.

4. These comments come from the original, unpublished version of Jeffers's preface to *The Double Axe* (1947), *The Selected Poetry of Robinson Jeffers*, 719–20.

Works Cited

Abbey, Edward. *Desert Solitaire: A Season in the Wilderness*. 1968. New York: Simon, 1990.

Alberts, S. S. *A Bibliography of the Works of Robinson Jeffers*. New York: Random House, 1933.

Aristotle. *Poetics*. Trans. S. H. Butcher. 1955. *Critical Theory since Plato*. Ed. Hazard Adams. New York: Harcourt Brace Jovanovich, 1971. 47-66.

Bloom Harold. *Shakespeare: The Invention of the Human.* New York: Riverhead, 1998.

Carpenter, Frederic I. *Robinson Jeffers.* New Haven: College and University, 1962.

Everson, William. "Harrowed Marrow." *Time,* 4 Apr. 1932: 63–64.

_____. Introduction. *Cawdor and Medea.* By Robinson Jeffers. New York: New Directions, 1970. vii–xxx.

Harvey, Gabriel. "From *Pierce's Supererogation* and *A New Letter of Notable Contents.*" *Elizabethan Critical Essays.* Ed. G. Gregory Smith. Vol. 2. London: Oxford UP, 1904. 245–84.

Home page. *Robinson Jeffers Association.* Robinson Jefferson Association, n.d. Web. 5 Sept. 2011.

Hubble, E. "Extra-galactic Nebulae." *Astrophysical Journal* 64 (1926): 321–69.

_____. "NGC6822, A Remote Stellar System." *Astrophysical Journal* 62 (1925): 409–433.

_____. "Photographic Investigations of Giant Nebulae." *Publications of Yerkes Observatory* 4 (1920): 69–85.

_____. "A Spiral Nebula as a Stellar System, Messier 31." *Astrophysical Journal* 69 (1929): 103–58.

_____. "A Spiral Nebula as a Stellar System, Messier 33." *Astrophysical Journal* 63 (1926): 236–74.

Jeffers, Robinson. *The Collected Letters of Robinson Jeffers, with Selected Letters of Una Jeffers,* 1890–1930. Ed. James Karman. Vol. 1. Palo Alto: Stanford UP, 2009.

_____. *The Collected Poetry of Robinson Jeffers.* Ed. Tim Hunt. 5 vols. Stanford: Stanford UP, 1988–2001.

_____. Preface, *The Double Axe and Other Poems. Collected Poetry of Robinson Jeffers.* Ed. Tim Hunt. Vol. 4. Stanford: Stanford UP, 2000. 428.

_____. *Rock and Hawk: A Selection of Shorter Poems by Robinson Jeffers.* Ed. Robert Hass. New York: Random, 1987.

_____. *The Selected Poetry of Robinson Jeffers.* 5 vols. Ed. Tim Hunt. Stanford: Stanford UP, 2001.

_____. *The Wild God of the World: An Anthology of Robinson Jeffers.* Ed. Albert Gelpi. Stanford: Stanford UP, 2003.

Karman, James, ed. *Critical Essays on Robinson Jeffers.* Boston: G. K. Hall, 1990.

_____. *Robinson Jeffers: Poet of California.* Brownsville: Story Line, 1995.

Olowin, Ron. Unpublished personal messages. 2005–2011.

Rothman, David J. "'I'm a humanist': The Poetic Past in *Desert Solitaire.*" *The Coyote in the Maze: Ed Abbey in a World of Words.* Ed. Peter Quigley. Salt Lake City: U of Utah P, 1998. 47–73.

Shakespeare, William. *Hamlet. The Riverside Shakespeare.* 2nd ed. Ed. G. Blakemore Evans, J. J. M. Tobin, et al. Boston: Houghton, 1997. 1183–245.

Strauss, Leo. *Natural Right and History.* Chicago: U of Chicago P, 1999.

Tennyson, Alfred. "In Memoriam." *A Collection of Poems by Alfred Tennyson.* Garden City: International Collectors Library, 1972. 318–422.

Thoreau, Henry David. "Walking." *Walden and Other Writings.* Ed. Brooks Atkinson. 1937. New York: Random, 1950. 597–632.

Vardamis, Alex A. *The Critical Reputation of Robinson Jeffers: A Bibliographical Study*. Hamden: Archon, 1972.

Vendler, Helen. "Huge Pits of Darkness, High Peaks of Light." *Robinson Jeffers Newsletter* 77 (1990): 13–22.

Wordsworth, William. "Lines Composed a Few Miles above Tintern Abbey." *The Poems*. Ed. John O. Hayden. 2 vols. London: Penguin, 1977. 357.

"Call me a ranger": Edward Abbey and the Exploratory Voice of *Desert Solitaire*[1]

David Copland Morris

Edward Abbey disliked the label "nature writer," but that is how his classic *Desert Solitaire: A Season in the Wilderness* (1968) is often shelved in the bookstores. He once wrote, "Much as I admire the work of Thoreau, Muir, Leopold, Beston, Krutch, Eiseley and others, I have not tried to write in their tradition. I don't know how. I've done plenty of plain living, out of necessity, but don't know how to maintain a constant level of high thinking" (*Journey Home* vii). I suspect that Abbey's fiercely independent soul recoiled from being grouped with writers whose names carried connotations of earnestness, reverence, and perhaps even piety: "Our nature writers are such a sober, solemn, misty-eyed lot. Rhapsody, except in minute doses, is always hard to swallow" (Introduction xi).

Despite the author's protests, I would argue that in *Desert Solitaire* Abbey is indeed a nature writer; and his dominant mode is earnest, even pious (though not in the self-righteous sense of the word), toward the overwhelming, soul-filling value he finds in nonhuman nature. He shares many nature writers' resistance to the nihilism that pervades so much of modern life and literature. In *Walden* (1854), Thoreau stated that "we are enabled to apprehend at all what is sublime and noble only by the perpetual instilling and drenching of the reality which surrounds us" (399), claiming shortly afterward that "be it life or death, we crave only reality" (400). Abbey echoes Thoreau more than a century later in *Desert Solitaire*: "I am here not only to evade for a while the clamor and filth and confusion of the cultural apparatus but also to confront, immediately and directly if it's possible, the bare bones of existence, the elemental and fundamental, the bedrock that sustains us" (6).[2] In addition to sharing this outward-looking focus on the natural world, Abbey constructs, like many nature writers, a powerful critique of the anthropocentrism—or the overweening human pride—that many believe are central causes of the environmental crisis.

While he is a genuine nature writer, Abbey is unusual among his ancestors and contemporaries of the genre in complicating his celebration of nature with provocative irony. He ultimately supports a celebratory vision of the western landscape in the novel by skillfully interweaving the voice of the irreverent ironist with that of the earnest rhapsodist. In addition to containing powerful Thoreauvian genes, Abbey's writerly DNA exhibits strong traces of Mark Twain. Two twenty-first-century nature writers influenced in turn by Abbey's complex voice—including his use of humor and his provocative, irreverent tendencies—are David Gessner (see the 2004 essay collection *Sick of Nature*) and Jordan Fisher Smith (in the 2005 book *Nature Noir: A Park Ranger's Patrol in the Sierra*). This ironical strain challenges the reverential vision by anticipating and expressing the secular doubt permeating the postmodern cultural context in which Abbey and his readers lived. Abbey's skeptical voice toughens and tempers *Desert Solitaire*'s ultimately celebratory message.

Whether one looks back toward writers like Muir and Jeffers, or at Abbey's contemporaries such as Lopez, Eiseley, and Dillard, one finds a reverential attitude toward wild nature. But none of these writers satirizes or complicates his or her own reverent voice like Abbey. True, there is satire and wit in all of them, but they approach their subjects with a nearly undiluted moral sincerity and a corresponding unity of tone. While they all are extremely compelling writers, none has access to the comic energy that gives *Desert Solitaire*'s environmental message its special force.

I find it helpful to place Abbey specifically (albeit impressionistically) within the context of these major literary stylists, who share essential features of his environmentalist worldview. Muir's almost superhuman exuberance in wild places never seems to flag, and he can be exhausting for the reader who finds him at times too insistent; remember Muir's friend Jerome Fay, marooned with the author one miserable and lonely night in an awesome snowstorm on Mt. Shasta. Both nearly died. Muir had overestimated Fay's mountaineering abilities in the same way he sometimes overestimated his reader's ability to sustain a sense of wonder equal to his own.

Robinson Jeffers's fierce, even sublime, pantheism fuses with his bitter misanthropy to form a voice as bracing as a salt wind off the cold Pacific. But sometimes, in reading Jeffers, I long for a modulating tone, a voice of human dimension. Yes, the banishment of human compassion from Jeffers's verse helps give it its distinctive power. Nevertheless, how welcome it is after reading Jeffers's work to come across a little poem like the following:

> OCTOBER WEEK-END
> It is autumn still, but at three in the morning
> All the magnificent wonders of midwinter midnight, blue dog-star
> Orion, red Aldebaran, the ermine-fur Pleiades,
> Parading above the gable of the house. Their music is their shining,
> And the house beats like a heart with dance-music
> Because our boys have grown to the age when girls are their music.
> There is wind in the trees, and the gray ocean's
> Music on the rock. I am warming my blood with starlight, not with
>   girls' eyes,
> But really the night is quite mad with music. (lines 1–10)

In these lines, Jeffers plays with, almost teases, his own dominant attitude and mood; the result is immensely appealing, like watching a lioness gently lick her cub. It may be revealing, though, that Jeffers left the poem out of his *Selected Poetry*. Did he see it as a moment of weakness, a deviation from his real work?

Abbey was profoundly influenced by Jeffers's poetry, as David J. Rothman reveals in his discussion of "the poetic past in *Desert Solitaire*" in Peter Quigley's 1998 collection *Coyote in the Maze: Tracking Edward Abbey in a World of Words*, which focuses especially on the echoes of Jeffers in Abbey's book. A case could be made, in fact, that Jeffers is the strongest influence on *Desert Solitaire*, stronger even than Thoreau. Abbey quotes Jeffers several times, and there are many more intertextual interpolations apparent to those who know the poet's work well. Indeed, Jeffers's *inhumanism* is like a steel reinforcing rod in the structure of Abbey's thought. Yet Abbey says in a late essay, "Like others, I admire Jeffers but I do not love him. He was not a wholly lovable man; not in his poetry: too grim, humorless, genuinely misanthropic, his entrails consumed by some secret bitterness. He told the truth in his work and nothing but the truth (a rare thing in poetry) but did not tell the whole truth" (*One Life* 72). After brooding for an hour during a pilgrimage to Jeffers's house in Carmel, California, Abbey says, "I feel the need for a different kind of outlook. I buckle myself into my motorcar and bear south again for the Big Sur coast. For Partington Ridge. For the spirit of Henry Miller" (*One Life* 73). In this statement is a clue to Abbey's own work, for he somehow fuses Jeffers and Miller in his own writing. This mixture is a major accomplishment, for while these writers are both profoundly Dionysian, they represent opposite poles within that sensibility. Unlike Jeffers, Miller is definitely not an inhumanist in temperament.

Though Abbey shares his Jeffersian inhumanism with Loren Eiseley, it would be hard to imagine two writers who sound more different than Abbey and Eiseley.[3] There is little of Henry Miller in the melancholy anthropologist. Eiseley's half-love for easeful death can soothe and captivate a reader, but one longs sometimes for the sound of brass to break through his mellow woodwind ensemble. And even while admiring the stoical strength of Eiseley's voice, one wishes occasionally that a vulgar cry of protest would wrench itself from the text. There is a beautiful modesty and sincerity in such volumes as *The Immense Journey* (1957) and *All the Strange Hours* (1975), but there is also something of the cleric, something repressed and at times even muffled; one finds nothing of this sort in Abbey.

What Barry Lopez says in his piece "Meeting Ed Abbey" is instructive: "Writers, in my experience, can be courteous toward each other to a fault, especially in private; but they inhabit different and private universes, and the will to remain in them is iron" (63). Lopez believes, however, that he and Abbey share "some unspoken sense of an opposition to a threat, a definition of which we largely agree upon" (64). What separates them is style and voice. Lopez's strength arises from beautiful modulation of tone in the middle register, a quiet and unforced sense of the dignity in his own character and in the unmolested natural world. His power is that of understatement, restrained passion. Abbey seldom writes in that middle register—what he feels, his essential passion, is given free rein.

Abbey has a problem with dignity; he is not at all reluctant to play the buffoon, the tenderfoot, the butt of the joke. The low comedy in his work (sexual and self-referential puns, mockery of tourists, etc.) places his flights of lyricism and caustic social criticism in a uniquely effective context. The comic context suggests that to experience a reverence for nature one does not have to be—what is the word?—as "decorous," as "genteel," as "distinguished" as the personae of Lopez and Eiseley. Abbey is in fact distinguished, but the word doesn't suit him at all. One cannot imagine a banquet host introducing Abbey as "our distinguished speaker," but the phrase would fit Lopez and Eiseley quite well. Also, I can hardly imagine Lopez mentioning Louis-Ferdinand Céline as one of his favorite writers, yet the near-insane Frenchman is one of Abbey's literary heroes. Still, in spirit Abbey remains closer to Lopez's reverence than Céline's nihilism. Ann Ronald—whose *The New West of Edward Abbey* (1982) was the first book-length study of Abbey when its first edition appeared—goes so far as to highlight the distinction between the author Edward Abbey and the narrator "Ed" in *Desert Solitaire*, even though the book purports to be nonfiction: "Viscosity," or resistance, Ronald claims, "awaits those who innocently believe the author is also the main character" (67). The playful, picaresque narrator may tilt toward Céline, while the more reserved, dignified author, before his death in 1989, more closely resembled the likes of Lopez and Eiseley.

And finally, as for Annie Dillard, Abbey said that though he generally admired her and recognized her power as a stylist, her prose touches the sublimely reverent note too frequently for his taste. Describing himself, Abbey says, "Some itch in the lower parts is always dragging me back to mundane earth among all you other denominators in the howling wilderness of American life" (*Journey Home* vii). You can hear some more of the sentimental good ol' boy, and also a more disagreeable sexism, in the following statement, from which I have taken the title of my article:

> I'll never make it as a naturalist. If a label is required say that I am one who loves unfenced country. The open range. Call me a ranger. Though I've hardly earned the title I claim it anyway. The only higher honor I've ever heard of is to be called a man. So much for the mantle and britches of Thoreau and Muir. Let Annie Dillard wear them now. (*Journey Home* xiii)

There seems to be a somewhat pejorative linking here of nature writing and effeminacy. I would argue that, when a writer pursues the sublime as fearlessly and often successfully as Dillard, she deserves the awe that she inspires in more than a few readers. In the view of many, an essay like Dillard's "Total Eclipse" is as successful as it is audacious in its sustained evocation of the sublime. In reading some of Abbey's comments on Dillard, it occurs to me that he recognizes in her his strongest competitor as a stylist. She even does things he cannot. For example, the mysterious intensity of many passages in Dillard's *Pilgrim at Tinker Creek* (1974) or *Teaching a Stone to Talk* (1982) is beyond Abbey's stylistic range. But Abbey's suspicion that nature writers (including Dillard) lack on the whole a certain leavening vulgarity—and that this lack constitutes some kind of limitation—seems well taken (David Gessner seems to be carrying a twenty-first-century banner in support of a new earthy vulgarity in nature writing). In my experience, a number of readers who connect with Abbey fail to be emotionally stirred by Thoreau, Muir, Eiseley, Lopez, or Dillard—perhaps because they find them too rarified in some way.

Abbey's multitoned quality causes him to stand out among modern environmental writers, although certain contemporary authors, such as the biologist-poet Sandra Steingraber, have demonstrated their own special blends of humor, self-reflection, and urgent social critique in recent years (see such books as *Having Faith*, 2003). The polyphonic voice of *Desert Solitaire* makes it difficult for opponents to identify and attack the ideological center of Abbey's polemical discourse; the multiple voices help refract and undermine the resistance of the skeptical reader. In *Desert Solitaire*, Abbey's celebratory tone bonds to an ironic one, demonstrating the problematic status of a naively reverent attitude in the postmodern world and enabling this particular book to become an alloy of distinctive strength.

I discern several kinds of voices in *Desert Solitaire* and would label them satirist, environmental advocate, lyricist, philosopher, scholar, buffoon, drunk, naturalist, and storyteller. Biographer James M. Cahalan explores Abbey's multifaceted personality in detail in *Edward Abbey: A Life* (2001), and in doing so shows the unusual range of Abbey's literary and political voices. Sometimes the voices exist in whole passages in pure forms, and sometimes they are fused in intriguing hybrids. But there is a mercurial quality to Abbey that makes him hard to pin down, a certain self-reflexiveness and doubleness. Not only are there multiple voices within the book as a whole, but within specific passages that seem, on the surface, to have a relatively pure voice there is often a vibrant instability. Here, for example, is a passage in which the satirist seems to predominate:

> We need more predators. The sheepmen complain, it is true, that the coyotes eat some of their lambs. This is true but do they eat enough? I mean, enough lambs to keep the coyotes sleek, healthy and well fed. That is my concern. As for the sacrifice of an occasional lamb, that seems to me a

small price to pay for the support of the coyote population. The lambs, accustomed by tradition to their role, do not complain; and the sheepmen, who run their hooved locusts on the public lands and are heavily subsidized, most of them as hog-rich as they are pigheaded, can easily afford these trifling losses. (35)

I sense great relish in Abbey's satirical attack. He is expressing a genuine anger about the way grazing occurs on public lands. He also offers an alternative to the senseless but widespread view that coyotes are somehow evil murderers—a theme picked up powerfully in Terry Tempest Williams's 1994 essay "Redemption," which earnestly criticizes those in the American West who fail to appreciate the ecological importance of predator species, concluding with the following observation: "My eyes returned to Jesus Coyote, stiff on his cross, savior of our American rangelands. We can try and kill all that is native, string it up by its hind legs for all to see, but spirit howls and wildness endures" (144). In Abbey's passage, though, there is a rather different voice, presenting something of a Twain-like delight in exaggeration and the reversal of expectations. This sense of fun pushes against the moralizing content of the passage and gives it a chewy, cross-grained quality. There is an almost palpable distaste for moral rectitude, together with an equally strong desire either to damn or to convert those who would thwart righteousness. This apparent contradiction, the righteous critique of self-righteousness, is perhaps more provocative than dogmatic—a point that Scott Slovic has explored in his chapter on Abbey's rhetorical and psychological tendencies in *Seeking Awareness in American Nature Writing* (1992).

A similar tension emerges when Abbey adopts a more professorial stance or plays the role of sober environmental advocate. In the following passage, he appears to take off his cowboy hat backstage and borrow some fake horn-rimmed glasses and a pointer:

Excluding the automobile from the heart of the great cities has been seriously advocated by thoughtful observers of our urban problems. It seems to me an equally proper solution to the problems besetting our national parks. Of course it would be a serious blow to Industrial Tourism and would be bitterly resisted by those who profit from that industry. Exclusion of automobiles would also require a revolution in the thinking of Park Service officialdom and in the assumptions of most American tourists. But such a revolution, like it or not, is precisely what is needed. The only foreseeable alternative, given the current trend of things, is the gradual destruction of our national park system. (65)

When compared to his more free-wheeling satire, the somewhat stuffy restraint of this passage becomes rather amusing. Abbey once commented in an interview that he prefers "writers who can range over a whole scale of tones and voices, who can go from the burlesque to the bawdy to the sublime, poetical" (*Resist Much* 36), but he did not explain exactly why. Perhaps, on some level, he simply savored the humor that emerges from such radical shifts.

Certain passages in *Desert Solitaire* do seem at first purely lyrical:

Dark clouds sailing overhead across the fields of the stars. Stars which are unusually bold and close, with an icy glitter in their light—glints of blue, emerald, gold. Out there, spread before me to the south, east, and north, the arches and cliffs and pinnacles and balanced rocks of sandstone (now entrusted to my care) have lost the rosy glow of sunset and become soft, intangible, in unnamed, unnameable shades of violet, colors that seem to radiate from—not overlay—their surfaces. (13)

Beautiful, graceful prose, no? But at the very core of this lyrical riff is an ironic, self-deprecating joke. Because the joke is a serious one, however (how could a human being presume to supervise such a vast, inhuman landscape, and what is the cost of such self-importance?), the passage becomes even more textured. If the whole of *Desert Solitaire* can be taken as a reflection on and critique of anthropocentrism, then this joke exemplifies one of Abbey's many stylistic tools. The whole thrust of the book evokes the otherness of the landscape and the value that inheres in its otherness. But it is true that humans have begun to destroy the land's beauty and integrity; therefore, it is indeed in Abbey's care. After all, as park ranger ("Call me a ranger") he stands for society's small gesture toward protecting such places as Arches National Monument, the setting of *Desert Solitaire* (which has more recently become Arches National Park). You could say that a main preoccupation in the book, in fact, is the debate over what "care" really means.

The quintessential Abbey shifts radically from one voice to another, deliberately complicating the tone of this meditation on caring:

> The magpies and jays squawk among the pinyon pines, which are heavy-laden with clusters of light-green, rosin-sticky, fresh, fat cones—we'll have a good crop of pine nuts this year. A variety of asters are blooming along the road and among the dunes; with yellow centers and vivid purple petals, the flowers stand out against their background of rock and coral-red sand with what I can only describe as an existential assertion of life; they are almost audible. Heidegger was wrong, as usual; man is *not* the only living thing that *exists*. He might well have taken a tip from a fellow countryman: *Wovon man nicht spraechen Kann, darueber muss man schweigen.* [Whereof one cannot speak, one must be silent.] (278–79)

A number of authors might have written this passage, until it reaches the mention of Heidegger—there, things take a surprising turn. Abbey not only implies that Heidegger would naturally come to mind in this context, but also flippantly suggests that the famous philosopher's thinking is obviously flawed. On one level, Abbey echoes Mark Twain's comic pose, whereby small-town common sense trumps intellectual pretension; on another, he genuinely subverts Heidegger's anthropocentric assertion of a sharp demarcation between human life and other life-forms. Abbey rejects Heidegger's claim of human superiority and his claim of humanity as a uniquely vivid or significant form of being. But the rejection, à la Twain, takes the form of the colloquially phrased advice that Heidegger might have done well to take a "tip" from Wittgenstein; the diction suggests that the two might have been fellow golf pros or ranch hands.

The whole performance in this scene evokes some 1930s movie, in which a character called "the Professor" gets wised up by the unlettered but street-smart protagonist. In reality, however, Abbey is far from unlettered. He evidently expects his reader to be familiar with Heidegger's philosophical notion of existence and to understand its anthropocentric bias. He also requires this reader to recognize the unattributed quotation from Wittgenstein's *Tractatus Logico-Philosophicus* (1921), and in German no less. In addition, he wants the quotation to be read in two different ways: 1) humorously, as a put-down of Heidegger's personal presumptuousness—as if Heidegger were one of Ranger Abbey's obtuse tourists, hopelessly blind to the reality in front of him; and 2) as an example in philosophy of the serious, exploratory stance that is appropriate when contemplating the limits of language and the mystery in all existence. James Cahalan and other scholars have detailed Abbey's formal training in philosophy, including his BA and MA in philosophy from the University of New Mexico and his Fulbright Scholarship at Edinburgh University in Scotland; but perhaps the difference between Abbey's approach to philosophy and that of many professional philosophers is that he felt such inquiry must start with an honest and sensitive account of experience, an account that he feels Heidegger does not give. This devotion to experience rather than a more bookish approach to deep ideas may well have been what drove Abbey to abandon his doctoral program at Yale.

One of the funniest and most delightful passages in *Desert Solitaire*, and one that highlights Abbey's uniqueness as a nature writer, is the following:

The cactus flowers are all much alike, varying only in color within and among the different species. The prickly pear, for example, produces a flower that may be violet, saffron or red. It is cup-shaped, filled with golden stamens that respond with sensitive, one might almost say sensual, tenderness to the entrance of a bee. This flower is indeed irresistibly attractive to insects; I have yet to look into one and not find a honeybee or bumblebee wallowing drunkenly inside, powdered with pollen, glutting itself on what must be a marvelous nectar. You can't get them out of there—they won't go home. I've done my best to annoy them, poking and prodding with a stem of grass, but a bee in a cactus bloom will not be provoked; it stays until the flower wilts. Until closing time. (28)

The passage begins in the conventional mode of natural history discourse, offering detailed physical description of a phenomenon in nature. But with the phrase "You can't get them out of there," Abbey deliberately shatters the genteel, almost Longfellow-like tone constructed out of phrases such as "marvelous nectar." He then becomes a kind of barroom bouncer, looking knowingly at the patrons, understanding their psychology all too well; "Until closing time" is placed at the end with perfect timing and rhythmic emphasis. Through this whimsical anthropomorphism, Abbey plays with the traditional rhetoric of nature writing. He also (seriously?—even sadly?) suggests a link between human and nonhuman life in the form of ungovernable destructive desire. Does the barfly in Abbey recognize the bee as his Dionysian twin?

When Abbey suggests, in a phrase quoted at the outset of this essay, that he is unable to "maintain a constant level of high thinking" required of the "nature writer," he is less than completely truthful. His thinking on the relation of humankind to nature is always penetrating and often profound, but he does refuse to maintain the rhetoric or appearance of sophistication. There is both self-effacing comedy and earnest reflection about human language in relation to nature in the dialogue below—Abbey and his friend Bob Waterman have camped in a remote wilderness area called the Maze, and as they sit by their campfire, they ponder the question of naming the unnamed but visually striking geologic formations that stand out in the landscape before them:

> Why call them anything at all? asks Waterman; why not let them alone? And to that suggestion I instantly agree; of course—why name them? Vanity, vanity, nothing but vanity: the itch for naming things is almost as bad as the itch for possessing things. Let them and leave them alone—they'll survive for a few more thousand years, more or less, without any glorification from us.
>
> But at once another disturbing thought comes to mind: if we don't name them somebody else surely will. Then, says Waterman in effect, let the shame be on their heads. True, I agree, and yet—and yet Rilke said that things don't truly exist until the poet gives them names. Who was Rilke? he asks. Rainer Maria Rilke, I explain, was a German poet who lived off countesses. I thought so, he says; that explains it. Yes, I agree once more, maybe it does; still—we might properly consider the question strictly on its merits. If any, says Waterman. It has some, I insist. Through naming comes knowing; we grasp an object, mentally, by giving it a name—hension, prehension, apprehension. And thus through language create a whole world, corresponding to the other world out there. Or we trust that it corresponds. Or perhaps, like a German poet, we cease to care, becoming more concerned with the naming than the things named; the former becomes more real than the latter. And so in the end the world is lost again. No, the world remains—those unique, particular, incorrigibly individual junipers and sandstone monoliths—and it is we who are lost. Again. Round and round, through the endless labyrinth of thought—the maze.
>
> Amazing, says Waterman, going to sleep. (288–89)

It is dizzying to trace the dialectical, point-counterpoint oscillation of Abbey's thought in this passage. Like a good inhumanist, he sees anthropocentric arrogance in the belief that naming is of any ultimate importance, and yet he recognizes that Rilke's idealistic position is not without its truth. Good ol' boy Ed agrees that Rilke's unmanly financial arrangements undermine his authority as an epistemologist and meta-physician, while Abbey the philosopher finds this disqualification somewhat absurd.

Beyond the comedic self-contradictions in this passage, Abbey seriously and succinctly illustrates an important philosophic problem: Words seem to call the world into being, but a preoccupation with the power of words to accomplish this awesome task causes us to lose the world again. And then, in the end, it is we who are lost. Abbey concludes with a playful pun, as if the entire naming/reality problem were a joke—which it may be—but of course it's a joke that has continually attracted thoughtful minds since antiquity, and bears an important relation to the larger (and ultimately unanswerable) question of anthropocentrism and humankind's relation to the environment.

It seems important to note, too, that Abbey is a writer and therefore shares with Rilke the fascination with the power of words to create worlds. What is more, the former graduate student in philosophy cannot help but be intrigued by the act of submitting the external world to rational analysis. I suspect that the antianthropocentric environmentalist in him feels guilty about his desire to play these potentially arrogant roles of the giver of names and the analyst. What is more, his working-class background, combined with his American bias toward individualism and self-sufficiency (not to mention his machismo), prevents him from fully embracing what Rilke represents. He is ambivalent, but this ambivalence results in rich, polyphonic comedy. Abbey uses multiple voices, partly as a rhetorical strategy to disarm readers who might resist the environmentalist elements of his message, and partly as an expression of his own sometimes contradictory feelings. After all, at the end of *Desert Solitaire*, he willingly sets out to resume the roles of social worker and barfly in Hoboken, New Jersey, the place where he spends six months of the year when he is not on duty as a ranger in Arches. And a place, needless to say, that is the antithesis of the Utah wilderness.

It must be acknowledged that some readers of Abbey find the complications and inconsistencies of *Desert Solitaire* suspicious. Tom

Lynch, for one, finds Abbey's part-time relationship to the Utah wilds a deficient substitute for making a true sustainable home in the desert, the kind of home created by Native Americans over previous centuries of residence. Lynch also has serious doubts about what he sees as Abbey's excessive glorification of individualism: "Abbey's vision of the Southwest, in spite of an environmentalist inflection, remains firmly configured by . . . his ethnic Anglo-American experience: [for Abbey] The West is, or at least it should be, a place of escape—a place where a man can ride away, alone, into the sunset" (103). SueEllen Campbell shares Lynch's reservations about Abbey despite the fact that *Desert Solitaire* is, in her words, "engaging," "well written," and "a book I like very much" (34). Like Lynch, she worries "about Abbey's constant emphasis on individualism—his title, his central solitude, his pervasive vision of the desert as a space of individuals" (45). And she sees this emphasis as part of a larger problem: "It's increasingly clear to me that environmental literature in general, and Abbey's book as an example, works partly by shutting out social and cultural complexities" (44).

Of course, devotees of environmental literature, and of Abbey as a practitioner of it, could easily turn Campbell's formulation around and argue that the main line of Western writing since Plato has in its emphasis on human society and culture often shut out environmental complexities. Clearly, environmental literature, as represented by writers like Abbey, is a tiny, tender sprout living in the immense shadow cast by the ancient branches of the dominant literary traditions.

In assessing the special contribution of nature writing to society today, Glen A. Love suggests:

Insofar as much contemporary literature—and criticism—has insulated itself from the biological and the natural world, nature writing seems to have responded to that lack, and to have provided a growing contemporary audience with that sense of an ecological reality-check which they do not find elsewhere. (203–4)

Love also observes that the postmodernist literary climate has not been a hospitable one for nature writing, and this is generally true. Yet Abbey effectively combines an ecological reality-check with his own postmodern linguistic playfulness. He is extremely engaging when he undermines the boundaries of genre, decorum, and discipline, and he thereby gains the power of the postmodern sensibility to question received meanings. But he shuns the emptiness and mean-spiritedness of much postmodernist writing. He was indeed a solitary creature in the postmodern desert, but he adapted to the environment, located his niche, and thrived.

Notes

1. This essay builds upon my previous study of Abbey's complex, ironic rhetorical style, "Celebration and Irony: The Polyphonic Voice of Edward Abbey's *Desert Solitaire*," *Western American Literature* (May 1993): 21–32.

2. All citations from Edward Abbey containing page numbers only are from *Desert Solitaire*.

3. Eiseley wrote a few extremely perceptive reviews of Jeffers many years before the publication of Eiseley's first major book in 1957, *The Immense Journey*. The pieces reveal Eiseley's profound engagement with the poet's *inhumanist* perspective. The Sierra Club photo-book *Not Man Apart* (1969) contains a foreword by Eiseley that displays his continuing fascination with Jeffers's work and career.

Works Cited

Abbey, Edward. *Desert Solitaire: A Season in the Wilderness*. New York: Ballantine, 1968.

_____. Introduction. *The Land of Little Rain*. By Mary Austin. New York: Penguin, 1988.

_____. *The Journey Home: Some Words in Defense of the American West*. New York: Dutton, 1977.

_____. *One Life at a Time, Please*. New York: Holt, 1988.

_____. "The Poetry Center Interview." Interview by James Hepworth. *Resist Much, Obey Little: Some Notes on Edward Abbey*. Ed. James Hepworth and Gregory McNamee. Salt Lake City: Dream Garden, 1985.

Cahalan, James M. *Edward Abbey: A Life*. Tucson: U of Arizona P, 2001.

Campbell, SueEllen. "Magpie." *Coyote in the Maze: Tracking Edward Abbey in a World of Words*. Ed. Peter Quigley. Salt Lake City: U of Utah P, 1998. 33–46.

Eiseley, Loren. Foreword. *Not Man Apart: Lines from Robinson Jeffers*. Ed. David Brower. San Francisco: Sierra Club, 1969.

Gessner, David. *Sick of Nature*. Hanover: Dartmouth CP, 2004.

Jeffers, Robinson. *The Collected Poetry of Robinson Jeffers*. Vol. 2. Ed. Tim Hunt. Stanford: Stanford UP, 1989.

Lopez, Barry. "Meeting Ed Abbey." *Resist Much, Obey Little*. Ed. James Hepworth and Gregory McNamee. Salt Lake City: Dream Garden, 1985.

Love, Glen A. "Et in Arcadia Ego: Pastoral Theory Meets Ecocriticism." *Western American Literature* 27 (November 1992): 195–205.

Lynch, Tom. "Nativity, Domesticity, and Exile in Edward Abbey's 'One True Home.'" *Coyote in the Maze*. Ed. Peter Quigley. Salt Lake City: U of Utah P, 1998. 88–105.

Quigley, Peter, ed. *Coyote in the Maze*. Salt Lake City: U of Utah P, 1998.

Ronald, Ann. *The New West of Edward Abbey*. 1982. Reno: U of Nevada P, 2000.

Slovic, Scott. *Seeking Awareness in American Nature Writing: Annie Dillard, Edward Abbey, Wendell Berry, Barry Lopez*. Salt Lake City: U of Utah P, 1992.

Smith, Jordan Fisher. *Nature Noir: A Park Ranger's Patrol in the Sierra*. Boston: Houghton, 2005.

Thoreau, Henry David. *Walden*. 1854. *A Week, Walden, The Maine Woods, Cape Cod*. Ed. Robert F. Sayre. New York: Library of America, 1985.

Williams, Terry Tempest. "Redemption." *An Unspoken Hunger: Stories from the Field*. New York: Pantheon, 1994. 143–44.

Loyalty to Place and Land Stewardship as Ecological Good Work in Wendell Berry's *The Memory of Old Jack*

Wes Berry

A moderately informed person who wishes to live in a healthy world might understandably feel anxious about the coming decades. A quick survey of major problems—detailed in such books as the *Plan B* series by Lester Brown of the Earth Policy Institute—reveals that we face declining sources of fresh water; decreased capacity to produce food, because of rising temperatures and the loss of fertile topsoil; increased desertification; oil shortages; the effects of climate change, such as melting ice and rising seas; accelerated species extinction; toxicity in the air, water, and soil; and a planetary population of six billion humans, which is predicted to increase to nine or ten billion before growth tapers off. And so forth. The piled-up problems seem so overwhelming that one is tempted to throw his or her arms into the air and exclaim, "I give up!" or just abandon hope and adopt a status quo lifestyle of consumption, waste, and frivolity. You know the tendency: spend hours on social media websites, watch a lot of television and sports, ignore what's going on outside the world of easy entertainments, spend lots of time shopping, and don't think much about the ecological costs of your consumption. Maybe recycle your beer and soda cans, since recycling is a convenient way to feel you are doing something to "help the environment."

Do you detect a bit of self-righteous indignation in my voice? Do I sound anxious? Guilty as charged. I don't have children, nor do I intend to, so I'm not worrying about the generations of my progeny to live on this planet after I sink back into the soil. But I do want future generations of humans to have access to the good stuff—clean air and water and forests and tasty, healthy food and compassionate companionship, abundant and beautiful birdsong, and the joy of animals. I want these things more than I want computers, cell phones, television, or cheap gasoline. Moreover, I want my students to know of the challenges facing humanity now and in the coming years, and I want them to care. I want my Kentucky students to know, for example, that their electricity comes from Appalachian coal burned in power plants, and that men employed by coal companies blow up mountains to get the coal—polluting streams and ruining the homelands of the people who live there—and that coal burning is the primary contributor to the greenhouse gases that spur climate change. I want my students to develop responsible lifestyles and lead examined lives.

Of all the environmental writing I have read to help me lead an examined life, the literary work of Wendell Berry has been the most influential. Just how influential has Berry's lifework been on American environmental writing? Consider this: Bill McKibben, an environmental journalist at the forefront of climate change research, dedicates his book *Deep Economy: The Wealth of Communities and the Durable Future* (2007) to Wendell Berry, because Berry's continued emphasis on the importance of sustainable settled communities props up (and precedes) McKibben's research into similar issues. Additionally, Norman Wirzba, editor of *The Essential Agrarian Reader: The Future of Culture, Community, and the Land* (2003), dedicates the book to Berry, whom he calls "mentor and friend." And again, Erik Reece, author of *Lost Mountain: A Year in the Vanishing Wilderness* (2006), quotes Berry's works throughout his own book of creative investigative journalism. In other words, after a half-century of writing and farming a singular piece of land in Henry County, Kentucky, Berry has the satisfaction of seeing the influence of his work surface in the works of other writers, writers who are making a positive difference in the world. Berry has delivered a consistent message for decades, in over forty books of essays, poems, short stories, and novels, and his lifestyle—being dedicated to his place—backs up his words. Because of this stability of character, Berry has become a hero to many who value conservation and sustainable agriculture. His life and work are a true model and inspiration for those who wish to live in a healthy world.

Increasingly since World War II, America has become a transient country, and Berry—both in his personal life and in his writing—has gone against that American habit of "moving on" or, as Huck Finn puts it at the end of his long narrative, "lighting out for the territory." Americans have been lighting out for the territory on a national scale since the Europeans first landed on the East Coast of what we now call the United States—moving westward, "conquering the wilderness," annexing Alaska and Hawaii, traveling to the moon. The interstate highway system was developed during the Eisenhower era, boosting rapid long-distance travel by automobile, and the growth of automobile-dependent suburban lifestyles followed. Many Americans have grown accustomed to living in one place and working in another, and as Wendell Berry's work shows, this transience generally carries with it considerable ecological and societal costs, such as the pollution resulting from our burning of fossil fuels. Berry points out how rural communities declined after WWII, as more and more people left farming and moved to cities. This decline in settled farming communities has corresponded with an increase in land being held by absentee owners—people who don't live in a place but make money from that place—and such absentee land holding raises the possibility that land will be poorly used.

Berry was born in Henry County, Kentucky, in 1934, and he grew up there. He left home for Lexington, not too far away from his native ground, where he studied at the University of Kentucky and earned both BA and MA degrees in English. Success as a writer led him to California, where he attended Stanford University as a Wallace Stegner writing fellow in 1958–59. In 1960, his first novel, *Nathan Coulter*, was published. Berry taught at New York University from 1962 to 1964 before returning to his home state, where he taught at the University of Kentucky from 1964 to 1977. In 1965, Berry and his wife Tanya moved to Lanes Landing Farm in Port Royal, a small farming community near the Kentucky River, where they continue to live (Merchant 7–10). Approaching five decades of permanent dwelling and fidelity to a place, the Berrys model the lifestyle that Wendell preaches in his prolific literary work—a lifestyle that counters the American habit of "moving on" that's become so common in modern lives.

Berry advocates sustainable agriculture and the importance of investing in healthy local cultures and economies. His cultural criticism, best expressed in his numerous essay collections, challenges the destructive habits of contemporary lifestyles. The habit of transience, for example, fosters the attitude that human beings can avoid responsibility for their actions by moving on to new places and other relationships. As a rejoinder to the irresponsibility that can accompany transience, Berry advocates fidelity to places and people. Berry's valuing of healthy communities encompasses the nonhuman world as well as the human, as he expresses in his essay "Health Is Membership," from the collection *Another Turn of the Crank*: "I believe that the community—in the fullest sense: a place and all its creatures—is the smallest unit of health and that to speak of the health of an isolated individual is a contradiction in terms" (90). We will best care for the world, Berry says, if we love the world; and people are most likely to love places they know intimately. Berry's alternative to the widespread destruction of land and human communities in modern life is, therefore, the regeneration of local cultures and economies. This is the number one motif and theme that links all of Berry's writing.

Because of the consistency of Berry's vision, and his multigenre oeuvre, choosing a single representative work is challenging. Ask someone to recommend a single representative text by Henry David Thoreau, and that person will likely recommend *Walden* (1854). Edward Abbey—*Desert Solitaire* (1968). Rachel Carson—*Silent Spring* (1962). Aldo Leopold—*A Sand County Almanac* (1949). Annie Dillard—*Pilgrim at Tinker Creek* (1974). Gary Snyder—a harder call, but probably *Turtle Island*, which contains both poems and essays and won the Pulitzer Prize for poetry in 1975. Berry's best known book is probably *The Unsettling of America: Culture and Agriculture* (1977), a collection of essays that, while central to Berry's work, may not be the best choice for someone just becoming familiar with his writing. A better choice is *Sex, Economy, Freedom, and Community* (1993), a collection of eight essays that represents Berry's vision eloquently. One finds here many of the ideas presented in *The Unsettling of America* in condensed form, more easily grasped by the beginning student of agrarian philosophies. Berry is one of our best essayists; he writes about complex cultural issues in a language accessible to a person of moderate intelligence. He avoids the jargon-laden prose too common in academic analytical criticism. Berry also writes fine poems in a clear voice, about rural living and fidelity to places and people, carrying on the themes one find in his essays. Perhaps most popular—I have heard these poems read on various occasions by a college president and university undergraduates—are Berry's "Mad Farmer" poems, spoken in the voice of a cranky farmer who, no surprise, sounds a lot like Berry himself. In "Manifesto: The Mad Farmer Liberation Front," the speaker urges us to thwart becoming passive consumers of industrial ideas and products, to avoid having our minds "punched in a card / and shut away in a little drawer," or having our bodies die for the profit of "they"—the unnamed captains of industry linked with big government and big military—by living a life that goes against the economic status quo of advertising and consumerism. The Mad Farmer urges us to

> every day do something
> that won't compute. Love the Lord.
> Love the world. Work for nothing.
> Take all that you have and be poor.
> Love someone who does not deserve it.
> . . . .
> Invest in the millennium. Plant sequoias.
> Say that your main crop is the forest
> that you did not plant,
> that you will not live to harvest
> Say that the leaves are harvested

---

when they have rotted into the mold.
Call that profit. Prophesy such returns.
Put your faith in the two inches of humus
that will build under the trees
every thousand years. (lines 12–16, 24–33)

The Christian allusions in these lines—"Take all that you have and be poor"—are typical of Berry's writing, which often draws on the best of Christian teachings, such as the values of neighborliness and peaceableness (see the essay "Peaceableness toward Enemies" from *Sex, Economy, Freedom and Community*). While Christian values inform Berry's work, Berry's brand of Christianity is not doctrinaire, but rather pragmatic. In the essay "Christianity and the Survival of Creation," Berry writes, "Our destruction of nature is not just bad stewardship, or stupid economics, or a betrayal of family responsibility; it is the most horrid blasphemy. It is flinging God's gifts into His face" (*Sex, Economy, Freedom and Community* 98). Berry criticizes the exploitative American economy, defined by global trade and absentee ownership, and encourages consumers to secede from this destructive economic system by buying good-quality, locally made products that honor the materials of Creation. An artist, Berry claims, does "good work" when he uses the materials of the earth in a respectful, sustainable manner.

As for fiction, and Berry has written plenty of it (thirteen novels and story collections), Berry's accessible and beautifully written novel *The Memory of Old Jack* (1974) serves as a good representative text, as it touches on many of the central subjects of Berry's work: the desirability of fidelity to places and people, the importance of passing down wisdom (especially farming wisdom) through generations, the necessity of doing "good work" by treating the materials of the earth with reverence, the value of being neighborly, and the desire for durable, healthy community life. This novel observes the Aristotelian dramatic unities, as it is set in one place on earth, takes place mostly during one day, and closely follows the actions of Old Jack, a retired farmer, through his slow last day in Port William, the fictional community Berry returns to over and over in various novels and stories. But this novel messes with the unities in its repeated flashbacks, as the mind of Old Jack slips, often with minimal authorial cues, into his complex and often challenging past. *The Memory of Old Jack* will be best appreciated by one who values theme, vision, character development, and setting over intricate plotting. There are no big explosions in this novel—no vampires or cliff-hanger jury trials, and no murders, espionage, or gratuitous sex scenes. This is a quiet, honest novel that explores the joys and frustrations of kinship, work, marriage, and aging, without the sensational plotting that Americans (and Brits, too) have come to desire in movies and popular genre fiction. Much of Berry's writing could be called *pastoral* in the fondness it expresses for rural living. Some might call this fondness "nostalgic," since many rural communities (and the vocation of farming in general) have declined greatly in population and prosperity since the Civil War, and increasingly in the twentieth century. But Berry's version of the pastoral isn't simple. These farm people live complex lives, suffering marital strife, financial losses, and the death of loved ones.

Jack Beechum ("Old Jack") was born in 1860, and most of the present-day action in the novel takes place during one day in September 1952, from early morning until evening. Jack was a man born to farming, meaning he was raised to it. Both his father and his grandfather were farmers, and at age twenty-five, with both parents dead, Jack bought out his sister's share of the family farm and began working hard on the land to put it back in order. "By Jack's time, the farm had been reduced by his father's money troubles to about a hundred and fifty acres," the narrator says, and what moved Jack was "a sense of the possibilities that lay yet untouched in his land. The rest of his own life seemed to him to lie unborn in the soil of the old farm" (29). The farm is Jack's lifelong companion. It challenges him and gives him the solace of work when domestic life, symbolized by the house in which his wife Ruth lives, sours. Jack is a kind of "natural man," or outdoorsman, reminiscent of such American characters as Huckleberry Finn and Rip Van Winkle, who prefers the green world of forests and fields to the confinement and civility of a household run by women. But this is a tricky claim, because Jack, unlike Huckleberry Finn, doesn't want to "light out for the territory." Jack was born on this piece of land in Kentucky, and that's where he wishes to dwell. "He had known no other place. From babyhood he had moved in the openings and foldings of the old farm as familiarly as he moved inside his clothes. But after the full responsibility of it fell to him, he saw it with a new clarity" (30). The farm becomes Jack's metaphoric lover, providing him the companionship lacking at home with Ruth. Berry suggests as much when midway through the story he describes how Jack struggles through years of economic hardship and looks upon his farm for the first time free of debt: "Clear and whole before him now he sees the object of his faith as he has not seen it for fifteen years. And he feels opening in himself the stillness of a mown field, such a peace as he has never known. . . . He has been faithful to his land, through all its yearly changes from maiden to mother, the bride and wife and widow of men like himself since the world began" (122). This language ties in with one of the key metaphors of Berry's writing, one that unifies his essays, fiction, and poetry: the metaphor of "marriage," which isn't just a formal bond between two people, but rather a harmonious unification of two people who are bonded to each other, connected with their community, and devoted to their place.

Revealed through flashbacks in the novel, Jack's life after his courtship of Ruth becomes complicated. They marry, and almost immediately Jack senses Ruth's disappointment with his ancestral farm and the old house they live in. Ruth comes from town people, and her family serves as a foil to the agrarian life Berry champions:

> Before Ruth was born her family's ambition had already turned away from the land of its home place toward the business of the town of Hargrave, following the myth of impending prosperity that hovered there. . . .

Their [hardware] business . . . seemed to them to promise ease and wealth such as they could not expect from farming, and once the Lightwoods had turned to the town they did not turn back. (42)

A major conflict in the marriage of Jack and Ruth arises because of this fundamental difference in expectations. Ruth is raised to value comfort; Jack is raised to value doing a hard day's labor on the land. Ruth dislikes the animal odors on Jack's body when he comes in from a long day of farm work; for Jack, such smells are a natural part of daily life in his place. Jack "was not a man who could be much dreamed upon; he lived too close to the ground for that" (42), the narrator notes, explaining Ruth's estrangement from him.

But the marriage disappointment goes both ways, as Jack is also disappointed with Ruth, who fails to provide for him the loving household he desires. Ruth's foil is Hannah Coulter, who makes a home with her new husband Nathan that contrasts sharply with the failures of the Beechum household. While Ruth begrudges having to live in an old house on the farm, Hannah relishes the challenge of repairing the run-down farm. In the four years Nathan and Hannah have lived on the farm, "they have labored at its renewal. The pastures have been cleaned up, the fences have been mended . . . four of the six rooms of the old house have been made livable" (75). Hannah "knows the deeper order of intention and labor," and she has sat many nights with Nathan planning the order of homestead renewal. "So much, at least, of what lies ahead of them they have desired, foreseen, planned, pictured in their minds. Against all that they cannot foresee, against all dread, this is what excites her and hurries her on" (75). Hannah stands for everything that Old Jack has desired in a mate throughout his long life. For example, after Hannah works in the kitchen all morning, preparing a big lunch for the hungry men who have sweated outside harvesting the tobacco, she gets a brief "moment of freedom" from the housework to go fetch Old Jack back to her house to eat with the tobacco workers, bringing him into the family/community ritual of the harvest he knows so well—and as she walks, "she feels full of the goodness, the competency, of her body that can love a man and bear his children, that can raise and prepare food, keep the house, work in the field. She is living deep in her body now as she goes under the hot, bright sky into the town of Port William" (79).

Through Hannah's point of view, we see how she represents for Jack the complete marriage of man/woman/community/land that he has always desired but not achieved. She "knows that he recognizes her out of pain and loss. She is what he has failed. She is his consolation and his despair. How much of his vision of the world comes right in the figure of a woman fulfilled and satisfied, her man's welcomer, at home in the world! She is his Promised Land, that he may see but never hope to enter" (79). Hannah is a "consolation" because Jack takes pleasure in seeing his kinsman, Nathan, fulfilled in his marriage; she's Jack's "despair" because she reminds him of his own marital failures. Of course, Jack is ninety-two years old at this point, and thus his chances of entering any female "Promised Land" are slender; but the point is that Hannah symbolizes the completion of "the country of marriage" (the title of one of Berry's poems): a perfect bond of people and place. And at the end of Jack's long life, this unfulfilled desire remains his primary regret. Even earlier in his life, at age forty-eight, after busting his body for fifteen years laboring to pay off bank debts incurred from an unnecessary, greedy purchase of a second farm—when he still had enough time to make things right—even then, as one part of his life is being renewed (the emergence from debt), the "country of marriage" eludes Jack. He and Ruth fail to communicate:

> If they could have spoken with some candor of themselves, with some mutual pleasure of their place in the world, looking ahead with concern or with hope, that would have made them both different lives and different deaths. But she could not offer, and he could not ask. That was his failure; he had not united farm and household and marriage bed, and he could not. . . . It was too late for a woman's love. And that was all that was lacking. (126)

Some feminists might take issue with Berry's marriage metaphor, and with language that seems to place women in a subservient position to men—for example, the idea of a wife as "her man's welcomer," suggesting that she's the one who stays at home and waits on the return of the breadwinning head of the household. I can also imagine feminists criticizing how Hannah views herself in relation to Old Jack as they walk with linked arms up the street on the way to lunch: "She is sturdily accompanied by his knowledge, in which she knows that she is whole. In his gaze she feels herself to be not just physically but historically a woman, one among generations, bearing into mystery the dark seed. She feels herself completed by that as she could not be completed by the desire of a younger man" (81). Does this passage put the woman in a subservient position? Is a man's gaze needed for a woman's "wholeness"? Can't Hannah be whole and complete unto herself? In Berry's world, which is in many ways traditional, a person can't be whole unto himself/herself. One achieves a kind of wholeness, as already noted, by forming bonds with other people (community) and a place (an essential part of that community), and by doing good work on that place and in that community. An even higher level of wholeness—that metaphor of harmonious marriage—occurs in the unification of land, household, and lovers.

In Berry's ideal vision, "marriage" means much more than two people bound by a religious or legal ceremony, and this is made clear in *The Memory of Old Jack* through two couples who serve as contrasting examples to the Nathan and Hannah marriage ideal: Lightning Berlew and his wife Smoothbore, and Jack's daughter Clara and the banker Glad Pettit. The contrast of these couples with the Nathan and Hannah union represents two types of economic systems: one based on material consumption and impermanence, and the other grounded in sustainable living and rootedness. The extractive consumer economy is represented by the tenant farmer Berlew and his wife, who prefer tinkering with an old automobile to doing an honest day's work. Mat Feltner, owner of the farm that the Berlews live on, offers Lightning a hog to fatten up for the winter, but Lightning is too lazy to keep a hog. We see the Berlews through the eyes of Mat, a hard-working farmer who, although disapproving of their laziness, understands part of the reason for that laziness: lack of permanence. In other words, since the Berlews don't own the land they live on, they have no permanent connection to it, "no interest in it, no hope from it. They live, and appear content to live, from hand to mouth in the world of merchandise, connected to it by daily money poorly earned" (13). Although the Berlews are shiftless—reminiscent of Erskine Caldwell's ignorant Jeeter family in *Tobacco Road* (1932) and the leisure-loving Tussie family of Jesse Stuart's novel *Trees of Heaven* (1940)—their lack of permanent connection to a place puts them in a similar position to the family of Will Wells, described in chapter four of *The Memory of Old Jack*. Will and his wife Marthy, both hard-working tenant farmers, make a home on Jack Beechum's second farm. They repair the place and make it productive with livestock and a garden. But ultimately, the Wells' lack of ownership causes disharmony in Will's relationship with the owner, Jack. "Will's work began to deviate subtly from Jack's directions and expectations. . . . In Will this was the result of a failure of interest that had been immanent all along in his knowledge that his labor formalized and preserved no bond between him and the place; he was a man laboring for no more than his existence" (61). Thus, even though the scale of work differs—Will being a much better worker than Berlew—these tenant farmers are linked in their lack of permanent connection to the place. Will's inability to own his own farm is tied to cultural and financial circumstances; sharecropping was a primary occupation for former slaves and their descendants after the Civil War, since these families lacked capital.

The second married couple, Clara and Glad, fails to satisfy the ideal marriage because the couple is disconnected from the farm and dependent on the consumer economy. Gladston Pettit of Louisville (his very name suggesting snobbery and finery) rolls into the countryside in his fancy automobile, "its immaculate gloss bearing like an insult the dust of the country roads" (133). Now that they are married, Glad and Clara pull the car up "to the very foot of the porch steps so that Clara could pass from the car into the house almost without touching the ground." Obviously, this symbolizes Clara's lack of rootedness to the farm and distance from her earthy father, to whom she's never been overly close. When Clara and Glad leave the farm, they take with them seasonal produce and meats, carrying them back to the big city in "the banker's gleaming machine to the satisfaction of such hunger as might be roused by the balancing of figures in a book" (133–34). This sarcastic attitude is Jack's perspective, and one senses that it's Berry's as well, especially if you read the Pettits alongside Berry's essay "Feminism, the Body, and the Machine," in which he claims that "the modern household is the place where the consumptive couple do their consuming. Nothing productive is done there. Such work as is done there is done at the expense of the resident couple or family, and to the profit of suppliers of energy and household technology. For entertainment, the inmates consume television or purchase other consumable diversion elsewhere" (*Art of the Commonplace* 67). Berry clarifies his critique of modern marriage by adding,

> I do not believe that "employment outside the home" is as valuable or important or satisfying as employment at home, for either men or women. It is clear to me . . . that children need an ordinary daily association with *both* parents. They need to see their parents at work . . . and then they need to work with their parents. . . . it matters a great deal that *the work done should have the dignity of economic value.* (68, emphasis mine)

In short, the Pettits fail to satisfy Berry's "country of marriage" ideal, while other rooted farm people in his fictional community—Nathan and Hannah, for example—succeed.

I should add here that this ideal of agricultural permanence is akin to Thomas Jefferson's hopes for an American democracy grown from the hard work, ingenuity, and thrift of numerous small permanent farmsteads. This is one version of *agrarianism* and the vision to which Berry subscribes. He spells this out clearly late in the novel, when Wheeler Catlett—"in a sense not so much a lawyer as a farmer who practices law" (107)—is introduced to wrap up the estate of the now-deceased Old Jack. We learn that Wheeler founded and for thirty years has operated a farming cooperative to help farmers find a market for their produce, "to assure a decent living, a chance to survive on their land. . . . It is a Jeffersonian vision, one might say, that the cooperative was founded to implement and preserve" (162). The writing turns didactic here (Berry's work is often didactic, but I forgive him, as I usually agree with him), as Berry describes the struggles of farmers in the twentieth century through the eyes of Wheeler, who sees the young farmers like Elton Penn and Nathan Coulter, "in whom the old way has survived," and who thinks about

> the troubles that probably lie ahead of them: an increasing scarcity of labor as more and more of the country people move to cities; the consequent necessity for further mechanization of the farms; the consequent need of the farmers for more land and more capital in order to survive; the consequent further departure of the labor force from the country; the increasing difficulty of preserving an agricultural economy favorable to small farmers as political power flows from the country to the cities. . . . Old Jack's death has raised anew and more starkly than ever the possibility that men of his kind are a race doomed to extinction, that the men Wheeler loves most in the world are last survivors. (163)

These old good farmers represent the second type of economy valued by Berry, one based on thrift, conservation, locality, and permanence. Berry presents his rules for good land use in many places, but nowhere more clearly than in the essay "Conservation and Local Economy" from *Sex, Economy, Freedom and Community*. A close reading of the essay helps one to understand the dominant themes of *The Memory of Old Jack*—indeed, allows us to better appreciate the consistency of Berry's vision, his metaphor of "the country of marriage," and the need for productive, stable rural households to thrive. "The pattern of land stewardship is set by nature," Berry explains.

> This is why we must have stable rural economies and communities; we must keep alive in every place the human knowledge of the nature of that place. Nature is the best farmer and forester, for she does not destroy the land in order to make it productive. . . . But we have not only the example of nature; we have still, though few and widely scattered, sufficient examples of competent and loving human stewardship of the earth. We have, too, our own desire to be healthy in a healthy world. (11)

This desire to live in a healthy world and the examples of good stewardship lie at the heart of Berry's complex pastoral novel. The novel is populated with characters bound by their faith and fidelity to each other and their place. Often these characters are men, fellow farmers who share work and pass on important farming knowledge particular to their place. The motif of "passing it on" is introduced early in the novel through Mat Feltner, age sixty-nine, who has depended on the older farmer, Jack, his entire life. "When Mat was born, Jack was already such a man as few men ever become. He has been faithful all those years. It is a faith that Mat has reciprocated in full. But Jack's faith has been the precedent and model. All his life Mat has had Jack before him, as standard and example, teacher and taskmaster and companion, friend and comforter" (10). Although not related by blood, Ben Feltner is a father figure to Jack, and later Jack becomes a father figure to Mat, who passes on the accumulated farming wisdom to his grandson Andy Catlett, soon going off to college. The hope of keeping the wisdom alive in the place depends in part upon the return of Andy after he finishes. "While they were still only children, Andy and [his younger brother] Henry became initiates of a way of life that was threatened and nearly done with in that part of the country, and of which they would be among the last survivors" (108). From a young age, Andy

---

and Henry went to work "in the fields that their kinsmen for generations before them had gone to work in," and the older men became
"their exemplars and taskmasters." "From that company of men, that
brotherhood of friends and kinsmen, his teachers, he glimpsed a vision
of human possibility that would not leave him" (108). Berry could be
talking about himself here, and indeed Andy Catlett is the likely fictional representation of Berry—the intelligent young man, "stubborn,
surly, intemperate, and generally extreme" (118), who leaves home for
college, packing along with him a deep respect for the honest lives of
the farmers he has learned from, perhaps to return to the community
later. Berry returned to his native ground and has made a home there
since 1965; he describes this return in the essay "A Native Hill," from
the essay collection *The Art of the Commonplace* (2002).

The conclusion of *The Memory of Old Jack* is fitting for a novel
about the value of doing good work within a community of kinsmen.
The final scene takes place in the stripping room, about three months
after Jack's death, as the men—including Andy, returned home from
the university for the winter holiday—strip leaves from the tobacco
plants in preparation for taking them to market. They reminisce about
Old Jack, the only person missing from the regular work crew. They
share some fun by quoting some of Jack's often-used phrases, like
"Where are you, son? Damn it to hell. It's *daylight*!" Then the men slip
into their own quiet reflections of Old Jack, and

> in the hush of it they are aware of something that passed from them and
> now returns: his [Jack's] stubborn biding with them to the end, his keep-
> ing of faith with them who would live after him, and what perhaps none
> of them has yet thought to call his gentleness, his long gentleness toward
> them and toward this place where they are at work. They know that his
> memory holds them in common knowledge and common loss. (170)

And so Berry concludes, with a few of the key motifs, that consistent
vision that defines his writing: the value of doing good work, represent-

ed by Elton Penn's holding out a beautiful stick of well-grown tobacco for Wheeler to see, and the value of doing that work within a community of people bonded by place and memory.

Works Cited

Berry, Wendell. *Another Turn of the Crank*. Washington, DC: Counterpoint, 1995.

_____. *The Art of the Commonplace: The Agrarian Essays of Wendell Berry*. Washington, DC: Shoemaker, 2002.

_____. "Manifesto: The Mad Farmer Liberation Front." *The Selected Poems of Wendell Berry*. Washington, DC: Counterpoint, 1998. 87–88.

_____. *The Memory of Old Jack*. 1974. Berkeley: Counterpoint, 1999.

_____. *Sex, Economy, Freedom, and Community*. New York: Pantheon, 1993.

_____. *The Unsettling of America: Culture and Agriculture*. San Francisco: Sierra Club, 1977.

Brown, Lester R. *Plan B 4.0: Mobilizing to Save Civilization*. New York: Norton, 2009.

McKibben, Bill. *Deep Economy: The Wealth of Communities and the Durable Future*. New York: Holt, 2007.

Merchant, Paul, ed. *Wendell Berry*. Lewiston: Confluence, 1991.

Reece, Erik. *Lost Mountain: A Year in the Vanishing Wilderness—Radical Strip Mining and the Devastation of Appalachia*. New York: Riverhead, 2006.

Wirzba, Norman. *The Essential Agrarian Reader: The Future of Culture, Community, and the Land*. Lexington: UP of Kentucky, 2003.

Reciprocal Spirituality: Human/Animal Interface in Linda Hogan's Multiple Genres _____

Barbara J. Cook

Through a variety of genres, Chickasaw author Linda Hogan seeks to encourage her audience to view the natural world from the perspective of traditional indigenous ways of knowing. Hogan's writing is often at the intersection of environmental matters and the treatment of American Indians, historically and currently, thus linking issues of environmental justice and social justice. Central to her exploration of environmental touchstones is the link between spirituality and the natural world for native peoples. She seems to have an intuitive connection with and understanding of animals and their stories. In a recent article in *Yes* magazine, titled "Our Animal Selves," Hogan writes:

> In our language, one term for animal is *Nan okcha*, which means, "all alive." We have songs for the animals, even a tick dance song. It is understood by traditional peoples that each kind of animal has its own expansive intelligence, each its own ways, own mind. The mind of the horse is not the same as the snake or crow. (6)

Throughout her work we find many of these animals. For instance, one focus that reappears in each of her novels is the conflict between indigenous spirituality, the Endangered Species Act, and human disregard of animals—see, for example, the bats in *Mean Spirit* (1991), the caribou in *Solar Storms* (1995), the Florida panther and young indigenous girl in *Power* (1998), and tales of whales, a magical octopus, and people connected to the mysterious sea in *People of the Whale* (2008). Many of Hogan's essays in *Dwellings: A Spiritual History of the Natural World* (1995) have appeared in anthologies or magazines and are not necessarily a cohesive grouping, other than as reflections of a consistent worldview. There is evidence throughout her work that Hogan looks to nature for spirituality, and it is quickly evident that hers is an earthly spirituality, as bats and birds fill the pages of *Dwellings*. Bats show us "how we can get . . . to the center of the world, to the place where the universe carries down the song of night to our human lives" (26, 28).

In *The Book of Medicines* (1993), Hogan divides the poetry collection into two sections, "Hunger" and "Medicines." The poem "Hunger" points to our failure to achieve a human/animal connection—men pull dolphins from the sea to "have their / way with them," comparing them to women even as they are unaware of a deeper hunger that holds them captive (18). The second half of the collection seeks to heal the human/animal disconnections found in the first half.

This essay points to Linda Hogan's importance within the field of environmental literature in her use of human/animal relationships and gender issues in general, but I will focus specifically on the novel *Power*, touching on examples in *Dwellings* and *The Book of Medicines*.

Hogan's writing draws on a traditional understanding of the interconnections within our world. She establishes the interdependence of land, animals, and humans, and draws attention to historic acts of destruction—driven initially by colonization and reinforced later by corporate and government decisions, human greed, and indifference to the environment. Her essays and poems reflect the traditional view of the world that she believes she was born with, and the importance she places on the interconnections of humans and the natural world. But it is in her fiction that Hogan most forcefully delineates the interplay between human actions and their impact on the land, animals, and vegetation. In her novels she draws on actual historical events and offers the reader insight into the repercussions of those events on individual communities. In doing so, she is acting on her belief that she has "to do something stronger than history to reach the emotions of readers" ("From the Center of Tradition" 116). To tell the stories, she begins with the history and embellishes in order "to create and put the imagery to work" (117).

In the Western tradition, history and time run in a straight line that "leads to an apocalyptic end" (*Dwellings* 93). Hogan reminds us that "stories of the end, like those of beginning, tell something about the people who created them" (93). Think about what our stories of the end say about us. We assume the "story of extinction" is unavoidable. Denial (or is it fear?) contributes to our estrangement from the earth. We seek to exploit the earth's resources; everything must be productive. It is, after all, inevitable—earth is man's domain until the apocalypse comes. This Cartesian divide between nature and humans is an underlying theme throughout Hogan's work. In addition to the unnatural abyss between the human and nonhuman world, her fiction focuses on the communal survival from the effects of the forces of history and the disregard for land, animals, plants, and people.

Her 1998 novel *Power* links the destruction of habitats and the systematic destruction of tribal communities. As in Hogan's other novels, she draws on a historical event: the 1983 killing of a Florida panther at the hands of James E. Billie, a Seminole tribal leader (for more information, see *United States v. Billie* 667 FS 1485 FL. Dist. Ct. 1987). Under the Endangered Species Act, it is a federal crime to kill an endangered species, the only exceptions being if the incident proceeds from some religious justification or if it transpires on Indian land. Already a controversial figure in the Florida Indian community due to his support of a casino being built on reservation land, Billie had been poaching with friends when he saw the panther's eyes shine in the dark and fired his weapon. He not only had friends take trophy pictures but later cooked and ate the animal. According to Hogan, the elders who were called in to testify were evasive. Although they did not agree with his actions, they chose not to challenge his authority as a leader of the tribal council (Castor 41).

In Hogan's narrative, she describes the Taiga, a fictional tribal community that numbers around thirty—the same as the number of Florida panthers believed to be alive. This common number links the fate of the tribe and the panthers, just as the destruction of the Everglades is linked to the decimated numbers of people and cats. Her two main characters are female, as are most of the tribal elders who seem to hover around at various times.

Omishto (which translates to "the One who Watches") is the sixteen-year-old Taiga narrator. She tells the story of her "aunt" Ama and her killing of the panther, linking the incident to a tribal myth that bears close ties to the Seminole mythology of Panther Woman. Omishto moves between two worlds: her Christian mother's more mainstream home and Ama's more traditional space, embedded in the natural world. But in one sense this could be a coming-of-age tale for Omishto, as she struggles to understand why Ama kills the panther and, more importantly, which world she wants to be a part of.

Omishto, like Ama, seems to have a special connection to the animals of the swamps. In the opening chapter, Omishto is in her favorite place, floating on a small lake in an open boat. As she nears the shoreline, she feels she is being watched. "I can tell. I feel it in my body. . . . an animal feeling, something—or someone—dangerous" (*Power* 2). Ama has told her that this is the territory of the cat and that "in the old way" both she and Omishto are relatives, kin, and members of the Panther Clan (3). Although Omishto has only seen one panther, which was treed by three boys—her mother says they are all gone, and if any are left, they are sick—she knows that "one finds its way through now and then. You can feel it more than see it, feel it more than smell it" (3).

Hogan suggests there is a pattern to her novels:

Every one of them has a return to indigenous knowledge systems, a person who says, "okay, I'm not going to be part of this other world, I'm going to return to the original way of thinking about the world." . . .Indigenous people know the environment. . . . They know how to keep that place intact. ("Sea Level" 170)

The characters in all of her novels are enmeshed in a natural world that is being destroyed. There is violence of some sort, and there is ultimately healing through a return to a traditional life based on respect for the natural world. Hogan provides hope that the natural world will be healed just as the people are healed. As Lydia R. Cooper points out in an article on *Power*, "Neither Ama nor Omishto associates the lapsed world with a particular government policy or industry, but instead they assume the symptoms to be part of a larger, more general human disease—a ubiquitous failure to recognize and respect the ancient 'rules' of ecological balance and mutual dependency" (Cooper 151). Hogan universalizes the "evil—the broken rules'" (151).

During a powerful hurricane, nature seems to be reinforcing its own power, and Omishto recalls that "the wind is a living force" (*Power* 28). Even the ancient Methuselah tree is uprooted. She looks down after the storm passes, and she is naked, "naked as the day I entered this world"—a symbolic rebirth. It is from this point that Ama and Omishto seem drawn into a reenactment of the old myth of the Panther Woman, who kills the panther to save the clan. And it is from this point that Ama's actions become a complicated puzzle that Omishto must come to understand as she decides how to lead her life. As Ama prepares for the hunt, she says, "Old Grandmother, I am coming" (49). The cat seems to be waiting for her, skinny, sick, and tattered. Omishto sees the killing as "cold-blooded" (70). Ama follows tradition—showing respect, making it a bed of leaves, sprinkling pollen—but Omishto knows it is not right and does not understand when Ama tells her it is "a sacrifice. It all is. This whole thing" (71).

Ultimately, it is the very violence of Ama's killing the panther that brings readers to question the validity, in a contemporary world, of following a path of violent atonement such as those found in native religious rituals. Ama cares for the dead panther after she kills it, but she does not follow the complete ritual, knowing that she will become a scapegoat herself. The proper disposal of the panther would mean presentation to the tribal elders. Ama does not do this because the panther had been starving and sick, and it would devastate the elders to see the condition of their "relative." As Omishto informs the reader,

"Ama said the old ways are not enough to get us through this time and she was called to something else. To living halfway between the modern world and the ancient one" (73). She tells Omishto not to tell the courts or the elders that the sacrifice of the panther reenacts the myth of panther sacrifice in order to restore ecological balance to the world. It is herself that she is sacrificing; she is "killing herself" symbolically.

Ama is quickly arrested for killing an endangered species and faces two trials—one by the "white" court, and then a community trial in front of the tribal elders. The first trial draws a large crowd, protestors, whites, Indians, and the media. Whereas Ama confesses, James E. Billie pleaded innocent on the grounds that he, as a Seminole Indian, was excluded from the authority of the Endangered Species Act, arguing that killing for religious ceremonies and hunting on Native American land were not prohibited. Billie claimed that he did not knowingly break the law, as he believed his actions to be within his rights under the freedom of religion clause of the First Amendment (Manning 3).

Ama mostly sits silently in the courtroom, confesses, and does not explain her actions. The tribal chairman comes in "to speak in defense of Ama" (*Power* 131). But Omishto begins to see even more clearly the divisions of the two worlds she is between. As the people watch Ama, they are studying her. "She's a curiosity. She is a human being of a different kind," writes Hogan (134). "'I killed it,' [Ama] says, as if to cut things short. 'I slayed it. . . . I knew what it was and I killed it'" (135). Watching Ama testify, Omishto realizes: "All those sheets of paper and she's saying it straight out and I can see they are convinced she is not sane. Or that she lies, that maybe she is covering for me or someone else, so they don't end the day here, don't listen deep enough" (135). She refuses to articulate her reasons for killing the panther, which she admits to thinking of as kin. Even as her lawyer gamely tries to defend her, she is believed to be "not sane" (135).

"Ama does not *reply* to the questions of the law," Pascale McCullough Manning argues.

Instead she declares herself. She does not attempt to stand outside the networking of power; she confesses, but she is her own confessional. It is Ama who stages the trial; she is the one who carries the panther's tracking device out of the woods, knowing that the biologists tracking the animal would notify the police; it is she who prepares Omishto for her role as witness. But Ama does not attempt to elude the law. Instead her confession is a text that subverts its own believability, placing her *outside* the paradigm of the confessional, for she proposes a new language of confession that stands apart from the convention whereby the confessor seeks to have her subjectivity reaffirmed by the authority or the power structure to whom she confesses. (4)

Manning notes Omishto's conclusion that she does not "like the way [Ama's] lawyer says 'Their world'—as he calls it—is different than 'ours,' meaning the one he and others like him have been shaped by, have inhabited" (*Power* 136). And, as Manning notes later, "The defense lawyer's speech begins with 'she believes' and ends with 'Their world'" (Manning 6). This again places Ama outside. She is an "other," just like the panther. Omishto realizes "that Ama is their animal" (*Power* 136); Manning pushes this further, arguing that

> she is their panther. To the jurors, Ama and the Florida panther are one and the same; both are endangered, both speak a language that the law solicits but cannot comprehend. In opposition to the evolved beings of the court, who live separate from their natural world, Ama represents the terrifying, encroaching natural world that science works to explain and map. (Manning 9)

In spite of Ama's refusal to defend herself, she is ultimately found not guilty, mostly due to lack of evidence; no one has found the panther's body, and thus there is no proof of whether the cat was actually an endangered species. Later in the novel, we find that Janie Soto, a tribal elder and the oldest and most traditional of the clan, has removed the body and the weapon so that no evidence would be found.

But as Ama tells Omishto, "It's not over yet" (*Power* 144). Her trial by the elders reaches a different verdict. Omishto knows that the elders need "the story," and she must testify again (160). She feels "both at home and a foreigner here in their presence. . . . In their eyes, I am the future. . . . I know our survival depends on who I am and who I will become. But this is all too large for me" (161). A male tribal elder, brought to the trial on a stretcher, questions Ama: "'You didn't bring the body of the cat to us.' It's an accusation, not a question. But this is what she should have done. Even I know this and I'm still a girl" (165). Once again Ama refuses to explain her actions, and the elders banish her from the community, condemning her to walk for four years. She has killed their kin, for they and the cat both are members of the Panther Clan.

Ama disappears, and Omishto retreats to Ama's house in the woods. Gradually, Omishto comes to terms with Ama's violent actions and realizes she must settle on the way to live her own life. She "realizes that she must choose between the civilized suburban world and the Everglades" (Cooper 154). Omishto comes to recognize that her isolation and loneliness will eventually destroy her and she chooses to join the Native community at Kili, "symbolically refusing to valorize Ama's violent atonement, and instead pursuing acts like singing and dancing that emphasize communal life and vibrancy rather than death and violence" (Cooper 154).

At first one may assume that Linda Hogan is rejecting the validity of traditional rituals in today's world, but as Lydia Cooper points out, *Power* does not "undermine native religious ideas altogether" (155). The narrative can be read as Hogan's rejection of the idea of regeneration through violence, or "substitutionary regeneration by which the world may be renewed through the sacrificial death of an animal or human" (155). After all, Omishto turns to the healing found in traditional song and dance within the Taiga community. *Power* can be read as reflecting the view that traditional rituals can be flexible, a view that seems foreshadowed by the hurricane's destruction of the ancient Methuselah tree, which for all of its strength over the centuries is an inflexible, rigid species. Indeed, tradition always has been evolving as circumstances and perspectives change. Ultimately, Omishto comes to understand but not condone Ama's act. In the process she comes to an understanding of faith. Connecting her Christian mother to their own traditional heritage, Omishto realizes that "the church is saving Mama, the old ways are saving the people at Kili. Ama is saving the world" (224). In reflecting back on a time when she, her mother, and her sister turned to the Taiga elders for shelter and security, she continues, "But I am saving myself being here, and in all these savings, the path of things is changed forever. And I can't help thinking that it's God Mama believes in, but it was the old people who saved us" (224).

Hogan describes her essays as having grown "out of my native understanding that there is a terrestrial intelligence that lies beyond our human knowing and grasping" (*Dwellings* 11). She writes "out of respect for the natural world, recognizing that humankind is not separate from nature" (12) and that the broken connection between the natural world and the human world appears not only in our language and myth, but also "in our philosophy of life" (52). Her writing places her squarely in the middle of ecofeminist discourse, a discourse that has evolved into a strong affinity with the tenets of the environmental justice movement. She writes in a 1982 essay in *Frontiers* that she does not consider herself a spokesperson for mainstream feminist groups, explaining that she feels that feminism is "a complicated issue for Indian women because what affects the women also affects the entire community" (1). As she points out, political and economic injustices are practiced by the dominant society against entire tribes, not against women only. As a result, Indian women struggle for survival and relief from oppression for the entire tribal community, and those struggles "take precedence over concerns about gender roles" (1). At the time of this early interview, and in her opinion, her statement clearly places her outside the theoretical framework of feminism.

In a 2002 interview with me, Hogan states that her views have shifted somewhat. She explains that there was a lot of conflict at the time she wrote the essay, and that tribal people were in despair and poverty and attempting to recover from a very long history. She explains:

> When feminists went to the reservation and took off their shirts for equal rights, or invaded the Yaqui reservation looking for Don Juan, it just didn't go over very well. Our struggles were separate from theirs. And the right to not wear a shirt was hardly an issue at all when we were watching enforced sterilization of our women, all children born in one time frame given up for adoption, hunger, etc. This, truly, was a continuation of genocide. And when people wanted to lay claim to our spiritual identity without having the knowledge systems to back it, that was another theft. ("From the Center of Tradition" 14)

She acknowledges that a lot has changed in the last few years and that she is "more of a feminist mind now. I especially think of it in terms of economics, work, and the ever increasing number of violent crimes" (14). Hogan links economics, violence, domination, and the interrelationships of human and nonhuman worlds to the need for a balanced ecosystem, a linkage that *is* echoed in ecofeminist discourse.

In *The Book of Medicines*, we find the central tenet of ecofeminist theory: Man's domination of nature parallels man's domination over women. For instance, in "Hunger," Hogan connects the hunger that crosses the ocean in ships to the European colonists: "The men who grew small as distant, shrinking lands" were left behind. Then she juxtaposes their treatment of nature and women:

> Hunger was the fisherman
> who said dolphins are like women.
> We took them from the sea
> and had our way
> with them. (lines 10–14)

This juxtaposition drives home the connection between the oppression of women and the oppression of nature. But in *Medicines* I believe Hogan is doing more than echoing early ecofeminist concerns; she is bringing to our attention a more indigenous, inclusive worldview, one in tune with the goals of ecofeminism.

Ecofeminism, however, is a complicated term. Definitions and understandings vary. In his discussion of the various facets of ecofeminism, John Dryzek has identified two philosophical ecofeminist approaches: cultural and social. As Dryzek points out, cultural ecofeminism is a rather romantic doctrine because its political program condemns one kind of human sensibility (male) while advocating another, more feminine sensibility that is "intrinsically more attuned to the nonhuman world" (179). This biological essentialism is rejected by an approach that Dryzek labels as social ecofeminism, which looks beyond a blanket condemnation of patriarchy and interrogates the structural social causes of the twin domination of nature and women while at the same time seeking a way that society might be organized differently (159). While social ecofeminism shares the cultural critique of patriarchy, its advocates are "more inclined to see patriarchy as one among a number of oppressions (also covering race and class) rather than the root of all oppression" (180). Thus, social ecofeminist activism, according to Dryzek, should "contemplate the causes of the domination of both women and nature that lie in the structure of states, economies, and social systems. . . . through collective political action and new social institutions" (189).

Linda Hogan's body of work falls within the realm of social ecofeminism as identified by Dryzek. Her rhetoric is inclusive and does not essentialize women and nature. Nor does she place the blame solely on men. She believes that she is also part of the problem. Her poetry addresses historical and social institutions and their oppression of nature and peoples. In "Sickness," she writes:

> I am the child of humans,
> I have witnessed their destruction inside myself,
> and crawled along the ground
> among fallen trees
> and long grasses. Down there,
> I saw disease (lines 15–20)

This "dis-ease," this disconnection of nature and humanity, is one that Hogan attempts to heal within her book of medicines by integrating various ways of knowing.

Ynestra King suggests that ecofeminism offers the possibility for "creating a different kind of culture and politics that would integrate intuitive, spiritual, and rational forms of knowledge, embracing both science and magic insofar as they enable us to transform the nature-culture distinction and to envision and create a free, ecological society" (23).

Hogan calls for society to heal, and she writes that "what we really are searching for is a language that heals" (*Dwellings* 59) the broken relationship between humans and the natural world. She seeks a transformation, a change in attitude. We want "a remedy that will heal the wound between us and the world that contains our broken histories" (76). We need "new stories" (94). She writes:

> In sickness are the stories of a broken world.
> . . . .
> I saw disease.
> . . . .
> It tried to take my tongue.
> But these words,
> these words are proof
> there is healing. (lines 10, 20, 26–29)

Hogan offers us new language and stories and attempts to connect our human world with the larger universe. Her poetry and essays work in the way that native ceremonies do, "showing us both our place and a way of seeing" (12). In this way Hogan is performing King's ecofeminism—uncovering the Cartesian divide of our culture through the integration of different forms of knowledge, and embracing both science and magic.

Hogan intertwines science and magic in her work. In an interview with Rachel Stein, she discusses her participation in the Native Science Dialogues: "Non-Indian thinkers and indigenous thinkers get together and talk about Western science and how it fits into the traditional worldview. We talk about similarities and differences in the knowledge systems" (Stein 114).

Her work makes these similarities and differences apparent. Hogan also draws parallels between our search for healing and traditional ceremony when she tells of the Navajo ceremony, the Upward Moving Way:

> The ceremony brings in all aspects of the growth of plants: the movement upward as the roots deepen, the insects beneath and above the ground, the species of birds which come to this plant. All aspects of the ceremony reveal a wide knowledge of the world. In order to heal, this outside life and world must be taken in and seen by the patient as being part of one working world. ("Great Without" 22)

An example of how she writes this "one working world" into being can be found in the essay "Walking" in *Dwellings*. One passage details the life span of a single sunflower and the life it supports during one season: While the flower is still a bud, ants gather aphids and sap; when the bud becomes a tender young flower, there is "a troop of silver-gray insects climbing up and down the stalk"; the flower turns its head to the sun "in the most subtle of ways"; and later there are bees fat with pollen, grasshoppers, lace-winged insects, a whole society. Hogan writes: "In this one plant, in one summer season, a drama of need and survival took place. Hungers were filled. Insects coupled. There was escape, exhaustion, and death. Lives touched down a moment and were gone" (157). By observing the details and intimacy of nature, Hogan connects with the natural world and at the same time with her ancestors (159).

In *Medicines*, Hogan writes,

> The first stem is growing like a vine.
> It holds the cure
> where you can reach through time
> and find the bare earth
> within your living hand. ("Other, Sister, Twin," lines 47–51)

The bare earth and the growing stem hold the cure, the healing. In "Flood: The Sheltering Tree," Hogan links the power of nature, embodied in rain, with past abuses and the possibility of reconnection with nature: "Where will it take us, time, water / the uneasy slope of this land" (lines 16–17). The flood isolates her speaker on a small raised patch of land and she

> . . . began to see again
> the beautiful unwinding field
> and remember our lives
> from before the time of science,
> before we fell from history (lines 23–27)

In this way, the natural world will bring us into contact with our ancestors and make us stronger, as Hogan tells us in "Carry":

> It was beautiful, that water,
> . . . .
> It says, come close, you who want to swallow me;
> already I am part of you.
> . . . .

> I will carry you
> down to a world you never knew or dreamed,
> I will gather you
> into the hands of something stronger,
> older, deeper. (lines 15, 24–25, 28–32)

One section of *Medicines* is called "Hunger." In this grouping of poems, Hogan calls attention to the hunger that lies in a town, a community, in reality in our world. She examines the causes of the sense of longing and hunger we face today, and points to the disruption of the relationship between the human and nonhuman world. Human misuse of the natural world creates restlessness:

> . . . He has been to war. He says
> with bamboo they do terrible things
> to men and women.
> I look at this bamboo.
> It did not give permission to soldiers.
> It is imprisoned in its own skin.
> The stalks are restless about this.
> They have lived too long in the world of men.
> They are hollow inside. ("Bamboo," lines 12–20)

We too are imprisoned in our own skins; but as Hogan writes elsewhere, skin is permeable. It allows for transformation. Hogan writes to create that transformation. In her fiction, poetry, and nonfiction, Hogan integrates history with the knowledge of nature that comes from close observation. She weaves science and traditional ways of knowing, the mystical and the spiritual, and envisions cultural transformation. Nicolas Low and Brendan Gleeson have pointed out that "social change on the scale which may well be necessary for global society to carry on the task of finding and delivering justice in and to the environment is likely to proceed in a somewhat piecemeal and incremental way" (3). In an interview with John A. Murray, Hogan claims, "The writing I do is politically centered because it is about a worldview that can't be separated from the political" ("Of Panthers and People" par. 34). Linda Hogan's work is indicative of the growth of awareness of ecological politics, and it provides one of those incremental pieces necessary to effect transformative social change.

Works Cited

Castor, Laura. "Hunting History and Myth in Linda Hogan's *Power* and William Faulkner's 'The Bear'." *Nordlit: Arbeidstidsskrift I litteratur* 12 (Fall 2002): 37–48.

Cooper, Lydia R. "'Woman Chasing Her God': Ritual, Renewal, and Violence in Linda Hogan's *Power.*" *ISLE: Interdisciplinary Studies in Literature and Environment* 18.1 (Winter 2011): 143–59.

Dryzek, John S. *The Politics of the Earth: Environmental Discourses.* New York: Oxford UP, 1997.

Hogan, Linda. *The Book of Medicines.* Minneapolis: Coffee House, 1993.

_____. *Dwellings: A Spiritual History of the Living World.* New York: Norton, 1995.

_____. "From the Center of Tradition." *From the Center of Tradition: Critical Perspectives on Linda Hogan.* Ed. Barbara J. Cook. Boulder: U of Colorado P, 2003. 11–16.

_____. "The Great Without: Humanity's Dislocation from Nature." *Parabola* 24.1 (1999): 21–22.

_____. "Native American Women: Our Voice, the Air." *Frontiers* 6.3 (1982): 1–4.

_____. "Of Panthers and People: An Interview with Native American Author Linda Hogan." *Terrain.org: A Journal of the Built and Natural Environments* 5 (Autumn 1999) Terrain.org. Web. 29 June 2011.

_____. "Our Animal Selves." *Yes!* Positive Futures Network, 9 Mar. 2011. Web. 18 Apr. 2012.

_____. *Power.* New York: Norton, 1998.

_____. "Sea Level: An Interview with Linda Hogan." *ISLE: Interdisciplinary Studies in Literature and Environment* 18.1 (Winter 2011): 161–77.

King, Ynestra. "The Ecology of Feminism and the Feminism of Ecology." *Healing the Wounds: The Promise of Ecofeminism.* Ed. Judith Plant. Philadelphia: New Society, 1989. 18–28.

Low, Nicholas, and Brendan Gleeson. *Justice, Society, and Nature: An Exploration of Political Ecology.* London: Routledge, 1998.

Manning, Pascale McCullough. "A Narrative of Motives: Solicitation and Confession in Linda Hogan's *Power.*" *Studies in American Indian Literatures (SAIL)* 20.2 (Summer 2008): 1–21.

Stein, Rachel. "An Ecology of Mind: A Conversation with Linda Hogan." *ISLE: Interdisciplinary Studies in Literature and Environment.* 6.1 (Winter 1999): 113–17.

Prodigal Summer: A Narrative Ecosystem[1]

Priscilla Leder

Barbara Kingsolver's novels have earned praise from readers who have repeatedly put them on bestseller lists, as well as compliments from critics, scholars, and other writers. The wide appeal of Kingsolver's fiction reflects the variety and scope of her concerns. As demonstrated in the 2010 collection *Seeds of Change: Critical Essays on Barbara Kingsolver*, her work can be located in many contexts, including gender, region, and disability studies. However, her most intense concern, the relationship between humans and the environment, grows from her rural childhood through her graduate studies in ecology and evolutionary biology, and reveals itself especially in her nonfiction. Her collected essays combine lyrical observations of the natural world with analyses of the environmental effects of practices and policies; her food memoir *Animal, Vegetable, Miracle* (2007) forms an essential component of the current wave of attention brought to bear on our food choices and their consequences. In her 1996 article on "New Voices in American Nature Writing," Lorraine Anderson points out that Kingsolver and others are "painting a more complex and realistic portrait of life, culture, and nature" in various regions of the United States (1162).

Of her fiction, the novel *Prodigal Summer* (2000) most strongly manifests her environmental concerns and emerges as a work of environmental literature. Suzanne Jones, for instance, calls the work "a blueprint for saving the small family farm and for restoring ecological balance in a southern Appalachian bioregion that is struggling to survive" (84). Kingsolver herself stresses the novel's emphasis on ecology. Responding to a reader's question about the work via the Harper Collins website, she advises, "I'd ask you to read slowly; this is the most challenging book I've ever given my readers. . . . My agenda is to lure you into thinking about whole systems, not just individual parts." Kingsolver not only depicts the Appalachian ecosystem of Zebulon Mountain; she also creates a narrative ecosystem by describing levels of distinct organisms and demonstrating how those organisms interact within and among those levels. She details the biology of a range of species, from producers such as chestnut trees to primary consumers such as Luna moths and keystone predators such as coyotes. The novel, Kingsolver tells us, is "not exclusively—or even mainly—about humans. There is no main character." Instead, she incorporates three human plots, layered like the different species, whose characters function as part of the same ecosystem.

Each plot occupies its own space, just as each species occupies its own niche. The headings that signal each plot identify a specific species— "Moth Love" (Luna), "Predators" (coyotes), and "Old Chestnuts." Nevertheless, each species appears in all three plots, and organisms and human artifacts circulate together. These interactions constitute Kingsolver's agenda: She asks us to "notice the sentence that begins and ends the book: 'Solitude is only a human presumption'" (FAQ). Whether they are aware of it or not, human beings are enmeshed and intertwined with their environment, and all the other species in it. Kingsolver illustrates this reality through her characters—the ranger who watches over the mountain and the visiting hunter; farmers who grow chestnuts and apples; aging neighbors at odds over propriety and pesticides; and a scientist adjusting to her life as a farmer's widow. Although the characters think of themselves as solitary, the narrative reveals the actual network of relationships that defines their lives. Krista Comer has noted in *Landscapes of the New West* (1999) that Kingsolver's novel *Animal Dreams* (1990) depicts a "gender-inverted American West . . . in which stereotypically female values like attachment, connection, belonging, community, and commitment vie with the old western masculine ideals of self-reliance, individualism, sexual sampling, mobility, and adventure" (145). Although not set in the West, *Prodigal Summer* continues the author's testing of gender expectations in the values and personalities of the novel's central female characters. The general development of the characters, however, moves from individualism to attachment, modeling the trajectory of evolving ecological consciousness.

Given the inevitable interaction among species in any ecosystem, every action has significant consequences. Nothing takes place alone, as Kingsolver reminds us with another sentence that both begins and ends the book: "Every choice is a world made new for the chosen" (1, 444). The characters in *Prodigal Summer* learn and develop through delicate, nuanced interactions—between their own biology and their consciousness, with each other, and between themselves and their environment, making new worlds with every choice. Repeatedly, Kingsolver reminds us that her characters are biological creatures—systems in themselves—by detailing their physiology, especially their sexuality. The elderly neighbors grapple with the pains and infirmities of aging; the widowed entomologist Lusa experiences the return of her monthly cycle, and with it an appreciation of her own physiology; and the ranger Deanna Wolfe and the hunter Eddie Bondo feel the pull of sexual attraction despite their opposing stances on environmental protection. The emphasis on sexuality, atypical for Kingsolver, reveals the interaction between biology and human agency. Deanna experiences her first sex with Eddie as "the body's decision, a body with no more choice of its natural history than an orchid has" (24). But her "body's choice" is also a conscious act—she invites Eddie to spend the night in her cabin. Later on, Lusa asserts the possibility of choice in the context of human biology by questioning the assumption that "dancing's basically just the warm-up act [to sex]." She acknowledges that "that's true for most animals. Insects do that, birds do, even some mammals. But we've got great big brains. . . . I think we could distinguish a courtship ritual from the act itself. Don't you?" (418).

Lusa's question to her nineteen-year-old nephew Rickie not only asserts her own ability to choose, but invites him to assert his own. Throughout *Prodigal Summer* characters negotiate with and attempt to educate one another. For instance, in each subplot, one of the key characters holds forth on the topic of interspecies relationships within an ecosystem, particularly emphasizing the hierarchical layers of predator species and prey species. The theme of predation is linked to the process of sexual reproduction. The apple farmer Nannie Rawley explains something called the "Volterra Principle"—the idea that predators reproduce more slowly than the species they prey upon—to her neighbor Garnett Walker: "That works out right in nature because one predator [insect] eats a world of pest bugs in its life. The plant eaters have to go faster just to hold their ground. They're in balance with each other" (275). This balance between predator and prey holds all the way up to the carnivores, such as the coyote at the apex of the pyramid. Killing coyotes and spraying with broad-spectrum insecticides, which kill predator insects along with the rest, disrupt this balance, resulting in the devastating, unchecked reproduction of rabbits or plant-eating insects. Kingsolver critiques such practices through her story, warning against destructive practices that fail to achieve their intended results.

In his book *Second Nature: A Gardener's Education* (1991), Michael Pollan distinguishes between the "wilderness ethic," which separates humans from nature, and the "garden ethic," which acknowledges the human presence in nature. "The Idea of a Garden," as Pollan puts it in the title of one of his chapters, is based upon the premise that it is impossible for humans to encounter nature without influencing what they experience by virtue of their own presence. The imaginative, metaphor-making human brain prevents us from engaging with the actualities of the world; as Pollan states, "We know nature only through the screen of our own metaphors" (227). The wilderness ethic, on the other hand, emerges from "the sense that nature undisturbed displays a miraculous order and balance, something the human world can only dream about" (214). The benefit of the wilderness philosophy is that it promotes a reverence for nature, but it also generates a false either/or that allows us to sacrifice whatever is *not* wilderness. In Pollan's words, "Americans have done an admirable job of drawing lines around certain sacred areas (we did invent the wilderness area) and a terrible job of managing the rest of our land" (223). More recently, writers such as the historian William Cronon have further eroded the notion of wilderness by pointing out that very idea of pristine places, never touched by human hands, is an artificial, ahistorical construct—true wildernesses essentially do not exist in the world.

If the either/or absoluteness of wilderness thinking seems problematic, following a garden ethic—which is the ethical paradigm in Kingsolver's novel—demands even more thought, in part because conscientious gardeners must adapt their practices to place. The good gardener, writes Pollan, must also be "in control of his appetites, solicitous of nature, self-conscious and responsible, mindful of the past and future, and at ease with the fundamental ambiguity of his predicament—which is that though he lives in nature, he is no longer strictly *of* nature" (232). In other words, gardeners must practice their craft responsibly in specific circumstances, aware always that "every choice is a world made new for the chosen." Through the experiences of her characters in this novel, Kingsolver shows both the limitations of the wilderness ethic and the constant vigilance—analogous to the interaction between human intellect and human physiology—that is necessary to maintain a garden or a larger farm.

The ranger Deanna Wolfe initially wishes to protect a mountain as pristine wilderness. The artificiality of this effort parallels Deanna's image of herself as a solitary being among thousands of living and extinct species. But her solitude is no more real than the boundary between the wilderness area and the Widener farm—both are imaginary constructs and therefore unstable. When Deanna begins her affair with the hunter Eddie Bondo, not only does her solitude end, but she begins to experience the inevitable interaction of humans and the environment. We read Kingsolver's novel as a work of environmental literature because it illustrates the complexity of human interactions with the nonhuman world, not because it advances a reductive "environmentalist argument." Her characters struggle to understand their relationships with each other and with the places where they live and their fellow species. The novel *explores* these complex relationships. This is the fundamental difference between a work of environmental literature and an environmental treatise or manifesto.

The sections of the novel focusing on Deanna's relationship with Eddie appear under the title "Predators," and the idea of predation— or hunting—recurs throughout. Eddie is interested in hunting coyotes, while Deanna watches and protects wildlife on the mountain. The two characters have in common their tendency to walk alone in the forest, and even their romantic relationship has the intensity and wildness of a predatory relationship. Deanna regrets the loss of independence that results from her attachment to Eddie, at one point expressing her aggravation at him for "me wanting you to come back." When he finds a favorite place of hers in an old chestnut tree, she exclaims, "That's my place!" and disagrees with his reply that "a few other people might have run across it . . . it's been lying there about a hundred years" (95). In behaving so possessively toward the tree and the mountain, Deanna undermines her idea that wilderness is public and open. She is similarly paradoxical in her simultaneous resentment of Eddie and attachment to him. Deanna's views of wilderness corroborate Michael Pollan's suggestion that wilderness areas with clear boundaries imply the possibility of ownership and control. This tendency to assume personal responsibility for a wild place that is, by definition, *not* one's own place illustrates the psychological and philosophical challenge of habitat protection.

Patrick D. Murphy observes that in Kingsolver's novel "male and female characters learn from each other, articulate ideas to each other, and engage in verbal and sensuous dialogues with each other and the interanimating world in which they grow" (202). Deanna retains her image of the mountain's pristine ecosystem, and Eddie retains his image of coyotes as killers of livestock, but their ongoing negotiations with each other represent the dialogue between opposing perspectives needed in order to produce a responsible, sustainable relationship between people and the natural environment. The characters adapt to each other and expand their perspectives. The possibility of changing ethical frameworks that emerges in fictional narratives such as

Kingsolver's implies to readers of the novel that they too might adjust their perspectives, so that they are not locked into static attitudes.

The novel represents the resolution of the negotiation between Deanna and Eddie not literally but symbolically with Deanna's pregnancy—perhaps future generations will be better caretakers of the land than the current generation. She no longer thinks of herself as solitary when she writes to Nannie Rawley: "I'm coming down from the mountain this fall . . . when it starts to get cold. It looks like I'll be bringing somebody else with me" (391). Once the child is born, Deanna will not be able to continue living on the mountain or keep the illusion of herself as a detached and appreciative observer of the natural processes surrounding her. Through her physical changes, Deanna realizes she is subject to the laws of biology—her knowledge of biology becomes internalized, visceral. Later, she will be responsible for helping her child become a reasoning person, conscious of his or her proper relationship to nature. Deanna's implicit trajectory in the narrative shows that she has replaced her role as solitary protector of the wilderness with a new role as a gardener.

Nearly eighty years old, Garnett Walker is the central character in "Old Chestnuts," one of the three major subplots in the novel. He maintains a small farm, comprising the last of his family's property. Most species of American chestnuts were lost to disease in the early twentieth century. Garnett, who has retired from his position as a teacher of vocational agriculture, now spends his time trying to develop a new blight-resistant chestnut strain. His point of view comes through clearly early in the novel when Kingsolver writes: "The grass-covered root cellar [built by his father and grandfather] still bulged from the hillside, the two windows in its fieldstone face staring out of the hill like eyes. . . . Every morning of his life, Garnett had saluted the old man in the hillside with the ivy beard . . . and the forelock of fescue hanging over his brow" (49). The face of the landscape seems to represent not only his own aging visage but also that of God. Garnett's salute shows respect for God's power.

Garnett believes that we are to "think of ourselves as keepers and guardians of the earth, as God instructed us to do . . . 'So God created man in his *own* image; . . . and God blessed them and said to them, Be fruitful and multiply, and replenish the earth, and subdue it'" (186). His sense that humans control nature comes from the idea that humans have been created in God's image. He argues with Nannie about the superiority of reason over the body and the hierarchy of humans above nature. Garnett believes that God-given dominion over nature is precisely what obligates humans to care for the natural world. Garnett's absolute way of thinking exemplifies what Michael Pollan calls the "wilderness ethic." Both Deanna's reverence for nature as an autonomous realm and Garnett's view of nature as a manifestation of God reflect the idea that "for many of us, nature is a last bastion of certainty; wilderness . . . something beyond the reach of history and accident," as Pollan puts it (218). Such certainly is not only comforting but, in a sense, irresponsible; it relieves people who think in terms of reductive absolutes from the obligation of making hard decisions about how to deal with the natural world.

Indeed, Garnett does have to make choices; he works hard to preserve the mighty chestnut trees, but in the process he annihilates insects with Sevin. Kingsolver's depictions of the personal aspects of Garnett's horticultural and spiritual struggles reveal the automatic, and consequently limiting, aspect of Garnett's thinking about his own biology and the natural world of which it is a part. He is frustrated with his dizziness, which he believes is a kind of "curse." He eventually learns from Nannie Rawley an exercise that stops the dizziness. As the narrative proceeds, Garnett's sense of superhuman self-control and control of nature breaks down, spurred by his interactions with Nannie. This deterioration of God-like perspective culminates in a comic scene. After becoming obsessed with a stranger leaning on the fence at Nannie's house, Garnett goes to confront the man with a shotgun, only to notice that "everything about him appear[s] unnatural," and that "he'd been jealous of a scarecrow" (423). Garnett has misidentified the scarecrow because of his limited vision, and this shortcoming parallels the limitations caused by his religious fervor. He manages to make light of his foolishness, though, when Nannie asks about the shotgun: "I didn't care for the way [the scarecrow] was looking at you in your short pants" (427). Just as Deanna eventually gives up her illusion of solitude, Garnett embraces Nannie and, as a result of his human interaction, progresses toward a more enlightened understanding of his interconnections with community.

Michael Pollan associates solitude with what he calls the wilderness ethic. Deanna and Garnett exhibit initially the sense of their own solitariness before eventually adopting the gardener's perspective of interconnectedness. Lusa, the main character of the third subplot of the novel, "Moth Love," has always thought of herself as a gardener. Even as a child, she imagined herself becoming a farmer (120). Concerning the gardener, Pollan writes that this perspective "accepts contingency" and "doesn't spend a lot of time worrying about whether he has a god-given right to change nature" (226, 228). Lusa loses her husband Cole in a truck accident after they've been married only a year. At this point, she has not yet fully adapted to her life on the farm or her place in a large extended family. She grapples with this loss and at the same time becomes increasingly devoted to the farm and the new family. She learns to appreciate nature's systems and understand human needs. Kingsolver's readers participate in various deliberations experienced by Lusa—and this is one of the essential purposes of environmental literature, as it helps to train readers to think about complex issues as they exist in the world, not only in the pages of fictional narratives.

An "ethic based on the garden would give local answers," according to Pollan. Local families have many goats on hand from abandoned 4-H projects and don't know quite what to do with them. Kingsolver walks readers through Lusa's process of deliberating about possible alternative crops for her farm with special attention to her decision to begin raising goats. The goats are an excellent local solution to Lusa's dilemma, because she happens to know, from her personal background (having a Palestinian mother and a Polish Jewish father), where to sell them. Her dialogue with Rickie about the goats is a mutually educational process that is more revealing of the deliberative process and more engaging for readers than an abstract analysis of local approaches to farming would be. This is one of the advantages a novel affords, introducing ecological ideas to audiences rather than providing the quantitative scientific, economic information or abstract philosophical ideas in the form of an essay. Kingsolver's work in general, and in *Prodigal Summer* in particular, depicts characters as they develop new understandings of themselves and their relationships to nature, and as they work through various dilemmas toward practical solutions. In the case of Lusa, she is willing and able to adapt to her new environment and family context. She tries to release "the burden of her aloneness" by embracing her husband's family, despite the fact that she seems foreign to them (and is, in fact, foreign in many obvious ways). One of the recurrent themes in Kingsolver's novels is adoption—the creating of new and expanded family units not only through biology, but through the welcoming of new partners and children. We can think of adoption as a mode of adaptation. Even the "adopting" of a relationship to a new place might be construed as an extension of this process—the making of necessary attachments. Lusa finds a way to survive following Cole's death by farming the soil and opening her heart to Cole's family. Using Pollan's vocabulary of gardening, we might say that Lusa has embraced "local answers" to her predicament.

During a particularly powerful dialogue with Rickie, Lusa subtly displays her open-mindedness and her willingness to consider new possibilities for herself and the land. They are discussing the similarities and differences between Jews, Muslims, and Christians. Rickie, who raises goats, cannot imagine eating them. But when he admits this, it prompts Lusa to consider keeping goats on her farm. As she thinks about this, she does something completely out of character: "She walked over and took the [cigarette] pack from him. 'Can I try this?'" (157). This gesture conveys a fundamental expression of solidarity with Rickie and the other farmers in the community: "If tobacco's the lifeblood of this country, I should support the project" (159). The lighting of a cigarette—her first ever—seems to symbolize Lusa's vulnerability, and in granting new authority to Rickie, this gesture enables him to assume a helpful, mentoring role, suggesting that neighbors have unwanted goats they could give her. Lusa is open to this opportunity provided by the environment, but she is not a passive participant in the brainstorming process. Drawing upon her own background, she dreams up a marketing strategy. Her cousin in New York, who works as a butcher for the Palestinian community there, could provide meat for traditional feasts using her organic goats. This solution to Lusa's farming dilemma grows from her basic willingness to talk to Rickie, despite their different perspectives. The essential willingness to negotiate, Kingsolver suggests, is one of the most important aspects of developing rational, responsible relationships with the natural environment and with human communities. As Lusa and Rickie share ideas, Kingsolver explains: "He was listening to her carefully. It made her listen more carefully to herself" (165). The process of negotiation results in new self-understanding, not only in encounters with new ideas.

The decision to raise goats is practical, and indeed essential. Lusa will be able to keep her farm because of the goats. These goats also represent an essential aspect of Kingsolver's food ethic. Elsewhere the novelist has written about the wasteful process of producing "food that's been seeded, fertilized, harvested, processed, and packaged in grossly energy-expensive ways and then shipped, often refrigerated, for so many miles it might as well be green cheese from the moon" ("Lily's Chickens" 114). Lusa avoids being wasteful through her abundant vegetable garden, canning the products of this "prodigal summer" for future use. As she explains to her sister-in-law, "Between this and my chickens, I may not have to go to Kroger's again till next summer" (*Prodigal* 375).

Lusa's garden ethic has both practical and aesthetic dimensions. She cooperates with plants and weather and soil to achieve basic sustenance, but there is something pleasing about the product as well. Her sister-in-law Jewel articulates this: "I swear, this is *pretty*. It looks like a woman's garden, some way. It doesn't look like other people's gardens" (375). The source of this beauty is more than gender, though—it has to do with Lusa's multicultural roots. The vegetables include not only common corn and carrots, but exotic fava beans, eggplant, and peppers. The multiple dimensions of the garden reflect an ethical commitment to cultural diversity that goes beyond the mere benefits of practical wisdom developed in different communities. Lusa expresses her identity by way of her gardening practices. In this way, she exemplifies what Patricia Klindienst reveals about the use of gardening to preserve ethnic identity in her book *The Earth Knows My Name: Food, Culture, and Sustainability in the Gardens of Ethnic Americans* (2006).

Cultural diversity can be carefully cultivated in families as well as in gardens, as Kingsolver demonstrates through the politics that play out in Lusa's farmhouse kitchen. Other female characters in the novel—including Jewel's mother and sisters—have spent their lives cooking in this place. It is only natural for them to resent Lusa, an outsider, who entered the family by marriage and who is, in many ways, foreign to the family. The fact that her husband, her closest tie to the family, is no longer even living accentuates Lusa's outsider status. The foundation for Lusa's eventual acceptance into the family comes as a result of the ordinary domestic processes of gardening and canning. The interactions between Jewel and Lusa while engaged in these activities signal crucial moments of diplomacy. Kingsolver suggests that it is possible to satisfy physical and emotional needs through the same processes—in this case, growing and preserving food. Having lost her husband, Lusa needs Jewel's company and support; Jewel, for her part, needs help with her children. Before taking steps to deal with these needs, people must recognize them. In her loneliness, Lusa is worried about spending her "nothing of a life in this kitchen cooking for nobody." Jewel immediately offers a solution to both her own problem and Lusa's: "I wish you'd make a pie for my kids once in a while. When I come home from work I'm so tired, I practically feed them hog slop on a bun" (114–15). What seems like a fairly mundane dialogue actually foreshadows the dramatic problem and resolution that will occur toward the end of the novel: Jewel is dying of cancer, and Lusa eventually offers to adopt her children, not only out of regard for Jewel but also out of affection for the children and their eccentricities.

Another feature of Lusa's growth as a character is her changing idea of property. As a result of this insight she comes to a new understanding of the family's perspective on what it means for her to keep the farm. Toward the end of the book, she realizes they do not bear animosity toward her; but they are concerned that they may lose their connection with the farm if she remarries. Lusa gradually comes to appreciate the family's attachment to the land. The solution here, as in other subplots within the novel, comes by way of children. In this particular narrative, she decides to adopt the children and stipulate that they will eventually inherit the land. They will live on the land with her, develop their own sense of attachment to the place, and thus achieve the mindset of true ownership that will enable them to maintain the family tradition of stewardship.

Truly attaching oneself to a parcel of land, for Kingsolver, does not mean possessing the land in a merely material sense. Lusa articulates her understanding of this: "This was still the Widener farm, but the woods were no longer the Widener woods, Lusa explained. They were nobody's" (439). The practice of mindful farming and gardening requires not only asserting one's hopes and claims upon the world, but accommodating the fundamental uncontrollability of the natural environment—its uncertainties and contingencies. At the novel's end, many uncertainties remain. Lusa could find another partner; Deanna's child may wonder where his or her father has gone; and Garnett and Nannie's aging bodies may give out. By inviting readers to speculate, Kingsolver reminds us again of the delicate, nuanced negotiations—with each other, between biology and consciousness, and between ourselves and our environment—that make for responsible action and make new worlds for chosen and chooser alike.

Note

1. A more detailed version of this article appears in the essay "Contingency, Cultivation, and Choice: The Garden Ethic in Barbara Kingsolver's *Prodigal Summer,*" *ISLE: Interdisciplinary Studies in Literature and Environment* 16.2 (Spring 2009): 227–43. The original essay also appears in slightly altered form in my edited collection *Seeds of Change: Critical Essays on Barbara Kingsolver*, published by the University of Tennessee Press in 2010.

Works Cited

Anderson, Lorraine. "New Voices in American Nature Writing." *American Nature Writers.* Vol. 2. Ed. John Elder. New York: Scribner's, 1996. 1157–72.

Comer, Krista. *Landscapes of the New West: Gender and Geography in Contemporary Women's Writing.* Chapel Hill: U of North Carolina P, 1999.

Cronon, William. "The Trouble with Wilderness; or, Getting Back to the Wrong Nature." *Uncommon Ground: Rethinking the Human Place in Nature.* Ed. William Cronon. New York: Norton, 1995. 69–90.

Jones, Suzanne W. "The Family Farm as Endangered Species: Possibilities for Survival in Barbara Kingsolver's *Prodigal Summer.*" *Southern Literary Journal* 39.1 (Fall 2006): 83–97.

Kingsolver, Barbara. "Barbara Kingsolver FAQ on *Prodigal Summer.*" *Barbara Kingsolver.* HarperCollins Publishers. n.d. Web. 5 July 2008.

———. "Lily's Chickens." *Small Wonders.* New York: HarperCollins, 2003. 109–30.

———. *Prodigal Summer.* New York: HarperCollins, 2001.

Kingsolver, Barbara, Steven L. Hopp, and Camille Kingsolver. *Animal, Vegetable, Miracle: A Year of Food Life.* New York: HarperCollins, 2007.

Klindienst, Patricia. *The Earth Knows My Name: Food, Culture, and Sustainability in the Gardens of Ethnic Americans.* Boston: Beacon, 2006.

Leder, Priscilla, ed. *Seeds of Change: Critical Essays on Barbara Kingsolver.* Knoxville: U of Tennessee P, 2010.

Murphy, Patrick D. "Nature Nurturing Fathers in a World Beyond Our Control." *Eco-Man: New Perspectives on Masculinity and Nature.* Ed. Mark Allister. Charlottesville: U of Virginia P, 2004. 196–212.

Pollan, Michael. "The Idea of a Garden." *Second Nature: A Gardener's Education.* New York: Dell, 1991. 209–38.

A Natural Alliance: Blending Nature Literature and Outdoor Education in the Integrated Outdoor Program

Jeff Hess

It's Wednesday, an early afternoon in May. The nearly forgotten sun has returned to incubate summer-lust. From the north bank of the Willamette River we look upstream and watch two teenage boys wade through the waist-deep current to a small island twenty yards from shore. The boys are shirtless, carrying fishing poles across the river on a school day. Who can blame them? A rustle alerts us to another fisherman nearby. He is obscured by the invasive reed canary grass between us. We watch him cast. He's focused, ignoring us. More teenagers are scattered down river; a few are alone, others in pairs or threes. Many are fishing, some for the first time. Two have fly rods and a dozen cast spinning rods, or try to figure out how they work. A group of girls are baiting treble hooks and tying lines to maple branches. An equal number have found solitary spots on rocks, logs, and under maples and cottonwoods. They're reading David James Duncan's *The River Why* (1983). The teenagers, sixty-six in all, are in school. They are students in the IOP, the Integrated Outdoor Program at South Eugene High School, and except for that blessed sun, this is a pretty normal day in class.

Seven years ago, Pete Hoffmeister and I had an idea to develop a program around our shared passions of reading, writing, and dirt cheap adventuring. Having watched our students being drawn more and more into "virtual" experiences, we didn't need Richard Louv to tell us that they had to be rescued from nature-deficit disorder. We knew they were starving to get back into the woods, to reconnect with their real environment, and to discover joy where there is no electricity, where achievement is fueled by carbohydrates, not hydrocarbons, where beauty is perceived through all five senses, and where interdependence is as obvious as a field of camas in May. To counter the perception of the fourth grader Louv quotes in *Last Child in the Woods* (2005)—the student who likes "to play indoors better because that's where all the electrical outlets are" (10)—we wanted our students to begin to accept Emerson's invitation to "enjoy an original relation to the universe" (1) and to experience both an intellectual and a physical connection to the literature they studied.

By the next spring, Pete and I had proposed the Integrated Outdoor Program to the curriculum committee at South Eugene High School, a public school in Eugene, Oregon. It would be a full-year program offered to juniors and seniors, and students would earn one credit each toward English and physical education. With an integrating theme of "our interaction with the natural world," the IOP would be a two-period block course at the end of the school day, alternating days of focus on English and physical activity, allowing us greater flexibility and giving students sufficient time to become fully engaged in either subject. We were fortunate that the committee and our administration saw value in what others might view as an outlandish proposal, and the next year the IOP began. At the end of its sixth year now, the class has passed its experimental phase and grown to the point that we have to turn away nearly as many students as we accept.[1] Not every one of our students buys in. Some still think reading is tedious. A few sneak off to play hacky sack under the bridge when the others are fishing, but most are fundamentally changed by a year in what they regularly call "the best class ever."

Genie Snyder, a 2009 graduate, said:

IOP changed my feelings about high school. IOP made me WANT to go to class. It made me realize that if you study what interests you, you will always do well. I took this with me to college and have been very successful. Because of IOP, I look at school as something I want to spend my time doing, not wishing I didn't have to do it. IOP really did change me.

Hannah Claussenius-Kalman was in the program in 2010 to 2011 and was selected to be a student leader in the fall of 2011. She added:

> Above all, IOP gave me confidence. Upon coming back to school after surviving the winter trip, I realized that while my friends had watched TV at home, I had nearly killed myself trying to get up a mountain that I was not in shape for. I couldn't have been more proud of myself.
>
> Now I can jump in a river without worrying about what will happen to me because I have learned what my body is capable of. IOP taught me how to do things I would have never done on my own.

Hannah came into the class academically confident and highly capable, but physically she was quite inexperienced and timid. Facing physical challenges and the fear of new experiences created a bridge linking her to the characters that we read about and the themes we examined. Many of our other students forge that connection in another direction: They are drawn to the class because of the activities, but are ultimately captivated by the literature through their shared challenges and outdoor experiences.

Reading and writing selections examine nature, adventure, personal growth, and environmental issues. We read novels, stories, memoirs, poems, songs, speeches, essays, magazines, and news articles. Longer readings include *Into the Wild* (1997), *Fall of the Phantom Lord* (1998), *Ordinary Wolves* (2004), *Desert Solitaire* (1968), *The River Why* (1983), *Desert Notes* (1976), *A Little More About Me* (1999), *Breaking Trail* (2005), *River Notes* (1979), *Affluenza* (2005), *Deep Survival* (2003), and *Indian Creek Chronicles* (1991). Writing assignments are varied and numerous. Much of the writing is based on the genres we study, including adventure nonfiction, personal accounts in nature, travelogue, nature-based essays and poetry, journal writing, and personal reflections.

When possible, physical activities parallel what we read about. They include rock climbing, tree climbing, introductory mountaineering, snowshoeing, bicycling, orienteering, swimming, kayaking, rafting, fishing, Frisbee, hiking, slack-lining, inline skating, roller hockey, trail running, shelter building, and a number of outdoor sports and games. Skills essential to the activities (using map and compass, knot tying, belaying, bicycle maintenance, white-water navigation, and others) are also part of the curriculum. Additionally, students spend a considerable amount of time working in, and creating, the IOP garden and outdoor classroom.

To establish a foundation for the course, we devote the first week to teaching and reinforcing the IOP ethics, which emphasize not only our pedagogical principles but also the interpersonal relationships that will be developed over the year:

Ethic #1: We are open to new people, new activities, and new ideas.

Ethic #2: We are willing to put others before ourselves.

Ethic #3: We believe that process is more important than product.

Ethic #4: We are grateful for our resources.

Ethic #5: We believe the world holds potential for positive change.

On each day of that first week, we roll our 70-bike phalanx one to six miles from school and focus our activities, reading, and discussion around one of the ethics. Day two brings us to the Willamette River. The river is one of several locations that we visit often during the year with the intention of helping our students develop close ties to specific places. On this first day at the river, we pick blackberries, read "Gathering Berries" by Aleria Jensen, and swim in the river. Three days later we return to the Willamette, this time under the bridge adjacent to a gravel plant, a spot frequented by people who leave evidence of their presence behind. Surrounded by dust, debris, and cacophony, we read former Oregon Governor Ted Kulongowski's 2004 plan to restore the river, and the students consider Kulongowski's proposal to "repair, restore, recreate" the Willamette River. At the end of a week spent establishing the ethos of the course, we begin the first of our three thematic units, and, as our student Jay Martin said, we commence "the experience that will change a group of indoorsmen into outdoorsmen."

Organizing the Curriculum Geographically

The year's curriculum is divided into three major sections: deserts, mountains, rivers, and a shorter fourth section, during which the students conduct projects in our outdoor classroom and garden. The readings focus on these ecosystems, and our activities prepare students to thrive there. At the end of each section, we take a three-day trip to celebrate the places they have read about and apply the skills they have developed. During the desert unit, students read Edward Abbey's *Desert Solitaire*, Barry Lopez's *Desert Notes*, and Jon Krakauer's *Into the Wild*. In the middle of that unit, we take our first three-day trip with the class. For the most significant test of the desert trip, the students are dropped off in small groups five miles from camp with maps, compasses, and a leader who will intervene only if they're heading to Idaho. They summit the closest butte, take bearings, determine their position, and then make their way back to camp through Ponderosa forest and dense stands of manzanita. We camp, without running water, on BLM land adjacent to a cave that the students explore. And since they are in high school (and because their teachers are perennially immature), there is an annual contest to see how many people can cram themselves into the pod at the end of the cave.

On Saturday morning, we get up before the sun, and each student finds a solitary place, as Abbey did, in "the center of the world, God's navel" (5). Individually, we watch the sunrise while rereading Abbey's sunrise scene in "The First Morning," when he longs to "know it all, possess it all, embrace the entire scene intimately, deeply, totally" (6). On their first morning in the Central Oregon desert, we want our students to share Abbey's desire to "know it all." That night, we gather in the cave, and Pete and I read aloud Abbey's chapter "Water," because parts of it are hilarious, and we are in the desert, washing dishes with dirt and using water only to cook and drink. We have brought water with us, but just the right amount. On the final day, we break camp and drive to a small rock-climbing area outside of Sisters, Oregon, where students boulder and top-rope climb, read and write in their journals, learn to slackline, and try to eat all of the food we have remaining.

Before our mountain trip, the students have read two memoirs: *Indian Creek Chronicles* by Pete Fromm, and Arlene Blum's *Breaking Trial*. The trip begins with a four-mile uphill hike on snowshoes. As soon as the students arrive at camp, they change into dry clothes and begin digging snow caves—their homes for the next two nights. The next morning, the student leaders are up early, eat, strap on snowshoes, and set off to follow their compass bearings and break trail to the summit of Fuji Mountain (Oregon's version). Thirty minutes later, we summon the sleep-deprived, blistered, and aching students from their snow caves and begin the seven-mile hike. At 7,144 feet, reaching the summit of Fuji Mountain isn't on many bucket lists, but for the majority of our students, who have summited nothing higher than Eugene's 2,052 foot Spencer Butte, this winter ascent is significant, and they are rewarded with a panoramic spectacle. From the summit of Fuji Mountain, they look out at the Central Cascade peaks from Mt. Jefferson to Mt. Washington, Three Fingered Jack, the Three Sisters, and Broken Top. To the South, Mt. Thielsen, "the lightning rod of the Cascades," stands alone waiting for another hit. The reflection of Diamond Peak glistens on Odell Lake to the west, and it seems almost possible to jump into Waldo Lake off Fuji's northeast ridge.

After returning from the hike, a former student of ours demonstrates fire building with a hand drill, then the students gather material and make their own fire in the snow (they get to use a lighter, but no paper), and finally we read London's "To Build a Fire" as a reminder to stay humble despite their recent successes living in the snow.

April is devoted to projects in the Student Outdoor Integrated Learning (SOIL) garden and outdoor classroom. While working on their projects, the students read Pam Houston's collection *A Little More About Me* and write about Houston's and their own experiences, transformations, and introspection. Five years ago, the IOP took control of a neglected courtyard within the school. What began as a 100' x 100' weed farm has become a vibrant outdoor classroom. In this space students plan, organize, and implement an annual project that will benefit the school and the future of the program. Since adopting the courtyard, IOP students have turned an overgrown, weed-infested, and unused space into a thriving garden with annual vegetables, perennials, fruit trees, berries, and native landscaping. Within the courtyard, the students have built a toolshed, a greenhouse, compost bins, a pond, two boardwalks, an arbor, a stone path, a raised meeting area (above the flood plain), and—most recently—a covered deck, where students can read and write in the rain, a tree house (another dry study area), garden furniture, a covered outdoor kitchen with a cob oven, a native plant garden, improved vegetable and fruit gardens, and a wetlands ecosystem around the pond. The benefits derived from garden projects are innumerable. Foremost, the work reinforces all five of the IOP ethics, while providing students an increasingly rare opportunity to produce something with their own hands.

As we near the end of the year, we pretend that Eugene's weather is warm enough to get back in the river. Previously, the students have read Abbey's "Down the River" in *Desert Solitaire* and have followed Chris McCandless down the Colorado to the Gulf of Mexico in *Into the Wild*. We finish the year with Barry Lopez's *River Notes* and David James Duncan's *The River Why*, and two weeks before school is out, we spend three days rafting and kayaking the Deschutes River in central Oregon, fishing its banks and hiking the butte nearest our campsite.

Alone, any one of the dozens of experiences students have in the IOP could be a high school highlight. However, it is the symbiosis of physical and mental processes, all in the fresh air, that cannot be duplicated piecemeal. Nature literature in general is appealing because it is real; it seems tangible. Yet, as written word, it is still fallible. As Abbey states in his introduction to *Desert Solitaire*, "Language makes a mighty loose net with which to go fishing for simple facts, when facts are infinite" (x). Integrating nature literature with physical activity in the outdoors, though, not only translates facts into a visceral experience, but also reinforces concepts within the writing and provides students with sensory experiences that lead to their own development as writers.

In his essay "My Advice on Writing Advice," David James Duncan writes:

> Many would-be authors refuse to take "Experience-It-Yourself" for an answer. They think Rilke and Doderer don't know what they're talking about, and that there *are* straight lines in life, and nifty shortcuts, and that they themselves are, by God, going to find them and so are never going to have to do anything as scary as be "truly without a name, without ambition, without help; on scaffoldings, alone with their consciousness."

Later in the same essay, he quotes Rex Stout saying, "If you're not having fun writing it, nobody's going to have fun reading it." Those two concepts are why we created the IOP, so that students could learn through their experience, and have fun doing it.

The IOP Bedrock—*Desert Solitaire* and Literature of Place

Over the six years of the program, we have added and subtracted texts each year. Abbey's *Desert Solitaire*, however, has been and will always be a mainstay. In the last three years, we have begun the year with *Desert Solitaire,* both to encourage deep thought after a summer of intellectual oxidation and to establish a framework on which to build the rest of the curriculum. Because of the overall mission of the IOP, our approach to the text is likely more experiential and less analytical than what may be found in many college literature courses. But if our students analyze less, they gain by heeding Abbey's advice to "get out of those motorized wheelchairs, get off your foam rubber backsides, stand up straight like men! like women! like human beings! and walk—*walk*—WALK upon our sweet and blessed land!" (291).

Three of Abbey's themes that we focus on are relationships with place, the relationship between nature and civilization, and solitude. A significant benefit to our focus on nature literature is the relative prevalence of common themes throughout the genre. Beginning with a canonical text like *Desert Solitaire*, we can subsequently follow its themes in other works throughout the year, as students are led toward an exploration of their own values, psyches, and perspectives on the natural world.

Some of our students enter the program with a considerable background in outdoor activities, but an increasing number begin the class with virtually no experience in nature. As they prepare to spend a year in an academic and experiential wilderness, it is fitting that they begin their journey by examining Abbey's "season in the wilderness." As Abbey opens their eyes to "the most beautiful place on earth" (1), they understand that they have been introduced to Abbey's main character. There may be no other people around, but Abbey is clearly not alone. To most of our students, children of the Pacific Northwest, the Southwest canyon lands are foreign territory, not their "most beautiful place." But Abbey tells us, "There are many such places. Every man, every woman, carries in heart and mind the image of the ideal place" (1). Developing a familiarity with place is central to the Integrated Outdoor Program. Being solitary, fully present, and attentive in a natural setting presents students with an opportunity for growth that is unlikely to occur in a classroom. Moreover, the awareness of comfort, safety, belonging, and stewardship that connects us to those places is essential not just to our own well-being, but also to the well-being of our planet.

In his essay "A Literature of Place," Barry Lopez writes:

> Over time I have come to think of these three qualities—paying intimate attention; a *storied* relationship to a place rather than a solely sensory awareness of it; and living in some sort of ethical unity with a place—as a fundamental human defense against loneliness. If you're intimate with a place, a place with whose history you're familiar, and you establish an ethical conversation with it, the implication that follows is this: the place knows you're there. It feels you. You will not be forgotten, cut off, abandoned.

After developing a literary connection to those places, we literally lead our students into them with the hope that they and the place will develop that intimacy essential for their mutual prosperity.

As Pete Fromm's memoir *Indian Creek Chronicles* begins, he is a greenhorn, completely unprepared for his seven-month sojourn in the wilderness. A number of hunters, guides, and an outfitter are camped nearby, and he regards them with awe for the apparent ease with which they navigate the territory that he still finds threatening. As winter sets in, however, he is thriving and confident. He has become intimate with his piece of wilderness, and he recalls "how the lion hunters had laughed at the wardens for being visitors. But the lion hunters were all gone now, too, and I was the only one who was still here, alone. . . . I was not just a visitor" (119).

Not only do visitors come and go, but in realizing that they can leave when they please, they are less likely to consider the effects of their passing. As the earth's animals, plants, waterways, forests, and atmosphere face increasing threat from human actions, the literature of place provides an essential bridge to begin reconnecting people to the land that sustains us. Lopez writes:

> I believe curiosity about good relations with a particular stretch of land now is directly related to speculation that it may be more important to human survival to be in love than to be in a position of power. It may be more important now to enter into an ethical and reciprocal relationship with everything around us than to continue to work toward the sort of control of the physical world that, until recently, we aspired to. ("A Literature of Place")

What Does It Mean to Be in Control?

"Control of the physical world," or the relationship between nature and civilization, is a second central topic of examination in the IOP. Once again, we start with *Desert Solitaire* and Abbey's polemic against industrial tourism. Abbey pits a conservationist argument—I'll also call it moral and logical—against a financial one. Our students, even the most radically minded, see Abbey's argument as logical but completely impractical. The notion of leaving cars behind is an uncomfortable cognitive stretch for them, but they absolutely cannot imagine the industrial complex conceding control of "The Natural Money-Mint" (62). They've all heard that "time is money," and have been constantly bombarded by the media equating possessions with happiness. "We are preoccupied with time," wrote Abbey. "If we could learn to love space as deeply as we are now obsessed with time, we might discover a new meaning in the phrase to *live like men*" (72). Our students feel the press of time. They do have other classes and other obligations, yet the contrast between discussing Abbey's polemic in our outdoor classroom, or at the base of a giant sequoia in Washburne Park, and discussing it in an air-conditioned classroom between physics and calculus is striking. Abstract thought and test results have their pedagogical places, and classrooms are neatly organized and convenient. But simply being outside allows our students a temporary respite from the clock, and their experiential integrated outdoor education inherently leads most of them to empathize with literary characters. That empathy, in turn, leads to a deeper degree of critical insight, toward both literary analysis and self-examination.

In her collection of essays *A Little More About Me*, Pam Houston describes her struggle to reconcile her obsessions with time, speed, and accomplishment with Bhutanese notions of what is truly important:

King Jigme Singye Wangchuk (the Bhutanese call him simply His Majesty) is famous for saying, "I don't want to increase the gross national product, I want to increase the gross national happiness." He says money makes people crazy, no matter how much of it you have, and happiness is all that matters. He has shut down all the country's lumberyards and strip mines, and has instituted a daily tourist fee (two hundred dollars per person) that more than picks up the slack. He strictly limits the number of tourists per year, is actively keeping television out of Bhutan, and has instituted a kind of Bhutanese Arbor Day, when every citizen is supposed to plant a tree. (258)

His Majesty and Ed Abbey would clearly get along.

While Houston races her companions to camp and is "inordinately happy" when she hears that the staff is discussing her walking stamina, she still counts the hours until the end of her trek. Her guide Karma "says I am crazy for counting the hours the way I do and living in the future. When you ask a Bhutanese person how long until something happens—the arrival at a destination, for instance—the answer will be, always, 'We will be there after *some time*'" (261). Houston hears Karma's message, but she is uncomfortable with the unfamiliar paradigm. Still, she presents that discomfort to her readers so that they can struggle along with her. Our hypocrisy becomes transparent in nature literature as writers force us to confront our habits and look honestly at our future.

The Potential for Positive Change—Alone and in Communion

Beginning with our first ethic—"We are open to new people, new activities, and new ideas"—and continuing throughout the year, we investigate the idea that substantive change cannot occur without the substantive reorganization of priorities. While nature literature is not strictly motivated by a political agenda, it can't be ignored that the protection of natural resources and the quest for monetary wealth are often in conflict. Many writers have referred to nature literature as a literature of hope, and as such it can potentially form a bridge to close that gap and look for common ground. As Abbey makes clear, continuing on a path of environmental destruction will only destroy that which makes us civilized:

> No, nature is not a luxury but a necessity of the human spirit, and as vital to our lives as water and good bread. A civilization which destroys what little remains of the wild, the spare, the original, is cutting itself off from its origins and betraying the principle of civilization itself.

If industrial man continues to multiply his numbers and expand his operations he will succeed in his apparent intention, to seal himself off from the natural and isolate himself within a synthetic prison of his own making. (211)

The writing and study of nature literature has, at its core, an intention—to help people to care about the natural world. Whether the words convey praise, dismay, or anger, the root is hope, and a class like the IOP offers hope to an age-group that often struggles to find it. The work that we do in our outdoor classroom, and the many other places that we visit, provides some balance to the incessant barrage of the media and consumer culture. As one of our students, Amelia Remington, put it, "I have felt myself growing *because* I am becoming less put together." In the IOP we follow the maxim that there is no bad weather, only inappropriate clothing. All year long, students go outside, get familiar with outdoor space, and grow in ways that are impossible between walls. They are invited to create new connections and discover new values and motivations as they step into Emerson's present sunshine: "Embosomed for a season in nature, whose floods of life stream around and through us, and invite us, by the powers they supply, to action proportioned to nature, why should we grope among the dry bones of the past, or put the living generation into masquerade out of its faded wardrobe? The sun shines today also" (1).

Every year in the IOP, a large group of students, virtually strangers, becomes a community. But many of our students first need to learn how to be alone—without gadgets—before they can develop empathy for that community. Once solitude becomes appealing, they can grow to understand that solitude needs to be nurtured and protected, in part to teach us how to care about where we live and whom we live with. The theme of solitude in nature is common to nearly every book we read. Beginning with Abbey's season alone, we then go to Lopez's solitary discoveries in *Desert Notes*. Chris McCandless goes *Into the Wild* and disappears into the Alaskan bush. Pete Fromm spends seven months alone in the Selway-Bitterroot Wilderness in *Indian Creek Chronicles*. Interestingly, though, while each of these writers goes into the wilderness at least in part for personal growth and discovery, each one also thrives on human contact.

Nature may be the ultimate sanctuary in which to contemplate, but we are still driven by a social instinct to share our lives and contemplations with other humans. Floating the Colorado with Newcomb, Abbey ponders the "utterly useless crap we bury ourselves in day by day . . . the constant *petty* tyranny of automatic washers and automobiles and TV machines and telephone!" (193). What would Abbey say about smart phones, iPods, Facebook, and Twitter? At the end of *Desert Solitaire*, he laments that he "too, must leave the canyon country, if only for a season, and rejoin for the winter that miscegenated mesalliance of human and rodent called the rat race" (330), but he then writes, "I grow weary of nobody's company but my own—let me hear the wit and wisdom of the subway crowds again, the cabdriver's shrewd aphorisms, the genial chuckle of a Jersey City cop" (331). Even in Arches, where instead of loneliness Abbey feels "loveliness and quiet exultation" (16), he still thrives in the company of the tourists, on the trail with Viviano and Roy, and even arguing "all night long" with the "comical Nazi," although he was simultaneously contemplating opening "his skull with a bottle of his own Lowenbrau" (332).

Chris McCandless's "great Alaskan odyssey" in *Into the Wild* was a solitary experience, but throughout the book we see him reveling in the company of others. According to his sister Carine, McCandless "always had friends, and everybody liked him" (107). He talked endlessly to the friends that he made as he traveled, and he corresponded with them after he moved on. In *The River Why*, Duncan's protagonist Gus creates an "ideal schedule" containing fourteen and one half hours of fishing a day and zero hours of "non-angling conversation" (58). His "ideal," however, soon disintegrates into virtual madness, from which he returns by discovering new people, new activities, and new ideas, as in IOP ethic #1.

While Abbey, McCandless, and Duncan's Gus all sought solitude, they could not remain in their hermitages. The wilderness was both their refuge and their classroom, and because they were also writers, their experiences gain meaning when shared with others. Therein lies the difference between the solitary writer and the hermit. The writer has a story, and the nature writer believes that story can make a difference to the world we live in.

David Barnhill addresses the notion of the nature writer moving away from society into solitude in his essay "Terry Tempest Williams and the Literature of Engagement":

> Nature writing certainly is at times about narratives of retreat and many writers explore consciousness of the natural world, but there are two problems with making this the principal and fundamental image of nature writing. The first is that it is, I think, inaccurate. Especially over the last forty years, since Rachel Carson's *Silent Spring* and the early writings of Gary Snyder, many writers have *not* turned their back on society and sought contemplation of nature but have linked nature writing with social life and ethical issues, and for many of them this is central to their work as writers. The second problem is that, in the face of environmental and social problems, such an image of contemplative retreat marginalizes nature writing and undercuts the social significance it *can*, it *does*, and it *should* have.

Nature literature by itself is often a point of merger between subject and form: politics and literature; beauty and activism; history and reform. In the IOP, we acknowledge those mergers and blend in the activities and environments that make the literature real. Fromm's humility and his sometimes self-deprecating narrative in *Indian Creek Chronicles* captivate our students. Despite his utter ignorance of the hardship he would encounter, and with virtually no preparation, Fromm ultimately thrives in his seven-month sojourn. But he devotes pages of the memoir to his bumbling ignorance and passes off his remarkable accomplishments with hardly a mention. Reading this, our students not only like Fromm as a narrator immediately, but feel more free to engage in new experiences, even if that leads to a bit of their own bumbling.

When the greenhorn Fromm is setting up his camp—"my home for the next seven months" (1)—the warden, his boss, suggests he tie off the guy line with a double half hitch:

> "A double what?"
>
> We traded places and he tied the tent up. Then he took me aside and demonstrated a half hitch. "Haven't you ever messed around with rope?"
>
> I shook my head and saw the wardens glance at each other. I tried harder not to appear stupid, but couldn't see why anyone would purposefully spend time "messing around with rope." (18)

Of course, the answer is obvious to Fromm's readers. It's also an obvious invitation to mess with rope in the IOP. As we discuss Fromm's narrative voice, his use of humor, and the expectations and tensions that have been created in the memoir's exposition, we also teach our students how to tie a double half hitch, a bowline, a fisherman's knot, an alpine butterfly, a clove hitch, and a trucker's hitch. As they tie knots, they connect Fromm's experience and their own and continue to reinforce the connectedness of all things. This is the basis of the IOP, and according to Lopez, it is the basis of nature writing:

> The real topic of nature writing, I think, is not nature but the evolving structure of communities from which nature has been removed, often as a consequence of modern economic development. It is writing concerned, further, with the biological and spiritual fate of those communities. It also assumes that the fate of humanity and nature are inseparable. ("A Literature of Place")

Nothing is separate in the *Integrated* Outdoor Program. We collect images, stack them upon each other, and see where they lead us. In Boyd Cave, a single headlamp illuminates a book and a mass of adolescents hangs on the words and each other. In Fuji Mountain, Jack, shirtless on the summit, wears his pale green long johns and a smile as wide as the view. In Tugman Park, and in the aftermath of touch rugby, we see mud-coated bodies, wet, cold, smiling. A mesa, fourteen miles north of Maupin, Oregon—Mt. Hood looming an arm's reach away, the river below just a flat ribbon, the rapids and our camp erased by the distance. Duncan's "line of light." Fairbanks bus 142 off the Stampede Trail. Abbey's snake dance. The embrace of a magnificent tree.

In Washburne Park, there is a 150-year-old sequoia known by some as "the Octopus." Its lower branches have been removed by the city, and it's a challenge even for rock climbers to get to the first branches, fourteen feet off the ground. We are in the park for today's class. The students scatter to read, and then write three haikus, illustrating scenes within the reading. Now it's time to move and play a little Ultimate Frisbee before the day ends, but several students are still in the Octopus. As I approach, I see they have dropped their folded poems to the ground eighty feet below them.

"Hey guys. We're going to play Ultimate," I say, but they don't respond. They're reading. I repeat myself, a little louder. One of them looks down.

"No," he says. "We're going to stay and read. We're in school, Jeff. Can you believe it? We're in school."

Note

1. South Eugene High School offers ten English courses to juniors and seniors. In 2011, 131 of South's 575 juniors and seniors registered for the IOP, and 80 were accepted.

Works Cited

Abbey Edward. *Desert Solitaire: A Season in the Wilderness.* New York: Ballantine, 1968.

Barnhill, David. "Terry Tempest Williams and the Literature of Engagement." *Introduction to Nature Writing.* U of Wisconsin Oshkosh, 2002. Web. June 2011.

Duncan, David James. "My Advice on Writing Advice." *Weber Studies: The Contemporary West* 21.2 (Winter 2004). Web. June 2011.

_____. *The River Why*. San Francisco: Sierra Club, 1983.

Emerson, Ralph Waldo. *Five Essays on Man and Nature*. New York: Appleton, 1954.

Fromm, Pete. *Indian Creek Chronicles: A Winter Alone in the Wilderness*. New York: St. Martin's, 1991.

Houston, Pam. *A Little More About Me*. New York: Washington Square, 1999.

Jensen, Aleria. "Gathering Berries." *Orion* (September/October 2007). Web. June 2011.

Krakauer, Jon, *Into the Wild*. New York: Anchor, 1997.

Kulongowski, Ted. "The Willamette River: Oregon's Legacy." *Oregon State Archives*. 15 Apr. 2004. Web. Sept. 2010.

Lopez, Barry. *Desert Notes: Reflections in the Eye of a Raven* and *River Notes: The Dance of Herons*. New York: Avon, 1990.

_____. "A Literature of Place." *Portland* (Summer 1997). Web. June 2011.

Louv, Richard. *Last Child in the Woods: Saving Our Children From Nature-Deficit Disorder*. Chapel Hill: Algonquin, 2005.

RESOURCES

Additional Works on Nature and the Environment____

Drama

The Tempest by William Shakespeare, 1610–11.
The Sea Voyage by John Fletcher and Philip Massinger, 1622.
Faust. Der Tragödie erster Teil (Faust. The First Part of the Tragedy) by Johann Wolfgang von Goethe, 1806.
Death of a Salesman by Arthur Miller, 1949.
Angels Fall by Lanford Wilson, 1983.
The Kentucky Cycle by Robert Schenkkan, 1992.
In the Heart of the Woods by Todd Moore, 1994.
Alligator Tales by Anne Galjour, 1997.
The Cripple of Inishmaan by Martin McDonagh, 1997.
Continental Divide by David Edgar, 2004.
Shadow of Giants by Matthew Graham Smith, 2004.
Odin's Horse by Robert Koon, 2004.
Song of Extinction by E. M. Lewis, 2008.

Fiction

The Sketch Book by Washington Irving, 1819.
The Prairie by James Fenimore Cooper, 1827.
Moby-Dick; or, The Whale by Herman Melville, 1851.
The Country of the Pointed Firs by Sarah Orne Jewett, 1896.
A Room with a View by E. M. Forster, 1908.
Kangaroo by E. M. Forster, 1923.
The Waves by Virginia Woolf, 1931.
Go Down, Moses by William Faulkner, 1942.
L'homme qui plantait des arbres (*The Man Who Planted Trees*) by Jean Giono, 1953.
The Milagro Beanfield War by John Nichols, 1974.
A River Runs Through It and Other Stories by Norman Maclean, 1976.
Aransas by Stephen Harrigan, 1980.
La Ronde et autres fait divers (*The Round & Other Cold Hard Facts*) by J. M. G. Le Clézio, 1982/2002.
The River Why by David James Duncan, 1983.
The Whale Rider by Witi Ihimaera, 1987.
Buffalo Gals, Won't You Come Out Tonight by Ursula K. Le Guin, 1994.
The Tortilla Curtain by T. Coraghessan Boyle, 1995.
Blanche Cleans Up by Barbara Neely, 1999.
Oryx and Crake by Margaret Atwood, 2003.

Forty Signs of Rain by Kim Stanley Robinson, 2004.
Returning to Earth by Jim Harrison, 2006.
Breath by Tim Winton, 2008.
The Other by David Guterson, 2008.
The Windup Girl by Paolo Bacigalupi, 2009.

Nonfiction

Letters from an American Farmer by Hector St. John de Crèvecoeur, 1782.
Les Rêveries du promeneur solitaire (*Reveries of a Solitary Walker*) by Jean-Jacques Rousseau, 1782.
The Natural History and Antiquities of Selborne by Gilbert White, 1789.
Nature by Ralph Waldo Emerson, 1836.
The Voyage of the Beagle by Charles Darwin, 1839.
Nature Near London by Richard Jefferies, 1883.
The Mountains of California by John Muir, 1894.
The Land of Little Rain by Mary Austin, 1903.
The Outermost House by Henry Beston, 1928.
A Sand County Almanac by Aldo Leopold, 1949.
The Singing Wilderness by Sigurd Olson, 1956.
The Immense Journey by Loren Eiseley, 1957.
Silent Spring by Rachel Carson, 1962.
Pilgrim at Tinker Creek by Annie Dillard, 1974.
The Desert Smells Like Rain: A Naturalist in Papago Indian Country by Gary Paul Nabhan, 1982.
Arctic Dreams: Imagination and Desire in a Northern Landscape by Barry Lopez, 1986.
Wild to the Heart by Rick Bass, 1987.
The Island Within by Richard K. Nelson, 1989.
The End of Nature by Bill McKibben, 1989.
Refuge: An Unnatural History of Family & Place by Terry Tempest Williams, 1991.
The Trail Home: Essays by John Daniel, 1992.
Where the Bluebird Sings to the Lemonade Springs: Living and Writing in the West by Wallace Stegner, 1992.
The Thunder Tree: Lessons from an Urban Wildland by Robert Michael Pyle, 1993/1997.
Staying Put: Making a Home in a Restless World by Scott Russell Sanders, 1993.
Memory Fever: A Journey Beyond El Paso del Norte by Ray Gonzalez, 1993.
Ecology of a Cracker Childhood by Janisse Ray, 2000.
Having Faith: An Ecologist's Journey to Motherhood by Sandra Steingraber, 2001.
Four Seasons in Five Senses: Things Worth Savoring by David Mas Masumoto, 2003.
Sick of Nature by David Gessner, 2004.

Planetwalker: How to Change Your World One Step at a Time by John Francis, 2005.
Healing with Herbs and Rituals: A Mexican Tradition by Eliseo "Cheo" Torres, 2006.

Poetry

Poems Descriptive of Rural Life and Scenery by John Clare, 1820.
"God's Grandeur" by G. M. Hopkins, 1877.
A Canticle to the Waterbirds by William Everson, 1968/1992.
Ghost Tantras by Michael McClure, 1969.
The Complete Poems of Emily Dickinson edited by Thomas H. Johnson, 1976.
Black Mesa Poems by Jimmy Santiago Baca, 1989.
Her Blue Body Everything We Know: Earthling Poems 1965–1990 Complete by Alice
    Walker, 1992.
New and Selected Poems, volumes one and two, by Mary Oliver, 1992/2005.
Garbage: A Poem by A. R. Ammons, 1993/2002.
The Darkness Around Us Is Deep: Selected Poems by William Stafford, 1993.
Words Under the Words: Selected Poems by Naomi Shihab Nye, 1994.
Agua Santa: Holy Water by Pat Mora, 1997.
Eating Bread and Honey by Pattiann Rogers, 1997.
The Life Around Us: Selected Poems on Nature by Denise Levertov, 1997.
The Monarchs: A Poem Sequence by Alison Hawthorne Deming, 1997.
Given Sugar, Given Salt by Jane Hirshfield, 2001.
Collected Poems and Plays by Rabindranath Tagore, 2002.
Time and Materials: Poems, 1997–2007 by Robert Hass, 2007.

Anthologies

This Incomperable Lande: A Book of American Nature Writing edited by Thomas J.
    Lyon, 1989.
The Norton Book of Nature Writing edited by Robert Finch and John Elder, 1990.
Literature and the Environment: A Reader on Nature and Culture edited by Lorraine
    Anderson, John P. O'Grady, and Scott Slovic, 1999/2012.
The Colors of Nature: Culture, Identity, and the Natural World edited by Alison
    Hawthorne Deming and Lauret E. Savoy, 2002.
A Place on Earth: An Anthology of Nature Writing from North America and Australia
    edited by Mark Tredinnick, 2004.
American Earth: Environmental Writing Since Thoreau edited by Bill McKibben,
    2008.
"A Booklist of International Environmental Literature," *World Literature Today*, co-
    ordinated by Scott Slovic, 2009.
Black Nature: Four Centuries of African American Nature Poetry edited by Camille
    T. Dungy, 2009.

General Bibliography

Adamson, Joni. *American Indian Literature, Environmental Justice, and Ecocriticism: The Middle Place.* Tucson: U of Arizona P, 2001.

Adamson, Joni, Mei Mei Evans, and Rachel Stein, eds. *The Environmental Justice Reader: Politics, Poetics, and Pedagogy.* Tucson: U of Arizona P, 2002.

Alaimo, Stacy. *Bodily Natures: Science, Environment, and the Material Self.* Bloomington: Indiana UP, 2010.

Armbruster, Karla M., and Kathleen R. Wallace. *Beyond Nature Writing: Expanding the Boundaries of Ecocriticism.* Charlottesville: U of Virginia P, 2001.

Barry, Peter. "Ecocriticism." *Beginning Theory: An Introduction to Literary and Cultural Theory.* Manchester: Manchester UP, 2002. 248–71.

Braddock, Alan C., and Christoph Irmscher, eds. *A Keener Perception: Ecocritical Studies in American Art History.* Tuscaloosa: U of Alabama P, 2009.

Branch, Michael P., and Scott Slovic, eds. *The ISLE Reader: Ecocriticism, 1993-2003.* Athens: U of Georgia P, 2003.

Buell, Lawrence. *The Future of Environmental Criticism: Environmental Crisis and Literary Imagination.* Malden: Blackwell, 2005.

Coupe, Laurence, ed. *The Green Studies Reader: From Romanticism to Ecocriticism.* London: Routledge, 2000.

DeLoughrey, Elizabeth, Renée K. Gosson, and George B. Handley. *Caribbean Literature and the Environment: Between Nature and Culture.* Charlottesville: U of Virginia P, 2005.

Dobrin, Sidney I., and Sean Morey, eds. *Ecosee: Image, Rhetoric, Nature.* Albany: SUNY P, 2009.

Estok, Simon C. *Ecocriticism and Shakespeare: Reading Ecophobia.* New York: Palgrave Macmillan, 2011.

Felstiner, John. *Can Poetry Save the Earth? A Field Guide to Nature Poetry.* New Haven: Yale UP, 2009.

Finseth, Ian. *Shades of Green: Visions of Nature in the Literature of American Slavery, 1770–1860.* Athens: U of Georgia P, 2011.

Gaard, Greta, and Patrick D. Murphy, eds. *Ecofeminist Literary Criticism: Theory, Interpretation, Pedagogy.* Urbana: U of Illinois P, 1998.

Garrard, Greg. *Ecocriticism.* London: Routledge, 2004.

Glotfelty, Cheryll, and Harold From, eds. *The Ecocriticism Reader: Landmarks in Literary Ecology.* Athens: U of Georgia P, 1996.

Goodbody, Axel, and Kate Rigby, eds. *Ecocritical Theory: New European Approaches.* Charlottesville: U of Virginia P, 2011.

Handley, George B. *New World Poetics: Nature and the Adamic Imagination of Whitman, Neruda, and Walcott.* Athens: U of Georgia P, 2007.

Heise, Ursula K. *Sense of Place and Sense of Planet: The Environmental Imagination of the Global.* New York: Oxford UP, 2008.

Huggan, Graham, and Helen Tiffin. *Postcolonial Ecocriticism: Literature, Animals, Environment.* London: Routledge, 2010.

Ingram, David. *The Jukebox in the Garden: Ecocriticism and American Popular Music since 1960.* Amsterdam: Rodopi, 2010.

Love, Glen A. *Practical Ecocriticism: Literature, Biology, and the Environment.* Charlottesville: U of Virginia P, 2003.

Lu, Sheldon H., and Jiayan Mi, eds. *Chinese Ecocinema: In the Age of Environmental Challenge.* Seattle: U of Washington P, 2010.

Lynch, Tom. *Xerophilia: Ecocritical Explorations in Southwestern Literature.* Lubbock: Texas Tech UP, 2008.

Malamud, Randy. *Poetic Animals and Animal Souls.* New York: Palgrave Macmillan, 2003.

Marshall, Ian. *Story Line: Exploring the Literature of the Appalachian Trail.* Charlottesville: U of Virginia P, 1998.

McMillin, T. S. *The Meaning of Rivers: Flow and Reflection in American Literature.* Iowa City: U of Iowa P, 2011.

Morton, Timothy. *Ecology without Nature: Rethinking Environmental Aesthetics.* Cambridge: Harvard UP, 2007.

Murphy, Patrick D. *Farther Afield in the Study of Nature-Oriented Literature.* Charlottesville: U of Virginia P, 2000.

Myers, Jeffrey. *Converging Stories: Race, Ecology, and Environmental Justice in American Literature.* Athens: U of Georgia P, 2005.

Newman, Lance. *Our Common Dwelling: Henry Thoreau, Transcendentalism, and the Class Politics of Nature.* New York: Palgrave Macmillan, 2005.

Oppermann, Serpil, Ufuk Özdag, Nevin Özkan, and Scott Slovic, eds. *The Future of Ecocriticism: New Horizons.* Newcastle upon Tyne: Cambridge Scholars, 2011.

Outka, Paul. *Race and Nature from Transcendentalism to the Harlem Renaissance.* New York: Palgrave Macmillan, 2008.

Rigby, Kate. "Ecocriticism." *Introducing Criticism at the 21st Century.* Ed. Julian Wolfreys. Edinburgh: Edinburgh UP, 2002. 151–78.

Rozelle, Lee. *Ecosublime: Environmental Awe and Terror from New World to Oddworld.* Tuscaloosa: U of Alabama P, 2006.

Ruffin, Kimberly N. *Black on Earth: African American Ecoliterary Traditions.* Athens: U of Georgia P, 2010.

Scheese, Don. *Nature Writing: The Pastoral Impulse in America.* New York: Twayne, 2002.

Scigaj, Leonard. *Sustainable Poetry: Four American Ecopoets.* Lexington: U of Kentucky P, 1999.

Sturgeon, Noël. *Environmentalism in Popular Culture: Gender, Race, Sexuality, and the Politics of the Natural*. Tucson: U of Arizona P, 2009.

Tredinnick, Mark. *The Land's Wild Music: Encounters with Barry Lopez, Peter Matthiessen, Terry Tempest Williams, and James Galvin*. San Antonio: Trinity UP, 2005.

Westling, Louise H. *The Green Breast of the New World: Landscape, Gender, and American Fiction*. Athens: U of Georgia P, 1998.

Willoquet-Maricondi, Paula, ed. *Framing the World: Explorations in Ecocriticism and Film*. Charlottesville: U of Virginia P, 2010.

Woodward, Wendy. *The Animal Gaze: Animal Subjectivities in Southern African Narratives*. Johannesburg: Wits UP, 2008.

CRITICAL INSIGHTS

About the Editor_____

Scott Slovic is professor of literature and environment at the University of Idaho, where he moved in 2012 after seventeen years at the University of Nevada, Reno. At Nevada, he served as director of the Core Writing Program and he also helped to create and coordinate the Graduate Program in Literature and Environment. He is the author of more than 150 articles concerning ecocriticism and environmental literature and has written, edited, or coedited sixteen books, including *Seeking Awareness in American Nature Writing: Henry Thoreau, Annie Dillard, Edward Abbey, Wendell Berry, Barry Lopez* (1992), *Going Away to Think: Engagement, Retreat, and Ecocritical Responsibility* (2008), and *The Future of Ecocriticism: New Horizons* (with Serpil Oppermann, Ufuk Özdag, and Nevin Özkan, 2011). From 1992 to 1995, he served as the founding president of the Association for the Study of Literature and Environment (ASLE), and since 1995 he has edited *ISLE: Interdisciplinary Studies in Literature and Environment*, the central journal in the field. He has been a Fulbright scholar in Germany, Japan, and China, and frequently travels to distant parts of the world to learn about "vernacular ecocriticism" and to support students and colleagues working in the field.

Contributors_____

Richard J. Schneider is professor emeritus in English at Wartburg College (Waverly, Iowa) and currently resides near the Adirondacks in upstate New York. He is the author of *Henry David Thoreau* in the Twayne United States Authors series (1987); editor of three books on Thoreau, including *Thoreau's Sense of Place: Essays in American Environmental Writing* (2000); and author of numerous journal essays on Thoreau.

Terry Gifford is Profesor Honorifico at the University of Alicante, Spain, and he is a visiting professor at Bath Spa University's Centre for Writing and Environment in the UK. For twenty-one years he was director of the annual International Festival of Mountaineering Literature, and he is now a trustee of the Mountain Heritage Trust. His pioneering books of ecocriticism include *Ted Hughes* (2009), *Reconnecting with John Muir: Essays in Post-Pastoral Practice* (2006), *Pastoral* (1999), and *Green Voices: Understanding Contemporary Nature Poetry* (1995, second edition 2011). His collected climbing essays were published in 2004 as *The Joy of Climbing*, and his seventh collection of poetry, *Al Otro Lado del Aguilar*, appeared in 2011. With Fiona Becket, Terry Gifford edited *Culture, Creativity, and Environment: New Environmentalist Criticism* (2007).

Priscilla Solis Ybarra is an assistant professor of English at the University of North Texas. She received her PhD from the Department of English at Rice University with specializations in Chicana/Chicano literature and ecocriticism. Her current book project, *Brown and Green: Mexican American Environmental Writing*, is the first study to engage a long-range environmental literary history of Chicana/Chicano writing. Dr. Ybarra's other publications on Latina/Latino environmental literature include an article in the journal *MELUS* (2009) and essays in the collections *Environmental Criticism for the Twenty-First Century* (2011) and *New Perspectives on Environmental Justice: Gender, Sexuality, and Activism* (2004), as well as a coauthored article in the MLA collection *Teaching North American Environmental Literature* (2008).

David Landis Barnhill's erosional life has taken him from the Sierra to the Cascades and the Blue Ridge, and now to the Central Sand Hills of Wisconsin, where he is director of environmental studies and professor of English at the University of Wisconsin Oshkosh. His publications include *At Home on the Earth: Becoming Native to Our Place, a Multicultural Anthology* (1999), *Deep Ecology and World Religions: New Essays on Sacred Ground* (coedited with Roger Gottlieb, 2001), and a two-volume translation of the Japanese nature poet Bashō (2004, 2005). Recent articles include "The Spiritual Dimension of North American Nature Writing," "The Social Ecology of Gary Snyder," and "East Asian Influence on Recent North American Nature Writing." His courses have included American nature writing, Japanese nature writing, and bioregionalism.

Ashton Nichols is the Walter E. Beach '56 Distinguished Chair in Sustainability Studies at Dickinson College. A professor of language and literature in Dickinson's English Department, he is the author, most recently, of *Beyond Romantic Ecocriticism: Toward Urbanatural Roosting* (2011). He is also the editor of *Romantic Natural Histories: Wordsworth, Darwin, and Others* (2004) and the web master of the hypertext resource *Romantic Natural History: 1750–1859*, a survey of the relationships between literature and natural history in the century before Darwin.

M. Jimmie Killingsworth is professor of English at Texas A&M University, where he teaches literature, rhetoric, and environmental studies. He is the author or coauthor of eleven books and over fifty scholarly articles and chapters, including *Ecospeak: Rhetoric and Environmental Politics in America* (with Jacqueline Palmer, 1992), which won the NCTE Award for Best Book of the Year in Scientific and Technical Communication, and *Walt Whitman and the Earth: A Study in Ecopoetics* (2004). He has also published general-audience essays on the natural world and the human experience of place, including the recent book *Going Back to Galveston: Nature, Funk, and Fantasy in a Favorite Place* (2011), with photographs by Geoff Winningham.

Tina Gianquitto received her PhD in literature from Columbia University (2003) and is an associate professor of literature at the Colorado School of Mines. She has published a book on women, nature, and science, *"Good Observers of Nature": American Women and the Scientific Study of the Natural World, 1820–1885* (UP of Georgia, 2007), as well as essays on Jack London and Mary Treat. She has an essay forthcoming in *Isis* on the British suffragist Lydia Becker and her correspondence with Charles Darwin. She has received fellowships from the National Endowment for the Humanities and the American Council of Learned Societies for a new project on Darwin's female correspondents and social reform.

Matthias Schubnell is professor and chair of the English Department at the University of the Incarnate Word in San Antonio, Texas. He teaches courses in Native American studies, the literature of the Southwest, Willa Cather, N. Scott Momaday, and literature and the environment. In addition to such books as *N. Scott Momaday: The Cultural and Literary Background* (1985) and *Conversations with N. Scott Momaday* (1997), he has published a number of studies of Willa Cather, often focusing on the environmental implications of her work.

Robert Bernard Hass is the author of *Going by Contraries: Robert Frost's Conflict with Science* (2002) and the poetry collection *Counting Thunder* (2008). He is the recipient of an Academy of American Poets Prize, an Associated Writing Programs Intro Journals Award, and a fellowship to Bread Loaf. He is currently professor of

English and theatre arts at Edinboro University of Pennsylvania, where he teaches courses in American literature, American nature writing, and Shakespeare.

Bert Bender taught literature at Arizona State University for thirty-three years. He is the author of *Sea-Brothers: The Tradition of American Sea Fiction from* Moby-Dick *to the Present* (1988), *The Descent of Love: Darwin and the Theory of Sexual Selection in American Fiction, 1871–1926* (1996), and *Evolution and "the Sex Problem": American Narratives during the Eclipse of Darwinism* (2004). In 2008, he published *Catching the Ebb: Drift-Fishing for a Life in Cook Inlet*, a narrative that recounts thirty summers of salmon fishing off the coast of Alaska and his life as a professor of American literature. He lives in Atascadero, California.

Brian Railsback is professor of English and the founding dean of the Honors College at Western Carolina University. He has published numerous scholarly articles and book chapters and has authored two books, *Parallel Expeditions: Charles Darwin and the Art of John Steinbeck* (1995) and *The Darkest Clearing* (a novel published in 2004). He coedited *A John Steinbeck Encyclopedia* (2006) and the Library of America edition *John Steinbeck, Travels with Charley and Later Novels* (2007). He won the 2006 Prose for Papa (Hemingway) Short Story Award. In 2004, he was named University Scholar at Western Carolina University.

David J. Rothman, a widely published poet and scholar, is director of the poetry concentration with an emphasis on versecraft at Western State College in Gunnison, Colorado, and also teaches at the University of Colorado at Boulder and the Lighthouse Writers Workshop in Denver. He holds degrees from Harvard, the University of Utah, and New York University. He served as president of the Robinson Jeffers Association from 2009 to 2011, and is the cofounder of the Crested Butte Music Festival and founding editor of Conundrum Press. His fourth volume of poems, *Go Big*, is forthcoming from Red Hen Press.

David Copland Morris teaches American literature, American studies, and environmental studies at the University of Washington, Tacoma, where he is an associate professor in the Interdisciplinary Arts and Sciences Program.

Wes Berry grew up among green hills, hardwoods, beef cattle, and tobacco fields in cave country, Barren River drainage, Kentucky, where he currently teaches at Western Kentucky University. He lives on a ridgeline near the confluence of the Green and Barren Rivers and is fixing up an old property, managing a small flock of laying hens, and fattening two duroc hogs. He specializes in twentieth-century American literature and environmental humanities, and has published essays on Walter Anderson, Wendell Berry, Cormac McCarthy, Anne LaBastille, Toni Morrison, Annie Proulx, Leslie Marmon Silko, and Barbara Kingsolver. His novel *Boating with the Dead* was a finalist for the Bellwether Prize for Fiction of Social Change in 2008. He is

---

currently working on a comprehensive guidebook to Kentucky's best smoked meats titled *Sweet Dreams of Kentucky Barbecue.*

Barbara J. Cook is an associate professor of English and women's studies at Mount Aloysius College in Pennsylvania. She has edited *From the Center of Tradition: Critical Perspectives on Linda Hogan* (2003) and *Women Writing Nature: A Feminist View* (2008). In addition to publishing articles in such volumes as *Restoring the Connection to the Natural World: Essays on the African American Environmental Imagination*, she guest coedited a 2007 special issue of *Studies in American Indian Literatures*, focusing on pedagogy.

Priscilla Leder is professor of English at Texas State University–San Marcos, where she has taught for over twenty years. She edited *Seeds of Change: Critical Essays on Barbara Kingsolver* (2010), and has published essays on Fanny Hurst, Julia Peterkin, Kate Chopin, and Sarah Orne Jewett, as well as on Kingsolver. She has taught in Belgium and Portugal as a Fulbright scholar.

Jeff Hess is codirector of the Integrated Outdoor Program at South Eugene High School in Eugene, Oregon. From 1989 and 1999, he taught a variety of subjects—from Advanced Placement literature to middle school Spanish, German, and PE—at Glendale High School and Middle School (OR). He has taught English, physical education, and health at South Eugene since 1999, and has coached track and field and cross-country throughout his teaching career.

Index